Theology and the Dialogue of Religions

Theology of religions is an area of theological reflection on inter-religious relations which raises fundamental questions not just for Christians but for all people of faith in a pluralist, post-modern world. How to practise a religious faith with integrity while respecting other claims to ultimate truth? Must 'the other' always be regarded as a problematic complication on the fringes of a Christianity-centred world? Is there a 'third way' between an all-dominating exclusivism and a tacit relativism? This book contributes to the debate about the place of inter-religious relations in the life of the Church by developing a 'theology of dialogue'. In offering a critique of much current thinking in this area, Michael Barnes SJ proposes instead a theology rooted in the themes of welcome and hospitality. He argues for a vision of Christianity as a 'school of faith', a community called not just to teach others but to learn from them as well.

MICHAEL BARNES SJ is Lecturer in Theology and Religious Studies and Academic Director of the Centre for Christianity in Inter-religious Dialogue at Heythrop College, University of London. His publications include *Religions in Conversation* (1989), *God East and West* (1991), *Walking the City* (1999), and *Traces of the Other* (2000).

Cambridge Studies in Christian Doctrine

Edited by
Professor COLIN GUNTON, *King's College London*
Professor DANIEL W. HARDY, *University of Cambridge*

Cambridge Studies in Christian Doctrine is an important series which aims to engage critically with the traditional doctrines of Christianity, and at the same time to locate and make sense of them within a secular context. Without losing sight of the authority of scripture and the traditions of the church, the books in this series subject pertinent dogmas and credal statements to careful scrutiny, analysing them in light of the insights of both church and society, and thereby practising theology in the fullest sense of the word.

Titles published in the series

Preface

More than ten years ago I wrote a book called *Religions in Conversation* which in their more mellow moments my friends tell me still has something to commend it. At the time I felt I wanted to contribute to a debate about what has come to be known as the theology of religions. The book fitted into the general category of a survey of a rapidly expanding field. In general that book was well received. One review even praised its intelligence (which pleased me) but criticised it for avoiding the awkward questions (which didn't). The nub of the criticism was that the author had found his way to the centre of a complex labyrinth but, once there, had little idea about how to get out again. Having pondered the issues at much greater depth since that relatively youthful excursion I feel I am now more happy to stay immured in the richness and complexity of inter-religious relations. The key questions, I am convinced, are not about the return and subsequent reflection – which remain comparatively straightforward – but how to cross over the threshold in the first place, how to get to the centre of a different and even threatening world, and how to remain there with a measure of Christian integrity.

This present study continues, and I hope deepens, that initial enthusiasm for the life of inter-faith engagement. I am confident that at some level it touches upon all the most important issues surrounding inter-religious dialogue and the place of Christianity in a multi-faith world – issues about Christ and Church, revelation, salvation and mission. This is not, however, a straightforward work of systematic theology. It will quickly become apparent to the reader that the dissatisfaction with much current thinking in this area which I hinted at in the earlier book has become a more blunt rejection in the present one. It is not so much that I find myself out of sympathy with the theological status quo in this area; it is rather that I am concerned that the challenge of other faith traditions, with all its complex ambiguities, should prompt Christians to exercise their theological imagination creatively and responsibly. To continue to treat people of other faiths as a 'problem' on the fringes of a still largely Christian world manifestly fails to do this. I am more concerned with a theology which arises from the various forms of dialogue with other religions, not with an exercise in preparing for such an engagement. To pick up one of the insights which has survived the transition from the earlier book relatively unscathed, I want to develop a 'theology *of* dialogue' rather than a 'theology *for* dialogue'.

The debate about the significance of religious pluralism for Christian faith involves a number of audiences. The present work originated as a doctoral thesis for the University of Cambridge and still retains traces of the demands of the academy. It has, however, been completely rewritten in order to reach a wider readership, both within the Church and in wider society. Inevitably there is a certain mixture of styles, and even genres, of theological writing, for which I can only crave the reader's indulgence. Some chapters are more obviously addressed to its former audience, particularly where philosophical questions about the nature of human subjectivity and relationality are involved. Others arise more directly from the contemporary experience of a Church committed to inter-faith dialogue. The book should be read as a dialogue between the two – hence the titles of the two parts, 'the returning other' and 'dialogue and God'. The rationale is explained towards the end of the first chapter. To anticipate briefly: there I argue that Christian discipleship in a multi-faith society can no longer afford to patronise others into a pre-determined scheme of things. The alternative, however, is not to close the borders or, more dubiously, to rub them out. It is to ask where God may be speaking across and between those borders. To answer that question adequately requires more than merely listening to the one whom Christians call the Word of God; it means attending to those complex processes which allow and sustain human relationships. What, I am asking, is the source of the dispositions and attitudes which are needed for life in a multi-faith society? How do Christians learn how to relate to the other?

Those last two words hold the book together. 'The other' is at once a post-modern term of mind-bending obscurity and the heart of the Gospel reality: stranger, neighbour, potential friend, with whom so much is shared yet who often represents a difference which can only be

Theology and the Dialogue of Religions

by

MICHAEL BARNES SJ

CAMBRIDGE UNIVERSITY PRESS

PUBLISHED BY THE PRESS SYNDICATE OF THE UNIVERSITY OF CAMBRIDGE
The Pitt Building, Trumpington Street, Cambridge, United Kingdom

CAMBRIDGE UNIVERSITY PRESS
The Edinburgh Building, Cambridge CB2 2RU, UK
40 West 20th Street, New York NY 10011–4211, USA
477 Williamstown Road, Port Melbourne, VIC 3207, Australia
Ruiz de Alarcón 13, 28014 Madrid, Spain
Dock House, The Waterfront, Cape Town 8001, South Africa

http://www.cambridge.org

First published 2002

Printed in the United Kingdom at the University Press, Cambridge

Typeface   *System*

A catalogue record for this book is available from the British Library

Library of Congress Cataloguing in Publication data

Barnes, Michael, 1947–
      Theology and the dialogue of religions / by Michael Barnes.
         p.   cm.
      Includes bibliographical references.
         ISBN 0 521 81077 9 (hardback) – ISBN 0 521 00908 1 (paperback)
         1. Theology of religions (Christian theology) 2. Catholic Church – Doctrines. I. Title.

      BT83.85 .B37 2002
      261.2 – dc21   2001037926

ISBN 0 521 81077 9 hardback
ISBN 0 521 00908 1 paperback

En hommage à mon ami

Daniel Faivre,

un véritable homme de dialogue

inter-religieux.

Contents

comprehended in the silence of faith. Between these two poles, the fragmented world of post-modernity and the pages of the scriptural witness, another other, the otherness of God is revealed. Part I of the book moves deliberately between the authoritative textual tradition of the Roman Catholic Church and the hermeneutical issues which the 'question of the other' raises. Part 2 sketches the outlines of a theology of dialogue which emerges from the Church's life of faith. But in the last analysis my theme is God and the various ways in which Christians, alongside persons who practise the ways of life inscribed in the great world religions, can speak about God. I make no apologies for writing as a convinced believer in the God of Jesus Christ. Indeed it is precisely because I am such a believer that I can also write, as much from my own experience as from my knowledge of the Christian revelation, about the other.

There is, inevitably, something autobiographical in any book, especially one which seeks to sum up a lengthy theological trajectory. Many teachers, colleagues and friends have contributed in different ways to this book. This brief note can include only the more recent. Among these the most important debt is owed to the supervisor of the original thesis, David Ford, who has been the benign godfather of so much of my thinking since he dropped the name of Levinas in my hearing during a lecture on inter-faith relations several years ago. I should also acknowledge the contributions of the examiners of the original thesis, Nicholas Lash and Rowan Williams, for the precision of their questions, the generosity of their comments, and the inspiration which they have always provided. For their help in transforming the text I am indebted to the editors of this series, especially Dan Hardy, and to Kevin Taylor of Cambridge University Press. I have received particularly generous support from Gwen Griffith Dickson and Bill Tomkiss who made heroic efforts to read and comment on various drafts. Many friends, colleagues and students, both at Cambridge and at Heythrop College in London, have made helpful noises and kept me from the grosser mistakes. My thanks for good conversation, important questions and equally important moments of relaxation, to Sarah Boss, Stephen Buckland, James Crampsey, Philip Endean, Laurence Hemming, Michael Ivens, John McDade, John Montag and Catherine Pickstock. A special debt is owed to Joe Laishley for his conscientious and imaginative criticism, to Gavin D'Costa for many useful suggestions, and to Graham Ward, who supervised my work at Cambridge in its initial stages and generously shared with me his enthusiasm for the thought of Michel de Certeau.

For helping me to root my theology in something more than the offerings of sundry libraries I owe a great debt to many friends and acquaintances from different faith traditions, both in Britain and India, especially Mr P. L. Soba of the Valmiki Sabha in Southall. I was extremely fortunate at an early stage in my research to benefit from a grant from the All Saints Educational Trust which made possible a trip to India. On that trip I was privileged to meet and get to know dalits and dalit theologians. My thanks are due particularly to Michael Jeyaraj, John Kumar and their colleagues at IDEAS in Madurai, V. Devasahayam at Gurukul and my Jesuit brethren at Arul Kadul, both in Chennai. Most especially I thank Antony Raj for long and stimulating conversation; X. Thamburaj for lending me his precious Abhishiktananda manuscript; S. Rajamanickam for sharing his immense learning about Roberto de Nobili; Sister Marie Rose at the Ananda Ashram, Kulitalai, for giving me so much material on Jules Monchanin; and John Packiaraj for good advice, generous hospitality, and for helping me negotiate the transport system in Hyderabad. I would also like to express thanks to the Teape Committee in Cambridge for inviting me to give the Teape lecture in India in December 1998. A month of lectures, from Delhi and Pune to Hyderabad and Chennai, proved to be invaluable in clarifying my thinking and for providing further opportunity to improve my knowledge of the Church and theological developments in the sub-continent. My only regret is that constraints of time and distance have made it impossible for me to do a rapidly changing scene full justice.

Final, and very inadequate, words of gratitude should be expressed to two good friends; firstly to Chris Roberts without whose constant interest this book would never have been finished; secondly, to my much revered colleague, Daniel Faivre, a self-confessed 'bombastic Frenchman', without whom it would never have been started. It was Daniel who got me involved in inter-faith relations in Southall many years ago. This book is respectfully dedicated to him.

Abbreviations

Documents of the Second Vatican Council

AG	*Ad Gentes* (Decree on Missions)
DH	*Dignitatis Humanae* (Declaration on Religious Freedom)
DV	*Dei Verbum* (Dogmatic Constitution on Divine Revelation)
GS	*Gaudium et Spes* (Pastoral Constitution on the Church in the Modern World)
LG	*Lumen Gentium* (Dogmatic Constitution on the Church)
NA	*Nostra Aetate* (Declaration on non-Christians)
SC	*Sacrosanctum Concilium* (Constitution on the Liturgy)
UR	*Unitatis Redintegratio* (Decree on Ecumenism)

Translations in this study are all taken from *Decrees of the Ecumenical Councils*, edited by Norman P. Tanner; London: Sheed and Ward; Washington DC: Georgetown University Press; 1990.

Other abbreviations

AS	*Acta Synodalia*
CBCI	Catholic Bishops Conference of India
DM	*The Attitude of the Church towards the Followers of Other Religions (Reflections and orientations on dialogue and mission)* (SNC)
DP	*Dialogue and Proclamation* (PCIRD)
DS	*Denziger-Schönmetzer*

ET	English translation
Exx	*Spiritual Exercises of St Ignatius of Loyola*
NBCLC	National Biblical Catechetical and Liturgical Centre (Bangalore)
PCIRD	Pontifical Council for Interreligious Dialogue
SNC	Secretariat for non-Christians
SPCU	Secretariat for promoting Christian Unity
ST	*Summa Theologica*

Part I

The returning other

Rethinking theology of religions

This is a book about what is sometimes called the 'wider ecumenism', about the place of Christianity in a world of many faiths, and about that contemporary development within Christian practice known as inter-faith dialogue.[1] But it is also, more broadly, about the ethics of discipleship, about the way Christians are to live in a multi-faith world. The two are obviously connected. Whatever I do, whatever I say, whatever I think, at some point my beliefs, and the practices to which they give rise, raise questions about the means which I use in developing relations with others; in brief, questions about power and control and the risk of violence done to the other. The result is a dilemma. How to remain faithfully rooted in my own Christian vision of a time-honoured truth and yet become open to and respectful of those committed to sometimes very different beliefs and values? Clearly this dilemma has serious implications, not just for how Christians are to live responsibly alongside their neighbours from other religious traditions, but for how the whole project of Christian theology is to be pursued in what I shall call an all-pervasive 'context of otherness'.

Not that such a dilemma describes a narrowly Christian agenda. In their different ways, all religious communities in the fast-changing secularised world of post-modernity face similar questions – about faith and tradition, loyalty and openness, about accommodation and the place of religion in civic society. But it is as a Christian theologian that I write, and with a Christian version of the dilemma that I am concerned. My conviction is that it is perfectly possible for persons of faith to maintain their

---

[1] 'Inter-faith' and 'inter-religious' tend to be used interchangeably; the former has inter-personal, the latter more inter-systemic, connotations.

own integrity while yet learning how to relate responsibly and sensitively to each other. Indeed, I would want to argue that it is *only* through maintaining that integrity in relationship that the harmony of a wider multifaith world can be promoted.

Possible but not easy. I write these words in the middle of a strongly multi-faith town in west London where difference and otherness is very definitely the context of everyday life. Over the last quarter of a century, immigration, mainly from the sub-continent of India, has drastically changed the religious and cultural profile of this part of the capital city. There is a flourishing mosque five minutes away at the end of my street; the biggest Sikh gurdwara outside Punjab is being built close by; between them sit two Hindu temples and a Buddhist vihara. There are, according to some estimates, more than fifty communities or groups of faith within a mile's radius of the railway station – itself remarkable for having signs written in English and Punjabi. More recently the influx of refugees and asylum-seekers, from parts of Africa and from Eastern Europe, has added an extra layer of multi-cultural complication. This is a world unimaginable just a generation ago, a world in which the ancient stereotypes of East and West no longer apply. To walk these streets is to become vividly aware that, for all the grand talk of globalisation, the global only ever exists within the local. Underneath the romantic image conjured by exotic fruit, fragrant aromas and multicoloured saris, the reality is more intractable. The tensions and rivalries of whole continents are forced to live cheek by jowl within single blocks.

In the middle of such a chaos of human religiosity, the mainstream Christian churches can be forgiven for feeling overwhelmed. One temptation is to retreat, to create safe enclaves in the middle of what often appears as a thoroughly hostile environment. Another is to seek to establish a comparable prominence with belligerent slogans and antagonistic rhetoric. But, for many Christians living in such an environment, another vision is beginning to make itself felt, a vision of a Church committed to mediation and the building of bridges between communities. That this is a more risky option is clear. In principle, faith is always 'inter-faith', formed and practised in relationship with others; at the heart of the Gospel is a message of peace and reconciliation which crosses all social and cultural barriers. In practice, of course, establishing a basis for positive relations is rarely straightforward. Even apart from considerable theological problems about how the mission which Christ gave to his Church is to be understood, communities are divided by age-old suspicions as well as by language and custom. The history of inter-religious relations, often a record of colonial exploitation and unresolved ethnic and inter-communal rivalries, makes a confused situation even more complex. The dangers of manipulation, by one party or the other, the possibilities for misunderstanding on both sides, are all too real. Emphasise distinctive-ness and you encourage a self-satisfied sectarianism; suppress it and you risk a fundamentalist backlash. On the streets of a town where difference is as glaringly obvious as the hoardings advertising the latest offerings from Bollywood, traditional Christian language about conversion, proclamation, even mission itself, becomes problematic. All of which is to repeat the dilemma, and to ask how Christians committed to a vocation which is nothing if not prophetic are to practise an ethic which would take seriously a responsibility for the peace and harmony of all God's creation.

A theological response

That is only the first of many questions which will be raised, like so many placards at a protest rally, throughout the course of this book. Most will turn out to be versions of the dilemma noted above. How to develop an ethical theology? How does a Church which is conscious of being called by God's Word of truth discharge that responsibility while, at the same time, remaining responsible before the demands of a religiously plural world? How, to use the language of Justin and Irenaeus, to discern in this context possible 'seeds of the Word'? It may be objected, of course, that it is easy to ask questions and to remain content with posing dilemmas. I shall not seek to answer that charge at this stage. I hope it will be suffi-cient to state that throughout this book I shall be concerned with prac-tice and with a theology which both emerges from the practice of faith and feeds back into it. And by practice of faith I mean both the liturgical and devotional roots from which the community's faith, its vision of its evangelical responsibility, springs *and* all those forms of engagement with others which faith supports and inspires. That does not mean that I shall be avoiding the theoretical; indeed at times the discussion of some of the more awkward philosophical and theological questions may appear to digress a long way from the practice of engagement with people of other faiths on the streets of our inner cities. That dilemmas, such as I have pro-posed, demand careful thought I do not doubt. But the point I want to stress at the outset is that there is more to questions and dilemmas than an intellectual challenge which theology is called upon to resolve. They are the very stuff out of which faith grows, the poles which define the limits of the language of faith, and pointers to what I shall call the 'possibility of God'. If, as I shall seek to argue, to do theology is to speak of God in response to God's Word, then the first task is to listen for possible 'seeds of the Word', what God may be saying in this new context of otherness. If nothing else, questions and dilemmas guard against the greatest temptation faced by the theologian, the tendency to seek premature closure, to put a limit on the extent of God's Word. More positively, the issue is what is to be learned for Christian faith and practice from the engagement with the other.

Open-ended questions about the possibility of God in the world of many faiths, questions once consigned to the fringes of Christian reflection, have emerged in recent years as a distinct area of theology, often referred to as the theology of religions. This term is problematic, for a number of reasons. In some accounts there seems to be no distinction between religions and 'religion', in the all-encompassing singular. Both are synonymous with 'universal' or 'world' theologies which seek to include the whole of the religious experience of humankind within a single scheme.[2] These remain, at best, utopian projects. Jacques Dupuis, who briefly draws attention to this point at the beginning of his magisterial survey of theology of religions, perhaps wisely prefers to speak of a 'Christian theology of religious pluralism'. To work from within a religious tradition such as Christianity, he argues, does not demand a parochial defensiveness. But neither does it require a levelling of all that is different and distinctive. The theological task is to work within an horizon which recognises through experience that commitment to one's own faith can – and perhaps must – grow through dialogue and conversation.[3] Certainly a 'universalist perspective' seems almost like a contradiction in terms; as we shall see shortly, supposedly 'neutral' positions usually turn out, on further inspection, to be heavy with their own particular ideological baggage. On the other hand, Dupuis's apparent willingness to assimilate all history to Christian history raises its own questions – again ethical as much as theological – about how, precisely, Christians are to 'leave room and indeed create space for other "confessional" theologies of religion, be they Muslim, Hindu or otherwise'.[4] Does not the project of

---

[2] E.g. Swidler 1987; Cantwell Smith 1981.

[3] Dupuis 1997:1–13.

[4] Dupuis 1997:7.

'theology of religions', with the adherence to the Christian meta-narrative which it implies, lead to the eradication of the otherness of the other?

A more immediate – because easily disregarded – problem with the term is the subtly subversive effect it has on the whole project of Christian theology. According to Dupuis, theology of religions as a 'distinct theological *subject*' dates from the early 1970s.[5] Before that, in most of the Christian churches relations with people of other faiths were considered within the doctrine of salvation.[6] The other was very definitely a theological 'problem' to be solved. In the Roman Catholic Church the major catalyst for change was, of course, the Second Vatican Council which shifted attention away from the question of the 'individual outside the Church' to a more positive assessment of the significance for the Church's own identity of the individual as a member of an historically and socially constituted religious community.[7] Once, not so long ago, 'they' were lumped together as 'non-Christians'; now they are Buddhists and Jews, Muslims and Hindus – people of distinct religious belief and practice, who have all assumed their own identities, their worlds no longer the distant fringes of a Christianity-centred universe. At the same time, the borders separating theology and its disciplines from the various branches of religious studies have become more diffuse. Theology and its 'publics' – to use David Tracy's term – can no longer be confined within the neat schemes of Church, the academy and society at large.[8] 'Other religions', other persons of faith, the all-pervading 'context of otherness', make legitimate demands on the theologian and force Christians to cross boundaries – whether they like it or not.

Pluralism and paradigms

More is at stake here than the emergence of yet another discrete area of study to be pressed into service within the ever-crowded curricula of universities and seminaries. A theology which would respond to the other

---

[5] Dupuis 1997:2–3 refers to V. Boublik's *Teologia delle Religioni* (Rome: Studium; 1973) as the first 'extensive study'.

[6] See e.g. Daniélou 1948; 1962; Eminyan 1960; Maurier 1965; Nys 1966; Sullivan 1992; and the extensive bibliography and discussion in Dupuis 1997:84–157.

[7] The shift is central to Dupuis's distinction between 'fulfilment theories' (e.g. de Lubac, von Balthasar) and those which seek to express 'the Mystery of Christ in the Religious Traditions' (e.g. Rahner, Panikkar). See Dupuis 1997:130–57.

[8] See Tracy 1982:6–28.

does not so much extend existing categories beyond the traditional limits of mission and Church as create new ones – notably dialogue and culture – which challenge *all* traditional categories. It is, however, by no means obvious that the truly revolutionary nature of this shift has been properly recognised. In recent years a large number of surveys and overviews have appeared which give a fairly consistent 'map' of the area.[9] Thus the language of what has come to be known as the 'threefold paradigm', 'exclusivism', 'inclusivism' and 'pluralism', is thoroughly familiar. This, however, has not been an unmixed blessing. As Gavin D'Costa points out, employed heuristically or pedagogically, the typology has its uses. Nevertheless, the fact remains that it is basically a simplification of a highly complex issue, 'forcing diverse materials into easily controlled locations'.[10]

What is meant by these three terms is fairly obvious: exclusivism privileges one's own tradition against all others; inclusivism patronises other traditions as lesser or partial versions of what is realised in only one; pluralism argues for the relativising of all traditions, including one's own. Now, understood in terms of theological *tendencies* which emphasise theological instincts or values – for example, the three theological virtues of faith, hope and love, which are to be developed within the actual process of dialogue – they can be understood not as mutually exclusive positions but as complementary perspectives which need somehow to be held together. In due course, I shall seek to argue in this way.[11] As used in the literature of theology of religions, however, they remain all too easily at the level of 'isms', theories which, as decidedly flat abstractions, have a limited purchase on the much more diffuse and emotionally freighted practices of engagement between the people who walk the streets of our multi-faith inner cities.

My major objection to this 'paradigm approach' to theology of religions is that it tends to serve the interests of the pluralist agenda only. This, of course, is the school associated with the name of John Hick and the theologians of what might be called the 'Myth of Christian

---

[9] See e.g. Knitter 1985; D'Costa 1986; Barnes 1989. The typology first appears in Race 1983. Race himself ascribes it to Hick. The most comprehensive account of Hick's own position is contained in Hick 1989:233ff. For Hick's earlier theological development and 'Copernican revolution', first adumbrated in Hick 1977, see D'Costa 1987:13ff. For a brief overview of a rapidly changing scene see D'Costa's essay, 'Theology of Religions', in Ford 1997:626–44.

[10] In Ford 1997:637.

[11] In chapters 7 and 8, following ideas suggested by Mathewes 1998.

Uniqueness' school. Hick's 'normative pluralism' claims to represent the only theologically plausible account of today's world of many religions.[12] So-called 'exclusivism' and 'inclusivism' are soon given the status of preliminary and inadequate adjuncts, leading inexorably to a theological 'crossing of the Rubicon' into the theologically more straightforward world of 'pluralism'.[13] This rapid reduction of theological history represents a very partial reading of the Christian encounter with the other. How adequate, for example, are terms like 'exclusivism' and 'inclusivism' for describing the work of Barth and Rahner respectively, the usual suspects rounded up to represent the contemporary traditions of Catholic and Reformed Christianity respectively?[14] That there is truth in what remains admittedly a sketchy outline is clear; Christianity has at times been both proudly exclusive and naively inclusive of the other. But this is not the whole story, and Hick's sometimes sweeping generalisations inevitably ignore elements of an important counter-tradition.[15]

Religions, culture and identity

On closer examination, the very attempt to cut through the complexities of centuries of dialogue, conflict and inter-religious rivalry, reveals a number of hidden presuppositions. Two may be noted at this stage. Firstly, to work as a normative thesis, some phenomenology of commonality must be established. It is, however, all too easy to slip from identifying a 'common context' within which spiritual or religious phenomena are discerned to speaking of a 'common core' to which such phenomena can somehow be assimilated. That there are many 'family resemblances' between religious traditions is clear: the mythical, the devotional, the scriptural, the ethical and so on. Any dialogue must be led by some initial assumptions about what makes for comparability. On closer examination,

---

[12] For a critique of 'normative pluralism' see my chapter on Religious Pluralism in the forthcoming *Penguin Companion to the Study of Religion*, edited by John Hinnells, London: Penguin; expected 2002.

[13] See e.g. Hick, 'The Non-Absoluteness of Christianity', in Hick and Knitter 1987:16–36.

[14] The subsuming of Roman Catholic theology of religions within the category of 'inclusivism' fails to distinguish between what might be called a 'universalist instinct' which is to be found in some form in most of the great world faiths (see the examples in Griffiths 1990) and the theology of religions associated with Karl Rahner, the thesis of the Anonymous Christian. As Rahner argues, this is a response to a dogmatic problem which is specific to Catholic Christianity. See e.g. Rahner 1966a; 1966b; 1978:311–21; Hebblethwaite 1977; Schwerdtfeger 1982; D'Costa 1985. As for the 'exclusivist' end of the spectrum, a great deal of nuance is needed, as is noted in Knitter 1985:73–119.

[15] See my comments in 'Religious Pluralism', in Hinnells, ed. (n12 above).

however, the putative basis of comparison is often put into question. Holy founders, for instance, do not fulfil the same role in all religions; nor do apparently common features such as sacred books and symbolic representation. Is there not a danger of forcing awkwardly unstable religious realities into a Procrustean bed of untrammelled homogeneity? It sounds plausible to invoke the imagery of paths up the same mountain or rivers flowing into the great ocean. But even such high-minded metaphors can turn out to be subtly oppressive. Ironically the very seriousness with which the particularity of the other is treated turns out to be so dominated by theory and so far removed from everyday practice that the other is not taken seriously enough.[16]

The covert shift from 'common context' to 'common core' raises the suspicion that the pluralist rhetoric, which would understand 'the religions' as different instantiations of the same genus, owes more to Enlightenment constructions of 'religion' than to observation of what Lash calls 'the ancient traditions of devotion and reflection, of worship and enquiry'.[17] The model by which Enlightenment rationalism identified discrete 'religions' was the deism which dominated the debate about the nature of Christian faith in the seventeenth and eighteenth centuries.[18] This, of course, gave a privileged place to a transcendent Absolute reality, the ultimate object of human understanding, and was rooted in what developed into an all-pervading dualism of sacred and profane. As God was set apart from the world, so the practices of religion came to be divorced from everyday living. It is a short step from the isolation of the essence of all human religion to the identification of all sorts of discrete phenomena, beliefs as much as practices, which are supposed to be typical of a particular dimension of human life known as the 'religious'.

Leaving the intractable, yet relatively insignificant, question of the definition of religion to one side, there is a very practical issue here for any community of faith seriously committed to engagement with the other. However similar beliefs and practices appear, it is by no means obvious that they spring from the same roots or represent similar motivations. Before the experience of a plurality of 'religions' constructed a generic concept called 'religion', human religiosity was inseparable from

---

[16] See e.g. Surin 1990; D'Costa 1990c.

[17] Lash 1996:21. On the 'creation of religion' in the early modern period and the effect this has had on theology and political thought through the privatising of faith see Cavanaugh 1995.

[18] On the genealogy of 'religion' see Lash 1996 who draws particularly on the historical work of Harrison 1990. See also Cantwell Smith 1963; Byrne 1998 and Smith 1998.

what in the West has come to be referred to as culture, those customary processes of remembrance and ritual by which a community identifies and protects itself. As Michael Paul Gallagher points out, 'a central crisis of culture today comes from the split between culture and religion over the last two centuries'.[19] The question being begged by an hypothesis which would bypass such complexities is precisely what processes are responsible for creating specific creeds and belief-systems from the total world-views of particular communities of faith.[20] With an essentially 'modern' self-confidence in its ability to comprehend the world, normative pluralism is unable to respond to the difficult conceptual issues of identity and relationality with which the practice of what has come to be known as 'inculturation' challenges the Church. This raises, in a different form, the ethical issue of power and control which dominates the contemporary debate about inter-religious relations.

Contradictions and ethical questions

There is a second irony here, for it is precisely this challenge which the reading of the Christian theological tradition by the 'Myth school' claims to address. Having bought into a secularised version of Enlightenment religiosity, normative pluralism can only repeat, rather than radicalise, that element of the Christian tradition which it so roundly criticises. The argument of the Myth school is that claims for the salvific effectiveness of Christianity over against the inadequacy of non-Christian beliefs are arrogant and morally unacceptable. Yet the very language in which the pluralist paradigm is couched remains that of the – Christianity-centred – salvation problematic. Hick, for instance, sets the exclusivist claim to a 'Christian monopoly of salvific truth and life' against the 'logical conclusion' to which observation of the 'fruits of religious faith in human life' inevitably leads. The great religious traditions, he contends, promote 'individual and social transformation' to 'about the same extent'.[21] Therefore any argument for the superior effectiveness of Christianity is simply misplaced. But this attempt to relativise all soteriologies masks a

---

[19] Gallagher 1997:23.

[20] Wilfred Cantwell Smith consistently refuses to reduce communities of faith to separate and definable 'religions'; see 1962; 1963; 1981. Harrison 1990 takes up Cantwell Smith's thesis in an account of the origins of the modern concept of 'religion' and the development of the 'history of religions' as a discrete object of study.

[21] Hick and Knitter 1987:23.

fundamental confusion. It is one thing to criticise versions of the thesis which insist that no one may be saved outside a particular tradition for being narrowly chauvinist; it is quite another to conclude that all ways to salvation are variations of a common theme. It simply does not follow that, because all religious traditions can be understood as ways to salvation, enlightenment or the saving knowledge of God, they are all equally valid ways. Moreover, in Hick's hands, what purports to be an objective, neutral and universal perspective looks suspiciously like a contradiction in terms. On the one hand, each religion is given equal soteriological value; on the other, a privilege is assumed by the pluralist 'system' itself.[22]

As a reaction against the chauvinism of a theology which would ignore all claims to truth in other traditions of faith, the normative hypothesis has a simplicity and an elegance which commands attention. But it also runs its own risks. By masking difference and otherness under an amiable mask of tolerance, it seeks to claim the moral high-ground for an all-encompassing vision. Such ethical self-righteousness turns out in the end, however, to be strangely unethical. More intractable questions about the manipulations inherent in theory itself, questions about power and control, are easily ignored. What sort of violence is done to the other by totalising forms of discourse – even the confessedly tolerant discourse of pluralism which grants everyone a place? From what position does the observer speak? How is such an abstraction, an apparent view from nowhere, possible? More awkwardly, if the other is genuinely other, different, strange and unknown, how can anyone claim to know the other as other, let alone speak *on behalf of* the other?

That the intentions of the Myth school are admirable is clear, but it is all too easy, in a multi-faith world, to seek to reconcile the claims of secular humanism with various forms of more or less strident religious revivalism by attempting to rewrite religious traditions in the light of some overarching universal vision. The more demanding challenge is to work within and between the living traditions, not to seek to extract from them some supposedly timeless essence. The religious communities which mingle on the streets of many of our cities manage a reasonably benign form of peaceful co-existence; genuine understanding is another matter. A certain degree of tolerance, the willingness to put one's own deeply held beliefs in brackets, may be essential if an engagement

---

[22] See Barnes 1989; Loughlin 1990; D'Costa 1996:74–82.

with the other is to begin. But tolerance can be an expression of the power of the stronger, a proscription on open-ended engagement which keeps people apart rather than enabling a full and frank exchange, with all the threats to security which the naming of prejudices involves. Religious beliefs, still more the communities which seek to practise them, do not describe neat, ordered worlds. And, however much exhortations are made about recognising common values, the sources of motivation in the particular traditions themselves are rarely touched. Indeed, particularity can all too easily be subsumed under an ethic of openness which quickly becomes rigidly ideological. By defining *in advance* the canons of acceptable religious value in a multi-faith world, the normative pluralist project has already determined, and therefore controls, the response which the other can make.

The post-modern context

What sort of alternative to such a pluralist-dominated theology of religions is possible? To read history as a more or less straightforward progress towards ever more 'reasonable' accounts of Christian faith is to reduce the role of theology to monochrome discussions about the reconciliation of 'family resemblances'. The other is still a 'problem' to be excluded, included or – more safely – 'pluralised'. Far from opening up theology to fresh insights, the 'threefold paradigm' settles it into a safe and predictable agenda. Even proposals for a 'fourth paradigm', which seek to break the mould, sometimes risk an uncritical collusion in the pluralist project.[23] That further proposals are needed, to break the current deadlock, is clear. But a distinction needs to be made between those which merely extend the terms of a now stagnant discussion and those which would question the assumptions on which it is based. The proposals which I intend to develop in this book are based on the different logical status of a theology which arises from reflection on the actual engagement with the other and on the whole complex process of inter-personal communication which is represented by the term inter-religious dialogue.

My first concern, therefore, is to register an objection to the terms of a modern, but now curiously dated, project which aims to include all that

---

[23] See e.g. D'Costa 1986:22–51; 1991; 1996; Barnes 1989:66–86; Loughlin 1990; 1991. For discussion of a 'fourth paradigm' see Ogden 1992:79ff.; Di Noia 1992:47ff. The concept of 'paradigm' depends, however, on an uncritical reading of Thomas Kuhn's *The Structure of Scientific Revolutions* which, as some of his critics point out, is itself ambiguous. (See e.g. Shapere 1964.)

exists within universal canons of reason.[24] After the manner of Cartesian foundationalism, the pluralist hypothesis presumes to establish a panoptic vision 'above the action'. What this misses is any sense of being itself part of the 'context of otherness': the historical and cultural complexity of the different religious traditions and their fraught and often destructive relations with each other.

The assumption that the mind can somehow surmount the created order is questioned by the cultural sensibility known all too vaguely as postmodernity. Sometimes regarded as an imprecise nostalgic eclecticism rooted in somewhat diffuse shifts in aesthetic awareness, sometimes defined more specifically as a reaction against the Enlightenment legacy and an incredulity towards master narratives, the post-modern is – more obviously – what comes 'after' the modern: an uneasy consciousness of reaching a limit, of standing apart from the familiar, and of being forced to wait in the middle of a period which has yet to define itself. Such a sensibility finds one expression in the ironic, playful, relativist terms typical of much contemporary Western thought. But it has also created a healthy critical historicism. In the words of Graham Ward, the post-modern names the unspoken 'myths and ideologies', notably the 'ideology of language', which have long attended modern thinking: '[t]he fetishization of the literal, the unacknowledged presupposition that language refers to things that are pre-linguistic, that words correspond to objects, that discourse is therefore concerned primarily with reference, with responding to and describing the objective nature of the world outside its system'.[25] This more conservative post-modernism – conservative in the sense of retrieving traditional forms of discourse and metaphor – opens up the possibility of a creative engagement with the otherness both of history and of culture. To that extent it makes common cause with another voice, one more typical of the East where 'the other' is less a philosophical conundrum than an ethical reality: the voice of the politically and economically marginalised and the religiously and culturally different.[26]

What price the theology of religions in this post-modern context of otherness? To anchor my all-too-brief generalisations in the thoroughly

---

[24] For an account of the beginnings of the modern project in the search for a spatialising *mathesis universalis* see Ong 1983, and Pickstock 1998:47–61. For post-modern theological critiques of modernity see Lakeland 1997:12–36; Ward 1997:xv–xlvii.

[25] Ward 1997:xvii, xxi.

[26] A theme to be developed in chapter 6. See also my discussion of the political dimension of dialogue in Barnes 1999:40–5.

prosaic reality of our fragmented and increasingly secular world, the question is no longer how the traditional Christian language of salvation and incarnation is to be accommodated to an 'other' reality. It is, rather, a matter of how religious discourse *of any kind* is to play a significant part in the process of building a harmonious multi-religious society. To put the point in more overtly Christian terms, it is to ask how Christians can speak of what they know in faith to be true without either relying on an uncritical use of modern 'myths and ideologies' or lapsing back into the oppositionalist discourse of ancient antagonisms. That, in brief, is the ethical *and* theological issue.

Being forced to live cheek by jowl with people who come from very different religious and cultural backgrounds undermines the uncritical self-assurance of the 'threefold paradigm'. This is not, however, to conclude that a post-modern sensibility towards the other somehow presents us with a ready-made alternative to the modern project of theology of religions. Indeed, to speak of 'alternative' theologies is to acquiesce in a fundamentally mistaken perception of the issue. If there is an alternative to a theology of 'other religions', it will emerge from a reflection on 'the other', not on 'religion'. I am, therefore, less concerned with explaining the 'problem' of religious pluralism than with understanding the meaning of the providential mystery of otherness for the life of the Church and for its practice of faith. My aim is not to continue a debate which has long since ceased to be creative, but – more radically – to learn how to read the engagement of Christian faith and the all-pervading context of otherness as revealing possible 'seeds of the Word'. Such a project is, I believe, more generous than that allowed by an approach to theology of religions which does little more than patronise otherness.

Responding to God's Word

What I seek to present is a theology of inter-faith dialogue which responds to the post-modern 'context of otherness'. I want to argue that theology of religions needs to be taken back into the centre of the Christian project of reflection on its experience of the Trinitarian God, the one who goes on generating meaning within the ever-changing flux of human relations through the creative interaction of Word and Spirit. Care needs to be taken, however, that such a project does not appear like some a priori essentialist scheme, imposed unceremoniously on some unsuspecting 'other'.

To begin from the practice of inter-religious dialogue is not an attempt to cut loose from the mainstream of Christian theological reflection, but, on the contrary, to recognise that dialogue is first and foremost a practice of *faith*; it springs from the same roots as the Church's liturgy, the story which Christians seek to tell. I shall seek, therefore, to give a theological account of practices of welcome and hospitality towards the other by rooting them in the formative experiences of the Christian community. In celebrating the Christian story the Church speaks by returning to its origins where it is made conscious of God's act of self-giving–for this and for *all* people. The liturgy is the sacramental act which narrates God's Word and which therefore gives Christians their identity as a people called to speak of what they know in Christ to be true. At the same time, in listening for 'seeds of the Word' Christians learn how to practise that form of waiting upon God's Spirit which mirrors Jesus's responsiveness to the Father. No arbitrary distinction between the two is possible. If all our knowing is relational and contextual–if, that is to say, every act of knowing relates the self to some other–then the encounter with another person, especially one who seeks to speak of what is true for all people, is in some sense an encounter with *the* Other, with God. But in what sense? And how to speak of such a relationship?

The Christian theologian is expected to speak out of the Christian meta-narrative without eradicating the otherness of the other. Emphasising the more ethical side of the dilemma, the task is to be respectful of otherness without slipping into the relativism of incommensurability. So far I have provided no more than dilemmas, questions and an initial sketch which will clearly need more careful elucidation as we proceed. But broad brush-strokes are necessary at this stage, if only that the properly theological questions – that is to say, issues about the nature and presence of God in a multi-faith world – may become clear. A reading of the Christian encounter with the other which stands 'above the action', making the participant in dialogue no more than an observer, risks premature closure; all too easily it domesticates the possibility of God. Indeed it is doubtful whether the trio of exclusivism, inclusivism and pluralism gives us anything more than a subtly prescriptive account of the actual practice of dialogue – let alone provides the motivation for serious engagement with the other. 'The first', as Rowan Williams puts it, 'rules it out in principle, the second makes a bid for ownership of all that is tolerable and recognisable in other traditions, the third allows no more than unquestioning co-existence'.[27] There is little risk here, no sense of mystery and no sign of a God who seeks to go on speaking God's Word in the demanding but richly rewarding 'middle ground' of human interaction.

This takes us back again to the opening dilemma. When the primary consideration is the development of a certain harmony between religious communities, it is all too easy to underestimate the difficulties of prac- tising an acceptably open and tolerant form of inter-faith dialogue. For Paul Knitter and Hans Küng, for example, inter-faith dialogue is essential for the cause of world peace and human liberation.[28] Their point of departure is the 'ethical' end of the dilemma: 'no peace among the na- tions without peace among the religions'. But peace has to be *made*; it can- not be proclaimed from on high. The question which the 'global ethic' project begs is how people of faith are to be motivated somehow to shift from a purely 'local' to a supposedly 'global' perspective. Such motivation can only come from within the religious tradition. Christians may not have an auspicious record of preaching and practising peace towards people of other religions, but there is no neat ready-made alternative which would avoid careful attention to the Christian concept of the self- communicating God and to what I called earlier the Church's evangelical responsibility to the other.

Dialogue and Radical Orthodoxy

If there is an alternative, a way of engaging with the other which does not do violence to the tradition of faith, it will emerge from reflection on the Christian experience of dialogue itself. But can 'dialogue' be understood in properly *Christian* terms? The term has connotations of a liberal ac- commodation which makes some theologians distinctly nervous. John Milbank, for instance, approaches my dilemma very much from the theological direction. As the title of the Radical Orthodoxy he has in- spired indicates, he is engaged in a quite thoroughgoing theological deconstruction of the whole project of inter-faith dialogue. The very language in which the pluralist paradigm is couched represents what he calls an 'ascription to modern liberal Western values [which] does not acknowledge the traditional and continuing political sub-structures

---

[27] Williams 2000:95.

[28] See 'Interreligious Dialogue: What? Why? How?' in Swidler *et al.* 1990:19–44; Küng 1993:xi–xii; Küng and Kuschel 1993; Knitter 1995.

which perpetuate these values'.[29] His comments draw attention to various presuppositions, especially about the relationship of theory and practice, which must attend any responsible theology of inter-faith encounter. But they also raise the question whether a largely intellectualist model of dialogue is adequate to describe the much more diffuse, laborious and even chaotic pattern of inter-personal and inter-community negotiation which is the reality of so much encounter between persons of faith.

I use that designation 'persons of faith' deliberately at this point to draw attention to another, if very different, example of premature closure – and to the problems incurred by any theology which would reflect on dialogue in a post-modern world. According to John Milbank, the post-modern context of otherness presents 'a moment of opportunity for theology'.[30] By refusing to recognise the autonomy of any secular realm, Milbank argues that a space is freed within which theology may speak. There can, therefore, be no Archimedean point of theoretical reason from which the world of religious pluralism is to be judged. Neither can there be any practical, ethical or political reason from which inter-religious discussion and negotiation may be conducted. All forms of supposedly neutral universal reason are culturally loaded and, therefore, forms of a discredited secular reason. The logic of Milbank's position is that the only alternative to a pluralism which invokes secular reason to judge between religious claims is criteria which arise directly from a restatement of Christian belief. Distinctly uneasy with assumptions that dialogue enables participants somehow to transcend the particularities of their own tradition, Milbank is also deeply suspicious of a hidden agenda which holds that 'dialogue gives a privileged mode of access to truth'.[31]

But why should dialogue be understood in this way? There is certainly something attractive about Milbank's insistence that the Church carries its own interpretation of history. Christians speak out of their faith in the God who speaks before them; the Christian language of faith does not *depend* on any dialogue with any other position. Milbank's meaning is clear when he opposes any form of correlational unfolding of the dialectic of sacred and secular to an Augustinian vision of the Church as the City of God, a realm of ontological peace. Whatever its manifest historical

---

[29] Milbank 1990b:175.

[30] Milbank 2000:41.

[31] Milbank 1990b:181.

failures, the Church sets out to be a source of harmony for humankind, a 'hope for community'.[32] Milbank thus presents us with a powerful riposte to the fragmentation of the post-modern and its potential for impending chaos. And, in so far as he brings a certain 'hermeneutic of suspicion' back into the practice of dialogue, his is an important reminder that Christianity is not about 'tea and nice conversation' but is based on claims to speak a truth which is subversive of all purely secular pretensions. His trenchant refusal to acknowledge a space independent of the Christian meta-narrative works well as a rejection of post-modern nihilism. But can religious traditions and world-views which have for the most part not been influenced by the values and vested interests of Western culture legiti-mately be assimilated so neatly to the realm of 'secular reason'?

What allows Milbank to lump religions and secular ideologies together is his idealised reading of Christianity as more post-modern than any other meta-narrative. For Milbank post-modernity presents Christians with a moment of opportunity, but this does not mean that they speak just one more discourse alongside others. In their refusal to draw boundaries, in their rejection of violence, they claim no territory of their own; theirs is the paradox of a 'nomad city'.[33] But, in a manner which is, ironically, all too similar to the 'global ethic' project, not to mention Hick's liberal pluralism, precious little attention is given by Milbank to the laborious and sometimes painful process by which peace is to be achieved. The ideal may be that of a Church on pilgrimage, a Church which is free from the constraints of structure and institution. But even so other-worldly a vision can become over-bearing, a covert violence which does not so much subvert secular pretensions as stand Hick-like 'above the action', avoiding the awkward demands of negotia-tion with other human beings. The danger, as some of Milbank's critics point out, is that the peace to which this Church is committed does not embrace difference but, through the force of a rhetoric delivered from on high, squeezes the very life out of it.[34]

For Milbank, dialogue has no theological significance; he is content with a minimalist 'mutual suspicion'.[35] The reality for a Church charged not just with bearing a message of truth but with listening for

---

[32] Milbank 1991:232.

[33] Milbank 1991:229.

[34] See e.g. Lakeland 1997:68–76, Reader 1997:133–49.

[35] Milbank 1990b:190.

the 'seeds of the Word' is considerably more complex. God's Word goes on being spoken – and not only in ways which the Church can presume to know. That there is a properly theological dimension to dialogue, that dialogue can indeed reveal something of God, is brought out by Emmanuel Levinas when he speaks about the 'God who comes to mind' in religion, in liturgy, and in the dialogue with the other person. Dialogue for Levinas is no unequivocal meeting of equals but, on the contrary, is founded in dissymmetry and difference. He wants to 'make it be felt that dialogue . . . is a thinking of the *unequal*, a thought thinking *beyond* the given'.[36]

In the Western philosophical tradition, as Levinas would remind us, the classic model of dialogue derives from Plato. A process of question and answer leads through the uncovering of ignorance to a fullness of understanding of a given topic.[37] For Levinas, however, dialogue is 'not merely a way of speaking', a method for uncovering truth, but a call to transcendence.[38] An initial distinction can, therefore, be made between two rather different ways in which the term dialogue is used, depending on whether the emphasis is placed on content or on form. In the first case, dialogue is described as a communication between two individuals who represent different communities of faith, speak a common language, and aim at some sort of consensus.[39] In the second, more ethical language is used to speak of the encounter which establishes a relationship between persons. If the former privileges the meaning of what is said over the act of speaking, the latter subordinates the issues discussed to the significance of the encounter itself.[40] In practice, dialogue is often justified as an end in itself by the potential understanding which the meeting enables.[41] It may be something of an interfaith cliché, but it remains none the less true, that dialogue takes place when *persons* meet – persons who are divided yet united by the asymmetries of language and discourse, the sensitivities of history and the tragic pathology of misunderstanding.

---

[36] Levinas 1998b:151.

[37] See C. Jan Swaeringen, 'Dialogue and Dialectic: The Logic of Conversation and the Interpretation of Logic', in Maranhao 1990:47–72.

[38] Levinas 1998b:147.

[39] For an excellent account of inter-religious dialogue conceived as debate or apologetics see Griffiths 1991.

[40] See Tanner 1993:3–6; Lochhead 1988:64.

[41] See e.g. Lochhead 1988:79–81.

Dialogue as critical generosity

It is in this sense of inter-personal engagement, with its ethical overtones, that I use the term 'dialogue' in this book. The now standard description of forms of inter-faith dialogue in the Roman Catholic Church puts 'the dialogue of theological exchange' alongside 'dialogue of life', 'dialogue of action' and 'dialogue of religious experience'.[42] No further analysis is given in official documents, no indication of how they relate to each other nor of where the distinctions come from.[43] The main issue is the relationship between what are seen as the complementary theological claims of 'dialogue' and 'proclamation', but in none of the documents is the one reduced to the other. Dialogue has its 'own integrity', consisting of a whole series of different activities, the practices of a missionary Church, but above all else 'a manner of acting, an attitude and a spirit . . . [which] implies concern, respect, and hospitality towards the other'.[44] The praxis of inter-religious dialogue, as Tracy says, 'does not merely bear a "religious dimension". It *is* a religious experience.'[45]

This is what makes inter-faith dialogue in all its many forms worthy of a more generous theological response than 'mutual suspicion'. If the Gospel really is about recognising and sharing the Good News of God's own act of welcome and hospitality, then theology has the task of telling that story in all its complexity and most unlikely manifestations. In this book I shall describe inter-faith dialogue as the 'negotiation of the "middle"'. I do not mean by this some sort of haggling or bargaining over positions of power but, more profoundly, a mediation of the context of otherness. For it is here that Christians find themselves and are faced with the multiple demands of the Church's evangelical responsibility. Negotiating this 'space between' is not, as Milbank seems to assume, a matter of engaging in some unprincipled debate between a series of competing but partial viewpoints from which, one hopes, truth will eventually emerge.

---

[42] The fourfold dialogue appears in Pope John Paul II's 1991 encyclical *Redemptoris Missio*, paragraph 57; and in two major Vatican statements on inter-faith dialogue: *Attitude of the Church towards the Followers of Other Religions*, published by the SNC, 1984; 27–35; and *Dialogue and Proclamation*, published jointly by the PCIRD and the Congregation for Evangelisation, 1991; 42–46. The order of the forms varies.

[43] See Sharpe's discussion of *Redemptoris Missio* and *Dialogue and Proclamation* in Burrows 1994:161–72. Speaking of 'discursive', 'human', 'secular' and 'interior' dialogue (originally in his 'The Goals of Inter-Religious Dialogue' in Hick 1974:75–95), he acknowledges his debt to the distinctions made by Taylor in 'The Meaning of Dialogue', in Jai Singh 1967:55–64.

[44] DM 29.

[45] Tracy 1990:98.

It is, rather, to recognise that all Christians speak out of a dimension of irreducible otherness which they encounter at the very heart of their own identity, the 'middle' of a world shared with others.

In the next chapter I will try to show that the Church is called constantly to recover the most significant example of this otherness, namely in its historical relationship with the people of the Old Covenant. Just as the encounter with the Jews reveals the other as both 'not the same' but not totally other either, so in other forms of interfaith dialogue Christians learn to recognise not an '*alter ego*', an extension of the self, with whom I share some sort of common essence, but one whom Buber would call 'thou', one who calls and to whom I must respond. Rather than a self-sufficient 'I' confronting an equally monolithic and unmoving other, some version of the Buberian 'it', dialogue always has an inter-personal dimension which makes it intrinsically ethical. The 'it' is a 'thou': not a 'thinking subject' or faceless other but the one who challenges and responds to challenge. The 'negotiation of the middle' is not, therefore, an examination of the space where persons meet, but entails exploration of the relationship which the space supports. This – to return to the point argued earlier – is a very different approach to theology of religions from that allowed by the normative pluralism thesis, a model which is irretrievably locked into the search for some overarching universal standard of rationality. However, it needs to be stressed that the alternative to such a model is not the postmodern nihilism which Radical Orthodoxy – quite rightly – seeks to resist. To reject the possibility of an Archimedean place to stand is not to end up imprisoned within particular limited horizons. It is to learn how to speak, how to communicate what we know, and how to learn from what we do not know. As William Placher puts it, '[i]n a particular conversation, we learn from a particular conversation partner, in a way shaped by our own previous assumptions as well as by the insights of the person to whom we speak'.[46]

Before briefly outlining something of the direction which this book will take, let me summarise the argument advanced thus far. A theology which arises from the inter-subjective experience of dialogue raises crucial questions from this facing of the other – about subjectivity, otherness and relationality. These questions are not, however, awkward complications to be sidelined, avoided or totalised into some grand theological

---

[46] Placher 1989:112.

scheme. They are intrinsic to a Christian faith practised in a spirit of welcome and hospitality.

I began by observing that the particular question of the relationship of the Church to people of other faiths is part of a much broader and more intractable agenda than is allowed by theologies of religions which are locked into the language of the normative pluralism project. The crucial questions which that relationship raises are not, in the first place, about salvation, Church and mission, but – more fundamentally – about what happens to Christian identity when the self encounters the other by cross-ing the threshold into another world. Missing from the current debate in theology of religions is any adequate account of the vulnerability of the self in face of the other. The none-too-hidden assumption is that inter-locutors are transparent to themselves, if not to the other, and that the difficulty of communication will be overcome once the 'right' language has been learned and the other becomes more familiar. The complex issues raised by inter-religious dialogue, in all its forms, beg questions about how identities are established – and how, and why, and to what, they adapt and change.

My point is that the relationship with the other has intrinsically the-ological dimensions. Christians are called not just to speak of the God who is revealed in Christ but to listen critically yet with generosity to what is spoken about God by the other. Christian witness to the God of Jesus Christ is rooted in the events which have formed the community – ultimately the Christian story of the Death and Resurrection of Christ. Christian 'action' is inseparable, therefore, from a certain 'passion'. What is required for a proper sense of Christian faith and practice in a plural-ist world is a theology which allows such a passivity, the experience of limitation imposed by otherness of all kinds, to speak of the Other – of God – within the context of a critical commitment to the good of all God's people.[47]

Christianity in a multi-faith world

My argument for a theology of dialogue – that is to say a theology which would seek to reflect on the Christian experience of existing in

---

[47] By passivity here I do not mean to imply the opposite of activity – some stripping of the self in face of a 'divine void'. With Rowan Williams, 2000:11, I want to argue for a contemplative *apophasis* which leads to a more complex 'discovery that one's selfhood and value simply lie in the abiding faithful presence of God, not in any moral or conceptual performance'.

relationship with the other – will develop cumulatively, in a number of overlapping stages. It will be obvious from what has already been said that I write from within the Christian theological tradition; more specifically I write as a Roman Catholic. The examples of inter-faith dialogue will be taken, for the most part, from the experience of that church. My theme, however, is the nature of Catholic Christianity in a multi-faith world – a Christianity which takes seriously its message of reconciliation for all people. If I start by exploring the Second Vatican Council's insights into the relationship of the Church with people of other faiths, it is not to ignore all other Christian traditions. The Council owed its existence as what Karl Rahner called a 'theological event' to a number of significant influences, many of them from outside the Roman Catholic Church itself. Some decades later, a narrowly 'denominational' interpretation of Vatican II seems quite inappropriate, and certainly foreign to the intentions of the generous-hearted Pope John XXIII who convoked the Council. At the same time, Vatican II did raise some awkward questions about how different ecclesial communities, and a fortiori different religious traditions, are 'related' or 'orientated towards' the People of God.[48] In due course, these questions will occupy us at some depth. What I want to stress here is that the perspectives which arise from the Council's theology of the Church as the people of God on pilgrimage and the call to discern the 'signs of the times' speak to, indeed *belong* to, the theological patrimony of all Christians.

Such perspectives encourage an awareness of the Church's own historicity and prescribe an imaginative engagement with contemporary culture. But in the first place they point to the primacy of Judaism for Christian self-understanding. Immediately, an issue of great delicacy presents itself. Judaism remains, in an important sense, other, and may not be reduced within an all-embracing Christian totality; indeed the risk of totalising the Jewish other is precisely the lesson taught by recent history, the history of the Shoah. For Paul, as we shall see in the next chapter, the constancy of God and the continuing validity of the promises made to the Patriarchs is the dominant issue which allows of no straightforward resolution. Is the Good News just for the Jews? If not, then what is to be said about them? Has God changed his mind? Paul's questions, theological *and* ethical questions about the relationship between Christianity and its Jewish other, cross the historical divide. They form the

---

[48] See LG 15–16.

dominating theme of *Nostra Aetate*, the Council's declaration on the relationship of the Church to non-Christian religions.

For all its blandness and brevity, *Nostra Aetate* is more than a hasty exercise in the updating of Roman Catholic thinking. In examining the process of its formation, we shall discern the beginning of a new vision of the way what was called earlier the catholic or universalist instinct is to be exercised.[49] We shall also find ourselves pointed towards a theology of revelation and, more importantly, towards the liturgical basis of all theology. Vatican II reminded the Church as a whole of its origins in the foundational event of the Death and Resurrection of Christ which is celebrated in the liturgy and through which the Church goes on renewing itself. For the Christian community to be faithful to this event entails a constant repetition; the words of the Christian narrative must be spoken again if the Church is to hear the Word and be led by the Spirit. But the present proclamation of the Word, whether through the liturgy or in public witness, can never be separated in any simplistic way from the traditions and structures which channel and, to some extent, precede the gathering of the community of faith. Each time, therefore, the liturgical repetition will be unavoidably different.

Paradoxically, then, to establish continuities is to be prepared to reckon with the constant rupture of continuity, to recognise the 'gap' which holds known and unknown, same and other, in continual dialogue. The question put to the Church is how it is to react to the 'context of otherness', how it can be at once faithful to what is known and sensitive to what is not known – but which may well be revealed through the other. As noted earlier, enormous conceptual issues about subjectivity and relationality are raised at this point; they will form the major consideration of chapters 3 and 4. The task of chapter 2, however, is to examine and establish the Church's 'primary relationship', the dialogue with Judaism – not just because it is the starting-point for the reflections which led to *Nostra Aetate*, but because it forms the matrix within which all Christian relations with others are situated.

From this arises what is in many ways the key question, whether this relationship of Christianity to its Jewish other is also formative of all other inter-religious relations between Christians and others. My response is not that one particular historical relationship provides a paradigm for understanding all other histories, but that that history changes

---

[49] See note 14 above.

the conditions under which the Church's history as a whole is viewed. In exploring the Church's relations with people of other faiths I shall employ Michel de Certeau's project of 'heterology'. As the term implies, this is a phenomenology of the other, what I shall call the 'returning other', other persons, other stories, other experiences, which, once marginalised to the borders of the known and familiar, manage somehow to insinuate themselves back into the centre of critical reflection. Its significance, as far as a Christian theology of religions is concerned, is to effect a certain pragmatic recovery of forms of otherness from the past which continue to affect the present.

In these pages, de Certeau is more than an occasional philosophical commentator. Historian, theologian, psychoanalyst, cultural critic, mystic of the everyday, his constant preoccupation is with the possibility of faith in a world which is made ever aware of the gap between representation and reality.[50] By reminding us that the present is always filled with traces of an other which cannot be resolved or removed in any simple way, he points us, however tentatively, in the direction of a theology which emerges from the 'context of otherness'. The image of the 'returning other' thus links the story of the Church's experience of religious pluralism with the more theoretical reflections on otherness and relationality in chapters 3 and 4. Here Emmanuel Levinas's philosophy of the other, and the engagement of Paul Ricoeur with his project, form the philosophical 'pivot' on which this study turns. For Levinas, all dialogue begins with a facing of the other as radically demanding. Perhaps more than for any other contemporary thinker, for him the encounter with another person is an opening to the Infinite. The ethical responsibility I am made to feel before the otherness of another person encourages me to think 'otherwise than being'.[51] Such a project is never less than paradoxical and provocative, bringing us to the heart of the 'context of otherness' and the philosophical questions it raises. How to account for a relationship with the other, to know the other *as other*, without assimilating the other to the category of sameness? How to avoid positing an alterity which is simply unknowable? Put another way – in the terms of Vatican II's account of inter-religious relations – how to discern signs of the Christian mystery, the gift of God himself, at the heart of particularity and difference?

---

[50] On de Certeau as theologian see especially the introduction to Ward 2000:4; also Bauerschmidt 1996a and 1996b.

[51] See Levinas 1991:3.

A theology which responds to these questions will be set between an activism which risks totalising the other and a passivity which can lead to a loss of self-identity. The aim must be to give an account of Christian subjectivity which would seek to respond ethically to the other. How is the responsible subject to negotiate with the other without resorting to acts of subtle manipulation or a more-or-less blatant violence? To explore what I shall argue is an intrinsically ethical issue, with all sorts of uncomfortable political 'edges', in chapters 5 and 6 I shall set this aspect of the Church's present experience alongside a more recent example of inter-faith engagement, the experience of the Church in India. The intention is to show how ethical sensitivity develops. De Certeau's perspectives on the practices of everyday life, in which the powerless fashion the trans-formation of the dominant cultural economy in order to adapt it to their own interests, will be used to develop the now familiar, but obscure, concept of 'inculturation'. The focus here is on the responsibility of the theologian. Religion, not just in India but in any part of the world, is an ambiguous force. The dilemma – to collude with injustice or to be committed to political agitation – is fraught with risk. By using de Certeau's method of narrating 'micro-discourses', in which he speaks not of 'the other' but of 'others' with their ever-developing and ever-changing relations with one another, I will take up the terms of a theo-logy of dialogue which emerges from within the practice of a community of faith committed to a life of constant 'negotiation of the middle'.

Principles and virtues

From the social context which forms the dialogue I return in chapters 7 and 8 to the dilemma with which I started and to the terms of a theology of welcome and hospitality. This is not concerned in the first place with enunciating theological responses to the 'problem' of the other. It is, rather, about the formation of principles, or – to be more precise – the virtues which will inform the practice of inter-faith relations.[52] The theo-logical virtues of faith, hope and love are formed within the Christian community by the prior dialogue which God initiates, by the generosity of God's self-giving. My aim is not, therefore, to develop a 'theology of

---

[52] Here I shall be following Alasdair MacIntyre's account of the virtues as dispositions or qualities necessary to achieve the goods internal to practices, and practices as forms of 'socially established cooperative human activity' which provide the 'arena in which the virtues are exhibited' (see e.g. MacIntyre 1985:181–225).

religions' – if by such a project is meant a discrete area of study within theology which seeks somehow to include the other in a conceptual world dominated by the same. Rather, I shall be guided throughout by a theology which takes seriously the Christian responsibility of hospitality to the stranger, the responsibility of narrating a story which neither totalises nor relativises – but, as Gerald Loughlin so beautifully puts it, 'imagines the possibility of harmonious difference and peace as the inner dynamic of the triune God'.[53] To do theology of religions in this sense means returning to the liturgical and sacramental practice of the Church's faith, and learning to recognise there the dimension of otherness within which *all* Christian theology is to be done.

Finally, let me state a principle which runs through this book. The Church speaks of what it knows in faith – that God has raised Jesus from the dead and thereby transformed the whole of creation. What the Church does *not* know is the total reality of what always remains other and utterly mysterious. Christians must, therefore, acknowledge this possibility: that God may act in the world in ways of which the Church does not know. Anything less would be to risk putting an arbitrary limit on the action of God; the Christian experience of the grace of God, of God acting freely and generously to create a people for himself, demands an openness to the Spirit at work in the world of the other. From the point of view of the practice of faith, the crucial question is how Christians are to keep faithful witness, hoping for resolution, while yet knowing that the future lies always in the hands of God alone, and in God's providential care. In the final chapter I shall, therefore, conclude with questions about how interfaith encounter is to be practised responsibly. My main concern, however, is with the terms of a Christian theology which can speak of God with integrity before the other. And for that I first need to give some account of recent teaching and recent experience.

---

[53] Loughlin 1996:21, commenting on Milbank's use of Augustine's musical metaphors to explain the singularity of Christian community; see Milbank 1991:227–8. The question of how such a harmony may be achieved is, however, left open.

2

Remembering the Covenant

On 8 April 1979, the Jesuit School of Theology in Cambridge, Massachusetts, awarded Karl Rahner an honorary doctorate. In response, Rahner gave a lecture in which he described Pope John XXIII's extraordinary exercise in 'updating' the Roman Catholic Church as 'the first major official event in which the Church actualized itself precisely as a *world Church*'.[1] What Rahner tries to present is, in his own words, a 'fundamental theological interpretation of Vatican II' – an interpretation, that is, which is 'suggested by the Council itself'. Vatican II was remarkable because for the first time in the history of the Church a genuinely 'world episcopate' gathered with the Bishop of Rome as the 'final teaching body in the Church'. Whatever its limitations, the Council marked the beginnings of a major shift of horizons. The influence of bishops from Asia and Africa, the demise of Latin as the language of the liturgy, and the emergence of particular local and more genuinely non-European churches, made the Roman Catholic Church as a whole more conscious of its 'world responsibility'.

This could, of course, be interpreted as no more than a belated attempt to reverse the introspective mentality dominant since the Modernist crisis. There is something to be said for such a view. Rahner, however, writes as a theologian. He is concerned with a theology of history, and particularly with the history of the Council as a theological 'event' in its own right. His point is not that the Council enabled Roman Catholics to recover a proper sense of their own identity, but that the true complexity of the title Catholic to describe the universal Church became apparent – perhaps for the first time. Picked out by Rahner for specific mention are

---

[1] Subsequently published as 'Towards a Fundamental Theological Interpretation of Vatican II'; see Rahner 1979c.

the two shortest – and most unexpected – of the Council's documents: on other religions and on religious liberty.[2] The former Rahner describes as a 'truly positive evaluation of the great world religions'. The latter reflects the same vision of the 'universal and effective will of God'. In all situations throughout the world the Church renounces the use of 'instruments of force for the proclamation of its faith which do not lie in the power of the gospel itself'.

It is the declaration on the relationship of the Church with other religions which speaks most clearly of this epoch of the 'world Church'. To call this document 'positive' is to draw attention to the fact that no longer are people of other faiths marginalised as an unfortunate complication on the fringes of a Church-centred world. Rather they have their own providential role to play in relation to the life and mission of a now world-orientated Church. Rahner's theological reading of history seeks, therefore, to understand this new process of engagement against the background of the brief period of Jewish Christianity and its encounter with the Mediterranean world of Hellenism and Roman civilisation. The significance of this earlier shift for today's Church is all too easily ignored. Just as Paul very consciously steered the infant Church away from its encounter with the purely Jewish world and established a properly Gentile Christianity, so with Vatican II a still very Western Church recognises the significance of other cultures and religions and the need to develop practices and theology which will adequately express its new responsibility. Rahner is not, however, just drawing a neat historical parallel. No historical event, as he says, ever repeats itself. On the other hand, Christian faith is a response to a God who reveals God – and goes on revealing God – through the particularity of historical events. Events as such may not repeat themselves, but God's Word does continue to speak through them. Paul's move to extend the preaching of the Good News beyond the Jewish world was not based on merely pragmatic or cultural considerations but, according to Rahner, has intrinsically *theological* dimensions. Rahner admits that we do not yet have an adequate theology of this first break, adding that 'perhaps that will only be worked out in a dialogue with the Synagogue of today'. Nevertheless, the second great shift in the Church's self-understanding, the contemporary dialogue with the great world faiths, has much to learn from

---

[2] Unexpected in the sense that neither appeared in the 'reduced list' of seventeen schemata which was proposed at the end of the Council's inconclusive first session in December 1962. See Hebblethwaite 1993:314–15. Both assumed independent status from under the 'umbrella' of ecumenism. See Stransky, 'The Foundation of the SPCU', in Stacpoole 1986:62–87.

the first – what might be called the Church's 'primary relationship', the dialogue between Christianity and its Jewish other.

Rahner's vision of a Church committed to discerning the 'seeds of the Word' in the movements of human history forms the basic framework within which I intend to work. In this chapter I shall be concentrating on the teaching about other faiths found in the various documents of the Second Vatican Council. *Nostra Aetate* represents a major watershed in the development of theology of religions. But, unexpected though it undoubtedly was, its significance lies not with any novel theology which it encouraged, but with the way it marks Rahner's 'second shift', reminding the Church as a whole of its first, and fateful, move towards the wider non-Jewish world.

Retrieving an older tradition

The question which will occupy us is the link between the two. To what extent can the first be understood as paradigmatic or formative of the second? It is not my intention to give an exhaustive analysis of Vatican II's various references to people of other faiths.[3] Rather, following Rahner, I shall be concerned with a theological account of the process by which the Church's public attitude towards the phenomenon of religious pluralism was irrevocably changed. The most important novelty of Vatican II, according to Alberigo, lies 'in the very fact that it was convoked and held'.[4] If the Council can be described as the single most important ecclesial 'event' of the twentieth century, it was not because of the depth of its theological insight into the nature of the Church, its 'updating' of the liturgy or its directives on missionary and pastoral practice. More profoundly, through the Council the Church was made conscious of the radical contingency of all human living and therefore of its own historicity.

The argument of this chapter is that in coming to terms with John XXIII's 'Jewish question' the Council was forced to reckon with suppressed aspects of the Church's history. The major effect of this retrieval has been to disturb the philosophy of history on which the Church's self-understanding, let alone its understanding of its relations with people

---

[3] See the new five volume history of the Council currently being edited by Giuseppe Alberigo. At the time of writing, volumes 1 (1995), 2 (1997) and 3 (2000) of the English version edited by Joseph Komonchak have appeared.

[4] See Alberigo, 'The Christian Situation after Vatican II', in Alberigo 1987:1–24; quotation from p. 24.

of other faiths, has traditionally been based. This philosophy, as John O'Malley reminds us, has been mainly concerned with the absolutising of particular events in order to emphasise continuity with the past and a more or less smooth progress through time.[5] Beyond a number of models which have been used in the past to plot the continuity of tradition, O'Malley suggests that Vatican II raises another possibility: reform by transformation or revolution, which implies 'at least a partial rejection of the past in the hope of creating something new'.[6] This is reflected in the uneasy tension detectable within many of the documents as much as within the process which was the Council as a whole: a tension between a return to, and renewal of, the sources of an ancient tradition, on the one hand, and a commitment to the reading of the 'signs of the times', the changes and differences within society and human culture at large, on the other.

The theologian who works in today's 'context of otherness' is committed to the inevitably laborious process of learning and understanding what is of God in a pluralist world. The question is how fidelity to the tradition can be maintained without lapsing into a tautological repetition which flattens out the ethical challenge of the relationship with what is other. Some attention needs, therefore, to be given to an account of the genesis of *Nostra Aetate* and to a critique of its theology of inter-faith relations. What follows, however, is not intended as a commentary on the text.[7] Rather, my intention is to set the document squarely within the Council's theology of revelation and the history of the Church's relationship with the Jewish people. In so doing I hope to raise a question about how this history is to be understood not just theologically but ethically. How is the 'New' to act with ethical integrity – without, that is, simply overwhelming and destroying the 'Old'?

Church 'within' and Church 'without'

The extent to which Pope John XXIII was aware of the theological complexities of the revolution he would unleash is only one of the more

---

[5] O'Malley 1971, 1983.

[6] O'Malley 1971:595. 'This is the style of historical thinking which has its remote origins in the Renaissance discovery of discontinuity' (ibid.).

[7] The most substantial commentary on *Nostra Aetate* is that by Oesterreicher in Vorgrimler 1969 III:1–154. The much briefer guide by Laurentin and Neuner, 1966, contains a clear and insightful account of the central controversy over the Jews. See also Henry 1966. For a critical non-Roman Catholic perspective see Ruokanen 1992.

intractable mysteries surrounding the interpretation of the Council.[8] Certainly he wanted a 'pastoral' Council which looked to internal reform and avoided condemnations. But pastoral could all too easily be interpreted, especially in a highly authoritarian Church, as 'canonical'. When the process of consultation began, many responses reflected a predictable inertia.[9] At the same time, there were signs of impatience with the status quo and calls for a theology which touched on social issues: the relationship between the Catholic Church and civil society, other Christians and – in missionary areas – non-Christians. The impasse was only resolved when a proper plan was introduced and the mass of material piled up by the various preparatory commissions was reduced to something more manageable.

The plan emerged from Cardinal Suenens's crucial distinction, between what concerned the *ecclesia ad intra*, the Church 'within', and what was appropriate to the *ecclesia ad extra*, the Church 'without'.[10] The Latin tags neatly summarise the Council's dilemma – the tension between different ecclesiologies which in due course led to Rahner's vision of the 'world Church'. How are the Church's internal relations, her self-understanding as a people called by God, to bear upon her external relations, her sense of sharing in God's own mission for the world? The first document to be promulgated, *Sacrosanctum Concilium*, on the liturgy, comes clearly under the '*ad intra*' heading. But, with its account of the liturgy as the summit and source from which the Church's power flows, it influenced so much of what was to follow.[11] By the end of the final session another '*ad intra*' text, the Dogmatic Constitution on the Church, *Lumen Gentium*, had been complemented by the more obviously '*ad extra*' Pastoral Constitution on the Church in the modern world, *Gaudium et Spes*. What began as a viable methodology for the Council's business assumed in due course

---

[8] Hebblethwaite 1994:339.

[9] See the summary of the *Conspectus* (index of the survey of *vota*) provided by Fouilloux, in Alberigo 1995:140ff., which neatly illustrates the principal theological concerns of the pre-Vatican II Church.

[10] Suenens's influence is discussed at length in J. Komonchak, 'The Struggle for the Council during the Preparation of Vatican II', in Alberigo 1995:342ff. See also Hebblethwaite 1993:300ff. The *ad intra/ad extra* distinction was originally made by Suenens in 1956 in a book later translated as *The Gospel to Every Creature*, Westminster: Newman Press, 1965. After reading of it in one of Suenens's pastoral letters, John XXIII used it in his radio broadcast on the eve of the Council, 11 September 1962. It subsequently formed the basis of schema 13 which was to become *Gaudium et Spes*.

[11] See *SC* 10.

intrinsically theological dimensions. From the ecclesio-centric obsession with a 'defensive wall' against the corrupting effects of 'erroneous opinions',[12] the Council sought to recognise and value the Church not just for its own sake but as a source of grace for the whole world.

The theological tone is set by the opening of *Lumen Gentium*. Pervaded by an eschatological vision of the whole of humankind gathered in Christ, it speaks of the Church existing 'in Christ as a sacrament or instrumental sign of intimate union with God and of the unity of all humanity'.[13] In this opening chapter, various scriptural 'figures of speech' point to the irreducible 'Mystery of the Church'. Then, in perhaps its most celebrated image, taken from St Augustine, the life of the Church is likened to a pilgrimage through a foreign land.[14] Charged with a responsibility for the salvation of humankind, the Church is no longer set over against but *in relationship* with what may appropriately be called 'other' – the world, other Christian communities, the great world religions. *Lumen Gentium* speaks of those who have not yet accepted Christ as being none the less 'ordered' or 'related' to the People of God.[15] What is implied by the word 'related'? And what does this say about the identity of the 'Roman Catholic Church'?

Vatican II rejects any simple equation of the visible community of the Church with the Mystical Body of Christ by saying that the latter 'subsists in' the former.[16] This was intended to preserve the normative status of the Church *vis-à-vis* 'separated Churches' whose ecclesial status is nevertheless recognised. They are accepted 'as sisters and brothers, with respect and love' (*UR* 3). This intra-Christian distinction caused a great deal of controversy, and a debate which cannot be pursued here.[17]

---

[12] See Fouilloux in Alberigo 1995:148–9.

[13] *LG* 1: 'veluti sacramentum seu signum et instrumentum intimae cum Deo unionis totiusque generis humani unitatis'.

[14] 'The Church "proceeds on its pilgrim way amidst the persecutions of the world and the consolations of God"'; *LG* 8: see St Augustine, *City of God*, XVIII, 51, 2.

[15] The Latin text reads: 'Ii tandem qui evangelium nondum acceperunt, ad populum Dei diversis rationibus *ordinantur*.' (*LG* 15; emphasis added.)

[16] 'Haec ecclesia, in hoc mundo ut societas constituta et ordinata, *subsistit* in ecclesia catholica' (*LG* 8). The debate which changed the word 'is' to 'subsists in' had the effect of avoiding the straight identification of the Body of Christ with the Catholic Church made by Pius XII in his 1943 encyclical *Mystici Corporis* – but, of course, left open any discussion of how the ecclesial status of 'separated churches' was to be related to the Catholic Church.

[17] The debate was concerned with reconciling the existence of the 'Church of Christ' as a visible 'fact of history' with the existence of ecclesial elements of sanctification and truth which can be found outside it. See Grillmeier's commentary on *LG* in Vorgrimler 1967 I:149–52.

But what of the other, wider relationship with non-Christian others? To what extent can one speak of a continuity between the experience of the Church and that of the 'whole human family in its total environment' (GS 1) without simply occluding or relativising one or other pole of the relationship?

Perhaps the complexities of Rahner's emerging 'world Church' can be expressed in terms of two complementary theological truths. The Church is Catholic because it is, in principle, the whole of humankind redeemed in Christ; at the same time, the Church exists not as some distant ideal but as *this* community of faith on pilgrimage with others. To put it another way, the Roman Catholic Church is a particular Christian community, but a community which exists not for itself but precisely *for others*; its identity is truly to be found only in and through the relationships it establishes with others. Suenens's distinction may be regarded as the key which unlocked the door to Pope John's vision of a 'pastoral Council'. But this is only to say that it set up, rather than resolved, the problem of the theological link between the inner life of the Church and its pastoral life and mission in the world.

The emergence of the text of *Nostra Aetate*

According to the Suenens scheme, *Nostra Aetate* fits into matter which concerns the Church 'without'. In its origins it is a good example of a pastoral concern which the Church had to exercise in order to address a serious wrong: not just the Holocaust or *Shoah*[18] but a history of Christian anti-Semitism. As it developed, however, from a brief chapter within the schema on ecumenism to an independent declaration on the attitude of the Church to non-Christian religions as a whole,[19] the

---

[18] In recent years the term 'Shoah', 'total destruction', has tended to replace the earlier 'Holocaust' which, according to many Jewish theologians, softens the impact of the historical event by imparting to it a distinct a priori theological meaning.

[19] In the evolution of *Nostra Aetate* five texts need to be distinguished. The very first 'preliminary study' of 1961, *Decretum de Iudaeis*, never reached the Council (text in Oesterreicher 1985:158–9); it was withdrawn to avoid political embarrassment following what Oesterreicher calls the 'Wardi affair'. (See Vorgrimler 1969 III:41–6.) The first draft introduced for debate, as section 4 of the schema on ecumenism (18 November 1963), was entitled *De Catholicorum habitudine ad non-christianos et maxime ad Iudaeos* (AS II/V, 431–2). A new draft entitled *De Iudaeis et de non-christianis*, sections 32–34 of the ecumenism decree, was debated 28–30 September 1964 (AS III/II, 327–9). The first fully independent text, *De Ecclesiae habitudine ad religiones non-christianas*, was prepared during the third session and accepted on 20 November 1964 (AS III/VIII, 637–41). The final text, *Declaratio de Ecclesiae habitudine ad religiones non-christianas*, was presented on 14 October 1965 and promulgated on 28 October 1965 (AS IV/IV, 690–96). The four conciliar texts are reproduced in Ruokanen 1992:121–31.

doctrinal implications for the Church 'within' made themselves felt. A regular theological minefield was unearthed – revealed as much by political issues of various kinds as by the undoubted fact that the Church was ill-prepared for a dialogue with Judaism, let alone for a theological debate about the values of non-Christian religions. It is thus that, more than any other Vatican II document, *Nostra Aetate* succeeds in bringing to light 'other' stories which challenge the theologian not just to reimagine history but to question the premises upon which a Christian theological history of religions must be based.

As is well known, the text owes its existence to a specific mandate from Pope John.[20] His request to Cardinal Bea to address the 'Jewish question' arose immediately from the visit of the French Jewish historian Jules Isaac.[21] Pressure from within the Church was all but non-existent; only the Jesuit professors at the Pontifical Biblical Institute asked for the subject to be dealt with. In Jewish circles, however, the news that the coming Council was preparing a statement on Jewish–Christian relations created a certain mood of apprehension. Previous Councils had notoriously taken punitive measures against Jews. What would this one do? And Bea was responsible for Christian Unity. Was ecumenism a new name for proselytism? The schema attracted more political controversy than any other proposal, especially from the Muslim countries of the Middle East.[22] From many of the Eastern-rite churches, too, there was a measure of opposition, ostensibly motivated by a prudent concern for the well-being of

---

[20] According to his secretary Loris Capovilla, 'it never entered Pope John XXIII's mind that the Council ought to be also occupied with the Jewish question and with anti-Semitism' until his private audience with Jules Isaac in the summer of 1960 (quoted in Stransky, 'Holy Diplomacy: Making the Impossible Possible', in Brooks 1988:51–69; quotation from p. 53). Yet there can be no doubt about his personal concern for the Jews. As Apostolic Delegate in Istanbul during the war, the future John XXIII helped many Jews escape from Nazi persecution. One of his early acts as pope was to decree that references to the Jews as 'perfidi' in the Easter liturgy be deleted – a small but none the less encouraging sign that attitudes were changing. See Hebblethwaite 1994:192–3; Oesterreicher in Vorgrimler 1969 III:6–8; Beozzo, 'The External Climate', in Alberigo 1995:392–7.

[21] Isaac put to the pope a series of measures which needed to be taken, among them the correction of false statements about the Jews in Christian teaching. He presented an extract from the 'Catechism of Trent', published after the Council in 1566. The text (quoted in Oesterreicher 1985:105–8) states that the reason for the suffering and death of Christ was the sin of humankind. Isaac's submission was that the accusation of deicide against the Jews did not accord with the tradition of Church teaching.

[22] Oesterreicher, in Vorgrimler 1969 III:18f., 39f., 81ff., 101ff., gives the details of Arab objections to a document which, so it was argued, intended to recognise the state of Israel and therefore supported Zionism. These led to the incorporation of the section on Islam into the original draft.

their people in a Muslim-dominated world.[23] The result was a delay, with the schema reappearing in a transformed version, including sections on Islam, Hinduism and Buddhism, in November 1964.

When *Nostra Aetate* was eventually promulgated in October 1965 it bore all the signs of its mixed parentage; it carried, and projected, different expectations. Two can be distinguished. The final expansion grew out of pressure from missionary bishops who formed what Peter Hebblethwaite calls the 'conscience' of the Council. One-third of the bishops at Vatican II came from Asia and Africa. Representatives of Rahner's 'world Church', they yet had to reconcile a universalist vision with the knowledge that they were in reality a minority in a sometimes powerfully non-Christian and even anti-Christian environment. For them, the document was a charter for a more positive missiology which would recognise that different cultures and different religions demanded different approaches to the living out and preaching of the Gospel.

At the same time, it is easy to lose sight of the fact that in its origins *Nostra Aetate* had a much more precise focus; despite the opening up of new inter-religious horizons, the context of the debate was the vexed question of the relationship of the Old and New Covenants. The intervention of Jews and Muslims, both before and during the Council, made it clear that the Church was no longer dealing with a purely internal theoretical question, the salvation of the non-Christian, but with the flesh-and-blood reality of real people, with their own history, traditions and theology. Even for professional exegetes and scripture scholars, Judaism had become a contemporary reality, not just an anachronistic relic.[24] What began as an attempt to heal the first great schism within the People of God almost foundered on the phrasing of the renunciation of the theological roots of anti-Semitism. In the interval between the third and fourth sessions, what Oesterreicher calls a 'holy war' raged.[25] Significantly, the first three and final sections were hardly touched; the

---

[23] Thus, for instance, during the September 1964 debate, Cardinal Tappouni, Patriarch of Antioch, criticised the text as 'not opportune'. See Oesterreicher 1985:216.

[24] The response of the Jesuits at the Pontifical Biblical Institute to the initial consultation argued that to refer to the Church as the authentic heirs of Abraham did not imply that the Jewish people as such have been rejected by God; rather, according to St Paul (Romans 11), the Jews remain the 'natural branches' which will in due time be grafted back into the single olive tree. A proper understanding of this passage and the overcoming of the defective exegesis of various New Testament passages (such as Matthew 27.25, 24.2; 1 Thessalonians 2.16; Romans 9.22) would go a long way to making any theologically justified versions of anti-Semitism impossible to sustain.

[25] In Vorgrimler 1969 III:101–22.

fourth, on the Jews, was greatly modified. The general effect was that something of the warmth and precise focus of the original draft was lost.[26] The gain, however, was in the extension of what Paul VI, in his highly influential first encyclical, *Ecclesiam Suam*, called a dialogue of love which would embrace all people of faith.

A reading of the final text of *Nostra Aetate* which fails to bear this contentious history in mind will detect only a certain portentous blandness. The first phrases reflect the Council's vision of a Church existing in relationship with others. What is to be noted – 'In our age, when the human race is being daily brought closer together and contacts between the various nations are becoming more frequent' (NA 1) – is the common humanity, single origin and final goal of the peoples of the world. Religions provide answers to the 'obscure riddles of the human condition', prompting various questions and eliciting in 'religions associated with the development of civilisation' the concepts and language which express 'a certain perception of that unseen force which is present in the course of things and in events in human life' (NA 2). Hinduism and Buddhism are both included here in a handful of unremarkable phrases, and the section finishes with a brief reference to 'other religions which are to be found throughout the entire world' (NA 2) which similarly bring peace and moral guidance.

The conclusion, however, has a double edge. The Church, it says, 'rejects nothing of those things which are holy and true in these religions' for they 'frequently reflect a ray of that truth which enlightens everyone' (NA 2). Nothing is said about what these elements of truth and holiness might be. Instead, the statement is immediately juxtaposed with another: 'Yet she proclaims, and is in duty bound to proclaim without fail Christ who is the way, the truth and the life' (NA 2). The implication is that, somehow, the two principles have to be held together. The paragraph ends with a powerful statement in which Christians are called upon to 'recognise, preserve and encourage those spiritual and moral good things'[27] found among non-Christians. The clarity of this exhortation is carried through to the end of the document. In the final section, the Council urges Christians to live

---

[26] Laurentin and Neuner, 1966:37–43, draw attention to the major changes: the loss of the phrase 'grato animo' in the opening sentence; the addition of a reference to the refusal of many Jews to accept the 'time of visitation'; the substitution of 'the Jews' for 'Jewish people' in order to avoid the political connotations of the latter term; the suppression of the term 'deicide'; the omission of the explicit 'damnat' with regard to anti-Semitism, in keeping with the express intention of John XXIII (so it was argued) that the Council issue no condemnations.

[27] 'illa bona spiritualia necnon illos valores socioculturales, quae apud eos inveniuntur, *agnoscant, servent et promoveant*' (NA 2; emphases added).

at peace with all people and comes out strongly against any discrimination based on 'race, colour, condition in life or religion' (NA 5).

Preceding this are two sections, the first on the Muslims, the second the original text on the Jews, now reworked as a meditation on 'the link whereby the people of the new covenant are spiritually united with the descendants of Abraham' (NA 4). A handful of guarded references to what Muslims and Christians hold in common – monotheism, prophecy, honour of Mary – leads to an exhortation to forget the past and work together. Nothing explicitly Islamic is mentioned, beyond a few of the attributes of God, the most glaring omission being that of the prophet Muhammad himself.[28] Judaism, however, the subject of so much theological and political controversy, is treated as a living tradition whose faith remains of crucial importance to the Church's self-understanding.[29] It is stated explicitly that the faith of the Church is rooted in that of the patriarchs and prophets. The Jews are still the Chosen People and therefore 'remain very dear to God'.[30] Rejected is any implication that they are as a whole somehow responsible for the death of Jesus.[31] Any further theology of the relationship of Jews and Christians is tentative. There is no specific reference to the Shoah. The state of Israel is not mentioned as a significant element in Jewish identity, nor is the Messiahship of Jesus as a determining element in the Christian. On the other hand, the introduction of the Pauline image of the wild olive branches grafted on to the ancient tree opens up the possibility of a more positive reading of the relationship of Jew and Gentile.

The theology of *Nostra Aetate*

The question whether this 'primary relationship' can be made the basis of the relationship between Church and other faiths will occupy us in due

---

[28] This section is theologically selective and avoids anything contentious between Muslims and Christians. See Farrugia 1988.

[29] Oesterreicher, who was involved in the process from its earliest days, sums up NA, 1971:17, as bespeaking 'the discovery, or re-discovery, of Judaism and the Jews in their intrinsic worth, as well as their importance for the Church'.

[30] 'adhuc carissimi manent propter patres' (NA 4). The use of the present tense throughout this section, to emphasise the *continuing* validity of God's Covenant with the Jews, is significant. See Oesterreicher 1971:24–5.

[31] The controversial reference in Texts I–III to 'deicide' gets a more biblically based and accurate theological presentation in the final Text IV. 'Although the Church is the new people of God, the Jews should not be represented as rejected by God or accursed, as if that follows from holy scripture.' The final version dropped the phrase on grounds of 'tact', says Laurentin, 1966:41, quoting the SPCU.

course. First, however, questions need to be asked about how *Nostra Aetate* is to be understood and assessed theologically. Even a review as brief as that given above indicates that several interests are at work. Different theologies can be detected. Despite its historical significance, the traditional question of the salvation of the non-Christian is the least prominent. In its opening account of the single community of peoples, *Nostra Aetate* speaks of their being gathered together by God 'whose providence, manifestation of goodness and plans for salvation are extended to all' (NA 1). The term *salus* appears on two further occasions, both with specific reference to the Church: once when speaking of the salvation from sins obtained through Christ (NA 4), and once when the Declaration finds the salvation of the Church 'mystically prefigured' in the Exodus (NA 4).

The salvation problematic is explicitly addressed not in *Nostra Aetate* but in the two documents on the Church. Here, as noted already, the context is the relationship of the Church and various others. 'There are those who without any fault do not know anything about Christ or his Church, yet who search for God with a sincere heart and, under the influence of grace, try to put into effect the will of God as known to them through the dictate of conscience: these too can obtain eternal salvation' (LG 16). The word which stands out here is 'can': all *can* – but not necessarily *will* – be saved. This reticent note masks an important theological principle. Care must be taken to ensure that the scope of God's salvific action in the world is not arbitrarily limited. Hence the wisdom of insisting that '[t]he Holy Spirit offers everyone the possibility of sharing in this paschal mystery *in a manner known to God*'.[32] But to admit that salvation is possible outside the Church is not to make the Church irrelevant for salvation. It is, rather, to restore a lost equilibrium in the Church's approach to the other. The text of *Lumen Gentium* begins with a vision of the Church called to shed the light that is Christ on all peoples. Despite its all-inclusive universalism, however, it still must add a cautionary note about the corrupting effect of evil and, therefore, the need to preach the Gospel 'to promote the glory of God and the salvation of all these people' (LG 16).

The effect of this shift of emphasis from the 'problem' of salvation outside the Church to the Church's role in the mystery of God's salvation offered to all is to contribute to the renewal of ecclesiology. As Francis Sullivan has shown, the old adage attributed to Cyprian, *extra ecclesiam nulla salus*, arose in the context of schism within the Church and was never intended as a

---

[32] GS 22; emphasis added.

condemnation of non-Christians as such.[33] Cyprian's point is that the Church is defined as a community of love; those who cut themselves off from the community of love destroy the sign of God's self-gift. In other words, they cut themselves off from the possibility of salvation. Later, as the Church became identified with Christendom, a visible political entity, it was all too easily set off against other 'non-Christian' entities. Cyprian's adage was hijacked and used to set up a divide between different communities of faith – not just schismatics and heretics, but also Jews and Muslims, who attacked the Church by their wilful refusal to believe. A more humble, more faithful understanding of the original sense would return to Cyprian's more positive intention. The controversy over the celebrated 'Boston Heresy Case',[34] for instance, has shown how much it is intended to express a truth which is primarily about the *Church*, not about salvation. 'What we have tried to show in this book', concludes Sullivan, 'is that it is only one way, and a very imperfect way at that, in which Christians have expressed their belief that God has given to his church a necessary part to play in his plan to save the world'.[35] The number of insistent exhortations to the Church to respect – even 'preserve and encourage' – the spiritual values found among people of other faiths, show that *Nostra Aetate* shares this hesitant shift from soteriology to ecclesiology.

To that extent, the theology behind *Nostra Aetate* reflects another, intimately linked, shift of emphasis within Vatican II: the recovery of missiology. When the Commission on Missions first met, it reflected the same Rome-centred obsession with canonical arrangements which marked the preparatory phase as a whole.[36] It took time for the idea to emerge that 'the missions' should be understood in terms of the single mission of the Church.[37] The powerful proclamation that 'the pilgrim

---

[33] Sullivan 1992:18–24.

[34] Sullivan opens his book with the case of Fr. Leonard Feeney, an overly zealous Jesuit who insisted on a literalist interpretation of Cyprian. For the Vatican's judgment in favour of the Archbishop of Boston see Roos and Neuner 1967:243–5 (DS 3866–72).

[35] Sullivan 1992:204.

[36] See Komonchak, in Alberigo 1995:192–6, who comments that during the Council the Roman missiologists were united in defending the 'traditional territorial approach to the missions'. In the Commission '[t]he chief discussions concerned the dominance of the juridical over the theological' (p. 196).

[37] The International Missionary Conference and the WCC had been moving in this direction for years. See the detailed discussion in 'Elements of an Emerging Ecumenical Missionary Paradigm', chapter 12 of Bosch 1991:368ff. Bosch traces the mutual influence of low (Protestant) and high (Catholic) ecclesiologies on missiology, quoting Moltmann 1977 to the effect that '[t]oday one of the strongest impulses towards the renewal of the theological concept of the church comes from the theology of mission'.

church is of its very nature missionary since it draws its origin from the mission of the Son and the mission of the Holy Spirit, in accordance with the plan of God the Father' (*AG* 2) is not in itself an insight which is original to the Roman Catholic Church. It reflects Barth's insistence that mission belongs to God himself.[38] In other words the Church does not *have* a mission, nor is mission something which the Church 'does'. Rather, mission is first and foremost an activity of God in which the Church is invited to participate.

At the same time, when the Council talks specifically about missionary activity, in the declaration *Ad Gentes*, the language is often practical – even pragmatic. There are a number of ways in which the Church bears witness to the truth of the Gospel: through pastoral work and ecumenism as well as through preaching and proclamation. A certain tension is apparent in the way the traditional missiology of '*plantatio ecclesiae*' is juxtaposed with a more open-ended prudential approach which acknowledges that the Church can only grow in stages, requiring time and patience, especially in those circumstances where direct preaching is impossible and 'works of charity' must suffice to make the Lord 'in some way present' (*AG* 6). Vatican II thus seeks to renew the Church's sense of mission while recognising that the form it will take must be adapted to particular conditions. *Nostra Aetate* is somewhat muted in this respect. The juxtaposition of respect for the other with the duty to preach 'Christ, who is "the way, the truth and the life"', is followed by the call to bear witness to the Christian faith and way of life 'through dialogues and co-operation with the followers of other religions'.[39] Nothing is said to indicate how these demands are to be practised.

It is, however, easy to detect tensions, differences and even contradictions. Largely because of their orientation 'without', and therefore their sensitivity to the complexity of mission in a pluralist world, documents like *Nostra Aetate*, *Ad Gentes* and *Gaudium et Spes* do have this much in common: they recognise that there are many contexts of God's action, all of which – somehow – have to be held together. As James Buckley comments,

---

[38] The Barthian influence on the 1938 International Missionary Conference at Tambaram, exercised through Hendrik Kraemer's *The Christian Message in a non-Christian World* was immense. According to Bosch, 1991:389–90, '[i]n a paper read at the Brandenburg Missionary Conference in 1932, Karl Barth became one of the first theologians to articulate mission as an activity of God himself'. (Barth's lecture was first published in 1932 as 'Die Theologie und Die Mission in der Gegenwart' in *Theologische Fragen und Antworten*, volume 3. Zürich: Evangelischer Verlag, 1957; pp. 100–26.)

[39] 'per colloquia et collaborationem' (*NA* 2).

'Vatican II does not permit us to live as if God only periodically intervenes and we ought occasionally to respond in our Scriptures, our worship, our common life as a Church, the non-Christian religions, the joys and griefs of our personal lives.'[40] It is true that little indication is given in the documents as to how the relationships between such contexts are to be maintained. But that practical question is less significant, perhaps, than the pressing dual responsibility which a 'world Church' must recognise, to live – however awkwardly – between the demands of the prophetic Christian vocation and the claims of the other to freedom and respect.

These claims have a very specific face. In *Nostra Aetate* salvation and mission are present as significant theological themes. What gives them a completely new dimension, however, is their subordination to the major issue of the Church's 'primary relationship' with Judaism. This links the document to a dimension of major significance in Vatican II: the biblical basis of theology itself.

There can be little doubt about the importance for the Roman Catholic Church of Vatican II's shorter dogmatic constitution, *Dei Verbum*, on Divine Revelation.[41] It grew out of the renewal of biblical studies without which *Lumen Gentium*, and so much else in Vatican II, would have been impossible. As an independent theological constitution in its own right, however, it is an important counter to what might otherwise have been an almost totally 'ecclesio-monist' Council.[42] The struggle in the Council over the text effectively signalled the end of the dominance of the 'Roman' school of theologians, but it also represents a new beginning.[43] *Dei Verbum* has no category of 'general revelation'; nothing is said about the natural knowledge of God beyond what is noted in the classic text from Paul, Romans 1.20 (*DV* 6). Rather, the primary mode of expressing revelation is the image of a relationship established by God through an act of self-communication summed up in Christ. Revelation is reserved for what God reveals of God in certain key moments in the history of salvation which are recorded in the Old and New Testaments.

---

[40] Buckley 1992:132.

[41] O'Collins 1993 traces the development of three different 'styles' of Catholic theology since 1965 back to the seminal influence of *DV*.

[42] The word is Ratzinger's; see his commentary on the history of the text, in Vorgrimler 1969 III:155–262, especially pp. 159–66.

[43] After the first session debate in which the original schema, *De Fontibus Revelationis*, was thrown out (reported in Hebblethwaite 1994:453–7) a new 'mixed commission' was set up by John XXIII consisting of members from the SPCU and the Theological Commission.

The shift away from the old two-source (scripture and tradition) theory of revelation and the concentration on a single source, Christ as the Word of God present in the Church, represents a crucially important doctrinal shift.[44] If *Lumen Gentium* is a reflection on the Church actively responding to the call of God in history and the world, *Dei Verbum* portrays the Church more passively *listening* to the object of its faith, the Word of God. But what, to repeat the question raised in the last chapter, is the relationship between such activity and passivity? How is the Word to be discerned in 'the words'? *Dei Verbum* raises a number of issues with which Roman Catholics are still struggling.[45] But its significance for ecumenical and inter-faith relations can scarcely be open to doubt.

No mention is made in *Dei Verbum* of non-Christian religions; still less is any consideration given to the possibility of revelation in other faiths. At the same time, the text's biblically inspired mode of presentation allows for the refiguring of the relationship of Church and the other, traditionally treated through soteriology, by a theology of God's self-revelation through the Word. 'Right from its prologue', as O'Collins points out, '*Dei Verbum* indicates how God's revelation and offer of salvation coincide. The council wanted to "set forth the true doctrine on divine revelation", because it wanted "the whole world to hear the summons to salvation" (DV 1).'[46]

Throughout *Dei Verbum* the language of the 'economy of revelation' and that of the 'history of salvation' are linked together.[47] The two are distinguishable but interdependent, different ways of looking at the same mystery; God's self-communication through words and deeds contains and makes present the reality of salvation for all people. The earlier versions of *Nostra Aetate* contain ethical imperatives about respect for the Jews backed by a biblical narrative which recognises their place in the history of salvation and their continuing intrinsic value before God. The later expansions have the same basic form. Thus, although the actual word 'revelation' only appears once (in reference to the Old Testament in section 4), the vision of a God who goes on revealing himself in his salvific

---

[44] See O'Collins 1993:49–51. Lash 1997 draws attention to the placing of chapter 1 of DV, on God's self-disclosure, *before* the chapter on the transmission of the Word in scripture and tradition.

[45] See especially Murray in Hastings 1991:74–83. By rejecting the 'two-source theory' of revelation DV raises questions about the authority of the magisterium, about the relationship of Word and sacrament, and about the use of scripture by the 'base communities'.

[46] O'Collins 1993:54.

[47] See DV 3, 4, 6, 7, 14–15, 17, 21.

love for all people is as central to *Nostra Aetate* as it is to *Dei Verbum*. God's providence and plans for salvation are intended for everyone 'until the elect be gathered together in the holy city which the bright light of God will illuminate and where the people will walk in his light' (*NA* 1).[48]

In the same paragraph, people are said to be linked according to what they hold in common, not least by the questions they ask of the different religions, the 'obscure riddles of the human condition' which disturb people's hearts. The questions seem unmemorable, but the passage has a certain inclusive logic, beginning with the origin of humankind in God and ending with that 'final unutterable mystery which takes in our lives and from which we take our origin and towards which we tend' (*NA* 1). From the more general 'perception of that unseen force which is present in the course of things' to the specific religious values in the four great faiths mentioned by name, *Nostra Aetate* acknowledges 'a ray of that truth which enlightens everyone' (*NA* 2). There may be no question of any special or independent revelation through non-Christian religions as such, but *Nostra Aetate* is bound to allow that God reveals God in and through the created order. It thus reflects the 'single source' theory of revelation of *Dei Verbum*: the revelation of the Word of God, spoken definitively in Jesus Christ, and the work of the Holy Spirit, bringing to fruition the 'seeds of the Word' in creation, represent together a single continuous action of God in the world.

Responsibility to the other

This is undoubtedly the great strength of *Nostra Aetate*. It engages with the dual responsibility of a world Church – to be able to speak of the relationship between same and other in a way which neither compromises the integrity of the former nor ignores the freedom of the latter. This is not novel. Even as sharp a critic as Ruokanen recognises in the document the 'traditional' Catholic approach, a 'natural law' form of argumentation which stresses the unity of God's action in the world.[49] To this extent, *Nostra Aetate*'s emphasis on God's continuing self-revelation reflects the 'open' ecclesiocentrism of *Lumen Gentium*. The same sort of emphasis on

---

[48] The scriptural reference added here is to the vision of the holy city in Apocalypse 21.23–4: 'the glory of God is its light, and its lamp is the Lamb. By its light shall the nations walk'.

[49] Ruokanen regards *NA* as leaning heavily on the traditional Thomistic theme of grace perfecting nature. See 1992:11ff., 55ff., 107ff.

the moral unity of all peoples before God is found in *Gaudium et Spes*, which speaks of the way God forms the natural law, 'to love and do what is good and to avoid what is evil', in the 'conscience of the human race' (*GS* 16, 79).

At the same time, this vision of the single religious community of humankind – the People of God centred on the Church – betrays a certain latent tendency to totalise the other. If this is to be avoided, questions have to be asked about the degrees of belonging between the visible community of the Church and other communities of faith. *Nostra Aetate* recognises what is at stake by raising in a new form the oldest of Christian theological dilemmas: Paul's question about what has happened to God's promises to his chosen people.

It was, of course, Paul the Apostle who first negotiated the shift to Rahner's 'second epoch' of the Church. The single most important scriptural text in *Nostra Aetate* is the Epistle to the Romans, Paul's great 'theological synthesis' addressed to a community of Jewish and Gentile Christians experiencing the tensions of marrying Old and New.[50] The original 'Decree on the Jews', dating back to 1961, is, if anything, stronger than the final text of the Declaration in seeking to express the sense of continuity between the Church and the People of the Old Covenant. A certain mutual dependence finds expression in the statement that 'the Church believes in the union of the Jewish people with herself *as an integral part of Christian hope*'.[51] The final version omits this, but adds the Pauline metaphor of the olive tree (11.17–24) from which the Church 'is nourished . . . [and] onto which the branches of the wild olive tree of the gentiles have been grafted' (*NA* 4). The full implications of Paul's sometimes tortured meditation on the fate of his former religious compatriots are not developed in *Nostra Aetate*. Enough is said, however, to indicate that the Declaration's interpretation of Romans is in line with that of recent Pauline scholarship – and for the same reasons.[52]

What is ultimately at stake, for the Roman community of the first century as much as for the contemporary Church, is not the justification of the individual but the very constancy of God and the unity of God's

---

[50] See Introduction to Dunn 1988; Harrington 1992:40ff.

[51] Text from Oesterreicher 1985:158–9 (emphasis added).

[52] As Stendahl points out, 1976:3ff., Romans is not primarily an exposition of the individual's relation to God, but a theological meditation about how the Jewish and Gentile Christians of Rome stand in relation to each other within the covenant purpose of God which has now reached its climax in Jesus Christ.

Covenant.[53] In grappling with this issue, the development of Paul's thought in Romans is hardly consistent – but that, as Sanders points out, would be to make the mistake of interpreting him as 'a philosophical theologian, concerned to get everything in the right hierarchical relationship to everything else', whereas he was, first and foremost, 'an apostle, an *ad hoc* theologian, a proclaimer'.[54] If the Judaism of Paul's time had been hopelessly corrupt or dominated by a theology totally at variance with the 'new' dispensation, Paul's task might have been easier. Neither was the case.[55] Paul's argument is not, however, that Jewish faith has been abrogated. Rather, he wants to make the point that the traditional covenantal faith of Judaism is to be defined more exactly as faith in Jesus Christ. What he is facing, therefore, is not a more-or-less straightforward replacement of one tradition by another, but the relationship between two similar ways of conceiving God's gratuitous acceptance of people through the Covenant. The antithesis, in other words, is not between a way of works of the Law and a way of faith in Christ. It is between a reading of the Covenant which would imply that God's promises are limited to the election of Israel and one which would provide for their *ultimate* fulfilment in Christ. This, for Paul, is what Jewish preoccupation with works of the Law as 'signs' of God's favour to Israel ignores, and what he himself proclaims as the Gospel, namely the salvation of the whole world which God has brought about through the Death and Resurrection of Jesus.

But how does Paul – the first example, perhaps, of the 'catholic instinct' – cope with what appears by any standards to represent an abrupt break, an antithesis between faith in Christ and the faith represented by his own Jewish heritage? How do the particularity of the promise and the universality of its intent stand together? How to explain the

---

[53] The developments in recent Pauline scholarship, represented most notably by the work of E. P. Sanders, rescue Paul from being interpreted through Lutheran spectacles by showing how the picture of a monolithic first-century Judaism based on works of the Law is historically false. Sanders, 1977:75, using a concept of 'covenantal nomism', which expresses the 'basic pattern of Rabbinic religion . . . how the participants perceived the religion to function', sees first-century Judaism as a religion of grace in which adherence to law is the *way* in which a response is made to a gracious God. In these terms Paul is not setting justification by law against justification by faith, but faith in 'covenantal nomism' against faith in Jesus Christ. According to Dunn, 1983:110; 1988:lxivff., 153ff., what Paul denies is not 'covenantal nomism' but what he sees in much Jewish practice, namely those 'works of the Law' which imply that God's favour extends only to those who 'wear the badge of the Covenant'.

[54] Sanders 1991:127.

[55] See Neusner 1978 for a favourable Jewish commentary on Sanders's thesis.

discontinuity, and the element of a new, decisive and unique revelation in the Gospel? However difficult to express, Paul wrestles with a dialectic of affirmation and negation. On the one hand, the promises made to Israel speak of God's faithfulness to the Covenant of Sinai, a Covenant which God goes on reaffirming throughout history. On the other hand, another historical story which overlaps with the first speaks of that human obstinacy and misunderstanding which comes to a head with the rejection of the one in whom those very promises are to be realised. Despite the evident paradox, Paul is guided by a passionate faith in God's constancy and by the sense of a certain continuity between the Covenant established with the elect of the 'old' dispensation and what has been revealed by God in Christ. If it is possible to speak of a 'resolution' within the sometimes tortured pages of the Epistle to the Romans, it comes not with the sort of logic which would recognise a complementarity, still less a symmetrical, relationship, between Old and New, but with a return to the God from whom the story originates. Paul's evident, but perhaps inexpressible, universalism breaks out with a great hymn of praise: 'O the depth of the riches and wisdom and knowledge of God! How unsearchable are his judgements and how inscrutable his ways!' (Romans 11.33).

There is, of course, no such paean of praise in *Nostra Aetate*. But by dwelling, albeit briefly, on the Pauline dilemma, the Declaration does at least allow for the most important expression of the 'catholic instinct': to avoid premature closure and allow God to be God. The text is hesitant. By seeking to hold together the two principles, a commitment to Christ, 'the way, the truth and the life', and an openness to the 'truths and values' in other traditions of faith, it acknowledges the need for a theology of the covenantal relationship which also allows an ethical response to the legacy of the Shoah. Any simplistic supersessionism which would reduce the Church's Jewish 'other' to an irrelevant rump is rejected. But, as Paul himself realised, to proclaim that God has done something 'new' in Christ must entail *some* form of supersessionism. *Nostra Aetate*'s version of the Pauline dilemma is clear: on the one hand, it affirms the validity of the 'ancient' Covenant; on the other, it wants to assert a smooth continuity between Old and New. Can the Church proclaim the uniqueness of Jesus as the Christ while simultaneously accepting that the Covenant with Israel has never been revoked? Or, to put it the other way round, can approval be given to the Jews as the 'people of the promise' without thereby negating the claims of Christians to be the 'new people of God' whose very *raison d'être* is to witness to the fulfilment of God's promises in Jesus?

The dilemma points us towards a complex question. How is a theology which would recognise otherness to be pursued? How can the Church think and account for her origins if they lie outside or beyond her own history? How, indeed, is it possible to 'think origins' at all? Paul's wrestling with the fate of Israel, so painfully obvious in the rhetorical questions which flash out from the pages of his Epistle to the Romans, is only the first in a long series of fateful engagements between what a later age has learned to call 'faith' and 'reason'. To find such a distinction in Paul the '*ad hoc* theologian', however, would clearly be anachronistic. Paul's theology arises not from the attempt to reconcile tradition with situation, but more directly from his own experience of the self-revealing God of Jesus Christ. There is a distinct rationality – or, perhaps better, wisdom – to which Paul's response to Christ points. But it does not resemble the calculative scientific reason of Enlightenment times which, all too easily, sets what O'Leary calls a metaphysical 'speculative drive for a comprehensive explanatory scheme' against the 'horizons of contemplation' opened up by the Gospel.[56] The question – for the Church of the 'third epoch' as much as it was for Paul – is not how to develop the great system but, more subversively, how to take on the 'mind of Christ' (Philippians 2.5).

This is what I mean by referring to the Council as a theological 'event'. There is more to Vatican II's version of Paul's dilemma than the reconciliation of theological principles. That the text is concerned with some such reconciliation is clear; soteriology and missiology seek to express a continuity with the best of tradition. The appearance of a theology of revelation, however, introduces a thoroughly subversive element, reminding the Church that its faith is through and through historical – based, that is to say, not on a priori metaphysical abstractions but on the particularity of its relationship with another historical community. The same lives uneasily in relationship with an other which may not be reduced to the same. The continuities for which faith naturally seeks, the signs of the constancy of the God of the Covenant, have to reckon with the discontinuities which challenge the limits of faith's 'horizons of contemplation'. At the very least, the 'speculative drive', which would presume to encompass all truth, has to give way to a more post-modern appreciation

---

[56] O'Leary 1985:79ff. O'Leary's critique objects not to the use of metaphysical language as such but to its limitations, in so far as it ends up working counter to the very movement it is supposed to support – the explication of faith.

that it always takes time for truth to emerge from an all-pervading 'context of otherness'.

Responding to the Shoah

The importance of *Nostra Aetate* is that it tells the story of this tentative shift in theological awareness. That this experience is of crucial significance for the process of everyday life in a fragmented multi-faith world becomes clear when we take the contemporary Jewish–Christian dialogue a little further. If it is the case that the historical relationship between Jews and Christians which began with the fateful split between Church and Synagogue represents the matrix out of which Christian identity grows, then what are we to say of 'other' others? How does Christianity's 'primary otherness' determine or constitute further relationships?

The first task is to attend to the Jewish–Christian relationship itself – especially with regard to the continued use of 'Covenant language'. Very roughly, three 'models' can be distinguished according to the relative emphasis they put on the theme of continuity and discontinuity.[57] 'Single-Covenant' models attempt to incorporate both Jews and Christians within the one covenantal relationship. 'Dual-Covenant' models distinguish two separate relationships with no necessary connection. 'Multiple-Covenant' models set Judaism and Christianity within a broader pattern of covenantal relationships.[58] This last is the most plausible to propose and the most difficult to defend, depending as it does on a straightforwardly pluralist reading of religious relations. Apart from the violence which it does to the Christian tradition, it also presupposes a panoptic vision which, as I tried to point out in the first chapter, is simply not possible. Of the first two positions, the 'dual' model has the advantage of proposing a certain complementarity for two distinct and separate traditions, but the disadvantage of being forced to drive a wedge between them.[59] Only the first position, insisting on the single Covenant, grapples seriously with the Pauline dilemma – and the crucial conceptual issue of relationality. Here the most promising version rests its case on the normativity of the various Covenants which supersede each other – the

---

[57] For a useful overview and critique of the main lines of this debate see D'Costa 1990b.

[58] I am grateful for the clarity of Paul O'Reilly's observations on this point.

[59] The most influential and persuasive version of the dual Covenant must be that of Franz Rosenzweig. See especially Novak 1989:93–113, and for a critique of Rosenzweig as a philosopher of dialogue, Barnes 2000:33–65.

Abrahamic, the Mosaic, the Davidic – finding not an absolute but a pro-
leptic fulfilment in Christ.[60] The question remains, of course, how it is
possible to acknowledge Paul's conviction that God has done something
new in Jesus Christ without simply evacuating the revelation to Israel of
all meaning. How, putting it in more Rahnerian terms, to marry the transcendental revelation of God as 'holy mystery' with the categorical instance of divine love made manifest in the Death and Resurrection of
Christ?[61]

It is not my intention to answer that key Christological question here.
I am only concerned at this stage with exploring possible avenues which
arise from the practice of dialogue itself. To that extent, it is important
to note that much Christian post-Shoah theology is set within the wider
context of the demise of the great conceptual systems of modernity.
Commenting on this phenomenon, Peter Ochs draws a distinction between what he calls post-critical theology and a more radical response
which operates from within a liberationist perspective. The latter theologians, he concludes, 'tend to let their reasoning, even if it concerns
specific political issues, speak before text or tradition'.[62] The former is a
much more diffuse grouping united in discerning the problem to lie
with 'the way in which the Gospel witness is received and transmitted'.[63]
As used by Ochs, the terms express George Lindbeck's project to reinstate a 'cultural–linguistic' model of theology based in biblical narrative
over 'modern' liberal foundationalism which seeks to fit Christian faith
within a wider framework of cultural norms and supposedly 'universal'
human experience.

In this regard, it is instructive to note a certain parallel between
Christian and Jewish reactions to the Shoah. Positions such as that
espoused by Richard Rubenstein, which works out of the conviction

---

[60] A robust variation on the single-Covenant thesis is proposed by John McDade who
argues that 'it will be an enrichment of Christian theology, rather than a diminution of its
claims, to recognize that Jewish faith is a *distinct focus of God's action* which, within our present
history, cannot be integrated in any simple fashion with Christian identity' (1990:21, emphasis
in original).

[61] For a lengthy discussion of these 'two moments in Christian theology', see Rahner
1978:176–321.

[62] 'Judaism and Christian Theology', in Ford 1997:607–25; quotation from pp. 619–20. For
the 'radicals' see especially Eckardt 1986 and Ruether 1974, who traces the roots of Christian anti-
Semitism to a high Christology which finds all truth revealed in the Resurrection.

[63] Ochs in Ford 1997:608. Ochs takes the term 'postcritical' from Lindbeck 1984. As well as
reflecting a fundamentally Barthian perspective, Ochs notes the influence on postcritical theology
of the 'non-rationalistic' Jewish philosophy of Rosenzweig, Buber and Levinas.

that after Auschwitz belief in a redeeming God is no longer credible,[64] beg the same question about theological method which Ochs notes with regard to the Christian radicals. According to Irving Greenberg, Rubenstein opts for an agnostic pluralism out of the mistaken desire, typical of 'a growing number of Jews since 1750, as well as Christians' to be 'right with modernity'.[65] If there is a post-critical parallel in Jewish theology, it is to be found in Fackenheim's resounding and ever-repeated call not to give Hitler posthumous victories.[66] For Fackenheim, this 614th commandment is a 'new Sinai', a moral imperative which traditional Jewish believers and agnostics alike can recognise: an imperative *not to forget* which returns Jews to the bedrock of the tradition. Like Rubenstein, Fackenheim recognises in the Shoah an unprecedented break with history but, unlike the former, he argues not for a rejection of the tradition but for a more radical rethinking of its fundamental themes. To mend the break with the past he seeks to counter passivity in the face of the inevitability of suffering with a typically Jewish active faith of resistance, a 'protest which *stays within* the sphere of faith'.[67] Abraham, Jeremiah, Job, all remonstrated with God. For Fackenheim, the 'voice of Auschwitz' commands the religious Jew to wrestle with God and – *contra* Rubenstein – forbids the secular Jew to use the Shoah as an additional weapon with which to deny him.

The Shoah will have a significant part to play in the next chapter, particularly in understanding the ethical 'first philosophy' of Emmanuel Levinas and his relentless insistence on the priority of the other in the formation of human subjectivity. At that point, the question of an

---

[64] According to Rubenstein the only way out of the scandal which would make the Jews as a chosen people play a determinative role in the self-revelation of God is to reject the categories on which such a pathology feeds. See Rubenstein 1966, 1992. In the earlier work (which was received as a Jewish contribution to the 'Death of God' theology) Rubenstein focuses on two historical facts, the Holocaust and the establishment of the State of Israel which means that Jews can live 'beyond ideology' in the joy and pain of the present without any need to seek 'pathetic compensation in an imaginary future'. The second edition shows a shift: the God of nature which Rubenstein expected to replace the biblical God of history has not taken over. Rather, after the 1967 Yom Kippur war, the rise of messianic movements emphasises how much the Shoah and Israel are inseparable, divinely ordained, a prelude to the messianic climax to Jewish history. For a trenchant critique of such developments, see the Jewish liberationist perspective of Ellis 1997.

[65] See 'Cloud of Smoke, Pillar of Fire', in Eva Fleischer (ed.), *Auschwitz: Beginning of a New Era? Reflections on the H*, New York: Ktav, 1977; reproduced in Roth and Berenbaum 1989:305–45. Greenberg himself attempts to reimagine history, linking Auschwitz with the 'recreation of the body of the people, Israel' after the manner of a 'new Exodus' (p. 336).

[66] See especially Fackenheim 1982.

[67] 'The Commanding Voice of Auschwitz' in Morgan 1989: 168–83; quotation from p. 171; emphasis in original.

'ethical theology' of religions becomes the dominant issue. What Ochs identifies as a distinction between radical and post-critical theologies is raised at this stage in my argument to illustrate possible resolutions to the theological dilemma with which I began, the dilemma which finds its most intractible formulation in Paul's agonising about what has happened to God's Chosen People. In Ochs's terms, the distinction is between responses which would *rewrite* the tradition and those which seek to *reread* it. Both look for a certain deconstruction of the tradition in favour of a more adequate response to an ethical challenge. But, if the former with its rejection of traditional doctrine still manifests an apologetic character which cannot but set the ethical apart from the theological, the latter returns to the experiential foundations of biblical faith, the linguistic constructions, metaphors and images of a particular historical culture, and seeks not an accommodation but a deeper understanding of the tradition through an engagement with the world of the other.[68] In this sense, the return to the language of tradition, which forms and supports the virtues and dispositions characteristic of a religious community, is at once ethical *and* theological. Such a 'postcritical rereading' of the New Testament witness seeks to return to the unresolved historical problematic of the Church's origins, so evident in Paul, and to do this, moreover, not apart from but precisely in dialogue with its Jewish other.

The implication of *Nostra Aetate*'s powerful call to 'recognise, preserve and promote those spiritual and moral good things' found among people of other faiths is that the Church must first discern what these 'good things' are; the Church has to learn the practice of discerning the 'seeds of the Word'. Such a practice is, properly speaking, a work of the Spirit with which the Church has to co-operate. In this sense, dialogue is less a 'means to mission' or another 'form of mission' than the animating spirit of openness to the other without which the Church as a missionary community in the post-modern world cannot exist. To see dialogue in this sense as an end in itself, is to shift attention from what I have called elsewhere a theology *for* dialogue, principles which prepare for dialogue and encounter, to a theology which arises from the complex dialogical experience itself, what might be called a theology *of* dialogue.[69] Of course, it is clear that the two cannot be neatly separated any more than the Pauline

---

[68] For a more consciously post-modern perspective based on 'narrativist' theology see Loughlin 1996:10–26.

[69] This distinction is developed at greater length in an earlier study, Barnes 1989:89ff. See also Dupuis 1997:200f., 377ff.

dilemma can be resolved with an unequivocal formula of words. My point, however, as noted in the previous chapter, is that much depends on what sort of distinction is made between the two: whether the emphasis is put on the beginning, and the establishing of relationships, or on the end, and some presumed resolution of difference.

Again, Paul's experience points the way forward. In an obvious sense, the dialogue only ever ends where it began, with God's utterance of the Word, in God. Only by entering again and again into this mystery of the God of justice and mercy who speaks out of darkness can the Church 'think origins'. But, strictly speaking, as the people of Israel – at their best – knew, God remains totally other. The Church's renewed experience of its Jewish other leads O'Leary to comment that 'as dialogue becomes increasingly inescapable the texture of Christianity becomes dialogal through and through, and its creeds appear as starting points in a quest which cannot be continued without the assistance of the other'.[70] But this return to the Jewish matrix of all Christian language about God again prompts an important question. If the self-revelation of God in Christ can only be properly understood in terms of the language and thought-forms of the Covenant with Israel, in what way does such a relationship inform or critique the developing relationship of the Church with the other great world religions?

Theology in the 'context of otherness'

This question takes us back to a tension with which so much contemporary theology is wrestling – what the Vatican Council recognised as the demand for a faithful renewal of the sources of tradition and a commitment in hope to reading the 'signs of the times'.[71] So far in this chapter I have considered the way the otherness of the Church's Jewish past returns in the shape of the Shoah to disturb the present; shortly we will need to consider the meaning of this 'theological event' and the question for wider inter-faith relations which it raises. For the moment, however, I want to stay with the 'horizons of contemplation' within which the Church seeks to tell its story in dialogue with the other. How – to invoke the Ochs distinction – responsibly to *reread* the tradition?

---

[70] O'Leary, 1985:208.

[71] This term, almost a slogan for the Council's agenda, appears with surprising infrequency in the texts. It occurs only once in *Gaudium et Spes*, 4, and in three other places: in the decrees on priestly ministry, 9; on the laity, 14; and on ecumenism, 4.

Both the shortest and the longest of the Council documents, *Nostra Aetate* and *Gaudium et Spes*, the massive 'Pastoral Constitution' on the 'Church in the world of today', are concerned with the ethical and pastoral challenges of a rapidly changing and thoroughly pluralist world. They have this much in common, that both started life not as theological position papers but with what may loosely be called the 'facts of experience' and the imperatives of respect for the other and willingness to learn. Within the Roman Catholic Church *Gaudium et Spes* has inspired liberation theology, restored pastoral theology and brought about a new development within missiology – that practice based on what has come to be known as 'inculturation'. None of these topics can be dealt with in any detail here. I refer to the Pastoral Constitution at this point because, like *Nostra Aetate*, it *raises* the critical theological issues rather than solving them. It also broadens the discussion, from the engagement with the Church's 'primary relationship' with the Jews to the 'context of otherness' within which all Christian relations are set. Openness to the other is the sine qua non of any theology, creating the context or the atmosphere in which theology is to be done. Unless, however, it also provokes sustained attention to the ethical and political issues which attend any relationship with the other, theology risks remaining at the level of a priori theory – a theology *for*, rather than *of*, dialogue.

Whatever its faults, *Gaudium et Spes* is remarkable for setting out a sacramental contemplative vision of a world in process of transformation by the Spirit of Christ. But its formation was just as fraught as *Nostra Aetate*. Opposition threatened at more than one point to reduce it to a 'pastoral declaration' with a series of 'appendix chapters'.[72] In the end, the view which finally prevailed gave theological principle and pastoral application equal status.[73] Likened at one point to a 'Noah's Ark' which contained material with no other place to go,[74] it should be read more positively as an attempt to develop a theological synthesis of the 'Suenens plan for the Council': to bring together what concerns the Church '*ad intra*' and the Church

---

[72] Vorgrimler 1969 v:38,69–70.

[73] See the 'explanatory note' which insists on the unity of the document, and footnote 1 in the Abbott edition of the Council documents, Abbott 1966:199. At the last November meeting of the Mixed Commission it was the Archbishop of Crakow, Karol Wojtyla, who asked that the term 'pastoral' in the title be carefully explained. Part 1, he said, is 'very pastoral in places, especially where it discusses the human person. Both parts must be seen in a pastoral light' (quoted in Rynne 1966:205). Hebblethwaite, 1993:421, notes the influence of Paul VI in ensuring that the text should be accessible, providing 'principles rather than solutions, direction rather than directives'.

[74] Vorgrimler 1969 v:38, 69–70.

'*ad extra*'. The inevitably repetitious collation of massive committees, the Pastoral Constitution is nothing if not a painstaking attempt to work through the insights generated by the whole extraordinary process that was Vatican II – not just those noted already from *Lumen Gentium* and *Dei Verbum* but, as Moeller concludes, those also from the liturgical constitution, *Sacrosanctum Concilium*, 'which is revelation announced, prayed, lived and conveyed to the People of God in and through the Church'.[75] Such a rooting of theology in liturgy would have been unthinkable in the neo-scholastic world of textbook theology, but it is precisely this return to the practice of faith which invites the Church to read the tradition against the background of the 'signs of the times' – and vice versa.

This is clearly an important, if problematic, shift of attention. *Gaudium et Spes* sums up the Council's abandonment of what, according to Ruggieri, can be called a 'deductivist outlook' and the adoption of an alternative: an 'inductive mindset'.[76] This decisive move away from an ahistorical approach to theology, which puts the Church *above* time, is the logical result of Vatican II's theology of revelation which, with its return to the 'single source theory' of the continuing action of the Holy Spirit in the Church, roots the Church more firmly *in* time.[77] More than any other document, it encapsulates John XXIII's hope that the Council would – again in Ruggieri's words – 'connect the truths of the Gospel with the demands of history'.[78] This shift, however, works two ways. Certainly, the emphasis on a contemplative sensitivity to the 'seeds of the Word', within the story the Church seeks to tell about itself, retrieves an important theological principle and an essential aspect of the sacramental tradition of Catholic Christianity. In a later chapter, I shall seek to elaborate on this point by exploring the roots of this tradition as the animating spirit of the Church. All I want to note at this point is that, in considering particular issues for the Church in its relations with the world '*ad extra*', *Gaudium et Spes* also focuses attention on the Church's life '*ad intra*' and therefore on the prior attitude of faith

---

[75] Vorgrimler 1969 v:70.

[76] See Alberigo 1987:97–8. See also Laishley's remarks on Vatican II's historical method: 'Unfinished Business', in Hastings 1991:215–20.

[77] According to Pottmeyer, in Alberigo 1987:32, there were 'two points of reference' which exercised a 'mutual control' over the Council's development: the return to scripture and attention to the 'world of today'. To these John XXIII added a third: 'the unity of Christians and the human race'.

[78] 'Faith and History' in Alberigo 1987:91–114. In exploring Vatican II's recovery of the biblical notion of faith anchored in history, Ruggieri seeks to show that the call to discern the 'signs of the times' 'throws light on the direction to be taken by . . . the hermeneutic of a renewed catholicity that excludes any desire for, any anticipation of, the disappearance or absorption of what is different from it' (p. 105).

before the complexity of life in the modern world, a faith which – as one of the great architects of the Council, Marie-Dominique Chenu, wrote at the time – listens to the world and learns how to recognise there the 'signs that the gospel is consistent with the hopes of human beings'.[79]

This notion of consistency is, however, highly problematic, and questions about discernment and the recognition of prophecy cannot be avoided. *Nostra Aetate*'s commitment to 'recognise, preserve and promote' the 'spiritual and moral good things' in other religious traditions demands – at the very least – careful attention to the 'seeds of the Word' in the world of the other. Similarly, in *Gaudium et Spes* the Church finds itself called to look at the historical situation of the modern world in order to elicit directives from it. Both are admirably dominated by a contemplative vision of a world in process of transformation by the Spirit of Christ. The Council's theological method arises from this vision, a version of the 'method of correlation'.[80] But any attempt to bring the resources of the theological tradition into dialogue with the present world of experience raises crucial issues for a theology which would reflect on the experience of dialogue and its implications for the Church's self-understanding as a community called together for mission.

The immediate issue is that of the objectivity of judgment. Where do the criteria for the proposed correlation come from? The assumption of an independent vantage-point, somehow distinct from both tradition and situation, ignores the fact that all judgments are particular, being rooted in time and place. The alternative, taking a position on either tradition or situation, betrays a similar naïveté: how can the one be disentangled from the other?[81]

---

[79] Chenu 1965:35.

[80] As stated by Tillich, 1951:3, the 'method of correlation' involves theology moving 'back and forth between two poles, the eternal truth of its foundation and the temporal situation in which the eternal truth must be received'. For an account of the dialogue between Tillich and Roman Catholic theology see 'Paul Tillich in Catholic Thought: the Past and the Future', in Bulman and Parella 1994:9–32. The main representative of the method of correlation – 'the two-source approach' – in theology of religions is Paul Knitter (see e.g. Knitter 1985:91–2).

[81] Ormerod, 1996, arguing against the use of the method made by Haight, 1990:195–210, draws on the work of Doran 1990, stressing the element of 'transformative praxis' in theology. Doran's point is that a distinction between tradition and situation cannot be made since both are 'already theological'. 'Correlational methods create first an artificial separation of situation and tradition, and then attempt conceptualistically to put back together what they have arbitrarily rent asunder. The situation cannot be understood apart from realities named by general categories, nor the tradition apart from realities named by special categories. And the one subjectivity of the theologian . . . is the single differentiated source of both sets of categories' (pp. 456–7). Doran himself is indebted to the work of Bernard Lonergan on the levels of conversion – religious, moral and intellectual (see Lonergan 1971:267–9).

That this is more than an abstract methodological point is shown by the peculiar difficulty which I noted in the first chapter with regard to inter-faith encounter. The negotiation involved demands not a formal correlation of concepts or points of view, but an engagement with persons which is logically prior to any such process. And persons not only bring a very particular history to the encounter, but ask questions which have ethical, and often political, implications. In other words, what I have referred to as a certain tension between the virtues of faith and hope is not to be resolved by an a priori theological strategy involving the comparison and contrast of concepts. This is not to say that theological debate is neither possible nor necessary. On the contrary. But, if it is to avoid a theoretical finality which places the other within a pre-defined Christian space, it must be made secondary to that practice of faith which forms persons in responsible relationship with each other.

Discerning the return of the other

My theme in this chapter has been the theological 'event' of the Council and the beginning of a new vision of the way in which all peoples can be said to be united in God. *Nostra Aetate* can easily be interpreted as an acceptably liberal form of Roman Catholic 'inclusivism' – a somewhat patronising attempt to find everyone a place, as if at some cosmic papal audience. More profoundly, Vatican II's various deliberations on people of other faiths can be understood as raising the question of 'the other' for a consciously universalist tradition. It is for this reason that *Nostra Aetate* in particular has to be read as a response to the question put to the Church in Rahner's 'third epoch', a question not primarily about how Christianity is to maintain credibility in a multi-faith world but, more importantly, about how a 'catholic' or universalist instinct, a generous tendency to include rather than exclude, is to respond when 'the other' enters into and disturbs what is familiar. In these terms, the achievement of *Nostra Aetate* and *Gaudium et Spes*, the shortest and the longest of the Council documents, is to take the key insights of *Lumen Gentium* and *Dei Verbum* – the Church as the sacrament of the eschatological People of God, witnessing to the promise of salvation which is revealed in Christ for all people – and to begin the process of reimagining the Church's history as the primary focus of God's *continuing engagement* with humanity.

History, in other words, is more than a pristine memory of the past which the Church somehow brings into correlation with the present.

History goes on being made – not in the sense that more and more 'events' have to be interpreted, but in the sense that the memory of the past is itself always being *re*-interpreted. The Shoah, for instance, has made the Church understand Paul's dilemma differently, more sympathetically. The disturbing return of the irreducible reality of continuing Jewish faith has done more than awaken ethical sensitivity; it has also shown that the Church's history is by no means a record of straightforward progress towards the eschaton. Once the possibility of divine action is not just allowed but affirmed in a particular case, the Church finds itself committed to something more than an apologetic theology, the repetition of a narrative which seeks to demonstrate the unbroken continuity between present and past. This is the most radical dimension of the Church's retrieval of a 'deductivist outlook'. In recognising the Jewish matrix of all their theology, a matrix which continues to exist independently of ecclesiastical control, Christians may no longer presume to speak as if they are in perfect possession of a panoptic vision. They must learn to live with the strangeness of the other – what is new, has been occluded, or simply forgotten.

A Christianity which would recognise this break and exist in responsible relationship with people of other faiths has to 'think origins', and indeed all its relations, in a more imaginative way. It is this shift away from the Hellenistic–Roman matrix of Christianity, Rahner's 'third epoch' of the Church, which is represented most powerfully by the engagement with the great world religions. What has changed with Vatican II, according to Rahner, is that the very sense of an unbroken continuity which can be unproblematically narrated from past to present no longer holds.

> None of us can say exactly how, with what conceptuality, under what new aspects the old message of Christianity must in the future be proclaimed in Asia, in Africa, in the regions of Islam, perhaps also in South America, if this message really is to be present everywhere in the world.[82]

The future contains a plurality of possible meanings and thus raises a variety of complex theoretical problems about authenticity and authorisation as well as about the limits of what has come to be called 'inculturation'. This is not to make a virtue of necessity, to accept that the 'seeds of the Word' are irretrievably lost in the fragmented post-modern world of

---

[82] Rahner 1979c:725.

competing meta-narratives. It is, rather, more positively to allow that the Church is – and always has been – a community charged with listening for the echoes of a Word spoken and disseminated not from some single controllable site but within the irreducible 'context of otherness'. Michel de Certeau, commenting on Jesus's command to the disciples to 'follow me', puts it like this:

> We have access to Jesus only through texts which, in talking of him, narrate what he awakened and hence describe only their own status as writings of belief or of those who have turned round to respond . . . No text, whether 'primary' or 'apostolic', represents anything other than a 'modification' (a writing) made possible by a call which cannot objectively be uttered in its own terms and which is recognized only gradually through successive conversions.[83]

'Heterology': disclosing the other

Christian texts, in other words, whether conciliar documents or Pauline letters, attempt to recapture and express something of that face-to-face encounter with the Word of God which establishes the faith of the Christian community. In seeking to understand this continuing process by which the Church seeks to come to terms with the other, I want to suggest that a way forward may be found by adopting de Certeau's somewhat elusive concept of 'heterology'.[84] De Certeau's all-consuming preoccupation is with the 'gap' between the object of faith, the Risen Lord of Easter faith, and the representations which the Church makes in order to continue to speak of that faith. But, however important it is to understand de Certeau's project in theological terms, he is first and foremost an historian who is concerned to lay bare the largely unspoken assumptions behind the act of historical interpretation. Radicalised by the 'events' of 1968 and by his growing engagement with Lacan, he brings historiography into a dialogue with

---

[83] De Certeau 1987a:288; translation from Ward 2000:227.

[84] According to Buchanan, 1996:483, 'heterology' is de Certeau's 'great unfinished project' and he admits that there is no way of knowing precisely what de Certeau intended by the term. De Certeau himself uses 'heterology' in a collection which has no original French equivalent: de Certeau 1986. For the three articles which Buchanan claims can be described as 'heterological' see Giard 1991. Tan See Kam, 1996:32, argues that in de Certeau's terms heterologies can be defined as 'countertraditions which can lead to (contrary to the "closed" epistemological field of History) "further possibilities of knowledge" . . . as well as to the unmasking of the technologies and tropologies by which History creates the simulacra of "others" out of its own fancy or its own obsession'.

psychoanalysis.[85] De Certeau reminds us that no historian is ever out-side history, but, through cultural background, political interest or psychological make-up, is involved in the process of production of his-torical data, those practices which have rendered the historian's pres-ent position possible. Since all historical material, from contemporary records to descriptive analysis, is radically contingent, historical inter-pretation must be set against the background of the society and cul-tural forms which have shaped its formation.

De Certeau does not, however, give us the 'broad sweep', the radical reinterpretation of whole epochs. He is more interested in the smaller scale processes by which difference is maintained within, or against, the established order. He attends in particular to moments of historical trans-formation or rupture; his texts are shot through with the disseminated voice of the other–whether discerned in diabolic possession or in the mys-tic's search for the 'lost body' of Christ–which insinuates itself back into the mainstream of reflection.[86] For de Certeau, the very act or process of 'doing history' always sets limits to the space of its operation which are inherently unstable. As he puts it, in characteristically gnomic fashion:

> In order to come into being, a science must resign itself to a loss of
> both totality and reality. But whatever it has to give up in order to
> establish itself returns under the figure of the other, from which it
> continually awaits a guarantee against that lack which is at the
> origin of all our knowledge.[87]

But de Certeau's historiography is also deeply ethical. As we shall see, it is full of resonances of Levinas's philosophy of the other.[88] His aim is to counter the totalising tendencies inherent in any a priori systematic discourse which, as he puts it, would disinter the dead only to bury them again in 'scriptural tombs'.[89] The act of writing, more than the spoken word, risks betraying its object, reducing it to a mere repetition of what is already known within the world of the same. De Certeau is thus con-cerned less with the retrieval of a lost or 'counter-tradition' than with

---

[85] See e.g. 'The Fiction of History: the Writing of Moses and Monotheism', in de Certeau 1988:308–54. De Certeau does not so much put the past *beside* as *within* the present. The two 'sites' do not succeed but overlay each other in a single time-frame, 'moving within the same polyvalent place' (p. 312).

[86] De Certeau 1992:81.

[87] De Certeau 1986:214.

[88] See e.g. De Certeau 1988:342f. For de Certeau's *'passion de l'alterité'*, see Giard's Introduction to de Certeau 1987a: xii.

[89] De Certeau 1988:2.

reflection on the nature and limits of the process of interpretation itself. The writing of history is always a writing from and about the present, and, just as the past is excluded from and yet finds its way back into the present, so the present will always intrude into any attempt to write about the past. In so far as it consists of such a writing of the past, *Nostra Aetate*'s retrieval of Judaism can therefore be described in de Certeau's terms as an otherness which returns to interrupt or 'haunt' the present.[90] De Certeau wants to show how conceptual issues of necessity and causality in historiography delimit the area of concern by including the other within the same, thus producing a 'tautology' which yet implies further stages of interpretation. This leads to 'heterology': the deconstruction or uncovering of unavowed forms of enclosure.

Practising hospitality to the stranger

Invoking de Certeau's distinction between tautology and heterology, we see that the dominant narrative of the Council documents, especially *Lumen Gentium* and to a lesser extent *Gaudium et Spes*, is concerned to include the other within the continuity of the history of salvation: a relatively benign version of the 'Catholic instinct'. In *Nostra Aetate*, on the other hand, a theology which would expect to assimilate the challenge of history by repetition of its own history finds itself facing a certain 'otherness' which can only be temporarily reduced. It inevitably returns in another form. The Shoah and the history of Christian anti-Semitism which it reveals introduce an ethical challenge, the presence of an other, which may not be totalised. The implication of the introduction of this 'Jewish context', both in *Nostra Aetate* and in the key doctrinal document *Dei Verbum*, is clear. The Church cannot understand itself without reference to the Jews, yet simplistic theologies of supersessionism are both ethically flawed and historically inadequate. Using the words of St Paul, *Nostra Aetate* says that 'because of their ancestors the Jews still remain very dear to God'.[91] In de Certeau's terms, the Jewish other is always returning, always present, 'haunting' the space carved out by the dominant Christian 'same'.

Something similar can be said about the way *Nostra Aetate* finds itself dealing with another history. The sometimes acrimonious relations

---

[90] For the image of 'haunting', see de Certeau 1988:2, 23, 25, 91, 231, 251, 345.

[91] Romans 11.28; see *LG* 20. The text continues: 'For the gifts and the call of God are irrevocable' (11.29).

between the Church and Islam, which speak of a history of conquest and crusade with effects lasting to the present day, also played their part in the process which led to *Nostra Aetate*. The inclusion of a paragraph on Islam and the recasting of the entire Declaration within the history of Indian religions and 'other religions which are to be found throughout the entire world' (*NA* 2) were made possible by the patient hidden work of scholars like the Arabist Louis Massignon and the Indologist Jules Monchanin. They were the ones responsible for keeping alive the voice of the all too easily forgotten other which yet continues to haunt the Church's history. The Pauline theology of Jewish–Christian relations arises from a particular history. There can therefore be no necessary or paradigmatic link between what is an appropriate theology to express that history and what would be appropriate to speak about relations between the Church and 'other others'. The inter-dependence of Judaism and Christianity is intrinsic to that relationship; such links as exist between Christianity and the religions of India and, more problematically, between Christianity and Islam, are determined by very different histories.[92] On the other hand, the *process* by which such heterologies are uncovered, is not particular to the relationships in question.[93] What might be called, following de Certeau, 'ethical heterology' – the practice, which finds expression throughout his work, of seeking ways for the other to speak – will take different forms in different situations.

For de Certeau, heterology is no passivity, but a work of hospitality towards the stranger which is expressive of Christian faith.[94] Later I want to take up various examples of this process of ethical recovery of the other by setting them explicitly within a biblically based theology of welcome and hospitality. Meanwhile, in concluding this chapter, let us briefly recall how the concept of heterology has been used so far to link Rahner's 'second shift' in the Church's history with the first.

I began this chapter with the event of the Council as an experience of the Church's own historicity which shifted attention from soteriology to revelation. I have tried to uncover within the text of *Nostra Aetate*

---

[92] See, however, the argument developed in chapters 5 and 6 which, by examining the contemporary dialogue with Indian religions, seeks to show that history, and therefore theology, is always being created.

[93] Ahearne, 1991:21, describes this process as a 'basic "heterological" law: the operation which draws up a limit to familiar space insinuates by the same movement foreignness into that space'.

[94] De Certeau 1987a:262.

the record of the Church's encounter with its own Jewish origins – Christianity's 'Jewish other'. The reaction of the Council to this disturbance of the more self-assured ecclesiology of the pre-conciliar era goes little further than the commending of theological and ethical principles. At the same time, I have also pointed out that the Council explored a number of images for the Church to account for the mystery of God's self-giving to humankind – most obviously that of the People of God to which all human beings are called to belong, and to which they are, therefore, 'related . . . in various ways' (LG 16).

This, however, only states the issue without resolving it: how does a universalist Church express this relationship without totalising the other? In a later chapter I will seek to argue that, however central the image of the People of God may be to the Church's self-understanding, it still needs to be complemented by another – that of the Church as sacrament, a sign of hope for all humankind. This is where the whole question of Christian identity, or to be more precise the process of identification, becomes an issue – an issue which will need some preparation through consideration of the concepts of subjectivity and alterity. Moving in the next two chapters from the guiding concept of de Certeau's heterology to Emmanuel Levinas's critique of the 'totalising' discourse of Western philosophy, I will take up his ethical 'first philosophy' and the response of Paul Ricoeur which this critique has provoked. In following the terms of this dialogue, my intention is not, however, to attempt an exhaustive treatment of the philosophical 'question of the other' – the history of which is, in Ricoeur's words, 'at the very least, intimidating'.[95] It is, rather, to show that a theology of dialogue, a re-reading of the tradition not over against but through the encounter with the other, has to be based on a reflection on the Christian experience of relationality itself. It is no doubt true that the Church lives by telling a story about where human beings ultimately and truly belong – in a life with God. This it does by pointing away from itself towards another. But even – perhaps especially – the most self-effacing of persons requires a strong sense of self.

---

[95] Ricoeur 1992:299.

3

Facing the other

In the first chapter, I briefly drew attention to the way the three-fold paradigm in theology of religions misreads the history of Christian engagement with people of other faiths as a progressive move towards a normative pluralism. I then went on in the previous chapter to explore the Jewish matrix within which all Christian theology has to be done. My point is that Christians cannot claim to possess an independent finality for their own vision of reality, for the symbolic language which they use has its roots elsewhere. Indeed, they cannot even claim to know the origins of that language except in so far as that language is mediated to them by an other. If this is correct, if Christian faith depends in some sense for its own coherence on the living tradition of Judaism, then the crucial conceptual issues for theology of religions are those which arise from *within* the experience of dialogue and encounter – not comparatively minor issues about commensurability and 'family resemblance', but issues about subjectivity and relationality.

The Jewish matrix for Christian theology shifts the terms within which the debate about the 'otherness' of people of other faiths is conducted. How is it possible to know the other *as other* – without, that is, risking the assimilation of the other to the category of sameness? How, on the other hand, does one avoid positing an otherness which is simply unknowable? My initial response to this dilemma is to seek a different approach to theology of religions: not an a priori theory of inter-faith relations but a reflection on what I am calling the 'negotiation of the middle'. To encounter another person, let alone a person of another faith, entails risk. At the very least, it requires a certain passivity in face of the other. It will also demand discernment of the Christian mystery, the gift of God himself, at the heart of particularity and difference. And it should eventually prompt us to ask what 'alteration' – change, becoming other – says about the nature of the person formed after the manner of Jesus Christ. What sense does it make to speak of a Christian practice of faith which risks the fragmentation of the subject?

Once this question is asked we are taken inexorably into the peculiarly post-modern concern – one might almost say obsession – with alterity. From Foucault's relentless uncovering of hidden power-structures to Derrida's dissection of textual *différance*, post-modernism searches the contexts, the margins and the edges of the known and familiar for what has been, consciously or unconsciously, repressed and occluded. Theology after the Shoah, post-colonialist liberation movements and, of course, the deconstructionist moves of much 'continental' philosophy, all contribute to a cultural sensibility which I described earlier as the uneasy consciousness of having reached a limit. Structures of knowing and authorisation are shown to be shot through by a continuing and irreducible otherness; the present is 'haunted', as de Certeau puts it, by a past which it can no longer control.

The experience of inter-faith encounter can be seen in a similar light: a plethora of faith traditions, old and new, forever reproducing themselves, forever in conflict, their constant 'alteration' challenging any claims to privilege on the part of one. Perhaps people of faith in a post-modern age are themselves condemned to haunt the fringes of the culture? An irrelevant and slightly irritating nuisance? Or a prophetic voice subverting the established status quo? Certainly it would be wrong to leap to the conclusion that the only alternative to the implied relativism of the post-modern is a more or less reactionary reinstatement of traditional forms of rhetoric. However we are to understand the complex process of self-identification, let alone 'alteration', same and other cannot be separated or related in any simplistic fashion. By choosing de Certeau as my guide through what in many ways appears like a post-modern morass I am not suggesting that he spares us the pain of negotiation and change. On the contrary, by multiplying the number of examples of the covert silencing or manipulation of the other, he asks the ethical question with ever-renewed insistence. Nor does the question lack a certain ambiguity for, as de Certeau also seeks to show, the other is needed for my own sense of self. Only the other can draw me out of a protective defence of the same into that never-ending yet life-giving journey which, he insists, alone makes faith credible.

What I have referred to, for the sake of brevity, as a 'theology of dialogue' is not, therefore, intended to replace one theory with another,

but to give an account of a Christian subjectivity formed through a practice of faith, the responsible relationship with other persons. This is not
to sidestep the theoretical in favour of an unprincipled pragmatism, but
to point to the danger of taking as a starting point an uncritical dualism
of 'same' and 'other'. If the threefold paradigm tends to set same and
other apart through the use of spatial metaphors, my argument is that
we are speaking not of a binary opposition but of inherently relational
concepts – what Plato called the 'great kinds' or categories of Being.[1] What
de Certeau's historiography shows is that the frontiers between 'now' and
'then' can never be irrevocably fixed within the terms of a totalising discourse. In a similar way, his image of the 'return of the repressed' suggests
that the Jewish other is 'other' only in the sense of being temporarily
forgotten or ignored.

In due course, we will need to consider how this – very particular –
relationship between Christians and Jews can be the basis for a theology
which would address the post-modern 'question of the other' in *all* inter-
faith relations. To anticipate briefly, I shall try to show that, when the full
social and historical reality of the other presents itself, the question shifts
from the reconciliation of tradition and situation towards the subjectivity of the theologian and to those virtues and dispositions which form
persons in responsible relationship with each other.

The more immediate questions, however, are philosophical. In what
follows, I shall seek to tease out the conceptual difficulties which attend
any account of otherness and the process of alteration by engaging with
the thought of Emmanuel Levinas. For Levinas, the 'question of the other'
is the guiding motif of a project which attempts to 'translate' 'Jewish' into
'Greek' thought through an engagement with the dominating post-
Kantian phenomenological tradition of Western philosophy. My intention here is not to critique Levinas's ethical 'first philosophy' as such, still
less to suggest that he provides an 'ethical alternative' for a theology of
religions. It is not so much the results of this intra-philosophical dialogue
which concern me, but the philosophical questions about relationality
which it raises.

---

[1] In *Sophist* 254b–259d, where the discussion is about the nature of 'sameness' and
'otherness', the Greek terms in question are neuter adjectives: *to tauton* and *to thateron*; see also
Timaeus 35b. Plato's *megista genē* are translated as 'leading kinds' in Ricoeur 1988:143 and 'great
kinds' in Ricoeur 1992:298. In the latter text, Ricoeur seeks to draw a clear distinction between
these 'metacategories' and 'the first-order discourse to which belong the categories or existentials
such as persons and things'.

An ethic of responsibility for the other

The question with which I want to begin comes from de Certeau's figure of the constant return of the other: how to allow for the inevitability of the 'alteration' of the subject without risking its fragmentation? Levinas asks the same question: 'How can a being enter into relation with the other without allowing its very self to be crushed by the other?'[2] Perhaps for the Christian theologian the question can be rephrased in christological terms: how are we to speak of the *kenosis* of Christ without implying a passivity which leads to a loss of self-identity? This is not the only reason why a dialogue with Levinas is fruitful for theology of religions. The issues surrounding a subjectivity formed in an ever-fractured relationship with otherness appear in all his texts. A dislocated Jewish émigré, educated in France and Germany in the intellectual crisis following the First World War, imprisoned during the Second, Levinas is both an insider and an outsider. If he is difficult to place philosophically, it is because the two sides of his work – philosophy and Talmudic commentary – mirror a life-experience set between different worlds.[3] What holds his work together is a deep questioning ethical sensitivity which puts the Other, the other person, at the heart of philosophy.[4]

In seeking to restore ethical thinking to a philosophical tradition which he believes has become fixated on forms of totalising ontology, Levinas points to the role which the relation with the Other plays in metaphysical reflection. This second-order 'ethics of ethics' – what might be called, following Rosenzweig, not ethics but 'metaethics'[5] – involves the

---

[2] Levinas 1987a: 77.

[3] As recent a survey of modern French philosophy as Matthews 1996 allows 'only cursory treatment' of Levinas. Descombes 1980 mentions Levinas only with reference to Derrida and deconstruction. Schroeder 1996, on the other hand, emphasises Levinas's contestation of the entire Western philosophical tradition, while Gibbs 1992, Cohen 1994 and Wright 1999 read Levinas primarily as a Jewish philosopher. Davis 1996 notes what he calls the 'Levinas effect: the difficulty of Levinas's texts permits his commentators to find in them a reflection of their own interests and attitudes'(p. 122).

[4] The convention is to translate Levinas's *autre* or *Autre* as 'other' and the personal *other person*, *autrui* or *Autrui*, as 'Other'. As Davis 1996:43 explains: 'the former confirms totality, the latter reveals infinity'. In this particular chapter I have tried to follow Levinas's usage. In the rest of the book I have tended to use only the lower case, except where it is clear that the reference is to the personal Other who 'reveals infinity'.

[5] Rosenzweig speaks of 'the basic characteristics of the sciences of God, world and man' as consisting of 'the metaphysical, the metalogical and the metaethical' respectively. See Rosenzweig 1970:89. Levinas never speaks of ethics as metaethics, but as a metaphysics (see e.g. Levinas 1969:43) – perhaps because he wishes to avoid any sense of a dialogical relationship of equals. He emphasises always the *ethical* relation which is established with the infinitely other.

establishment of what Levinas calls a 'non-allergic relation with alterity'.[6] In his enigmatic term, ethics is an 'optics', by which he means a '"vision" without image . . . a relation or an intentionality of a wholly different type'.[7] In face of the Other, the active subject becomes passive – 'subjected' or responsive to the Other. By being responsible before the face of the Other, the subject is to be made aware of the dangers of self-betrayal through the desire for totality – *and* to be opened to the possibilities for human existence contained in the 'idea of infinity'. The first part of this task, the critique of 'Greek' philosophy, is relatively uncontroversial; the second, the project to establish a metaphysics of the 'Good beyond Being', far more problematic. For Levinas, however, they are inseparable: two interdependent sides of a phenomenology of inter-subjectivity.

It is important to ask why this should be so. While there is only the occasional allusion to the Shoah in Levinas's philosophical works, it somehow simmers beneath the surface. The epigraph to *Otherwise than Being* is dedicated to the memory of 'those who are closest among the six million murdered by the National Socialists besides the millions and millions of human beings of all confessions and all nations, victims of the same hatred of the other humans, of the same anti-Semitism'. And *Existence and Existents* was put together in the prison camp – which accounts, says Levinas, for the 'absence of any consideration of those philosophical works published, with so much impact, between 1940 and 1945'.[8] While making for an intriguing parallel with Rosenzweig's masterpiece, *Star of Redemption*, which began life on the battlefield in the dying months of the First World War, it is also a reminder that Levinas's philosophising is anchored in personal experience, as well as that of a people. Levinas accepts the Shoah as the 'explicitly Jewish moment' in his work, but he also regards it as a paradigm of gratuitous human suffering.[9] As such it raises an enormous moral – and philosophical – problem, for how is it possible to understand what is beyond understanding, to make sense of the

---

[6] Levinas 1969:47.

[7] Levinas 1969:23.

[8] Levinas 1978:15.

[9] In an interview given in 1986, Levinas said that: 'If there is an explicitly Jewish moment in my thought it is the reference to Auschwitz, where God let the Nazis do what they wanted. Consequently, what remains? Either this means that there is no reason for morality and hence it can be concluded that everyone should act like Nazis, or the moral law maintains its authority . . . The essential problem is this: can we speak of an absolute commandment after Auschwitz? Can we speak of morality after the failure of morality?' (in Bernasconi and Wood 1988:168–79; quotation from pp. 175–6).

apparently meaningless?[10] In Levinas's opinion, the Holocaust brought with it not the death of morality but the end of theodicy – a largely intellectualist project aimed to make suffering bearable. Although not involved in inter-faith dialogue as such, his project takes its rise from the same ethical concern which inspired *Nostra Aetate* – and leads to the same questions, about a subjectivity formed in face of an irreducible alterity.

The instinct behind Levinas's project – a deeply Jewish sensitivity to the needs of the 'sojourner, the fatherless and the widow'(Deuteronomy 14.29) which puts the Other first – is nothing if not an important corrective to overly systemic accounts of alterity. For Levinas, phenomenological intentionality can all too easily become reduced to an increasingly *self*-conscious account of knowledge, with all the disastrous consequences for human relations which are written into the history of this century. Levinas's meta-ethics attends to the non-intentional and develops an account of the self constituted by its relationship with an otherness which presents itself as more than the simply strange or unusual, but as that which precisely transcends all a priori self-justifying categories. At this point, the subject lives not by finding a place, however significant, for the other *within* the totality of existence, but by responding to the relation which is established with that which is *outside* the self. Thereby the subject is constituted as responsible, capable of responding to the initiative of the Other. Of the many questions which Levinas's project raises, the one which concerns me is whether the 'instruction' of the Other leaves the self free to respond rather than being constrained by a sense of guilt for its own inadequacy. Is it possible for Levinas to avoid replacing the violence which would make the same the centre with the more subtle, but equally constricting, violence which would paralyse the self – what Gillian Rose criticises as a 'passivity beyond passivity'?[11]

My argument in what follows is that the terms of the problematic of same and other with which Levinas engages are already set by Husserlian phenomenology and that, despite – or perhaps because of – this legacy, Levinas is implicated in a neo-Kantian transcendentalism which leaves him always deeply suspicious of an account of phenomenality anchored in the visible, but equally uneasy about giving *any* account of

---

[10] Maurice Blanchot ends his article, 'Our Clandestine Companion', in Cohen 1986:41–50, with the comment: 'How can one philosophize, how can one write within the memory of Auschwitz of those who have said, oftentimes in notes buried near the crematoria: know what has happened, don't forget, and at the same time, you won't be able to' (quotation from p. 50).

[11] Rose 1996:13–14.

the numinous on the grounds that to do so is to fall back into immanence and ontology. The result is that his own account is perilously dualistic.

This, however, does not make an engagement with Levinas irrelevant to the questions raised above. On the contrary, as a Jewish philosopher committed to the 'translation' of Hebrew or 'non-Greek' thought into the Western philosophical tradition, he gives voice to de Certeau's image of the other which returns from the past to 'haunt' the present. Levinas's is a prophetic voice, warning of the dangers of totalising discourses and, in the interests of preserving the ethical relationship with the other, encouraging a healthy reticence in the theologian. But is he more than a prophet? This chapter proposes a 'first reading' of Levinas in which I want to show the limits of a purely philosophical engagement with alterity. My criticism of Levinas, therefore, is not that he takes us in the wrong direction, but that he does not take us far enough. This chapter portrays Levinas in dialogue with other philosophers – with Husserl and Heidegger, with Rosenzweig and Buber, and lastly with Derrida. But dialogue for Levinas, as noted in the first chapter, takes us '*beyond* the given';[12] the *results* of dialogue are less significant than the continuing and fundamentally *ethical* encounter which the practice of dialogue promotes. In the next chapter, I will attempt a 'second reading', in dialogue with Paul Ricoeur, which will seek to broaden the concept of alterity, setting it within the history and social context which form the self in relationship with what is other. The first task is to outline the terms within which that dialogue takes place.

Heterology as a philosophical project

Earlier I explained the term heterology, as coined by de Certeau, under the figure of the other who continues to 'haunt' the present. Wlad Godzich, in his Foreword to the collection of de Certeau's essays entitled *Heterologies*, tells us somewhat portentously that the term refers to a 'philosophical countertradition that, in short-hand, could be described as being deeply suspicious of the Parmenidean principle of the identity of thought and being'.[13] Whatever the form of such a countertradition, it is clearly beyond the scope of this book. My aim here is rather more limited:

---

[12] Levinas 1998b:151.

[13] Wlad Godzich's Foreword, 'The further possibility of knowledge', to de Certeau 1986:vii–viii.

to explore the issues surrounding Levinas's project to establish what I referred to in the last chapter as ethical heterology. Following Levinas, the fundamental question is in what sense the ethical relation with the other can be understood as *pre*-original, as anterior to ontology.[14] There is, however, a teasing perplexity or an element of *aporia* behind this project which is neatly expressed by Ian Buchanan. 'Traditionally, "heterology"', he says, 'designates that branch of philosophy concerned with the other as that which philosophy relies on without being able to comprehend'.[15] The term is, of course, thoroughly paradoxical. 'The other' cannot be inscribed within a '*logos*', within a theory, or it ceases to be other; at the same time, philosophy cannot but work within the horizon of otherness, an horizon which it always works to fill. For de Certeau, then, heterology is less a 'theory of the other' than a phenomenology: a description of the logic peculiar to the post-modern experience of limitation in face of the other and the practices of negotiation which this experience calls forth.

For Levinas, such a phenomenology is to be put to a very precise purpose – the overturning of the pretensions of the Western philosophical tradition which always tends to resolve the relationship of same and other in favour of the former. At least since the time of Descartes, the preoccupation with sure foundations has resulted in what Levinas calls a 'narcissism' which gives the other a largely instrumental role in the self-establishing of the subject. The other is never more than the 'limit' or 'boundary' over against which the same maintains its sense of identity through time. The other is always subsumed by the same; the alternative would be for reason to be dominated by the irrational. The other is, therefore, always conceived as a 'problem' for the same – essentially, as Descombes puts it, 'only one particular instance of the reduction of being to representation. The *esse* of others becomes reduced, like every other *esse*, to the *percipi*.'[16] It is precisely this assimilation which Levinas resists.

Despite the complexity of the philosophical discussion which he has provoked, Levinas's basic message is simple. In whatever I do and say I am faced by other persons who put my self-sufficiency into question. This basic conviction leads Levinas to develop a phenomenology of the other which questions the solipsistic tendencies of the philosophical tradition

---

[14] See 'Ethics as First Philosophy', published in *Justifications de l'éthique*, Bruxelles: Editions de L'Université de Bruxelles, 1984; pp. 41–51; translated by Sean Hand in Levinas 1989:76–87.

[15] Buchanan 1996:486.

[16] Descombes 1980:22.

and, most notably, the account of same and other which he inherits from his teacher Edmund Husserl. What Levinas tries to establish is a fundamentally different way of thinking, based not on the workings of intentional consciousness but on the primordial *ethical* experience of human subjectivity.

Levinas's relationship with Husserlian phenomenology is, however, ambiguous. More than fifty years after his original studies with Husserl, Levinas still believes 'the essential truth of Husserl' – 'the possibility *sich zu besinnen*, of grasping oneself, or of getting back to oneself, of posing with distinctness the question, "Where are we?", of taking one's bearings'. This, for Levinas, is phenomenology in the broadest sense, the project of tracing thoughts and intentions back to the 'whole horizon at which they aim'.[17] That horizon must, in a paradoxical way, 'include' the other. The problem which will continue to occupy Levinas is how this is possible without reducing the other to the 'merely' different. In the first place, however, the 'problem of the other' is Husserl's.

The Other as 'Alter Ego'

Husserl's project seeks a way through the epistemological perplexity contained in forms of 'naturalism', making the real equivalent to 'nature', and 'psychologism', the belief that the private data of consciousness provide the basis of knowledge.[18] The *Cartesian Meditations*, which Levinas translated into French in 1931, belong at the end of Husserl's 'middle phase', and represent something of a turning point in his thought.[19] Originally a series of lectures in honour of Descartes, they are subtitled 'an introduction to phenomenology' and represent a patient reworking of some of Husserl's major themes. Like Descartes, Husserl sets out to seek the basis of indubitable knowledge; like Kant, he develops a transcendental idealism, an inquiry into the 'conditions of possibility' for a priori synthetic judgments. The nature of consciousness is to be determined by its

---

[17] Levinas 1985:30.

[18] See Jacques Taminiaux, 'Immanence, Transcendence and Being in Husserl's Idea of Phenomenology', in Sallis *et al.* 1988:46–75.

[19] According to Macann, 1991:3ff.: '[i]t is conventional to distinguish three main phases in the development of Husserl's thinking, the phases of a pre-transcendental, a fully transcendental and a genetic phenomenology'. Macann notes that Husserl thought of himself as a 'perpetual beginner', always prepared to rethink answers to Kant's question – how are objects of experience possible?

intentionality; consciousness by its very nature is consciousness *of something*. All realities are pure phenomena, the only data from which we can begin. They appear in the mind in the form of unchanging and invariable types or essences. Through the careful reductive method of *epoché*, putting into brackets everything beyond immediate experience, intentional consciousness effects an eidetic intuition, the act that makes objects present to the subject. It is this theory of intuition which, according to Levinas, enables Husserl to overcome the Kantian duality of a passive faculty of sense and an active faculty of understanding.[20] For Husserl, *epoché* reveals a transcendental ego which through its intentional acts is the source of objective knowledge of the world.

This intuiting transcendental ego, the source of apodictic certainty, is similar to Leibniz's concept of the self-contained monad which mirrors the world to other monads. In the fifth of the *Cartesian Meditations*, Husserl faces the problem of solipsism which the constitution of the transcendental ego raises. The experiencing subject is both an object *in* the world and the source of consciousness *of* the world. On the one hand, as my 'natural environment', the world is ordered round me as centre. Temporally and spatially I am at the centre with everything and everyone, near and far, dependent on me, in so far as they *appear* to me. On the other, the world is 'present at hand', independent of me. As Theunissen puts it, I both 'bring order' to the world and seek to 'have my place in the world'.[21] Thus phenomenology becomes an 'egology'; the phenomenological reduction reduces the world to its being *for me*. This is what leads Husserl to push his Cartesian doubt even further:

> When I, the meditating I, reduce myself to my absolute
> transcendental ego by phenomenological *epoché* do I not become
> *solus ipse?* . . . But what about other egos, who are surely not a mere
> intending and intended *in me*, merely synthetic unities of possible
> verification *in me*, but, according to their sense, precisely *others?*
> Have we not therefore done transcendental realism an injustice?[22]

Phenomenology reveals that the world is full of 'other egos' who have a similar capacity to constitute and be constituted by the world. As I relativise the world, so do they; as I fit them into 'my' world, so they fit me into theirs. There exists, then, a class of beings who exist not 'for me' but

---

[20] Levinas 1995:116ff.

[21] Theunissen 1984:27–8.

[22] Husserl 1950:89.

'for themselves'. This experience of alternative centres of consciousness means that there are other subjects, which are essentially inaccessible to me. As Macann puts it: 'How am I to keep on tracing the source of all meaning giving activities back to the self while still doing justice to the existence of other selves who, moreover, must still be regarded as alternative sources of meaning giving activity?'[23] Husserl's response is nothing short of a sustained analysis of the experience of being in relationship with the other. I may never know the other as other (or we would occupy the same place), but the fact of *relationship*, the coexistence of monadic egos, cannot be doubted. Empathy and imagination are therefore to be employed to develop an 'analogizing apperception' which mediates between the ego and the other who is therefore constituted as an *'alter ego'*.[24]

Being in relation

Whether or not Husserl's complex argument is a philosophically coherent solution to the problem of solipsism is not clear. The constant reworking of the theme in the fifth meditation, not to mention the amount of manuscript material devoted to the topic of inter-subjectivity, shows that Husserl himself was never entirely satisfied.[25] More important, for the purposes of this discussion of the 'question of the other', is to note that the problem is inherent in the phenomenological method itself, and in the disjunction between intentionality and phenomenality. On the one hand, Husserl takes the essentially Cartesian subject as the guarantor of certainty; on the other, he insists that the very nature of intentionality is to be conscious of that which is *outside* itself. His solution to the dilemma amounts to a reflection on the experience of *inter*-subjectivity; to be is *to*

---

[23] Macann 1991:28.

[24] Ricoeur explains Husserl's strategy as a 'question of transforming the objection of solipsism into an argument' (see Ricoeur 1967:118). The object is to exclude everything which might have the nature of a subject so as to arrive at a quite distinctive sphere of immanence – a 'sphere of ownness'. This is a logical move. Husserl refuses to consider the *inter-subjective*, which remains something of an enigma, before the subjective. Thus he says, 1950:94, that '[i]n this pre-eminent intentionality . . . there becomes constituted an ego, not as "I myself", but as mirrored in my own Ego, in my monad. The second ego, however, is not simply there and strictly presented; rather is he constituted as "alter ego".'

[25] See the discussion in Macann 1991:27, 115ff. Opinions on the coherence of Husserl's arguments in the *Cartesian Meditations* vary. Derrida, 1978:124, defends him against Levinas's charges that he suppresses the other; for Husserl, says Derrida, '"other" already means something when things are in question'. Ricoeur, 1967:115, 139ff., is less enthusiastic; Bell, 1990:215ff., finds Husserl's approach an 'uneasy amalgam of the old and the new'.

be in relation. Underlying the complexities of argument is a simple insight: the recognition that every centre of consciousness is intrinsically related to other centres of consciousness. What complicates matters is the fact that this experience is not primordial. The other is not directly accessible, not 'here' but 'there', and has to be mediated in some form.[26] It is the impossibility of establishing such a 'mediation' which will exercise Levinas – the fact that the other is always made dependent on a *'tertium quid'*, a 'middle and neutral term' which, he objects, is always controlled by the same.[27]

As a commentary on Husserl, Levinas's *Theory of Intuition* is important less for the way it presents the phenomenological method which underlies Levinas's relational thinking, than for showing how Husserl's concept of consciousness is an attempt to make more precise and primordial Descartes's *cogito*. According to Levinas, for Husserl the existence of consciousness does not follow necessarily from the positing of the *cogito*; it is rather the existence of consciousness that 'allows' a *cogito*. Husserl is, therefore, concerned with the nature of the sort of 'existence' which applies to the *cogito*. For Levinas, Husserl's step beyond Descartes consists in his not separating the knowledge of an object from its being; it entails a recognition of the 'mode of its being' – which means analysing the intentions of the life which is directed towards the object. In Levinas's interpretation, the strength of Husserl is that he proposes a 'fundamental ontology' which seeks the meaning of being as it arises *in each particular case*. The weakness is that he is still too theoretical.[28] For all its careful attention to the conditions of relationality, Husserl's theory presumes on the power of reason to understand all domains of human actuality. The form of outward manifestation with which what is other is presented to me may not be a variant of the same. What of the radical *strangeness* of the other? How is one to perceive the meaning of those acts with which the other contests my very capacity to reflect that meaning? These are the questions which will lead Levinas to 'reverse' Husserl, making the other not an *alter ego*, but precisely that which the ego *is not*. For Husserl the idea of the other is already present in intentionality prior to any particular encounter. For Levinas the relation with the other is not to be derived from any capacities which we may possess in ourselves; the other is radically 'exterior' to our experience.

---

[26] Husserl 1950:108–9.

[27] Levinas 1969:43.

[28] Levinas 1995:157. This is the point contested by Derrida 1978:124.

The terms of Levinas's phenomenology of the other are, therefore, set by Husserl. This 'legacy' privileges an epistemology which intends particular concrete phenomena but betrays a tendency to be 'forgetful of its horizon, of its implicit content and even of the time it lives through' – what cannot simply be controlled by acts of the will.[29] Levinas remains profoundly dissatisfied with the equation of the phenomenal with the visible. What of the conditions of possibility of the *non*-intentional, what can yet be said to 'appear' albeit as the undisclosed 'horizon' against which all appearance takes place? Whereas, for Husserl, the intention is always assumed to be adequate to the intended object, for Levinas, intentionality always goes beyond its object; it 'already presupposes the idea of infinity'.[30] Human subjectivity is established through the welcome which is given to the other – a welcome in which the Cartesian idea of infinity becomes an issue for the same. In his critique of the philosophy which has led to Husserlian 'egology', Levinas finds in the third of Descartes's *Meditations* a glimpse of an all too easily ignored 'counter-tradition' in Western philosophy: the idea of God, the 'supremely perfect and infinite being' which exceeds the capacity of thought yet 'does not do violence to interiority – a receptivity without passivity, a relation between freedoms'.[31] The subject exists in a relationship with Infinity, and is not destroyed by it.

This is a crucially important idea for Levinas, raising the possibility of an answer to his own question: 'How can a being enter into relation with the other without allowing its very self to be crushed by the other?'[32] Just as significant is the Platonic concept of the 'Good beyond Being'.[33] Above the human concern for the knowledge of the true is placed the call of the Good, an exteriority which is also the revelation of

---

[29] See 'Ethics as First Philosophy', in Levinas 1989:79.

[30] See the Preface to Levinas 1969:26–7, where Levinas introduces Descartes's 'idea of the infinite'. The 'idea of infinity' is not just to be distinguished from the 'idea of totality' but given a philosophical primacy as emerging from the *primordial relationship* of same and other.

[31] See Levinas 1969:211. Levinas emphasises that the infinite is not a theme or an object, yet in revealing itself it enables a relation with the subject to be established. Descartes's argument both establishes the subject and points towards the existence of God. Levinas quotes the final paragraph of the third meditation, in which Descartes ponders on the 'incomparable beauty of this light', and comments that it represents 'the expression of this transformation of the idea of infinity conveyed by knowledge into Majesty approached as a face' (1969:212).

[32] Levinas 1987a:77.

[33] *Republic* 6.509a–b. 'The good . . . may be said to be the source not only of the intelligibility of the objects of knowledge, but also of their being and reality, but is beyond it, and superior to it in dignity and power' (translation by H. D. P. Lee; London: Penguin, 2nd edn, 1974; p. 248).

the other, and which in its relentless proximity overcomes the complacency of the totalising self.[34] Levinas is not, however, interested in
developing some version of the Cartesian ontological argument for the
existence of God. The Idea of the Infinite as an awareness which exceeds
our capacity to conceive is not the ultimate source of certainty but, rather,
an argument *against* the adequacy of human consciousness to itself. In
such an idea is described a passivity which is prior to the certainty of the
cogito. Or, as Levinas puts it:

> The placing in us of an unencompassable idea overturns this
> presence to self which is consciousness; it thus forces its way through
> the barrier and checkpoint, it confounds the obligation to accept or
> adopt all that enters from without. It is thus an idea signifying with a
> significance prior to presence, to all presence, prior to every origin in
> consciousness, and so an-archic, accessible only in the trace.[35]

The question Levinas will have to face is how a phenomenology of this
'an-archic trace' can be made philosophically coherent. For the moment,
however, we need to stay with his critique of Husserl and with a more
immediate question: how is it possible to overturn the primordial character of phenomenological intentionality? In his commentary on the
Cartesian Meditations, Paul Ricoeur – noting the shift which has occurred
in Husserl's thought, from the other as a purely psychological problem
to its more primordial role in the fifth meditation – says that '[i]n this
respect the problem of the Other plays the same role in Husserl that the
divine veracity plays in Descartes, for it grounds every truth and reality
which goes beyond the simple reflection of the subject on itself.'[36] For
Husserl, subjectivity can only be thought in and through relationality; as
points in space can only be understood as related, so there can be no self
without an other. Levinas, however, with his suspicion of totalising discourses, sees the other not as the ultimate condition of possibility which
somehow supports the self, but as a pre-original encounter which
undermines self-reference.

In emphasising the accusative mode in which the self is formed in
response to the priority of the other, he argues for a clear distinction
between *need*, interpreted in a Husserlian instrumental sense, and *desire*
which challenges any sense of satisfaction the self might gain from 'using'

---

[34] Levinas 1969:33–40.

[35] Levinas 1998b:64.

[36] Ricoeur 1967:115.

the other for its own purposes. What Levinas criticises here is an insidious complacency which separates need from that desire which seeks to transcend self-centred categories by responding to the other.[37] Beyond the controlling totality of need opens up an infinity of desire. The initiative lies always with the other. *Totality and Infinity* is a sustained effort to think through these ideas.

Ethics as 'first philosophy'

The ethical 'catalyst', however, – the 'first philosophy' which fuels the phenomenology of *Totality and Infinity*, established not by self-assertion but by passivity in face of the other – emerges from a deep-seated and life-long contestation of Heidegger.[38] Levinas's unease at the way Husserl instrumentalises the other into providing the ultimate support of selfhood is confirmed by what he calls Heidegger's 'evasion'.[39] Ethics is subordinated to ontology.

Levinas admits that his critique of Husserl is already deeply influenced by Heidegger's 'powerful and original philosophy'.[40] The immediate attraction of Heidegger's phenomenological ontology is that it shifts attention away from Husserl's transcendental idealism to the historical facticity of *Dasein*, for which 'in its Being, that very Being is essentially an *issue*',[41] and which becomes, therefore, the 'site' for the revelation of the truth of Being. Heidegger overcomes the intellectualism of Husserl by proposing to analyse the ontological significance of the existence of a *Dasein* which is already constituted as *Mitsein* – 'there with us [*mit da sind*] in Being-in-the-world'.[42] For Heidegger the Being of *Dasein* is always a *Being-with-others*. 'Others' are included within the

---

[37] Levinas 1969:117.

[38] *Existence and Existents* (1946) and *Time and the Other* (1947), as their titles indicate, are both engagements with the Heidegger of *Being and Time*. In the 1983 lecture entitled 'Transcendence and Intelligibility', 1996:149–59, Levinas restates his opposition to the privileging of an epistemology of presence and 'Heideggerian critiques of metaphysics which proceed from the will to power' (p. 154).

[39] Without mentioning him by name, Levinas's 1935 article *De L'Évasion* is marked, says Jacques Rolland, by 'the latent conflict with Heidegger'. See Introduction to Levinas 1982:14. Levinas speaks of the concept of 'the ancient problem of Being as Being' as not only 'the obstacle which free thought would be able to overcome . . . but as an imprisonment from which one tries to escape' (1982:73).

[40] Levinas 1995:lv–lvi.

[41] Heidegger 1962:117.

[42] Heidegger 1962:152.

world, 'those from whom, for the most part, one does *not* distinguish oneself – those among whom one is too'.[43] The problem of solipsism which dogged Husserl does not, therefore, occur for Heidegger because he does not *begin* with a potentially solipsistic transcendental ego.[44] What is less attractive to Levinas is that in Heidegger's terms 'others' have no ontological significance *in their own right*. At best they are a subordinate feature of the priority given to *Dasein*; at worst, the unquestioning *Da* of my *Dasein* becomes the 'usurpation of somebody else's place'.[45] The question which continues to preoccupy Levinas is whether Heidegger's ontology does any more than depict an essentially solitary *Dasein along-side* others, an heroic figure of mastery always seeking control of what Levinas sees as the essentially ungraspable mystery of otherness. Heidegger's search for an all-inclusive view of things through a neutral impersonal vision fails to allow for the destabilising experience of otherness and is the example par excellence of the Western philosophical tradition's quest for a totalising universal knowledge.[46]

Levinas's early enthusiasm for Heidegger as a path beyond Husserl gives way to 'a profound need to leave the climate of that philosophy'; at the same time he is governed by 'the conviction that we cannot leave it for a philosophy which would be pre-Heideggerian'.[47] Levinas's Jewish background and experience explain something of that ambiguity. In many ways their respective projects run parallel. Both seek to rethink the terms in which metaphysics has been set and are faced with the same fundamental questions: Heidegger with the 'forgetting of Being', Levinas with what he sees as the 'forgetting of the Other'.[48] Such a neat

---

[43] Heidegger 1962:154.

[44] See *Being and Time* p. 155 where Heidegger emphasises, against Husserl, that others are not apprehended by a 'primary act of looking at oneself'; rather, 'others are encountered *environmentally*' – through the act of being-together in the world.

[45] 'Ethics as First Philosophy', Levinas 1989:85.

[46] Levinas's article, 'Philosophy and the Idea of the Infinite', Levinas 1987b:47–59 (originally published as 'La philosophie et l'idée de l'Infini', *Révue de Metaphysique et de Morale*, 62, 1957; 241–53), contains some of Levinas's strongest anti-Heideggerian polemics, criticising Heidegger's atheistic paganism for its lack of any ethical basis: 'When he sees man possessed by freedom rather than possessing freedom, he puts over man a neuter term which illuminates freedom without putting it into question. And thus he is not destroying, but summing up a whole current of Western philosophy'(p. 51).

[47] Levinas 1978:19.

[48] This makes Peperzak's comment, 1993:17, that their perspectives are so different 'that it may remain doubtful whether we can understand their thoughts as answers to one and the same question' seem extreme. Nearer the mark is the assessment of Ward, 1995:123, that Levinas's work is a 'Jewish midrash on Heidegger's'.

juxtaposition can, however, be misleading. Levinas reacts against Heidegger rather than responds to him, setting 'philosophies of communion' in which the other is 'side by side' against his own version of ethical relationalism where the other confronts the same 'face-to-face'. How different these positions are is not my immediate concern; the correctness of Levinas's interpretation of Heidegger is less important than the perception he has formed that *Being and Time*–which fifty years after his initial confrontation he can still call 'one of the finest books in the history of philosophy'[49]–is also a defining moment in the disastrous history of the occlusion of the ethical in Western thought. Levinas's antagonism towards Heidegger is based on more than personal prejudice.[50] Heidegger represents for him the unacceptable side of Western philosophy: its totalising of the other.

A 'Jewish moment' in 'Greek philosophy'

At the same time he is convinced that it is impossible to become 'pre-Heideggerian'; the 'Jewish moment', the otherness which intrudes into the totality of Western philosophy, is set in Heidegger's shadow. Levinas's philosophy is transcendental in its aims, tracing experience back to its conditions of possibility, but it is also deeply dialogical in its method–a dialogue which necessarily includes Heidegger. If Levinas is to be treated as a Jewish philosopher, as Robert Gibbs has argued,[51] it is not just because he writes with the Shoah in mind, but also because he is heir to a tradition of thought which includes Rosenzweig, Hermann Cohen and the Buber of 'I and Thou'.[52] Throughout the essays and broadcasts collected as *Difficult Freedom*, Levinas reflects on the prophetic vocation of the Jew. In the aftermath of the Shoah, the particularity of Jewish identity becomes clearer–but also its universality. Jewish monotheism is not a version of some general sense of the numinous; on the contrary, it breaks with such conceptions, establishing a certain type of atheism. 'Here', says Levinas in a talk entitled 'A Religion for Adults', 'Judaism feels very close

---

[49] Levinas 1985:37–8.

[50] In this regard see the revealing incident narrated by William J. Richardson in his article 'The Irresponsible Subject', in Peperzak 1995:123–31. See also Barnes 2000:14–15.

[51] Gibbs 1992:10ff.

[52] For the context of dialogical philosophy see Bergman 1991. The significance of Rosenzweig, both as philosopher in his own right and as an influence on Levinas, is acknowledged in a number of works, especially Handelman 1991; Gibbs 1992; Cohen 1994.

to the West, by which I mean philosophy'.[53] To follow the teachings of Judaism is not at variance with the intellectual quest of 'Greek' philosophy. As a philosopher Levinas wants to bring divergent views to bear on the traditional study of the Jewish sources, while as a Jewish commentator on the Talmud he is concerned with maintaining the particularity of Judaism and its concept of a God revealed through the ethical. The two roles are not contradictory, for Levinas tells us that he is simply following one of the great teachers of nineteenth-century Lithuanian *yeshiva* Judaism, Rabbi Hayyim of Volozhyn, who wrote that 'a Jew is accountable and responsible for the whole edifice of creation'.[54] This responsibility for the other is the witness the Jew bears before the world.

There is more to the tension in Levinas's writing between the 'Greek' and the 'non-Greek' than in the distinction between 'purely' philosophical works and 'Hebrew writings'.[55] It is, rather, indicative of a commitment to the work of translation, a task of engagement with the dominant philosophical tradition which he inherits from Rosenzweig.[56] As Rosenzweig 'translates' Hegel, so Levinas seeks to do the same with Husserl and, more problematically, with Heidegger. What is at stake for Levinas is nothing less than the future of philosophy itself. If Hegel expected philosophy to encompass all revealed religion, Rosenzweig sought the salvation of philosophy in the restoration of the concept of revelation. This is the catalyst for Rosenzweig's dialogical philosophy which seeks to bring three central concepts – God, Humanity and World – into a complex correlation where each

---

[53] Levinas 1990a:15.

[54] Levinas 1990a:50–1. Levinas continues: 'There is something that binds and commits man still more than the salvation of his soul. The act, word and thought of a Jew have the formidable privilege of being able to destroy and restore whole worlds.' Rabbi Hayyim ben Isaac of Volozhyn's great work is the *Nefesh ha'Hayyim* (*The Soul of Life*); translated by Benjamin Gross, with an introduction by Levinas, into French (*L'Âme de la Vie*, Paris: Editions Verdier; 1986). Cohen, 1994:131, comments that 'what attracts Levinas to this text . . . is [the] basic thought that the Above and the Below, the divine and the human, are linked through human ethical behaviour. Human ethical behaviour has cosmic implications.' Levinas writes of Rabbi Hayyim and *Nefesh ha'Hayyim* in 'In the Image of God', in Levinas 1994b:151–67.

[55] This is Levinas's own term for the regular Talmudic readings which occupied him from 1960. Robert Gibbs, 1992:157, clarifies the 'Greek' – 'non-Greek' distinction as one of 'modes of thought; it is not a historical claim'. In her introduction to *Nine Talmudic Readings*, Anne Aronowicz says that Greek is Levinas's 'metaphor for the language Jews have in common with the inhabitants of the Western world' (p. ix).

[56] In a letter of 1 October 1917, Rosenzweig writes to Rudolf Ehrenberg: 'The true goal of the mind is translating; only when a thing has been translated does it become truly vocal, no longer to be done away with. Only in the Septuagint has revelation come to be at home in the world, and as long as Homer did not speak Latin he was not a fact. The same holds good for translating from man to man' (quoted from Glatzer 1953:62–3).

is linked and understood *through* the other. Not that this is intended to develop a self-enclosed system; truth for Rosenzweig is eschatological – 'we never see the truth until the end'.[57] The inter-relation of the three elements extends throughout time; the whole of Being is 'relational life'. Following in Rosenzweig's footsteps, Levinas says the future indicates 'a relation with Eternity' which is 'not the disappearance of the "singular" into its general idea, but the possibility for every creature to say "we" – or, more exactly, as Rosenzweig puts it, it is the "fact that the *me* learns to say *you* to a *him*"'.[58] Rosenzweig's complex analyses of the complementarity of Christianity and Judaism do not interest Levinas. He is more concerned with 'translating' the philosophical wisdom affirmed by Judaism. Thus, in drawing attention to two 'typically Jewish elements' in Rosenzweig's account – God's commandment, which precedes love, and the role of the human person as the agent of redemption in the world – Levinas seeks to insinuate a 'Jewish moment', an ethical or relational element, into a philosophical tradition dominated by the Husserlian epistemology of presence.[59]

Philosophy for Levinas is always more than the 'love of wisdom' – the desire for comprehensive knowledge of beginnings and ends. In *Otherwise than Being* the terms are reversed; he speaks instead of philosophy as 'the wisdom of love at the service of love'.[60] Human subjectivity is to be thought relationally. By this, however, he does not mean a form of Husserlian analogising apperception, but a conceptuality of the self which neither exercises mastery over, nor unites with, the other. Again, the crucial question is whether such an 'ethical translation' can be made philosophically coherent.

The ethical priority of the Other

It was Rosenzweig, says Levinas, who inspired one of his central concepts – the opposition to totality.[61] *Star of Redemption* begins with a challenge to the

---

[57] Rosenzweig 1970:398. The three theological dimensions of Rosenzweig's system – creation, revelation and redemption – need to be understood in *temporal* terms (see Barnes 2000:48–51).

[58] Levinas 1990a:191–2.

[59] 'Even though redemption comes from God', says Levinas, 'it has an absolute need of this intermediary man' (see Levinas 1983:38).

[60] Levinas 1991:162.

[61] Levinas, 1969:28, notes simply that *Star of Redemption* is 'a work too often present in this book to be cited'.

all-powerful Hegelian system:

> All cognition of the All originates in death, in the fear of death.
> Philosophy takes it upon itself to throw off the fear of things
> earthly, to rob death of its poisonous sting, and Hades of its
> pestilential breath . . . But philosophy denies these fears of the
> earth.[62]

In the totalisation set in motion by Hegel and continued by Heidegger,
persons are subordinated to 'the Whole of history' and the person of the
philosopher to the 'system of truth of which the person is but a moment'.[63] Such a reduction has enormous ethical consequences, of which
the Shoah is only the most obvious; more subtle, but no less insidious,
however, is the contradiction inherent in the concept of totality. As a phe-
nomenologist, Levinas works from the particularity of experience. Death,
for instance, cannot be totalised; it remains 'absolutely unknowable', an
experience of otherness – where every assumption of possibility is rendered impossible, but 'where we ourselves are seized'.[64]

Levinas's account of death as a moment of pure passivity is set very
clearly in contrast with Heidegger's portrait of 'authentic existence' as
'supreme virility'. His immediate point is to contest Heidegger's analysis
of *Dasein* as 'ecstatic', a subject whose horizons extend into the past and
future, and whose present relationship with the world is instrumental,
described in terms of the use of 'tools'. For Levinas such 'ecstasy' resides
not with an act of *Dasein* but with the 'instant' or event which marks the
beginning of beings within Being.[65]

Prior to the various modalities of being – fatigue, indolence, effort, let
alone any act of perception – is the '*il y a*', 'there is', a 'horrifying silence'

---

[62] Rosenzweig 1970:3–4. In an interview, 1985:76, Levinas notes that Rosenzweig's 'radical
critique of totality . . . starts from the experience of death; to the extent that the individual
included within the totality has not vanquished the anxiety about death, nor renounced his
particular destiny, he does not find himself at ease within the totality or, if you will, the totality has
not "totalized" itself. In Rosenzweig there is thus an explosion of the totality and the opening of
quite a different route in the search for what is reasonable.'

[63] Levinas 1990a:188.

[64] Levinas 1987a:70–1. Levinas's own footnote to this section should not be ignored. 'Death
in Heidegger is not, as Jean Wahl says, "the impossibility of possibility" but the "possibility of
impossibility". This apparently Byzantine distinction has a fundamental importance.' What Levinas
appears to mean is that Heidegger seeks a heroic objectification of death, and therefore a totalising
control, whereas for Levinas death is the unknown, mystery, simply an *impossibility*. See Heidegger
1962:294,307; Levinas 1969:235.

[65] 'Does not Being in general become the being of "a being" by an inversion, *by that event
which is the present* (and which shall be the principal theme of this book)?' See Levinas 1978:17–18
(emphasis added).

which somehow surrounds consciousness – 'a density, an atmosphere, a field, which is not to be identified with an object that would have this density'.[66] In some ways '*il y a*' is Levinas's version of the Heideggerian '*es gibt*' – the sense of the impersonal anonymity of Being. Levinas, however, seeks to maintain a crucial difference from Heidegger.[67] For Heidegger, *Dasein* manifests a fundamental anxiety before a Being which is, precisely, 'gift' or 'given', and becomes the object of care.[68] For Levinas, however, there is no sense of the generosity of the Heideggerian '*es gibt*'. He stresses the impersonality and anonymity of the expression; the subject cannot be identified. Instead he wants to speak of some pre-conscious state, which can only be identified intuitively by deliberately paradoxical expressions such as presence within absence or Being without beings, or oxymoronic metaphors like the 'rumbling silence'.[69] 'It' disturbs, bringing with it not an 'anxiety' about a collapse into nothingness, but the horror of a continuity without interruption. Like Heidegger, and against Husserl, Levinas wants to reinstate the priority of Being to consciousness of Being; unlike Heidegger, for whom the forms of *Dasein*'s contingent existence are identified as the modes of comprehension of Being, Levinas seeks to analyse the conditions which allow the notion of an existent subject to arise *within* Being. Such a subject can only be understood in terms of the priority of the other.

Levinas is concerned, therefore, with a radical translation rather than an ethical critique of Heidegger's 'ecstatic' *Dasein*. In the Preface to the 1979 edition of *Time and the Other*, Levinas recalls the central project of what he refers to there as a 'phenomenology of alterity': the analysis of encounters which have a 'certain *alterity-content*'.[70] Once themes of nourishment and enjoyment have been established, themes which emphasise that only the

---

[66] Levinas 1978:64.

[67] See Preface to the second edition of *Existence and Existents* (not translated in Lingis's English edition): 'It was never either the translation or the copy of the German expression' (p. 10).

[68] See translators' note to *Being and Time* p. 255, referring to Heidegger's insistence that the expression *es gibt* is used deliberately to express the essence of Being: '[Heidegger] writes: "for the 'it' which here 'gives' is Being itself. The 'gives', however, designates the essence of Being, which gives and which confers its truth." He adds that the "es gibt" is used to avoid writing that "Being is", for the verb "is" is appropriate to entities but not to Being itself.'

[69] In Levinas 1985:47ff., conversations with Philip Nemo, Levinas uses multiple similes ('It is something resembling what one hears when one puts an empty shell close to the ear, as if emptiness were full, as if the silence were a noise.') to speak of this primordial 'there is' which is 'neither nothingness nor being' but which somehow 'exists' prior to the 'event' of consciousness. See Davis 1996:22ff.

[70] Levinas 1987a:35–6.

subject fully 'at home' in the world can be disturbed by the 'event' of otherness, he turns to the theme of solitude, repudiating 'from the start' the Heideggerian conception 'that views solitude in the midst of a prior relationship with the other'.[71] For Levinas, such an ontology of a *pre*-original other is a contradiction. Death, for example, is never a 'now'. It is future and therefore *ungraspable*. His concern is for the 'now'. This is marked by the suffering which endures the nearness of death and which marks the reversal of the subject's activity into passivity. Death signifies not because, as in Heidegger, it brings the final test of heroic capacity, but because it marks the onset of that moment when we are no longer *'able to be able'*.[72]

The ambiguity of this impossibility which yet becomes possible breaks the subject's sense of solitude before the *il y a*. Death, in other words, is the prime analogue of the social encounter with the total mystery of another person. For Levinas, the Other is not an Husserlian *'alter ego'*, but a trace of that alterity which threatens always to disrupt 'philosophies of communion'.[73]

Dialogical and transcendental ways of thinking

But how to speak of the other without lapsing back into ontological language? Levinas's alternative to Heidegger's philosophy of communion is an ethical relationalism: the Other 'in front' or face to face. This 'I–Thou' relationship, however, is not to be taken, says Levinas, in Buber's sense of a 'reciprocity . . . between two separated freedoms'.[74] Despite the fundamental spiritual affinity between them, Levinas is a long way removed from the Hasidic mysticism which so much occupied Buber; he distrusts what he considers the easy way Buber moves from philosophical to theological thinking. They at least agree that truth cannot be totalised into an intentional content but emerges from the prior context of the 'I–Thou' relation. The 'I–It' relation fits Husserl's scheme of intentional consciousness, while the 'I–Thou', says Levinas, 'designates what is not intentional but what for Buber is rather the condition of all intentional

---

[71] Levinas 1987a:40.

[72] Levinas 1987a:72–4.

[73] Levinas 1987a:74–5.

[74] Levinas 1987a:93–4. Levinas's relations with Buber are complex, as Bernasconi's detailed analysis of Levinas's interpretation of Buber shows. See '"Failure of Communication" as a Surplus: Dialogue and Lack of Dialogue between Buber and Levinas', in Bernasconi and Wood 1988:100–35.

relations'.[75] However, Levinas objects that Buber's reading of the 'I–Thou' tends to be a reciprocal relationship, not accounting for difference, nor allowing for the thinking of the Infinite 'beyond Being' which is Levinas's main concern.

This is the crucial difference between them. Levinas is uneasy with any concept of the other which can be implicated in a totality. Buber's version of transcendentalism seems content to trace otherness back to the 'immanent sphere' of the 'I–Thou' relation. As Theunissen explains, compared with Husserl, for whom intersubjectivity is an issue which arises within a particular epistemological framework, for Buber 'the problem of "dialogical life" is the problem pure and simple . . . The explication of dialogical life is supposed to lay the foundation of ontology'.[76] 'In the beginning', says Buber, 'is relation'.[77] The 'I–Thou' and the 'I–It' 'do not signify things, but they intimate relations'; they 'do not describe something that might exist independently of them, but being spoken they bring about existence'.[78] For Buber, human beings live life as a dialogue in which otherness is constantly being mediated *between* the I and the Thou who coexist in an identity-in-difference. The concept of the 'between', the site of the dialogue in which I and Thou are established in relationship, is the key to understanding Buber's intention. The ontology he wants to work out Theunissen calls the '*ontology of the between*'.[79] For Buber, the intersubjective relation is formed within the overarching unity of Being. He allows for the 'event' which sees the beginning of beings within Being, but, in presupposing a symmetrical process which brings the I–Thou into a unity, begs the question of how the two terms of the relation know each other in the first place. Levinas asks, therefore, whether Buber does any more than *point* to the site, the 'between', in which the other is to be encountered. He is here more Heideggerian than Buber: 'Man does not meet, he is the meeting.'[80] Levinas

---

[75] See 'Martin Buber and the Theory of Knowledge', in *The Philosophy of Martin Buber*, edited by Paul Arthur Schilpp and Maurice Friedman; La Salle Illinois: Open Court; London: Cambridge University Press, 1967; pp. 133–50. Originally in German, 'Martin Buber und die Erkenntnistheorie', in *Martin Buber, Philosophen des 20. Jahrhunderts*, Stuttgart: Kohlhammer, 1963; pp. 119–34. See Levinas 1989:59–74; quotation from p. 63.

[76] Theunissen 1984:269

[77] Buber 1958:32.

[78] Buber 1958:15.

[79] Theunissen 1984:272; emphasis in original.

[80] See 'Martin Buber and the Theory of Knowledge', in Levinas 1989:66.

agrees with Buber that there can be no interposing of a *tertium quid*, a third 'shared' conceptuality, between same and other; but he finds Buber's position not ethical enough – his other more a friend in a common project than the stranger who demands a response. In an essay on dialogue, subtitled 'Self-Consciousness and Proximity of the Neighbor', Levinas says that:

> Simultaneously, in dialogue is hollowed out an absolute distance between the I and the You, absolutely separated by the inexpressible secret of their intimacy . . . On the other hand, it is also there that unfolds – or intervenes, disposing the *I* as I and the *you* as you – the extraordinary and immediate relation of dialogue, which transcends this distance without suppressing it or recuperating it . . . Here is a way of acceding to the other different from that of knowing him: to approach the neighbor.[81]

Levinas's thought is therefore dialogical, in the sense that the source of meaning is given in the relationship with alterity, but more radically transcendental than Buber's in insisting that the nature of subjectivity must be understood through a phenomenology which gives priority to alterity in the forming of that relationship. The question is whether it is possible to bring together these two ways of thinking without simply creating another totality.

To do this Levinas needs to show that in the self-reflection of the ego on its world there is *already* a 'trace' of something which ruptures its equilibrium. He brings together elements of the alterity analysed in earlier writing and synthesises them with a more thoroughgoing attention to experiences of human relationship which introduce a sense of plurality into existence. Such concern with forms of 'relative otherness', however, is not, as Peperzak notes, a simple matter of setting egotism over against 'a moral law of altruism'.[82] By analysing the intentionality of the subject encountering the unfamiliar through the radical asymmetry of the relationship with the other, Levinas builds a unified discourse which has as its thoroughly paradoxical purpose to point *beyond* its own unity to an ultimate horizon 'elsewhere'. It is this dimension of existence which Levinas describes as the ethical, a dimension which has a certain 'religious' character – not in the sense that it is characterised by the numinous

---

[81] Levinas 1998b:144.

[82] Peperzak 1993:137. 'Ego is *at the same time* turned and returned to itself by the spontaneous egoism of its being alive . . . *and* transcendent, that is, exceeding its own life by desiring, i.e., by a nonegoistic "hunger" of generosity for the Other' (emphases in original).

or the sacred, but in a very specific sense allowed by Levinas: that which unites same and other without constituting a totality.[83]

Totality and Infinity: the 'epiphany' of the Other

This is why the Idea of the Infinite is so important for Levinas. The quality of this 'religious bond' transcends all immanent totalities available within nature. Every phenomenal experience includes within it an element of *self*-consciousness, but in its openness to the other there is also an awareness of 'something more', a further possibility or element of surprise. Something other enters the internal finite world of relations which cannot be reduced to that world as it exists as a system or be accounted for by a process of self-projection.

In *Totality and Infinity*, the argument is cumulative, a labyrinthine narrative in which subjectivity is seen to emerge through a constant dialogue with an alterity both related to, yet not encompassed by, the same. 'The I is not a being that always remains the same, but is the being whose existing consists in identifying itself, in recovering its identity throughout all that happens to it.'[84] The other appears, first when the self is 'at home', then in the state of recollection, being prepared to wait on an uncertain future. Here Levinas uses feminine metaphors to describe a 'delightful "lapse" of the ontological order. By virtue of its intentional structure gentleness comes to the separated being from the Other.'[85] Levinas's point, however, is not to set the 'feminine' against the 'masculine', metaphors of 'home' against metaphors of 'public space'.[86] Rather, the need for security and a habitation within which to feel 'at home' reveals the presence of an other.

Most importantly, the other appears in the face-to-face encounter – the key event in a journey from the rustling of the '*il y a*', through the *jouissance* of possessing the world to the enigma of an eschatology which would break the bounds of totality. Certain themes signify this primordial experience of the face to face. Behind the erotic relationship of lovers, for instance, is

---

[83] 'We propose to call "religion" the bond that is established between the same and the other without constituting a totality' (Levinas 1969:40).

[84] Levinas 1969:36.

[85] Levinas 1969:150.

[86] Whether such diverse categories or aspects of existence are typical of the way women and men think is not the immediate point – though Levinas has been roundly criticised for his entrenchment of gender stereotypes. The most celebrated critic is de Beauvoir 1970. See also articles by Luce Irigaray, Catherine Chalier and Tina Chanter in Bernasconi and Critchley 1991. Cohen, 1994:195–6, has produced a brief but robust discussion of these and other texts.

experienced a transcendence in which alterity is touched but not reduced to some sort of monistic fusion. The other is revealed in the vulnerability of the face and the nudity of the body, yet for all the passion of the moment remains apart, pointing to an undetermined future.

The face commands because in its vulnerability it reveals the asymmetry of the relationship between same and other – by which Levinas means that 'my' existence is submitted to the ethical priority or 'height' of the other. The face says quite simply: you shall not kill, you shall not *efface*. Levinas quotes a Jewish proverb which

> says that 'the other's material needs are my spiritual needs'; it is this disproportion, or asymmetry, that characterizes the ethical refusal of the first truth of ontology – the struggle *to be*. Ethics is, therefore, *against nature* because it forbids the murderousness of my natural will to put my own existence first.[87]

The face is not some qualitatively different phenomenon which sets a divide between same and other – for such a distinction would be to make its alterity a difference within a 'community of genus' – but an *epiphany*, a movement of the Infinite exterior to the same. The face of the Other is not just seen and therefore known; rather it challenges the very capacity to know, and so to appropriate to the same. What Levinas calls the 'tautology' of the ego's preoccupation with itself is overcome by facing it with the alterity, the disarming transcendence, of its own existence.[88]

Pressing the limits of language

This aporetic concept of the 'infinite other', with its spatio-temporal categories of 'priority' or, to use one of Levinas's earliest neologisms, '*excendance*',[89] makes the construction of what I have called 'ethical heterology' problematic. To put our earlier question in a different form: what sense can it make to speak of what is '*before* the totality', '*beyond* everything' or, more precisely, '*outside* Being'?

At the beginning of this discussion, I noted that Levinas's contestation of the philosophical tradition risks a dualism of same and other. Ricoeur

---

[87] 'Dialogue with Emmanuel Levinas', in Cohen 1986:24.

[88] Levinas 1987a:55–6.

[89] Levinas 1982:73; see also the Preface to Levinas 1978:15. Davis, 1996:18, comments that this is 'not transcendence which implies a willed ascension to the higher reaches of Being, but an *exit from* or *exceeding of* Being without direction or ultimate goal'.

makes the same point rather more positively. Levinas, he says, dares a reversal of the traditional priority: from 'the statement "no other-than-self without a self", substituting for it the inverse statement "no self without another who summons it to responsibility"'.[90] The analogising *tertium quid* is what Levinas will not allow; the other remains always *exterior*. The problem is not just that Levinas's project takes place, as Ricoeur notes, 'at the crossroads of ethics and ontology',[91] but that there is no meta-ethical language which is not already implicated in the ontological language of such concepts as subjectivity, causality and freedom. Levinas seeks to use the language of the tradition in order to deconstruct it, to use Husserl to reverse Husserl. This, as Derrida points out in his lengthy critique of *Totality and Infinity*, is precisely what is impossible; the 'move beyond or above', he says, presumes the very things transcended.[92] Levinas's overcoming of ontology is dependent on the totalising ontology it seeks to overcome. Derrida asks: can one both step outside the language of a tradition, in order to critique it, *and* develop a different way of thinking about that tradition, in order to take it in another direction?[93] If Levinas begins to think *within* the terms of the tradition he must inevitably rethink it in these terms too. Derrida's argument, as Simon Critchley puts it, is that there are

> certain necessities within philosophical discourse which all
> philosophers, Levinas and Derrida included, are obliged to face ...
> [A]s the resources of metaphysical discourse are the only ones that
> are available, one must continue to use them even when trying to
> promote their displacement.[94]

---

[90] Ricoeur 1992:186ff. Ricoeur's discussion at this point is centred on the Aristotelian concept of *philia*, the 'ethics of reciprocity', and the disparities between the activities of giving and receiving in the establishment of selfhood.

[91] Ricoeur 1992:189 n24.

[92] See Derrida 1978:111. Although Cohen (in 'Derrida's (Mal) reading of Levinas'; Cohen 1994:305–21) takes the line that Derrida has ignored Levinas's fundamental ethical concern, Bernasconi's argument (in 'Levinas: Philosophy and Beyond', in Silverman 1988:233–58) that Levinas is already aware that the underlying issue is to do with language, is borne out by the shift Levinas makes from the residually ontological language of *Totality and Infinity* to the more deconstructive approach of *Otherwise than Being*.

[93] Derrida defends both Husserl and Heidegger against Levinas's critique. He objects that to make of the *alter ego* a projection of the transcendental Ego somehow within my control is to mistake Husserl's intentions. 'Husserl does not cease to emphasize that this is an absolute impossibility' (Derrida 1978:125). And, according to Derrida, Levinas's opposition to Heidegger simply reproduces Heidegger's language; Levinas only 'confirms Heidegger in his discourse' (Derrida 1978:142).

[94] Critchley 1992:14–15.

Derrida's critique supports my basic contention that Levinas is locked into the terms of a phenomenology which risks a certain dualism. The problem for Levinas is that the one thing that the phenomenological method leads Husserl to assume – namely the possibility of an intentional consciousness by which the ego intuits the other through means of analogical apperception – is the one thing that Levinas will not permit. For Levinas, the primordially ethical experience of the other is distorted by a cognitive model which sees the relationship of persons as a variant, in degree but not kind, of the relation of subject to things.

There is, however, something of a vicious circle in any attempt to construct a meta-ethical alternative. The presence of the other demands an ethics but an ethics which would be more than an exercise in prudential self-interest demands the presence of the other. But, to repeat the questions which have run through this chapter, how to allow the other to appear? Or, to return to a point made in the first chapter, how to allow the other to speak *as other*? Levinas contests a model of relationality based on a monistic fusion, a relationship which depends on grasping and power. Equally, however, he resists any attempt to establish a relation modelled on the classic form of the Socratic dialogue between two subjects. Levinas objects that this would be to presume that, however different two subjects or the two terms of a relation may be, 'they can ultimately be rendered commensurate and simultaneous, the same, contained in a history that totalizes time into a beginning or an end, or both, which is presence'.[95]

Speaking 'otherwise than being'

Otherwise than Being, written with Derrida in mind,[96] is a further and more complex attempt to answer the ethical question which this aporia of the other raises: how to speak of Infinity without creating another Totality? By seeking to use the phenomenological method against itself, Levinas is left with no option but to search out the conditions of possibility for the self-communication of the other. Is this to be discovered in the future – what is not yet known? In which case, how does one recognise what is other without already having some idea of otherness? Or is it that which

---

95 From 'Dialogue with Emmanuel Levinas', in Cohen 1986:19.

96 See the discussion of *Otherwise than Being* as a response to Derrida's 'Violence and Metaphysics', in Bernasconi, 'Skepticism in the Face of Philosophy', in Bernasconi and Critchley 1991:149–61.

has always existed, pre-existing our attempts to know, and therefore
something which has to be recalled from the past? In which case, how
does one avoid falling back into the Husserlian problematic and reducing Being to consciousness of Being?

Rather than attempt to make the deconstructive interruption of
alterity some sort of ontological basis of subjectivity, Levinas seeks to
show that the experience of alterity, the prior condition which makes the
pursuit of truth possible, disallows any finished process of signification.
Thus he begins *Otherwise than Being* with a question – 'what is *Being's
other?*'[97]

The answer is not given as the opposite of Being, its negation or nothingness, nor even as 'to be otherwise', but more enigmatically as '*otherwise
than being*'. The adverb points to an 'other way' of existing or relating to
the other. Levinas tries to show how the act of responsibility before the
face of the Other can describe a relation to what lies 'beyond essence'. This
is not, however, a reversal of his earlier project so much as a repetition
or intensification. His whole argument turns on a distinction between a
subjectivity of the totalising self which always returns to self-presence
leaving nothing outside self, and a subjectivity which arises from a contingent experience in which self is literally 'subject' to the other, its self-
presence constantly ruptured by 'a past more ancient than any present'.[98]
He opposes, in other words, a potentially solipsistic self-affirmation with
a thorough-going self-abnegation to the point of substitution before the
face of the other.

In *Otherwise than Being,* by overstating the case 'to the point of
paroxysm' Levinas produces the effect of a break 'with regard to the idea
of exteriority in the sense of absolute otherness' – as Ricoeur puts it.[99]
The immediate aim of this strategy is a critique of what might be called
a 'residual Husserlianism': the attempt to establish the subject through
an intentionality which 'places' the other. For Levinas, every intentional
act of self-identification entails a 'saying', making the self a theme and
the other an object of thought. But in face of the other this establishing
of the self as a *beginning* is destabilised; the said becomes 'unsaid'.

---

[97] Levinas 1991:3.

[98] See Levinas 1991:24. The shift of emphasis discernible in *Otherwise than Being* from future
to past makes explicit a point raised by Derrida in 'Violence and Metaphysics', p. 94. Derrida
wonders 'whether history itself does not begin with this relationship which Levinas places beyond
history. The framework of this question should govern the entire reading of *Totality and Infinity.*'

[99] Ricoeur 1992:337.

To use Levinas's particular language, the 'ethical' diachrony of the trace of alterity punctuates the 'ontological' synchrony of an otherwise self-constituting subject, challenging the egotism and self-reference of the same.[100] Or, to put it more simply, the responsible self is always subject to the other. This is the only relationship which Levinas will allow.

The vocation of philosophy – a 'first' and a 'second reading'

The extent to which the phenomenological analyses of *Totality and Infinity* have been superseded or corrected by the deconstructive approach of *Otherwise than Being* cannot be pursued here. In the next chapter I will argue that in the latter text Levinas seeks the proper vocation of philosophy as 'the wisdom of love at the service of love';[101] if the tradition of philosophical thinking has the thoroughly ethical purpose of reducing the element of betrayal of the unthematisable in the act of Saying, then it will seek not so much to say 'something new' as always to go on *repeating* the terms of the tradition in order to uncover the 'old question' of the other which the Said risks suppressing. In a 'second reading' of Levinas I hope to show that, understood in performative terms as a text which allows for the return of the other without reducing the other to a theme, *Otherwise than Being* opens up a possible dialogue with theology.

The object of this 'first reading' has been more modest: by developing a critique of Levinas's project as essentially philosophical 'translation' to show that the question raised by the experience of inter-faith relations is the same as that addressed by Levinas's project of 'ethics as first philosophy'. De Certeau's figure of the constant return of the other leads us to ask how the subject can be 'altered' – 'made other' – without being fragmented. How successfully does Levinas answer this question?

There is an inner consistency to Levinas's project; the other is not just 'different', that which the conscious subject is not, but that which, entering the world of the same through the 'diachrony' of the trace, resists all mastery and totalisation, all reduction to the same. To that extent, Levinas's philosophy of the other leaves us with an important consideration for a theology of dialogue. The insistence on ethical responsibility is a

---

[100] The term 'diachrony' is not so much opposed to 'synchrony' as deconstructs it, much like the relation between the concepts of Totality and Infinity. For Levinas, 1999:173, diachrony describes the primordial alterity of time itself which disturbs the 'synchrony of all eternal presentness'.

[101] Levinas 1991:162.

direct challenge both to the grosser forms of exclusivism and to the more subtle forms of patronising violence which seek to encompass the other within a self-fulfilling totality. Moreover, Levinas makes us acknowledge that the 'middle' within which the inter-faith dialogue takes place is an ethically demarcated space. Through phenomenological analyses which illustrate how much human subjectivity is formed in the presence of a disturbing otherness, he argues that the idea of the Infinite in us cannot be understood by the epistemology of presence. Entering consciousness through the epiphany of the face-to-face encounter, the other constrains the same to act responsibly. Levinas's commitment to what I have called 'ethical heterology' rather than the tradition of a self-centred ontology thus emerges as an important counter to the individualism which would found any commonality in the power which the 'I' can wield over 'others'. In short: to understand who 'I' am as subject I need to recognise that I exist in responsible relationship to what is other than or different from me.

Strangely, however, for one so deeply concerned for the recovery of the ethical in philosophy, Levinas shows little interest in the actual *practice* of ethical relations. To pick up a distinction of de Certeau's, Levinas is a critic of the sort of self-regarding 'strategy' which seeks to command the single shared space in defence of power-relations, but has little to say about the calculus of 'tactics' by which people seek to develop a degree of plurality and creativity within the constraints of a particular place.[102] This alone must raise serious questions for a theology of religions which would be committed to the responsible discernment *and* realisation of a universal vision of the common good. The alternative to a juxtaposition of competing totalities cannot be an anodyne refusal to risk the labour of negotiation of the 'middle'.

Nevertheless, Levinas remains profoundly uneasy about bringing same and other into a relationship which might compromise the primordial 'height' or '*excendance*' between them. What Levinas leaves us with, in Gillian Rose's evocative terms, is a 'holy middle' rather than a 'broken middle'.[103] This 'holy middle' appears to be what is left once the past has been renounced and the future deferred as 'eschatology': a present meeting or dialogue which lacks any 'epistemology of recognition' because it seeks to avoid contamination with the messiness of the phenomenal. 'Holy middles corrupt', says Rose, 'because they collude in

---

[102] De Certeau 1984:29–42.
[103] See Rose 1992:277–8.

the elimination of the broken middle.'[104] If Rose is right, then she has uncovered a very precise area of weakness at the heart of Levinas's project: his insistence on transcending the autonomy of the subject by a substitution in favour of the other. If same and other are kept in a state of constant suspended passivity, then the establishing of any relationship with the other becomes impossible.

There is, then, a prescriptive element in Levinas's account of subjectivity which makes the establishment, let alone continuing negotiation, of such a relationship problematic. Ethical critique restricts totalising activity on the part of the same, and recognises the constructive role of the other in the formation of human relationships. This, however, is at the risk of paralysis before the other who, in the logic of Levinas's thought, has the major formative role in the constitution of the subject – to the extent of grounding subjectivity in the act of substitution for the other. This is not to say that the concept of responsibility, so central to Levinas's project, does not have its place in a philosophical analysis, only that the other, for which responsibility is taken, is, in Levinas's terms, necessarily beyond analysis. The sharpness of his dichotomising of 'same' and 'other', says Rose, misrepresents alterity, for '"the Other" is equally the distraught subject searching for its substance, its ethical life ... [I]t is the inveterate but occluded *immanence* of one subject to itself and other *subjects* that needs further exposition.'[105] It is by no means just the powerless who are defensive or passive.

My 'second reading' intends to press this point further and to link it with the complex experience of relationship with persons who come from 'other' faith traditions. To put 'other' in inverted commas here is to make the point, with Husserl and Derrida and against Levinas, that the very concept of otherness implies that there is some relation *already* established which enables us to use the language of difference in the first place – even and perhaps especially a 'resistant' difference. This is what leads Ricoeur to ask: 'Would the self be a result if it were not first a pre-supposition, that is, potentially capable of hearing this assignment?'[106] If with Levinas we try to speak of the Other in ethical terms as the one who confronts or challenges, then we still need to ask with Ricoeur: how is this 'challenge' to be recognised? *Who* is it that speaks?

---

[104] Rose 1993:49.

[105] Rose 1993:8.

[106] Ricoeur 1995:126.

4

Learning something of God

As I sought to describe it in my introductory chapter, there is more to 'dialogue' than an exchange of ideas which leads to a consensus. Broadened to include moments of inter-personal encounter which give rise to a diffuse variety of forms of discourse, the experience of dialogue turns out to have an irreducible – and, therefore, in Levinas's terms – an ethical character. It is not just the moral authority of Levinas's Jewish experience which draws our attention to the horizon of responsibility against which the other is to be encountered. His relentless insistence on the asymmetrical nature of the ethical relationship contests the *naïveté* of an unproblematic 'openness' by stressing the infinite obligation that the relationship with the other person opens up. All of this seems very persuasive and promising for the future of inter-faith relations, especially where history and culture conspire to prevent rather than enable communication across the divide. Levinas sensitises us to power-differences and the latent areas of violence which underlie all relations with the other.

The question, however, is whether his project enables him to defend subjectivity *and* establish a non-totalising account of alterity, or whether it just leaves him locked within the polarities of same and other. As the discussion in the previous chapter tried to show, it is impossible to speak of a relationship with what is other without dropping back into the language of the totality. Is it possible to make coherent this shift from ontology to ethics as 'first philosophy'?

Rather than pursue this question directly, my purpose in this chapter is to continue questioning the presuppositions within which Levinas works and to broaden the context of debate. Set against his philosophical account of the 'question of the other' is the guiding concept I take from the experience of inter-faith relations as a faithful practice of responsible encounter described earlier: the other is always 'other *than*' something or someone else. 'Same' and 'other' are essentially relational categories; they cannot be reified or understood apart but exist in relationship. But, even where same and other are taken as relational categories, the concept of 'the other' is often ambiguous. Sometimes it refers to the second with respect to a first; sometimes, to invoke a distinction of de Certeau's, it is the 'entire circumference with respect to a center which generates it'.[1] In these terms, to speak of 'the other' is to relate the same to the whole horizon of intelligibility within which the practices of living and learning are set. Such an image follows Levinas in making plain that the 'negotiation of the middle' cannot be understood as a controlling strategy from which the knowing subject can somehow be extracted; the subject is called to responsibility before the other. But it also seeks to avoid a dualism of same and other by placing the negotiation within a more complex and primordial otherness, namely the history, the language, and the culture within which the subject is formed.

A phenomenology of the 'returning other'

It is this more complex sense of otherness that de Certeau's repeated figure of the 'uncanny ghost' of the past which resists control by 'haunting' the present is intended to illustrate. De Certeau's preoccupation with the way the other resists assimilation has certain Levinasian overtones to it. Like Levinas, he does not allow a theory of the other, which would risk reducing the other to the same. Where, however, Levinas has difficulty in accounting for the relationship between same and other without some form of an analogising 'tertium quid', de Certeau proposes 'heterology', a phenomenology of the 'returning other' which the same can neither avoid nor overcome. This is what Jeremy Ahearne, commenting on de Certeau's historiographical method, says he finds 'tempting to call a basic "heterological" law'.[2]

What this phenomenology amounts to is a sequence of overlapping stages by which the other insinuates itself back into the world previously controlled by the same, disrupting the status quo and demanding further interpretation. The initial stage in which the same recognises common ground and attempts to enclose the other within the space it dominates is followed by the disorientating irruption of alterity. However much the

---

[1] De Certeau 1987b:29.

[2] Ahearne 1991:21.

other may be turned into an object of discourse, such displacement eventually re-emerges in reflection, provoking an indefinite series of reinterpretations. To speak in terms of same and other as relational categories means, therefore, that that which is taken to be other can never be left unexamined, still less cut out by the powerful in order for them to maintain a persuasive representation of the world. The point of my account of the Church's experience of relations with its Jewish other was to illustrate precisely this truth. The Christian self is formed in response to the Word of God who calls the Church together as that community of faith whose identity is found in the practice of narrating the Christian story. But the Word is not ours to command; the Spirit 'blows where it wills'. The practice of witness to what is known is therefore inseparable from another practice, that of listening for the 'seeds of the Word'.

Understood in this way, the figure of the 'returning other' has major implications for the way we understand Christian personhood. In this regard, my first reading of Levinas was, at best, ambiguous in its conclusions. What Gillian Rose somewhat dismissively refers to as Levinas's 'Buddhist Judaism'[3] springs from his desire for a philosophy which will eliminate a violent colonising of the other.[4] Thus, for Levinas, philosophy – 'the wisdom of love at the service of love' – is called to reduce the ever-present danger of the betrayal of what is ineffable.[5] As noted earlier, Levinas gives us an ethics based on the *event* or fact of revelation, but with nothing revealed except ever-repeated prescriptions.

For Rose, however, violence is an unavoidable consequence of the interaction of human beings in society at every level. Any attempt to think through, let alone make judgments about, the relationship with the other involves the possibility of mistake. But, just because such negotiations, philosophical as much as any other, fail, it does not follow that they must, or indeed can, be renounced. Politics must beware the siren voice of the totalising 'holy middle', a peace imposed before its time. For Rose the 'middle' is always broken, a fact which has philosophical, and theological, consequences. As Rowan Williams puts it, in powerful advocacy of Rose's project:

> [t]o recognize misperception is to learn; to learn is to reimagine
> or reconceive the self . . . And the insistence on a sociality never

---

[3] Rose 1996:37–8.

[4] Thus Levinas, 1993:15, in a lecture on the place of Buber in contemporary Judaism says that 'philosophy seeks, after all, to avoid violence'.

[5] Levinas 1991:162.

'mended' in a final way . . . raises . . . a religious question; not the facile and tempting question of law's relation to grace, but the harder one of how the experience of learning and of negotiation can be read as something to do with God.[6]

How can Christian theology respond positively to Levinas's warnings about the dangers of totalising the other without being forced into a fragmenting passivity? Ricoeur's engagement with Levinas, as I have already noted, attempts to resolve the aporia of alterity by encouraging a constant reimagining of the trace of the other as the very basis of subjectivity. If Levinas speaks of a 'hyperbolic exteriority', and risks thereby the effacement of self, Ricoeur defends self-esteem by using the terms of interiority and conscience. For Levinas, subjectivity is to be established through the act of responsible substitution before the other. For Ricoeur, self does not know self directly but through the act of self-attestation in the face of experiences of passivity or alterity. Hence in this chapter what I intend is a second reading of Levinas – this time in dialogue with Ricoeur. My aim will be to describe the terms or stages of a phenomenology of de Certeau's 'returning other'. I am going to begin, however, with Ricoeur's critique of Levinas. To the question to which this chapter leads – whether a narrative account of subjectivity simply raises another form of synchronic totalisation, albeit in a theological guise – I shall respond with Levinas's concept of time as diachrony, essentially the 'event' or 'moment' beyond synchronicity which expresses the absolute temporal separation of same and other, in order to keep the strictures of his ethics responsibly in view.

The ethical process of self-identification

Although discussed in detail in only two major sections, the influence of Levinas throughout the ten studies that make up Ricoeur's *Oneself as Another* is acknowledged.[7] Following Levinas, Ricoeur wants to allow for the 'ethical primacy of the other than self over the self';[8] at the same time he seeks to avoid the prescriptive extreme to which he feels Levinas's position tends, risking 'the substitution of self-hatred for

---

[6] Williams 1995:9.

[7] See Ricoeur 1992:189, n24. In Ricoeur 1998:6, reflecting on the 'duality' of his biblical and critical interests, he notes the similarity of his life-project to that of Levinas.

[8] Ricoeur 1992:168.

self-esteem'.[9] In setting the same over against the other, he argues, Levinas fails to allow for any process of self-differentiation in 'the middle', the site of negotiation. Ricoeur's dialectic of *idem* identity and *ipse* identity is an attempt to express this differentiation.[10] Both terms are concerned to resolve the problematic of an existence which endures across time; but, whereas the former speaks of personal identity through categories of the permanence of substance, the latter takes up the more ethical discourse of self-constancy: 'that manner of conducting himself or herself so that others can count on that person'.[11] In the self-attestation 'Here I am', one becomes a responsible witness before the other.

Despite the tentative nature of the book's structure, *Oneself as Another* can be read as a single extended meditation on the essentially ethical process of human self-identification, charting the 'endless task of understanding accomplished only after painful critiques of the self'.[12] Ricoeur seeks to steer a path between the extremes of Cartesian foundationalism, with its obsessive search for a sure 'place to stand', and the post-modern 'shattered *cogito*' where, thanks to Nietzsche, Descartes's 'evil genius' has gained the upper hand.[13] Together with his earlier study, the three volume *Time and Narrative*, which in many ways *Oneself as Another* repeats through a different set of mediations, Ricoeur sets out his own version of relational subjectivity. So far from seeking to defend a concept of self which occupies the 'place of foundation',[14] he makes a virtue of necessity by arguing, more radically, that selfhood can only be understood in dialectical relationship with a range of

---

[9] Ricoeur 1992:168.

[10] *Oneself as Another* begins with three converging intentions: the problematic centrality of the self-positing 'I', the distinction between two meanings of 'identity' (*identity as sameness* or *idem*-identity, and *identity as selfness* or *ipse*-identity), and the dialectic between *self* and *other than self*. The crucial point, to which Ricoeur returns throughout his text, is that '[a]s long as one remains within the circle of sameness-identity, the otherness of the other than self offers *nothing original*' (p. 3; emphasis added). The influence of Levinas is already apparent here as Ricoeur argues that it is the experience of otherness which demands a differentiation between solutions to the problem of personal identity based on the fait accompli of self-subsisting permanence and those which allow of no a priori resolution, being based on the faithful interpreting of life through the refiguring of narrative. Without wishing to drive a wedge between the two, Ricoeur opts for 'self-constancy' rather than 'self-consistency', a point which has its origins in Levinas's theme of promise-keeping and responsibility (see Ricoeur 1988:249; 1992:165, n32).

[11] Ricoeur 1992:165.

[12] Van den Hengel 1994:461.

[13] Ricoeur 1992:12–13.

[14] Ricoeur 1992:318.

experiences of otherness. If the issue is about what gives unity to a life lived in face of the other, Ricoeur adopts a narrative solution.[15] This is in line with his consuming interest in the capacity of language to reorder the experience of the reader.[16] As historical beings we are characterised by an ability to 'emplot' life, to develop descriptive and imaginative strategies to keep us in possession of a constantly refigured identity. Like Levinas, therefore, Ricoeur begins with a self which is summoned by the voice of the other. But, unlike Levinas, he sees a need to set such a call for justice not *over against* the struggle of the *same* for recognition and mastery, but *within* the search of the *self* for an authentic living out of the 'ethical intention' – as Ricoeur puts it – *'aiming at the "good life" with and for others, in just institutions'*.[17] If Levinas shows little interest in the actual practice of ethical relations, for Ricoeur they are philosophically of crucial importance.

In the seventh, eighth and ninth studies of *Oneself as Another*, Ricoeur distinguishes a teleological ethical aim from deontological moral norms. To the former he gives a certain priority, while admitting that it can only be reached by way of the latter which has the function of testing action through universalisable maxims.[18] Hence the importance of the 'practical wisdom' which informs conflictual situations and returns 'to the initial intuition of ethics, in the framework of moral judgement in situation'.[19] At issue in this lengthy discussion is a version of the hermeneutical circle I detected in Levinas's thought at the end of the last chapter. Does ethics presuppose the other, or vice versa? In my first

---

[15] Ricoeur 1992:158–60. In dialogue here with MacIntyre about what gives unity to fragmentary practices Ricoeur draws attention to the 'thorny problem' of connecting story to life, raising a question – how do the 'thought experiments occasioned by fiction . . . contribute to self-examination in real life?' – to which we will return later.

[16] See Ricoeur's remarks on the composition of *Time and Narrative* in Ricoeur 1998:83-4. His previous study, *The Rule of Metaphor*, ends with the creative reorganisation of language through metaphor but leaves, he says, a 'link missing' in the final chapter: 'the role of the reader'.

[17] Ricoeur 1992:172ff.; emphasis in original.

[18] Ricoeur 1992:216ff. The basic orientation here is a radical reading of Kant's categorical imperatives in the context of the 'true problem for us': the 'propensity for evil' which challenges the limits of autonomy and freedom (p. 216). Hence Ricoeur's own maxim: 'Act solely in accordance with the maxim by which you can wish at the same time that what *ought not to be*, namely evil, will indeed *not exist'* (p. 216).

[19] Ricoeur 1992:240. Ricoeur's brilliantly evocative example from one of the 'voices of nonphilosophy: that of Greek tragedy' (p. 241), Sophocles' *Antigone*, does more than illustrate the dialectic between Aristotle and Kant. It also presses the limits of philosophical discourse, moving from ethics to the poetics of tragedy in graphic illustration of the inevitability of conflict in the aspiration to live the 'good life'.

reading of Levinas's dialogue with the phenomenological tradition, I noted his objections to the Heideggerian 'philosophy of communion' – the other 'side by side' rather than 'face to face'. For Levinas, Heidegger completes a Western tradition which swallows up the other in a collective representation.[20] Levinas can at least agree with Heidegger that Man is not a 'being' among 'beings', but *Dasein*, 'being there', in the sense that Man's vocation is to be the one who discloses Being. For both, subjectivity is never 'given' but always in process of revision. They disagree profoundly about the place of the other. In this dialogue there is no doubt where Ricoeur's sympathies lie.[21] Nevertheless, in raising the 'delicate problem of the epistemological status of attestation'[22] Ricoeur finds himself seeking an important mediation between the two.

Recognising difference: the otherness of passivity

Levinas's position, set so firmly against Heidegger, allows the Other to command the same as a 'master of justice' – to use Ricoeur's term.[23] But, in his concern to maintain the asymmetry of the relationship, Levinas allows no reciprocity. Ricoeur objects that such an initiative establishes no relation at all. He argues that only a self rooted in what he calls 'self-esteem' is capable of recognising – let alone responding to – the Other. He is therefore unhappy with Levinas's account of the self before the encounter with the Other as 'a stubbornly closed, locked up, separate ego';[24] this he takes as illustrative of Levinas's general strategy, particularly in *Otherwise than Being*, to ground ethics in the language of 'hyperbole, to the point of paroxysm'.[25] For Ricoeur, however, the self is not constituted purely in substitutionary response to the diachronic incursions of the Other, but equally by the attestation which it brings on its own behalf. However much the former may challenge and inform the latter, the self is still responsible

---

[20] Levinas 1987a:93.

[21] Ricoeur's critique of Levinas is at once an attempt to explicate Levinas's engagement with Heidegger and an exercise in mediation. According to Peter Kemp, in Kearney 1996:41–61, Heidegger analyses the attestation of self without the injunction of the other; Levinas claims the injunction by the other without allowing the attestation of conscience.

[22] From 'Emmanuel Levinas: Thinker of Testimony', in Ricoeur 1995:108–26. The sentence continues: 'which is an assurance, without being a doxic certitude, an assurance always bound to acts' (p. 117).

[23] Ricoeur 1992:189.

[24] Ricoeur 1992:337.

[25] Ricoeur 1992:338.

before itself and its history. Thus, against Heidegger's attestation which 'risks losing all ethical and moral significance' and Levinas's 'injunction which risks not being heard and the self not being affected', Ricoeur finds a middle position, proposing 'the third modality of otherness, namely *being enjoined as the structure of selfhood*'.[26]

What does he mean by this? To recognise otherness as otherness, not-self, is to accept that there is some relation already established which enables the recognition of difference. This recognition may indeed be 'broken', fraught with all sorts of ambiguities and in constant need of mending, but it is rooted in highly complex processes of present and past interaction with forms of 'otherness' inscribed in 'experiences of passivity, intertwined in multiple ways in human action'.[27] In proposing an ontology of the self, Ricoeur suggests 'as a working hypothesis what could be called the *triad of passivity and, hence, of otherness*':[28] recognition and respect for the otherness of one's own body, for the otherness of other people, and for the otherness of conscience which remains always the judge of the self. Whereas, for Levinas, the other is very specifically revealed through the face of another person, Ricoeur recognises a broader phenomenology of alterity, allowing that otherness appears in a number of forms. To put it another way, if Levinas privileges an otherness or passivity before the face of the Other, for Ricoeur, activity and passivity are interrelated in complex ways. Every human act affects and is affected by the other.

The 'primary otherness' is embodiment[29] – a point which recalls and takes further the account of ego and *alter ego* in Husserl's fifth *Cartesian Meditation*.[30] Like all experiences of alterity there is an enigmatic quality in the way the body mediates between self and world, known and unknown. The second passivity is found in the intersubjective relation. Here Ricoeur argues, following Husserl, for an 'analogical transfer from myself

---

[26] Ricoeur 1992:3 54–5. See Kemp in Kearney 1996:41–62.

[27] Ricoeur 1992:318.

[28] Ricoeur 1992:318.

[29] Ricoeur 1992:327.

[30] Towards the end of the *Cartesian Meditations*, Husserl appears to be moving away from the analysis of the problematic of ego and *alter ego* to a different sort of discourse with distinct touches of what Ricoeur will develop. To understand the world in intersubjective terms, Husserl is saying, one must first lose it; only through each unique individual being prepared to put his own life 'in doubt' will a true community between 'others' emerge (p. 157). Here he recognises that there is more to the subject characterised by the quality of 'empathy', *Einfühlung*, than the Cartesian concept of a fixed substratum.

to the other [which] intersects with the inverse movement of the other toward me'.[31] But he also seeks to allow for Levinas's strictures on a self-positing foundationalism by balancing Husserl's other as 'alter ego' with Levinas's other as radical exteriority. Between the exalted and humiliated *cogito* lies the hermeneutics of the self based on attestation – a dialectic of trust and suspicion. The otherness of conscience, the voice which summons to responsibility, is also an attestation of self to itself. In Ricoeur's account of human identity or, to be more precise, the process of self-identification, action is never separated from passion, same is always kept in relationship with other. Thus '*Idem*-identity', in its concern to maintain the continuity and coherence of the individual, sets self over against the other, whereas '*Ipse*-identity' gives us the subject in dialogue with the other, where it is challenged and shaped anew by a complex and pluriform otherness in which it is always and already embedded.

The significance of the other for the self

But what does alterity signify for the self? The crucial question for the Christian theologian is whether what Levinas calls the 'trace of the other' can be understood in the traditional Patristic terminology of 'seeds of the Word'. To repeat an earlier question: in what sense can we speak of the other revealing 'seeds of the Word', as in some sense a *locus* of God's self-revelation? *Nostra Aetate* simply juxtaposed principles of good practice derived from a theological tradition committed to an inclusive universalism; nothing was said about *how* the Church saw itself as 'related' to other communities. My aim in this discussion of Ricoeur's debate with Levinas is to outline the terms of such a relationship. Ricoeur argues that selfhood cannot be thought apart from alterity, that a responsible self-attestation is rooted in a dialectic of action *and* passion.

Ricoeur thus provides not just an important critique of Levinas's insistence that the other is always exterior, beyond the totality of what can be encompassed by thought, but a theoretical basis for the practices of negotiation and hospitality. In these terms, theology of religions demands not a version of the 'method of correlation', which sets the subject above 'tradition' and 'situation', but a far more risky enterprise which would speak of a self implicated in both and called, therefore, always to be responsible before the pressures of history, culture and politics.

---

[31] Ricoeur 1992:335.

How can Levinas help the theologian here? In the first place, Levinas warns us that any theology risks betrayal, a collusion in the totalising of language. Levinas allows that the subject may bear a sincere witness to the Infinite – 'inasmuch as the same is for the other . . . to the point of substitution as a hostage' – and that such a witness gives rise to a saying.[32] Thus, in the final pages of *Otherwise than Being*, he returns firmly to a phenomenology which would root human subjectivity in response to a trace of the Infinite, and to a God who addresses each person in his or her particularity. At the same time, however, Levinas fears the shutting up of the glory of the Infinite in the word God. What he resists is not the concept of revelation as such, but theology turned into an idolatrous system of thought – the 'said in which everything is thematized' – which would absolve the subject of his or her infinite responsibility for the other.[33]

Levinas thus challenges totalising tendencies in general. But it is not just this element of ethical critique which makes his project strangely enriching for the theologian committed to reimagining the terms of the relationship with people of other faiths. Despite his stated antipathy towards theology, the deconstructive language of *Otherwise than Being* brings his project as a resistant discourse which operates within – more properly, against – the terms set by the dominant philosophical tradition very close to theology. In what follows I want to argue that attention to the rhetorical nature of Levinas's language enables us to understand his project in what I shall call 'liturgical' terms as a faithful and obedient repetition of the tradition. This is the beginning of a theology of dialogue: a reflection on a subjectivity formed in responsible relationship with the other. How far can Levinas take us in developing such a theology? Again, as I have already noted, he is not interested in the labour of an ethical negotiation, still less in discerning 'seeds of the Word' revealed in the space of the 'middle'. For this we must turn to Ricoeur who is more at home than Levinas with the signification of feelings.

Revelation and the 'logic of superabundance'

Although in his ethical thinking Ricoeur is deeply influenced by Levinas, he is also suspicious of Levinas's account of God as the 'master of justice'. For Levinas, 'ethics is an "optics"', by which he means an unmediated

---

[32] Levinas 1991:145–51.
[33] Levinas 1991:183–5.

vision of the Other.[34] The imperative revealed in this encounter presses the limits of the linguistic resources available to the philosophical tradition and contests the centrality of the Greek logos with the 'Jewish logos' of substitution, in order to 'hear a God that is not contaminated by Being'.[35] For Levinas, this God is a distant God who 'hides His face and abandons the just man to a justice that has no sense of triumph'.[36] By contrast, Ricoeur's instinct is always to discern the surplus of meaning promised by the return of the other. For Ricoeur, love, sympathy and solicitude introduce an element of mutuality into the esteem which characterises the relationship of self and other.[37]

In reflecting on this theme, Ricoeur tells us in an essay on the Great Commandment that he found 'an unanticipated source of help' in Rosenzweig's *Star of Redemption*. His comment is worth quoting at length:

It may be recalled that this work . . . is divided into three sections, corresponding respectively to the idea of creation (or the eternal before), revelation (or the eternal moment of encounter), and redemption (or the eternal not yet of messianic expectation). Coming to the second section, revelation, the reader may expect to be instructed concerning the Torah, and in a sense this is what happens, but the Torah, at this stage of Rosenzweig's meditation, is not yet a set of rules. Rather, it becomes so, because it is preceded by the solemn act that situates all human experience in terms of the paradigmatic language of scripture. And what is the most apt symbol for this imposing of a primordial language on the human sphere of communication? It is the commandment to love. Yet, contrary to our expectation, the formula for this commandment for Rosenzweig is not that of Exodus, nor that of Leviticus, nor that of Deuteronomy, but rather that of the Song of Solomon, which is read at every Passover celebration. Love, says the Song of Songs, 'is as strong as death'. Why does Rosenzweig refer to the Song of Solomon at this place? And with what imperative connotation? At the beginning of this section on revelation, he considers just the intimate colloquy between God and an individual soul, before any 'third' person comes on the scene, which is taken up in the section on redemption. His

---

[34] Levinas 1969:23,29. Elsewhere, 1990a:17, he explains that ethics is 'not the corollary of the vision of God, it is that very vision. Ethics is an optic, such that everything I know of God and everything I can hear of His word and reasonably say to Him must find an ethical expression.'

[35] Levinas 1991:xlii.

[36] See 'Loving the Torah more than God', in Levinas 1990a:142–5.

[37] Ricoeur 1992:193–4.

insight is to show in this way how the commandment to love springs from the bond of love between God and the individual soul. The commandment that precedes every law is the word the lover addresses to the beloved: Love me! This unexpected distinction between commandment and law makes sense only if we admit that the commandment to love is *love itself, commending itself*, as though the genitive in the 'commandment of love' were subjective and objective at the same time. Or, to put it another way, this is a commandment which contains the conditions for its being obeyed in the very tenderness of its objurgation: Love me![38]

This *prior* conversation which God has with the individual soul reveals the bond of love which makes the Torah more than a set of rules but the gift of God himself, the 'source of *unknown* possibilities'.[39] Ricoeur argues that this economy of the gift allows us to develop what he calls the ethical 'logic of superabundance' which both disorients and yet reinforces the utilitarian tendency of the 'logic of equivalence'.[40]

Let me briefly anticipate my conclusion at this point. What is at stake here in this dialogue between Levinas and Ricoeur is a concept of revelation which recognises the possibility of such a 'logic of super-abundance'. How can this recognition be extended beyond the action of God discerned in the familiar events and experiences of the privileged tradition of faith to include those questions which the other puts to that tradition – questions which, if de Certeau's 'heterological law' is correct, are themselves already present or implicit in that tradition? In drawing attention to the way Vatican II speaks of God's continuing self-revelation to all peoples, I noted how *Nostra Aetate* responds to the ethical challenge of the Jewish other by reflecting on Paul's great 'theological synthesis' of Old and New in the Epistle to the Romans. As a contemplative rereading of the tradition, Paul's meditation on the constancy of God becomes para-digmatic of a theology of dialogue, a theology committed both to a faithful account of the events which inspire faith and to the continuing labour of what Rowan Williams calls 'learning about our learning'.[41] My argument is that a second reading of Levinas in dialogue with Ricoeur

---

[38] Ricoeur 1996:27; emphasis added; reference to *Star of Redemption*, p. 202 (see also Ricoeur 1992:194 n32).

[39] Ricoeur 1996:33. Emphasis in original.

[40] Ricoeur 1996:34–7. Ricoeur's argument here is based very much on Jesus's sayings in Luke 6.27–38 (see also pp. 38–9, n14).

[41] Williams 2000:132.

emphasises the essentially liturgical nature of this project. To pursue this point it is necessary to ask what is meant by liturgy in this context and how it modifies my first reading of Levinas.

The God who is revealed: obedience to tradition

When Levinas speaks of revelation in the Jewish tradition it is in terms of a certain 'rationality' of obedience which is traced back to the love of neighbour.[42] In revelation, through the epiphany of the face, 'the Other is the first intelligible'.[43] In desire for the Other which transcends self-serving need, I discover that I am not enclosed within myself, but am already *for the other*, ready to be hostage, a substitute. The heart of Jewish integrity, in face of the greatest of moral challenges, the enormous evil of the Shoah, says Levinas, lies in faithfulness.[44]

This theme of faithful obedience rather than speculation about the nature of God is at the heart of Levinas's Talmudic readings. Essentially an oral tradition, Talmudic commentary points in two directions at once: towards the Jewish tradition, into which one can withdraw to be 'at home', and towards the 'religious dimension' wherever it may appear in the world at large. Exegesis of the texts, in other words, arises from the exigencies of everyday life. This is not, however, to reduce it to a form of correlation. Levinas talks about a 'liturgy of study', by which he means the never-ending response which obedience to the Torah demands.[45] Such study is necessary if the texts themselves are not to become the object of idolatry but to go on nourishing understanding and wisdom.[46] For Levinas is suspicious of any spiritual experience which would divert attention from the Torah. In Talmudic commentary he is quite prepared to use the imagination in bringing the text to bear on contemporary issues, but presupposed in this process is a prior commitment to the tradition represented by the text. Before one knows what the teaching amounts to, one is guided by the

---

[42] Levinas 1994b:146. '[T]here is the primordial importance in Judaism of the prescriptive . . . the revealed is welcomed in the form of obedience . . . This obedience cannot be reduced to a categorical imperative in which a universality is suddenly able to direct a will.'

[43] 'Signature', Levinas 1990a:294–5. This brief autobiographical memoir summarises many familiar themes, finishing with the ultimate sense of responsibility: 'in this substitution not only *being otherwise* but, as freed of the *conatus essendi, otherwise than being*'.

[44] See 'Useless Suffering', in Bernasconi and Wood 1988:156–67.

[45] See 'Contempt for the Torah as Idolatry', in Levinas 1994a:59.

[46] See the introduction to Levinas 1990b by the translator, Anne Aronowicz; especially p. xxii–xxvii.

conviction that a teaching exists in the texts to be interpreted, that the very 'warp of being' is somehow concealed there.[47]

When, for instance, Levinas comments on the giving of the Law (Exodus 19.17ff.) he makes great play of how the people *did* the Law first and then subsequently came to understand it. To accept the Torah, because it represented 'the good', before reasoning about its meaning, because it is 'the true', appears contrary to reason. This might be true of 'Greek' reason, says Levinas, but not of 'Hebrew' reason. What he calls the 'deep structure of subjectivity' emerges from this paradox of knowing by doing, this 'upside down order' which 'underlies any inspired act, even artistic'.[48] But, as Tamra Wright comments, this is not a matter of '*praxis* as opposed to theory, but a way of "actualising without beginning with the possible", a way of "knowing without examining" '.[49]

For Levinas, such obedience before the tradition of faith is the very heart of the religious practice of Judaism. In the collection of writings on Jewish faith entitled *Difficult Freedom*, he tells an ancient rabbinic story in which three opinions are given in answer to the question: which verse contains the whole of the Torah? The first two opinions are familiar: 'the Lord our God is One' and 'love your neighbour as yourself'. The third is not: 'sacrifice a lamb in the morning and another at dusk'. It is this unexpected third opinion which is given approval, making the story read like a piece of deliberately disorientating hyperbole. Levinas uses it, however, to link the practice of ritual with that of justice. The second answer, he says, 'indicates the way in which the first is true, and the third indicates the practical conditions of the second'.[50] Through daily acts of fidelity to the law, the commandments of God are met and justice is done. At the end of the Preface to *Difficult Freedom*, Levinas speaks of the hunger of the Other as sacred; commitment to the Other is at the heart of Jewish identity – and what makes for the title of the book. He concludes that this deeply Jewish ethical commitment to service of the Other 'with no thought of reward . . . is the original and incontestable meaning of the Greek word *liturgy*'.[51] Liturgy is not to be confused with the singing of psalms or the practice of cult. Nor is it a mechanical recitation of ancient

---

[47] See Levinas 1990b:xxix.

[48] Levinas 1990b:42.

[49] Wright 1999:142; see notes on pp. 169–70.

[50] Levinas 1990a:18–19.

[51] Levinas 1990a:xiv.

texts. As obedient response to the divine command, Levinas insists that liturgy is 'ethics itself'.[52]

Liturgy as repetition and deconstruction

The word 'liturgy' literally means the 'work of the people', with connotations of the worship duly offered to God.[53] More precisely, liturgy manifests what Michael Purcell calls a 'cruciform structure', bringing together and realising 'in a single moment' vertical and horizontal dimensions, a divine service and a human service. Putting this in Levinas's terms, Purcell argues that Levinas's insight – that liturgy manifests an essential structure as a work which is *for*-the-Other' – brings worship and ethics together 'in mutual indispensability'.[54]

Levinas develops this liturgical metaphor in order to counter the tendency to neutralise the other by recognising the priority of the same's indebtedness to the other. In his terms, the word liturgy describes a 'work' (œuvre) which has something of a passive quality, a work in which the subject is acted upon by the other, or, as Levinas puts it, *'a movement of the same unto the other which never returns to the same'*.[55] The essential image used here is that of the Abrahamic journey, Levinas's 'ethical' alternative to the 'Greek' Odyssey which always returns the other to the same. For Levinas, there can never be a return to the same for the other is always pre-originary or 'anarchic', beyond the totality. Thus, any movement or work of the same is always dependent on or subsequent to the priority of the other; any relationship with the other can only be expressed by the use of goods which have already been given. In other words, any work of the same, any act of justice or generosity, is only possible because of the prior work or movement of the other. In Levinas's terms, before becoming work as action, which the autonomous individual accomplishes, it

[52] In an article entitled 'The Trace of the Other', originally published in 1963 (see Levinas 1986:350).

[53] See Jungmann 1975:851; Bouyer 1965:41ff.

[54] Purcell 1997:145. Much of Purcell's argument revolves around Derrida's discussion of the aporia of the gift. Derrida asks 'what would be a gift that fulfils the condition of the gift, namely that *it not appear as gift . . . ?*' (see Derrida 1992:27; emphasis added). In other words: what do we mean by saying a gift is 'given' if by accepting a gift we enter into an economy of indebtedness which annuls the *gratuity* which defines the gift as gift? Purcell argues that the 'gap' which the aporia opens up between 'gift which is thought, named and desired and that which refuses to show itself within the economy of knowledge' is the gap between same and other – or, in Levinas's terms, between totality and infinity.

[55] Levinas 1986:348 (emphasis in original).

must be accepted as an accomplishment which summons the same to responsibility before the face of the Other. In these terms, Levinas would remind us that the 'work of the people' is a work which *makes* the people before it is a task which the people do.

In my first reading, Levinas's project was shown to be implicated in the same phenomenological language which he seeks to deconstruct. I argued that 'meta-ethical' or relational language cannot be substituted for ontological without begging the question of how it refers to the other. A second reading makes Levinas's translation of 'Greek' philosophy more radically Jewish. He seeks to overcome the aporia of the other by proceeding after the model of a Talmudic 'liturgy of study' to repeat the language of the tradition but, at the same time, to subvert it by pressing the questions which it fails adequately to address. In *Otherwise than Being*, as I have already noted, Levinas's method is different from *Totality and Infinity*, but the change to what I have called a liturgical approach is not just a reaction to Derrida's critique. In *Time and the Other*, Levinas forbade the 'third term', a 'tertium quid', the means by which Heideggerian ontology tries to bring same and other into correlation.[56] In 'The Trace of the Other', written soon after *Totality and Infinity*, we find him speaking of the trace of the other in terms of the passive-yet-active œuvre of liturgy. This is described as the 'third person who in a face has already withdrawn from every relation and dissimulation' yet is immediately transfigured into the hyperbolic language which makes Illeity 'the whole enormity, the inordinateness, the infinity of the absolutely other'.[57]

Such language is familiar from my first reading. The style of Levinas's writing – an ever-spiralling renuancing of increasingly obscure terms and images – seems deliberately intended to disallow any finished process of signification. Both Levinas's major texts seek to articulate what might be called an 'ethical wisdom' which is contained in the experience of alterity, the prior condition which makes the pursuit of truth possible. In *Totality and Infinity*, the inadequacy of a model of knowledge as comprehension or possession is shown up by the inquiry Levinas undertakes into the conditions of possibility for ethical experience. He continues to use phenomenological language to describe various 'strata' surrounding the primordial vision of the face of the Other. In *Otherwise than Being*, he embarks on an exploration of 'liturgical language' which presses us 'to

---

[56] Levinas 1987a:94: 'a collectivity that is not a communion'.

[57] Levinas 1986:356.

a move is crucial, and points to the major difference between Levinas and Ricoeur. Levinas argues for an obedience before the tradition but has no interest in the past except as the 'immemorial'; his is a 'meta-ethics' which justifies the passivity of the present 'holy middle'. For Levinas, says Ricoeur, the past is the 'past of the moralist . . . compelling but not revealing'.[70] Ricoeur, on the other hand, takes Levinas's ethical demand with the utmost seriousness, but also seeks to establish a relation with the other as constitutive of self. His ethics would seek to mend the 'broken middle' by motivating us to 'think more and speak differently'.[71]

Taking time to mend the 'broken middle'

By discussing *Oneself as Another* before the earlier *Time and Narrative* in the first half of this chapter, my intention was not just to enable a second reading of Levinas but to show that Ricoeur's dialectic of *idem* and *ipse* identity with its ethical discourse of self-constancy makes an important corrective to Levinas's emphatic insistence on a subjectivity established through substitution. In this second part I want to turn to the thesis of *Time and Narrative*, in which Ricoeur argues that it is through the practice of narration that the destabilising experience of temporality is overcome, in order to show how Ricoeur's interest in the capacity of language to refigure and make significant the nature of human existence allows for a nuancing of Levinas's concept of liturgy.

Ricoeur's project, which like Levinas's is set within the terms of the Western engagement between Hebrew and Greek patterns of thought, devotes only the occasional aside to other cultures and traditions.[72] Nevertheless, his overriding concern for a subjectivity recovered through time enables us to discern within his account of the practice of narration a way of understanding experiences of negotiation of the 'broken middle' – not just intellectual exchanges but more informal interpersonal encounters, involving meetings, visits, pilgrimages, acts of

---

[70] Ricoeur 1988:124–5.

[71] Ricoeur 1988:274.

[72] Although sensitive to the issues raised, Ricoeur is reluctant to enter directly into an inter-faith discussion. In a reply to Bernard Stevens's article 'On Ricoeur's Analysis of Time and Narration', in Hahn 1995:499–506, which begins with questions about Buddhist concepts of time, Ricoeur suggests that the 'fables of time' of the second volume of *Time and Narrative* allow other possibilities for speaking of the experience of eternity, and that these might open doors 'onto the thought of the Far East' (p. 508).

think Being otherwise'. Here, as Charles Reed points out, Levinas uses a strategy he has learned from Descartes. The 'effusive glorification of God at the end of the third *Meditation*' contains an 'important linguistic device': a 'rhythm of transcendent excess and its counterbalancing analysis' both of which are necessary to the philosophical project.[58] Thus the 'Abrahamic journey' does not end, *cannot* end, in some sort of blissful contemplation of the 'Good beyond Being' – for this would be to presume to be able to comprehend, to encompass, Being through *logos*. Through language, produced in the face-to-face encounter, the 'abyss of separation' is not filled – indeed, says Levinas, it is confirmed. But the very exteriority of language, the fact that the interlocutor can never be held within 'inwardness', means that the discourse is forever being repeated as the interlocutor 'arises again behind him whom thought has just apprehended'.[59] In a reference to his own text, Levinas adds that philosophy 'in an essentially liturgical sense, invokes the Other to whom the "whole" is told, the master or student'.[60]

The use of this liturgical metaphor is revealing. It underlines graphically the danger that language will confine its theme, and the need therefore for what has been said constantly to be repeated – the act of 'saying' continually 'unsaying' what has been 'said'. As Levinas puts it at the end of the Preface to *Totality and Infinity*, 'it belongs to the very essence of language . . . to restate without ceremonies what has already been ill understood in the inevitable ceremonial in which the said delights'.[61] There is, however, a further point here. Liturgy is not performance for its own sake, in obedience to the prescriptions of tradition. The 'logic' of continuous performance only makes sense in the face of an irreducible otherness which challenges the betrayal of thematisation. Any discourse, even a liturgical narrative, *is* inadequate to its purpose and must always be re-said. But it must also be 'un-said'. The particular meanings which the process of interpretation gives, and which risk betrayal, must be deconstructed in order to return to the face in which meaning originates. In the face, Levinas says, existent and signifier are as one. The face is not a mask which reveals and conceals; it *is* the person who signifies by his or her presence. The condition of possibility of the Said is the Saying, the act of

---

[58] Reed 1986:78.

[59] Levinas 1969:295.

[60] Levinas 1969:295.

[61] Levinas 1969:30.

signification which precedes the Said, and which is 'equivalent to . . . presenting oneself in person'.[62] Said and Saying, however, can never be contemporaneous, any more than the person signified in the face and the subject who faces the other can occupy the same space or the same time as the other. There is a 'gap' between us. But in responding to the call of the Other I am committed to making and remaking the relationship in a manner which is appropriately described as liturgical – and, in the sense in which Levinas uses the term, 'religious': 'the bond that is established between same and other without constituting a totality'.[63]

Listening for 'other others'

Liturgy as the responsible practice of the tradition before the face of the Other provides a powerful metaphor for understanding Levinas's project, but how successfully does it avoid 'constituting a totality'? The danger with any liturgy is that it can become 'mere' ritual, the locking of a community of faith into a formulaic and unquestioning repetition. Our second reading is intended to bring out more clearly the element of 'translation' in Levinas's project, broadening the scope of phenomenology to include the typically ethical orientation of Judaism towards truth, the other and God.[64] Here the 'end of philosophy' – or, at any rate, the end of a purely 'Greek' philosophy – is taken up and celebrated as ethics. Levinas's aim is to make divine and human service mutually indispensable; the same is always 'for-the-Other'. This, however, is at the risk of producing 'holy middles' in which, as Rose puts it, 'Revelation is opposed to a totalized history of "Western metaphysics".'[65] This raises the question: does Levinas's 'liturgy of study' translate, or simply replace or overlay one tradition with another?

Despite his insistence that his philosophical texts can be read without any knowledge of the Bible, the context out of which Levinas speaks is, as Bernasconi says, 'in some sense a Jewish experience'.[66] This is not to

---

[62] Levinas 1969:262.

[63] Levinas 1969:40.

[64] Gibbs 1992:171ff. 'Levinas offers a deeply Jewish justification for the task of correlating the Jewish and the philosophic concepts. Here is an other of philosophy reaching out toward philosophy in order to provide it with what it cannot get from itself (or at least what it has not previously provided for itself)' (Gibbs 1992:172–3).

[65] Rose 1992:278.

[66] Bernasconi 1995:84.

---

take away from the measure of his achievement w concludes, is to develop a philosophy that arises philosophical experience of persecution – and which c ent itself as a 'model' for the 'millions of all confessio that are victims'.[67] Nevertheless, determined not Heideggerian', Levinas never looks beyond a dialogu and 'non-Greek'; in fact, in an off-hand moment he ca the rest – all the exotic' as 'dance'.[68] In seeking to the-Other', how consistent is he with his own principl others', not just the various dimensions of otherness draws our attention, but the other conceptualities and the Jewish and Western philosophical traditions son shall see in later chapters, have *already* contributed altered the terms of the dialogue which Levinas atten

My first reading of Levinas was an attempt to give ing other' of Judaism. What, following Ricoeur, can otherness' gives birth to a theology of religions by dist the same. But, however powerful a voice, it risks rema prescription alone: an ethics which refuses a politics. difficulty of presenting any specific experience as univ the language of persecution risks developing a certai which only fragments the self. The question for a ful – to return to Rowan Williams's phrase quoted at t chapter – is how the discerning of the trace of the oth terity can be understood as 'something to do with G allowing others to speak without their voices being language appropriate for describing one culturally s

Resolution of the aporia of the other is only poss dialogue are willing to enter into relationship thereby to risk change or alteration – in Ricoeur's t another. For a properly relational account of hum must be what Ricoeur calls 'a presumption of tru bearers of meaning without which the past would construction. For Ricoeur, human subjectivity is a by the past'; we are never 'at the beginning of the p

---

[67] Bernasconi 1995:85.

[68] In an interview, see Mortley 1991:18.

[69] Ricoeur 1988:227.

hospitality in which there may well be little verbal exchange – as having 'something to do with God'.

Let me first preface this discussion by a brief summary linking the guiding concept of an ethical heterology with my second reading of Levinas. In proposing a theology of dialogue, my argument started with de Certeau's figure of the 'uncanny ghost' which 'haunts' the present, disturbing the totalising tendencies inherent in any systematic discourse. This, I contend, comes much closer to describing the sense of risk to, and the possibility of enrichment for, the subject which arise from the interfaith encounter than anything to be found in a priori theories of a self-constituting subject. In reminding us that same and other are *relational* categories, not the poles of a dualism, de Certeau returns us to the problematical issue of knowledge of the other. He does not, however, look for an overarching theory but works through 'local interventions' intended to undermine 'founding oppositions'.[73] Without a 'place to stand', the powerless still find ways to negotiate the 'space of the middle' through tactics of resistance which challenge the strategies of the powerful to stand above or outside time. Thus it is that for de Certeau the theoretical question of *how* the other is to be known gives way to the more perplexing question of the significance of the other for the same – a significance which depends not on establishing an alternative position of power but on what he calls 'a clever *utilization of time*', watching and waiting for the opportunities for action to arrive.[74]

In responding to this question, I have resorted to the lengthy detour with which Ricoeur reworks the terms of a relational subjectivity in dialogue with Levinas. Although, as I have shown, Levinas's project tends inevitably to dig itself into the aporia of the other, it can be fruitful in helping us understand the irreducibly ethical character of the face-to-face encounter. In Levinas's terms, the destabilising moment of entry into the world of the other can be likened to the threat of the '*il y a*', what he calls the impersonal objectless 'density' or 'atmosphere' which threatens existence. This is countered firstly by the labour which would establish home and, most powerfully, by the epiphany of the face. By using the language of liturgy to express the movement of the same towards the other, Levinas makes the point that the two 'moments' cannot be synchronised. Time cannot be understood as if it were a sort of unbroken

---

73 Maclean 1987:84.

74 De Certeau 1984:34–9.

thread extending backwards and forwards from a 'controlling' present; the same is not in control of the present, let alone the past and future which remain always other.[75]

Subjectivity recovered through time

The problem with analysing relationality in terms of spatial metaphors is that space, as de Certeau points out, can all too easily become the base of totalising power. Hence, in *Otherwise than Being*, Levinas places a growing emphasis on the diachrony of the other's movement towards the same. Steven Smith suggests that the greater prominence given to this theme in Levinas's later text is to rule out the presumption that the other's command simply intersects with a present of which the same is somehow the master.[76] Levinas wants to stress that the other is not 'in a place' but evidenced only in the *trace* of an immemorial past which disrupts the present. The identity of the self comes to it despite itself, from the outside, as an election. If the other is always prior to me, existing before me, he is saying, then the only way I can become a subject is by putting myself in place of another – *becoming* an other. It is in order to disturb a Husserlian egology that Levinas resorts to the hyperbolic language of substitution, the self being hostage to the other, to signify 'the very subjectivity of a subject, interruption of the irreversible identity of the essence'.[77] Subjectivity is not a self-presence, not even an 'other-presence', but an election by the diachrony, precisely the *non*-simultaneity and *non*-presence, revealed by the other. If with Husserl the other cannot occupy the same place as the same, with Levinas the other is never the contemporary of the same. The subject does not surmount the potential loss of identity by somehow asserting itself throughout that set of temporal phases called 'life'. Rather we are held 'in the middle', subject in the present moment to a past opened up by an alterity which can be described as 'anarchy' – not *dis*-order but beyond the ordering capacity of the self.

Setting this in terms of Levinas's liturgical language, we need to note that, for him, subjectivity has its 'anarchic origins' in the disruptive

---

[75] Levinas begins *Time and the Other* by stating that his aim as to show that 'time is not the achievement of an isolated and lone subject, but . . . the very relationship of the subject with the Other'(p. 39). At the end he explains the relationship as absence – not the absence of nothingness, 'but absence in a horizon of the future, an absence that is time'(p. 90).

[76] Smith 1983:167ff.

[77] Levinas 1991:13.

diachrony effected by the incursion of the other. Ricoeur, on the other hand, wants to develop a synchronic subjectivity in which a version of Levinas's diachronic call of the other is subsumed into the more primordial responsibility of the self before history and culture. In other words, if for Levinas the self is never autonomous but always directly 'subject' to the 'glory of the infinite', for Ricoeur the subject's autonomy is always mediated by a particular situation. As Gadamer puts it, '[w]e always find ourselves within a situation, and the work of throwing light on it is never entirely finished'.[78]

Ricoeur's project, as noted earlier, is set within the self-reflexive tradition of phenomenology but seeks to integrate hermeneutics as a variation or development within the phenomenological method. Thus hermeneutics for Ricoeur is not a matter of reconstructing an autonomous text, but a process of entering into a relationship with the world opened up by the text. In this respect, Ricoeur finds that the failure of a self-constituting consciousness is compensated by a dialogue with what Gadamer calls 'historically effected consciousness'.[79]

In developing a concept of the 'mediating subject', Ricoeur's debt to Levinas is clear; identity is not the 'achievement' of an isolated self, but the product of an inter-subjective process in which the activity of the work of interpretation combines with 'the three great experiences of passivity'.[80] Ricoeur moves away from the language of Husserl's phenomenological problematic of the coexistence of separate transcendental egos, to the hermeneutical language of testimony in which the self is continually summoned to respond to the voice of the other. In place of the ego, concerned only for the maintenance of its own continuity in time, arises the self formed in dialogue with the cultural symbols and narratives sedimented in the traditions of communities over periods of time.

Negotiation of the 'middle'

What might be called a 'narrative subjectivity' emerges as a process of mediation between different philosophical accounts of time discussed at length in the three volumes of Ricoeur's *Time and Narrative*. At stake here

---

[78] Gadamer 1989:301.

[79] Gadamer 1989:299–307. In their Introduction, the translators draw attention to the 'key concept *wirkungsgeschichtliches Bewußtsein* which we have translated as "historically effected consciousness"' (p. xv). It has a double meaning: not just 'affected' by history but also 'brought into being – "effected" – by history and conscious that it is so' (p. xv).

[80] Ricoeur 1992:355.

is the temporal character of human experience. 'Purely' philosophical accounts of time, Ricoeur tells us, collapse into a whole series of aporias; time can neither be reduced to consciousness nor be given a coherent account without it. He thus sets out to show that the contrast between phenomenological perspectives, with the emphasis on the 'subjective' process of perceiving time, and the cosmological, with the emphasis on the 'objective' state of time as all-encompassing, is only ever resolved by a reflective application of the contrasting yet complementary narratives of history and fiction. Each perspective presupposes the other while yet concealing it; the cosmological cannot be measured except by the contingent subject, while the phenomenal always has to be referred back to some objective standard by which the passage of time is calculated. According to Ricoeur, the act of narration is a third mediating perspective which, by developing forms of mimetic activity, engages variants of the two major perspectives and brings them together into a unified discourse. Ricoeur's account of 'narrative identity' offers an alternative without reverting to a totalising subjectivity. In what Genevieve Lloyd calls a 'poetic resolution', he brings the experience of time and the activity of narration into a correlation: 'time becomes human by being organized after the manner of a narrative; and narrative in turn is meaningful to the extent that it portrays features of temporal experience'.[81] Such an argument, Ricoeur admits, is circular. Not, however, a vicious but rather a 'healthy circle': narrativity and temporality reinforce each other.[82] On the one hand, human time is always organised after the manner of a narrative; on the other, narrative is meaningful to the extent that it portrays the temporal character of human existence.

A narrative account of personal identity is made possible by the emplotment of that which somehow endures in the midst of what passes away. By enabling acts of memory and anticipation – whether through historical reconstructions of the past or fictional imaginative projections from the present – we make some sense of the disarming passage of time. The paradigmatic example for Ricoeur comes from Augustine's concept of the *distentio animi* which picks up and arranges the threads of memory into some self-stabilising form of 'autobiography', the narration of a 'self'. In Ricoeur's terms, we make a 'configuration out of a succession'.[83] Life

---

[81] Lloyd 1993:11.

[82] Ricoeur 1984:3.

[83] Ricoeur 1991:22.

has a 'pre-narrative capacity' or we would be incapable of grasping the form of a story, its 'followability'. But such a prefiguring has to be both configured in the present and transfigured by an imaginative application which bridges the gap between story and life. That is to say that, in addition to the configuring act of 'the well-told story', there is the transfiguring activity of reading which makes particular intellectual and emotional demands on the imagination. As the point of intersection between the world of the text and the world of the reader, the act of 'following' the story is the critical creative moment in which elements of the known or expected come up against what is unknown or innovative.

Yet the paradox of time remains. It endures, but it also passes and continually breaks through our attempts to understand, let alone 'narrate', it. If the strength of narrative is that it enables the plotting of a story, the weakness is that such narratives are themselves inherently unstable. Several plots can be woven from the same events. And the significance of discrete elements in any narrative is bound to change as different perspectives – and other narratives – are brought into view. Ricoeur admits this limitation, but argues that such a pluralism can be turned to advantage, allowing imaginative variations appropriate to the genre of the novel to bring out the unresolved questions at the heart of historical narrative. As a practice of the search for '*ipse*-identity' the construction of narratives remains at the level of what Ricoeur calls a 'thought experiment by means of which we try to inhabit worlds foreign to us'.[84] Such variations, however, do not evade but rather enable the crucial moment in the process of self-identification – what he discusses at greater length in *Oneself as Another* as the act of self-constancy, the attestation 'Here I stand.'

Ricoeur's whole project is, in many ways, summed up as a commitment to extending the limits of the self-reflexivity of 'hermeneutical phenomenology'. What I refer to as 'narrative subjectivity' is never, for Ricoeur, the 'achievement' of an isolated ego but the product of the intersubjective dialogue between self and other through which, after the manner of the Freudian *Durcharbeitung* of psychoanalytic therapy, the self finds itself in and through the otherness of the stories which it tells.[85] As Ricoeur himself puts it, the goal of the 'whole process of the cure' is to 'substitute for the bits and pieces of stories that are unintelligible as well

---

[84] Ricoeur 1988:249.

[85] See Kathleen Blamey, 'From the Ego to the Self', in Hahn 1995:571–603.

as unbearable, a coherent and acceptable story, in which the analysand can recognize his or her self-constancy'.[86]

This principle of a form of 'analogical mirroring', which Ricoeur takes from Husserl's fifth *Cartesian Meditation*, applies as much to history as to works of fiction. A truthful chronicle of the 'traces' of the past and the imaginative restructuring of temporal experience in a novel – the one, says Ricoeur, tending to 'blunt the edges' of the philosophical *aporias*, the other 'sharpening its sting'[87] – operate at different ends of a literary spectrum and make different demands of the reader, but in practice they overlap and raise the same questions, about truth, reference and meaning.[88] Something similar can be said for two complementary dimensions of a theology of dialogue. A faithful witness to the story which the community tells, both about its origins and about its history of engagement with the other, goes hand in hand with the imaginative retelling of that story as it finds itself mirrored in other cultures and reflected in the stories that others in their turn tell about themselves. If what motivates all narration is the *aporia* of time, making the other never the contemporary of the same, then theology faces the same challenge as Levinas's 'translation' from a Jewish to a Greek logic. His diachrony of the anarchic other underlines the provisionality of the concordance brought about through acts of narration and reading. The process of narration which establishes subjectivity has to be repeated, or, rather, constantly rebuilt and reinforced in response to different encounters with the other.

To link up with what has been discussed in the first half of the chapter, my argument is twofold: that such a repetition begins with the faithful obedience to the terms of the tradition which Levinas calls a 'liturgy of study', but that it opens up and demands further stages of interpretation. In explicating de Certeau's 'heterological law', which I described at the beginning of this chapter as a sequence of overlapping stages by which the same is disrupted by the return of the other, let us turn finally to Ricoeur's reworking of Plato's categories, the dialectic of the 'leading kinds'.[89] Ricoeur's intention, he tells us, is to 'say something meaningful about the past in thinking about it successively in terms of the Same, the Other and the Analogous'.[90]

---

[86] Ricoeur 1988:247.

[87] Ricoeur 1988:138–9.

[88] Ricoeur 1985:158–60.

[89] *Sophist* 254b–259d (see chapter 3, n1).

[90] Ricoeur 1988:143.

My intention here is to say something meaningful, 'something to do with God', for a theology of dialogue by applying Ricoeur's version of the categories to the inter-faith experience of the negotiation of a shared space.

Discerning the trace of the other

The first strategy, which Ricoeur associates with the thought of R. G. Collingwood,[91] sees history as a 're-enactment' of the past in the present. Historical construction is a work of the imagination which brings the world revealed by the trace and the world of the historian into a correlation which thereby annuls the sense of temporal distance. This, however, is precisely the problem: change and continuity through time cannot be thought by what amounts to an atemporal idealism. Reacting against Collingwood, says Ricoeur, 'many contemporary historians see in history an affirmation of otherness, a restoration of temporal distance, even an apology for difference pushed to the point of becoming a sort of temporal exoticism'.[92] Here we move into the sphere of the post-modern in which the prejudice of present interests has to be unmasked. Amongst Ricoeur's examples is Michel de Certeau for whom, as noted earlier, the desire for mastery inherent in the practice of historical writing is itself problematic. In so far as a philosophy which recognises that 'the past is what is missing, a "pertinent absence"' can make for a positive critique of the totalising ambitions of history, Ricoeur finds much to admire here, but, he asks, does such a 'negative ontology of the past' do justice to what is positive about the persistence of the past in the present? At the end of de Certeau's labours he finds the enigma of the trace of the other 'more opaque'.[93]

Far from dismissing these attempts, however, Ricoeur then proposes to bring them into line with 'a leading kind that itself associates the Same and the Other . . . the Analogous, which is a resemblance *between relations* rather than between terms per se'.[94] A 'tropological' approach to the

---

[91] Ricoeur 1988:144–7, commenting on Collingwood's *The Idea of History*, New York: Oxford University Press, 1956.

[92] Ricoeur 1988:147.

[93] Ricoeur 1988:149–51. Ricoeur allows that his notion of the debt which the historian owes to the past 'has some kinship with the one which runs throughout the work of Michel de Certeau' (p. 312, n42). With his concern to develop the 'logic of superabundance' he wants to place less emphasis than de Certeau on the experience of loss as a 'figure of otherness'. They are, nevertheless, in fundamental agreement that 'the writing of history does more than play a trick on death' (ibid.).

[94] Ricoeur 1988:151 (emphasis added).

dialectical relationship of same and other sees historical narrative in metaphorical terms as 'standing for' or 'taking the place' of the past. This resort to metaphor has the effect of closing the 'gap' between history and fiction. The demands made on historians and novelists in terms of truth and reference are clearly different; both, however, are caught up in what Aristotle in the *Rhetoric* would call a 'strategy of persuasion' which through the use of linguistic devices seeks to impose on the reader the 'force of conviction . . . that upholds the narrator's vision of the world'.[95] Instead of replacing the first two approaches, this focus on the role of metaphor turns their 'complex interplay' into a series of 'successive filters' through which the search for the truth of the past must move. This analysis of history in terms of 'three moments' in a single activity rather than a series of conflicting approaches has the effect, thinks Ricoeur, of combining Levinas's enigma of the trace, the deeply ethical 'signification without a signified', with a solution to the problematic of temporal distance. The trace unfolds itself across time through the traditional narratives which are inscribed in culture. Not only do these carry the trace of the past, they are also responsible for forming present consciousness of the past. The two have to be thought together. To borrow from Gadamer's powerfully stated opposition to the tradition of Romantic hermeneutics with its projection of a thoroughly unhistorical 'human nature': '[u]nderstanding is to be thought of less as a subjective act than as participating in an event of tradition, a process of transmission in which past and present are constantly mediated'.[96] If the dilemma can be stated as 'uncrossable distance or annulled distance',[97] the solution is a Gadamerian 'fusion of horizons' in which narrativity and temporality – to return to the central thesis of Ricoeur's study – mutually reinforce each other.

Understanding and reimagining history

With Ricoeur's 'three-moment' dialectic, which both questions and extends the limitations of the same–other relationship, the terms of a theology of dialogue begin to emerge. As the aporias of time are resolved by an imaginative discourse which brings into play the processes of 'reduction to the Same, the recognition of Otherness and the analogizing

---

[95] Ricoeur 1988:177.

[96] Gadamer 1989:290 (emphasis in original).

[97] Ricoeur 1988:220.

of apprehension',[98] so the theology which takes its rise from the experience of inter-faith dialogue – being set in the 'middle', between same and other – will utilise a similar dialectic to reimagine a history of inter-faith relations in which traces of the other are discerned as possible 'seeds of the Word'. By bringing different modes of self-identification into a correlation, Ricoeur's engagement with Levinas adds a hermeneutical 'detour' to their shared phenomenological project; with his attention to the fictional element of historiography, he makes for a further mediation between de Certeau's heterology of the past which haunts the present and Levinas's anarchic other which signifies without appearing. But how far – to return to Levinas's problem with which we opened the chapter – can such a project be extended without simply creating another totality?

What Ricoeur does is to attempt a mediation between the phenomenological 'subjective' form of time and the cosmological or 'objective' form, with a third – historical time.[99] This, he says, is a 'creation' which emerges from the shadow of the overarching concept of 'mythic time', the attempt to hold together the various celestial, biological and social rhythms of human experience. Ricoeur gives tantalisingly little attention to the way ritual both forms and expresses mythic time, preferring to focus exclusively on its function as a 'relay station' between 'the order of the world and that of ordinary action'.[100] Historical narrative has its own techniques for fixing time, 'reflective instruments' such as calendars and genealogies, by which the passing of time can be anchored and measured. It is significant, however, that, when Ricoeur probes further into the historian's act of fixing and following the traces of the past, he finds himself dissatisfied with the purely linear trajectories of time which often result and introduces Levinas's concept of the anarchic trace which 'signifies something without making it appear'.[101] For this reason, 'mythic time', in the form now of the imaginative variations played by fictional writing, makes its reappearance. Fiction provides a 'treasure-trove' of variant forms of discourse which compensate for any overemphasis in

---

[98] Ricoeur 1988:157.

[99] See Ricoeur 1988:104ff. The Kantian nature of Ricoeur's project emerges when he talks here about the conditions of possibility of the historian's 'intellectual tools' – 'or, rather, their conditions of significance'. He is indebted to Gadamer's concept of *Horizontverschmelzung*, bringing together the horizon of the interpreter and the horizon of the text through a *third* horizon, a fresh perspective different yet clearly dependent on the other two.

[100] Ricoeur 1988:106.

[101] Ricoeur 1988:125.

historical writing on linear models of time. In other words, around the fixed points of 'historical time' fiction develops an imaginative discourse which serves to heighten the significance of particular moments and to bring the past into a correlation with the present. Ricoeur admits the significance of the mythic idea of 'great time' which holds together the multiple recurring rhythms of life in all its forms, but his main interest is philosophical – 'the discernment of the universal conditions of the institution of the calendar'.[102] The particularity of the worlds which history and sociology of religions describe, and the possibility that such worlds might subvert a universalising thesis, are not considered.

As a more systematic account of de Certeau's 'heterological law' – essentially a recognition of the provisionality of all attempts to speak of the other – Ricoeur's account retains a certain validity. Relationships are always dialectical: my action affects the other, but I am also affected *by* the other. On the other hand, Levinas's warning, that Ricoeur's supposedly 'successive filters' do not allow of a neat synchronic process, expresses an important reservation. The process of inter-faith dialogue, in all its many forms, is never a straightforward negotiation of an unproblematic 'middle'. It remains, as Gillian Rose insists, always 'broken'.

Voices of abundance and reticence

Ricoeur concludes *Oneself as Another* with a greater 'equivocalness of the status of the Other on the strictly philosophical plane' than Levinas, with his conviction of the fundamental asymmetry of all human relations, would allow:

> Perhaps the philosopher as philosopher has to admit that one does not know and cannot say whether this Other, the source of the injunction, is another person whom I can look in the face or who can stare at me, or my ancestors for whom there is no representation, to so great an extent does my debt to them constitute my very self, or God – living God, absent God – or an empty place. With this aporia of the Other, philosophical discourse comes to an end.[103]

A similar reticence appears at the end of *Time and Narrative* where Ricoeur returns to the 'two archaic inspirations' of Western thought, the Hebraic and the Greek, behind which can be heard the voices of Augustine and

---

[102] Ricoeur 1988:104–6.
[103] Ricoeur 1992:355.

Aristotle, the sources of the phenomenological and cosmological perspectives on time which he has sought to bring together into a 'discordant concordance'.

This conclusion is remarkable for the very hesitancy with which Ricoeur sums up and reinstates the inscrutability of time and admits the limitations of his narrative resolution. He points to other literary genres within the Hebrew Bible, notably Wisdom literature, which show that 'narrative is not the whole story'.[104] Israel remains for Ricoeur the most powerful example of the self-constancy of *ipse*-identity which is derived from a tradition of founding events recorded in texts. Nevertheless, all narratives are particular and have a particular defining context. This alone argues against succumbing to what Ricoeur calls the 'Hegelian temptation'.[105] A community of faith, such as Israel, can still speak of discerning a unity in historical experience without presuming to have mastered the 'supreme plot'. Here Ricoeur's method wins out over content; the systematic discussion of a series of *aporias* does not itself constitute a system. The very particularity of narratives precludes such claims to mastery without, at the same time, disallowing both the right and the duty of a community rooted in historical consciousness to go on searching for the ideal vision of the meaning of history 'with its ethical and political implications'.[106]

Behind this reticence can be detected the voice of Levinas – the voice of Hebrew reason translated into Greek. Despite his scant regard for 'other others', it is precisely Levinas's Jewish perspective which subverts the pretensions of the synoptic totality by emphasising the diachronic incursions of the other. Levinas reminds us that the beginning of any story is arbitrary and particular; we cannot, to repeat, 'think origins' in any absolute sense. The act of saying which becomes said must always be unsaid and returned, in a manner which I have argued may appropriately be described as liturgical, to its origins in the ancient traditions which form a community of faith. But, again as Levinas would remind us, the mere repetition of familiar words and phrases can become a way of enforcing predictable outcomes. Liturgy can be subtly subverted into becoming a counter to the threat of the other by locking the community safely into a given tradition and providing a ready evasion of responsibility. When

---

[104] Ricoeur 1988:272.

[105] Ricoeur 1988:193.

[106] Ricoeur 1988:274.

Ricoeur's 'three-moment' dialectic is read against that particular 'context of otherness' which is inter-religious engagement, a different possibility is raised.

Destabilising encounters and dialogues with people of other faith traditions involve a movement – literal as much as metaphorical – over the threshold into a world where one's sense of identity is questioned; in a very real sense they can be considered liminal experiences.[107] To speak, however, of 'three moments' is not to suggest a temporal progression. Rather the self-attestation which would seek to synchronise all experience is constantly undermined by Levinas's diachrony of the trace. If there is a 'first moment' in a Christian theology of religions, it arises from the strictly anarchic otherness to which the living tradition of Judaism witnesses; in faithfulness to that trace of the Infinite, Judaism continues to 'haunt' the process of Christian self-identification. This can perhaps be considered analogous to Ricoeur's 'primary otherness', the passivity of embodiment: a closeness which yet demands the acknowledgement of difference. Such an experience of 'oneself as another', sharing yet strangely divided by a tradition which is, in a very real sense, a 'broken middle', forces us to return to the sources of the language of faith in a repetition of the foundational experiences which have formed the community. There the laborious process of learning and relearning the language of faith face to face with the other has to begin again.

Such an account of the Christian self has clearly got 'something to do with God' – with its promise of a continuing revelation of 'seeds of the Word'. Ricoeur's dialogue with Levinas finishes with the '*aporia* of the Other [where] philosophical discourse comes to an end'.[108] His reticence is, however, not the end of the story; the 'logic of superabundance' reminds us of a further perspective within which the successive filters of the imagination seek to go on telling the Christian story. I do not intend to follow Ricoeur in his account of the self in the 'prophetic

---

[107] See C. Jan Swearingen, 'Dialogue and Dialectic: the Logic of Conversation and the Interpretation of Logic', in Maranhao 1990:47–72. This commentary on dialogue as a liminal experience depends on the anthropological work of Victor Turner (see especially 1967 and 1969). In such a liminal encounter with the other can be discerned a ritual-like movement involving entry, consecration and return which has a certain similarity to Ricoeur's dialectic. Firstly, one responds to the invitation to cross by stripping away elements of one's previous life; secondly, one is initiated into what is new in the society one is temporarily part of and perhaps confronts something 'other' about oneself; thirdly one returns to translate the experience into a form comprehensible to the familiar world.

[108] Ricoeur 1992:355.

vocation' of the Jewish and Christian traditions.[109] It is important, however, in returning to the question which runs through this book – how a
universalist tradition can avoid totalising the other – firstly to note the
reticence with which Ricoeur approaches the topic of biblical hermeneutics. His remark that those who take up the Christian life 'are not led by
their confession either to assume a defensive position or to presume a superiority in relation to every other form of life'[110] is a welcome reminder
that theology is always ethical in Levinas's sense – that is to say, developed
from the relationship with the other, not prescribing the terms that that
relationship must take in advance. At the same time, the Christian story
of the 'economy of the gift', which I shall seek to develop through a theology of dialogue rooted in the biblical themes of hospitality and welcome,
does not suppress but positively enhances the stories told by others.[111] As
James Fodor puts it:

> Ironically, it is the Christian virtue of humility and not the modern
> liberal democratic ideal of tolerance which is genuinely open to the
> otherness of the stranger. For Christian humility cultivates a love for
> the particular in a way that does not negate the stranger or hide from
> itself its own temptations to coercion, its own lust for power, its own
> proclivities to sin.[112]

The question for a theology of dialogue is not how the otherness revealed
at the heart of selfhood can be synchronised into a more or less grand
strategy, but how, more radically and yet more humbly, a certain passivity in the face of the other is to be recognised as *intrinsic* to the Christian
vocation itself.

---

[109] At the end of the introduction to *Oneself as Another*, Ricoeur explains his decision to
exclude the final lectures from the published version as an 'asceticism' which allows a proper
autonomy to philosophical discourse (p. 23–4). The first of these lectures, 'The Self in the Mirror
of Scripture' is unpublished; the second is published in English translation by David Pellauer as
'The Summoned Subject in the School of the Narratives of the Prophetic Vocation', in Ricoeur
1995:262–75.

[110] Ricoeur 1995:263.

[111] Ricoeur 1996.

[112] Fodor 1995:20.

Dialogue and God

5

Telling the Christian story

I am arguing for an account of Christian subjectivity practised before the self-revealing God in responsible relationship with persons of another faith. Such an account recognises that the subject is constantly altered in face of the 'returning other' and therefore raises the question with which the last chapter ended – how 'a certain passivity' can be considered an intrinsic dimension of Christian selfhood. The concept of the self fragmented in face of the other has, of course, become a cliché of postmodern discourse. I have therefore concentrated on the very different, yet intimately connected, ethical philosophies of Levinas and Ricoeur, philosophers with roots set deep within their respective religious traditions and sharing a common concern to engage philosophically with some of the terrible events of the twentieth century.

In Levinas, Fackenheim's 'voice of Auschwitz' – the 614th commandment forbidding posthumous victories to Hitler – is never far away. As a Jewish philosopher concerned with an 'ethical translation' of the 'Greek' tradition, he writes in a performative mode which, I have argued, can be described as liturgical. In practice, liturgy for Levinas is the constant repetition of the Torah which, in study and learning rather than the ritual of the synagogue, calls the individual to responsibility for the Other. In philosophical terms, this translates as the maintenance of the tension between Saying and Said, the witness of Saying constantly deconstructing the 'violence' and 'betrayal' inherent in the discourse of the Said. The centrality of this concept of liturgy to Levinas's project has already been noted. For him, liturgy – 'a movement of the same unto the other which never returns to the same'[1] – is ethics itself. Faithful yet responsible practice of liturgy is not a way of enforcing predictable outcomes but of

---

[1] Levinas 1986:348.

developing a certain 'ethical rationality' or wisdom which cannot be reduced to, and therefore controlled by, consciousness.[2]

Ricoeur's project, by contrast, is less a translation than a mediation, an insistent engagement with the philosophical tradition which he traces back to 'the clash within me between my Protestant upbringing and my intellectual formation'.[3] Like Levinas, Ricoeur resists Husserl's idealism by positing the historicality of all human experience, and his version of a 'hermeneutical phenomenology' is similarly inspired by an ethical concept of the self as summoned to self-scrutiny by the other. But, whereas for Levinas the other is radically exterior, for Ricoeur the other is already mediated by symbols and inscribed in the texts of tradition. If Levinas is dominated by the voice of the other, two voices seek to make themselves heard in Ricoeur's writing: the voice of suspicion, always seeking a mediation in the 'conflict of interpretations' involving philosophy, literary theory and theology, and the voice of restoration which would seek to extend the possibilities for human living by a creative engagement with 'another world' to which tradition testifies.[4] Ricoeur is concerned not just to restore the richness and variety of metaphorical and figurative modes of speech, but to investigate how forms of narrative, whether history or fiction, succeed in redirecting or restructuring experience – in other words, how language transforms the reader of the text, turning him or her into what he calls a 'border-crosser'.[5]

This liminal dimension of the transfiguring act of reading the text reminds us of a distinction implicit in the argument of the last chapter: between ritual as a resolution of otherness in favour of the same, and liturgy as a celebration of gift which yet allows the other to break into and challenge the world established by ritual. If Ricoeur's mediation between the polarities of same and other by way of analogy in his 'three-moment' dialectic shows how narrative restructures experience, Levinas makes them rather less than *successive* filters'. The Levinasian echoes in the retrieval of the 'Jewish other', with which my account of *Nostra Aetate* concluded, is a reminder that the process of self-identification is never finished and always liable to be disturbed by the disarming sense of an

---

[2] See Barnes 2000:30–2.

[3] Ricoeur, 'Intellectual Autobiography', in Hahn 1995:5.

[4] See Williams 2000:133–4.

[5] Ricoeur 1998:87. Ricoeur says he owes the term 'border-crosser' to Hans-Robert Jauss and to 'what has been termed the school of "reception" '.

anarchic otherness. Levinas's project to establish ethics as 'first philosophy' may be problematic, but this is not to say that his insistence on the priority of the other does not contain an essential corrective to overly systemic theological accounts of relationality. To enter into a relationship with the other, still more to negotiate the world of the 'broken middle', is to have such uncritical universalism questioned, and to be forced to confront a certain anarchic otherness in oneself. As Levinas never ceases to remind us, I am never in control of my beginning, any more than I know my own death. Life is lived in face of the other.

Earlier I raised what is in many ways the crucial issue which runs through this book – the question of how the 'primary otherness' of the Church's relationship with Judaism can be considered determinative of the Church's relations with 'other others'. The point I have tried to make is that there is more to the Jewish matrix of Christian theology than a source of symbols and metaphors for the divine economy which can be quarried for their 'proper' Christian purpose. Christian discourse about God is anarchic in Levinas's sense. Its beginnings lie not with the story the Church tells about certain events in first-century Palestine, but in the 'context of otherness' which God alone establishes. This is what makes the 'middle' both 'holy' and yet 'broken', the place of God's single con- tinuous action of creation and redemption. The Word which God speaks and to which the Church responds is one with the continuing action of God's Spirit in the world – however difficult that continuity may be to ex- press. Like Paul agonising about the constancy of the God of the Covenant, the Church recognises a dual responsibility. Christians look, as it were, in two directions at once, with no choice but to go on generously responding to the mystery of God's self-gift wherever it is discerned. Once understood in this way, any hard and fast distinction between the very particular responsibility Christians experience before the Jewish people and what they come to recognise in face of the different yet no less de- manding engagements with Muslims, Buddhists, Hindus and other peo- ple of faith, appears problematic. Just as the continuing history of the Church's engagement with the Synagogue makes ethical demands on the way the Church seeks to tell its story, so the history which the Church is in the process of establishing with other communities must have a simi- larly ethical dimension. How, then, to bring a version of Levinas's 'ethi- cal rationality' into theology? How to learn 'a certain passivity' which is one with the responsible speech the Christian is called to exercise before the other?

Speaking of the other

These questions raise the topic of Christian personhood or subjectivity. In due course I want to argue that the Christian's dual responsibility is to be learned by returning theological reflection about the other
to the liturgical and sacramental practice of the Church where all theology has its origins. The mystery of the self-giving God which the
Church celebrates is the primary 'context of otherness' within which
all the negotiations which form us in relationship with others take
place. Christian subjectivity, in other words, is formed both by a faithful repetition of the language of faith and by a hopeful facing of an
irreducible other. But it is not at all obvious how the two can be held
together without covertly subsuming the latter within the former. Before proceeding, therefore, a measure of repetition of what has gone
before may be in order.

One can only conceptualise the other by linguistic representation, a
practice which is fraught with the dangers of betrayal and violence.
Whether we employ the ceaseless deconstruction of Levinas's spiralling
antitheses or work in the very different medium of Ricoeur's narrative of
self-attestation, the fundamental problem is how to speak of an existing
yet always elusive relation between same and other. By definition, the
other is incapable of articulating its otherness. Thus Gayatri Chakravorty
Spivak asks, in an article as critical of post-modern forms of discourse as
of the Orientalism they seek to deconstruct, 'can the subaltern speak?'[6]
The context in which this question arises will occupy us later in this chapter, and more fully in the next, when we turn to the recent history of the
Church in India. I raise it at this stage in order to link my earlier discussion about the 'question of the other' with the theological dilemma with
which I started and, more precisely, with the project of 'ethical heterology' to which, as I have argued, it leads. What is the significance of the
other for the same? Or, to use de Certeau's own terminology, how can
'countertraditions' lead to 'further possibilities of knowledge'?[7] That this
is an ethical, and not just a purely conceptual, issue is acknowledged by
de Certeau when he says of his own major concern that historians 'can
neither be satisfied with describing the fact by blindly postulating its
meaning, nor can they admit an unfathomable meaning which could be

---

[6] Spivak 1988.

[7] See Tan See Kam 1996:32.

conveyed by any kind of expression'.[8] In speaking on behalf of the other, the historian has to be prepared to take the responsibility and ethical risk of interpretation – in Ricoeur's terms to marry the 'gap' between novel and history, between imaginative and factual modes of narration.

The same ethical challenge which faces the historian must apply equally to the theologian. The historian is concerned with getting the past to challenge the pretensions of the present perspective through the writing of an 'other history'.[9] The discourse of the theologian is also heterological. It can never be enough to repeat the tradition in the language of the tradition, or the otherness instantiated in liturgy is domesticated to the sameness of ritual. The task is to allow the other to speak *as other* – by which I mean not just the other person but the whole 'context of otherness' within which all theology is done.

So far I have sketched a possible way forward in terms of 'ethical heterology'. In some ways, de Certeau's largely descriptive method feels like an idiosyncratic mix of Levinas's ethical responsibility before the face of the Other and Ricoeur's insistent mediation of the otherness revealed through historical and cultural contexts. As I have noted earlier, de Certeau never uses any 'meta-language' nor invokes some overarching theory. Instead he tells particular stories which analyse the logic to be discerned in the everyday practices by which people learn how to negotiate with others. Such stories, what might be called 'micro-discourses', can be understood in Ricoeur's terms as narratives which allow lives to be 'plotted' across time. But de Certeau's real interest is with the fissures, gaps and breaks implicit in such narratives which challenge any neat resolution of Ricoeur's 'filters of the imagination' in favour of analogy and metaphor. Ricoeur is certainly right in his central conviction that language is a mode of communication between persons before it is a means of representation. To that extent, *pace* Derrida, speaking comes before writing. Or, as Raimon Panikkar would put it, the dialogue of persons precedes and makes possible the dialectic of ideas.[10] Nevertheless, there is always the danger that the *logos* of philosophy in its concern for universal truth will relativise and reduce the disorderly

---

[8] De Certeau 1988:140.

[9] See O'Hanlon 1988; Pandey 1994, especially p. 221. The same problem is faced by the anthropologist. Thus Buchanan, 1995:22, speaking from the perspective of cultural studies, argues that the 'orthopractic question: can a just ethnography be written?' (raised in different ways by Talal Asad, Edward Said and James Clifford) is also a 'complex philosophical question: can the other speak *as* other?'

[10] Panikkar 1984.

yet life-giving world of metaphorical speech. This is why de Certeau comes close to Levinas in developing his version of the 'heterological law': the other always returns to reinscribe an anarchic absence within the space which philosophy works to fill. What Ricoeur speaks of as the 'aporia of the Other'[11] which brings philosophical discourse to an end is taken up by de Certeau in terms of the descriptive phenomenology of 'micro-discourses'. This method is quite explicitly ethical; the central image of constant departure and return puts the self-constituting subject into question. But it is also more implicitly theological, in that the journey is made in response to the Word God utters before us.

Already I have developed one important heterology, the 'event' of Vatican II and the story of the re-emergence at Vatican II of Christianity's Jewish other. Without a sense of this 'primary otherness', the Church's identity as that community of faith which is called to mediate the Good News of God's redemption through a variety of relationships with 'other others' could not be established. The achievement of *Nostra Aetate* was to record this shift in the Church's self-understanding. Little, of course, was said about how the Church was to express its relationship to other communities. In a sense that was left to practice and to the Christian wisdom of people engaged in the 'negotiation of the middle' – inter-faith dialogue in all its forms. But this is only to say that, if Christians are to live responsibly in the 'context of otherness', they have to learn how to discern there the 'seeds of the Word'. How Christian wisdom, more exactly the theological virtues of faith, hope and love, are to be formed and practised will occupy us in a later chapter. Before moving to that topic I want to stay with de Certeau's determination not to turn the engagement with the other into a totalising system. 'Ethical heterology', as I have tried to argue, is not a theory but a descriptive phenomenology. If such a project is genuinely to allow the other to speak as other, then – as de Certeau insists – it can only be pursued through particular 'micro-discourses' or studies which yet reveal a certain logic of practice in the way people respond to a present 'haunted' by the other.

A 'world Church' and the other

How is such a 'logic of practice' to emerge from *within* the dialogue? My interest is specifically in the effect that an open-ended engagement with the other has on Christian personhood. If it is the case that Christians are

---

[11] Ricoeur 1992:355.

called to respond to the Word by telling the story of their origins, then they have to concern themselves not just with the way that that story has to be related to origins which are strictly 'other', but also with the way that same story must be constantly adapted in response to the ever-changing demands of history and culture in the face of others' stories. The task, then, is to find a way of speaking of a continuity between the 'primary otherness' of Judaism and different forms or levels of engagement with 'other others' without simply totalising the lot into the history of the same. I intend to proceed in two complementary directions. In this chapter, I shall focus on the inter-personal dimension of de Certeau's heterological project; in the next I shall set this first level or stage of 'a certain passivity' before the other within its wider social and, more precisely, its ecclesial context. What links them together is ethics – in Levinas's sense. An ethical sensibility develops in response to the other, a consciousness of always existing in responsible relationship.

If de Certeau's phenomenology of the returning other is correct, then we are to expect a constant growth in this sensibility, as the subject seeks to respond to the traces of the other which continue to haunt the present. The heterology I want to pursue in the rest of this chapter has its origins in Vatican II's *Gaudium et Spes* – like *Nostra Aetate* one of the more unexpected results of the Council. As noted earlier, the Pastoral Constitution seeks to root the Church in the modern world, to be a Church which would address the 'signs of the times' by bringing the truths of the Gospel into a dialogue with the needs of the present day. There can be little doubt about the impetus which *Gaudium et Spes* has given to liberation theology in Latin America.[12] Strangely, however, its impact on political theology in Europe has been relatively limited.[13] This may be because its reading of history reflects a Church too comfortable with the intellectual challenge of a world shaped by Enlightenment values. What it misses, as McDonagh points out, is a sense of the tragic dimension of European life in the fifty years leading up to Vatican II – 'above all the chilling

---

[12] The exact grounding of Liberation Theology in its Latin American context is open to much debate. Latin Americans themselves tend to locate it firmly in their own soil and history (see Dussel 1992:391–402). The Latin American conference at Medellín in 1968, which gave a powerful impetus to the emergence of liberation theology, took as its theme 'The Church in the Transformation of Latin America in the Light of the Council'. Galilea, in Alberigo 1987:59–73, especially pp. 63–4, speaks of the 'undeniable influence of *Gaudium et Spes*' in enabling the Latin American Church to 'incarnate evangelization in history'. Gutiérrez's seminal paper, 'Hacia una teología de liberación', from which sprang his *Theology of Liberation*, was given one month prior to Medellín; it contains explicit references to *Gaudium et Spes*. See text in Hennelly 1990:62–76.

[13] See McDade, in Hastings 1991:422–43.

counter-sacrament of the Holocaust'.[14] In *Nostra Aetate*, Christianity's Jewish other very much haunts the text. *Gaudium et Spes*, with its sweeping self-confidence, is more obviously tautological.

Yet here, too, the other returns in an unexpected way. Arguably the most significant theme covered in *Gaudium et Spes* is the relationship between faith and culture. This has led to a rich explosion of inculturated 'local' theologies in the post-conciliar period.[15] In one sense, what the word 'inculturation' describes is simply a new term for a familiar experience. Any missionary faith – Islam and Buddhism as much as Christianity – has to consider complex yet essentially practical questions not only about the limits of adaptation to local circumstances, but also about how its own meaning is to be communicated.[16] In another sense, it is the experience which is new and which generates a new sensitivity to relations once safely stereotyped into a forgotten corner. A Church committed to living alongside people from different cultures and faith traditions finds itself having to do more than just adapt to a new situation; it must also discern what the new situation may reveal as a 'sign of the times'.

The most widely quoted definition of inculturation is ascribed to the Jesuit General, Pedro Arrupe. In a letter to the Society of Jesus in 1978 he speaks of inculturation as

> the incarnation of Christian life and of the Christian message in a particular cultural context, in such a way that this experience not only finds expression through elements proper to the culture in question, but becomes a principle that animates, directs and unifies the culture, transforming it and remaking it so as to bring about 'a new creation'.[17]

The particular value of this 'incarnation model' (which can be traced back to the Council itself[18]) is that it makes of inculturation something more radical than adaptation to changed circumstances, a matter of 'translating' given words, as if the Gospel is merely a text. Rather, if the Gospel is 'the Word' which God roots in the world through the action of the Spirit

---

[14] McDonagh 1985:90.

[15] See 'The Effect of the Council on World Catholicism', in Hastings 1991:310–97. The literature of 'local theologies' is enormous, as evidenced by Part 4, the section on Latin American, African and Asian theologies, in Ford 1997:405–76.

[16] See Biernatzki 1991:17.

[17] *Acta Romana*, 17, 1978; 256–81. See the further explanation offered by Roest-Crollius 1978.

[18] See AG 22; GS 58.

and goes on bringing to fruition throughout time, then clearly more is at stake in the practice of inculturation than some more-or-less mechanistic refashioning of an infinitely versatile truth. Culture is, of course, a notoriously slippery concept with various connotations, and *Gaudium et Spes* oscillates uneasily between culture in its anthropological and its more aesthetic sense.[19] However, the ambiguity which discloses a heterology lies less with any particular meaning of the word culture than with the tendency to instrumentalise it, to make it a 'thing' set apart from the everyday processes of engagement with persons of faith.

Now the point I want to press here is the ethical and political issue of the construction of culture. The shift in the meaning of 'culture', which Raymond Williams describes, from the 'active cultivation of the mind' to a 'configuration' of the spirit of a people, has had a profound effect on the way the other has been identified.[20] It is instructive, for instance, to note that this shift coincides with the beginnings of the Romantic movement, and with what Raymond Schwab in his magisterial study of Europe's 're-discovery of India and the East' calls the 'Oriental Renaissance'.[21] Anouar Abdel-Malek's brief but perceptive account of the origins of Orientalism brings out the political dimension of Europe's fascination with the East. Like Schwab, who notes that the rapid growth of oriental studies at the beginning of the nineteenth century was part of a much wider explosion of the physical and natural sciences, Abdel-Malek ascribes the phenomenon of Orientalism to the European humanist desire to broaden the classical concept of Greek culture to include the Islamic 'other'.[22] However, this romantic eurocentrism tended, he says, to become dominated by

[19] See *GS* 53 where the connotations of the term 'culture' are described rather than defined. Gallagher 1997:38 notes 'three levels of meaning': the older sense of 'self-cultivation', a more anthropological view as embodied in social systems, and 'an explicit recognition of the plurality of cultures'.

[20] According to Williams, this shift in meaning begins in the latter part of the eighteenth century as a response to the Industrial Revolution. 'From Coleridge, and later from Ruskin, the construction of "culture" in terms of the arts is seen to originate' (1987:61). In Matthew Arnold's definition, quoted by Williams, culture refers not just to 'the arts' in general, but to the object of aesthetic enjoyment, the intellectual and spiritual life of the individual: 'a pursuit of our total perfection by means of getting to know . . . the best which has been said and thought in the world' (see *Culture and Anarchy*, Murray: London, 1869; p. viii). At almost exactly the same time the term becomes synonymous with the object of study of the new science of social anthropology. Here the classic form comes from Edward Tylor: '[t]hat complex whole which includes knowledge, belief, art, morals, law, custom, and many other capabilities and habits acquired by man as a member of society' (see *Primitive Culture*, London: Murray, 1871; p. viii).

[21] Schwab 1984.

[22] Abdel-Malek 1963:102–40.

another interest: that amalgam of scholars, businessmen and adventurers whose only objective was to generate an understanding of the 'other' in order to pursue European interests. Behind the intellectual history of Europe's engagement with the East can be detected what Edward Said calls a 'missing dimension . . . the political one, much sadder and less edifying than the cultural one'.[23] Once reduced to an object of study, the oriental other becomes stamped with an identity of an essentialist character.[24] The idealist connotations which the term culture has developed have resulted in the identity of the other being determined not within its own terms but by the self-sufficient projections of the dominant power. Culture, whether intended in the descriptive or normative sense to list observable ways of acting in society or in its original meaning as a practice of self-cultivation, is never neutral; it always takes account of the relationship with the other.

This debate about inculturation would have been impossible without the voice of African and Asian bishops who made up the 'conscience of the Council' – a voice which began to surface in the course of the Vatican Council and has so much marked the post-conciliar period.[25] In the next chapter, when we turn in more detail to the experience of the Church in India, this background of Orientalism and the complex question of how identity is established and maintained in the 'middle' will become crucially important. The problems which face such an ethical and relational account of Christian subjectivity are clearly demonstrated by the experience of the Church in India where the empowerment of local churches has formed a vigorous, if problematic, reaction to what are often perceived as the orientalist tendencies of a eurocentric Church. As this particular example illustrates, in the 'context of otherness' any inter-faith dialogue is now inseparable from issues of poverty and justice.[26]

---

[23] Said 1993:235.

[24] Thus, according to Said's celebrated thesis, the imperial pretensions of Europe were pursued not just through military and economic power but by a whole mode of discourse: 'Orientalism' – a universalising and self-validating historicism, a praxis similar to patriarchy in which the Orient becomes Europe's feminine, and preferably silent, other (see Said 1978; 1986).

[25] See, for instance, the intervention of Archbishop Simon Lourdusamy of Bangalore who complained that 'the description of man in the schema applied to industrialized areas of the world . . . "but what about the greater part of humanity, in Africa, Asia and Latin America?" ' (from Wiltgen 1967:254). For an account of another Indian bishop's experience of the Council and attempt to implement its thinking see Fernandes 1997.

[26] Thus Pieris, 1988a and 1993b, advocates a paradigm for theology of religions which recognises the 'magisterium of the poor'. Theology in Asia will be based on the inseparable realities of the poverty and religiosity of the people.

Whatever is to be said about the development of liberation theology in Latin America as a counter-cultural movement, the form it takes in India is bound up with the response to people of other faiths and to a history of missionary engagement which retrieves forgotten perspectives for understanding the relationship with the other.

The second part of this chapter discusses such a retrieval, a 'micro-discourse' which shows how an active witness to the other goes hand in hand with a more passive willingness to wait upon the other. The example of the Jesuit missionary, Roberto de Nobili, to inculturate the Gospel in seventeenth-century India is linked with more recent experience of 'ashramic spirituality' and the practice of Jules Monchanin and Henri le Saux. Theirs is a graphic illustration of that adaptability to changed circumstances which is demanded of life in the 'middle' shared with the other. The aim, however, is not just to describe a Levinasian alternative to the orientalist mode of identifying the other over against the same. My point is that inculturation is not some bright idea dreamed up on the back of post-Vatican II enthusiasm. It has roots set deep in the traditions of Catholic Christianity.[27]

The practice of inculturation: an Indian heterology

Roberto de Nobili (1577–1656) arrived in India in 1605 and spent most of his life as a missionary in the city of Madurai in South India.[28] As a student in Rome destined for India, he was inspired by the letters of the extraordinary Matteo Ricci, who worked as mathematician, astronomer and theologian in China from 1583 until his death in 1610.[29] Responsible, however, for the direction of Jesuit missionary work was Ricci's

---

[27] See Andrew C. Ross's criticism of David Bosch's *Transforming Mission* in 'Alessandro Valignano: the Jesuits and Culture in the East', in O'Malley *et al.* 1999:336f. Admittedly written from a Reformed perspective, Bosch's otherwise comprehensive survey has one entry on 'The Gospel and Culture', in which 'accommodation' (Roman Catholic), and 'indigenization' (Protestant), are discussed as nineteenth- and early twentieth-century strategies for transmitting largely 'Western theology' to the 'mission field'. Catholic experience, particularly in Asia, is overlooked. Ross argues that a couple of mere 'asides' on Ricci and the early Jesuits are misplaced under the 'Medieval Roman Catholic Paradigm' and represent a 'massive lacuna . . . and a distortion of the Roman Catholic tradition'.

[28] The best-known and most accessible account of de Nobili's life is contained in Cronin 1959. Cronin's work, however, is based largely on the more extensive account contained in Saulière 1995, originally published in instalments in the magazine *New Leader* (Madras) in 1956–7. The editor tells the chequered story of the relationship between the two works in his introduction. For a summary of de Nobili's life and a detailed account of his Tamil works, see Rajamanickam 1972a.

[29] On Matteo Ricci and the early Jesuit missions in the Far East, see especially Ross 1993.

novice-master, Alessandro Valignano, who was Visitor of the Jesuit Missions in India and the Far East from 1573 until 1606.[30] Valignano was an energetic administrator, but he was also an imaginative and inspiring figure without whose influence Ricci's achievements would have been impossible.[31] His contact with China convinced him of the importance of learning the language and becoming familiar with the Confucian classics, if only as a matter of courtesy to a civilisation in which respectful demeanour, self-control and decorum were valued so highly. He was not so impressed by the peoples of India. His immediate judgment was that they lacked 'distinction and talent'. Their society was fragmented by caste, the rigidity of which he condemned as 'diabolic superstition', and he was less than optimistic about the prospect of converting people in whom he found such a poor aptitude for religion. He acquired a better opinion of the St Thomas Christians; he hoped they might form the nucleus for conversion of the higher castes.[32] Later, after his contact with the Far East, he modified his initial judgment.

When de Nobili arrived in Madurai in 1606, he ran into prejudices far more deep-rooted than Valignano's hasty first impressions and against which he had to battle for much of his life. St Francis Xavier, the greatest of the first generation of Jesuit missionaries, working through interpreters, had impressed the unsophisticated fisher-folk of the Malabar coast by the sheer force of his personality. De Nobili saw that, to make any impact on the leaders of a highly stratified society, he had to not only learn their language, but also find ways of adapting himself to the culture in which that language was set. He started to live as a 'Raja-sannyasi', a high-caste holy man, hoping thereby to become acceptable within Brahmanical society. This scandalised the established order of the Church in India – and many of his Jesuit brethren. De Nobili argued, however, that the adoption of Brahmanical customs in his personal lifestyle was a question not just of the etiquette of self-presentation, but of the *only* way in which Christian faith could be represented to such a society.

Much of the voluminous correspondence which passed painfully slowly from India to Rome and back again between the years 1606 and 1622 was concerned with whether the high castes could retain the traditional signs of their status – particularly the wearing of the thread which

[30] See Schutte 1980/85. Further material, mainly letters, in Moran 1993.

[31] See Ross in O'Malley *et al.* 1999:343.

[32] Schutte 1980, volume 1:129–35.

traditionally marks the 'twice-born' castes. Such customs de Nobili considered belonged 'solely to the political or profane order'. His opponents argued otherwise. De Nobili's defence was that his method of adaptation was simply following the practice of the early Church. Most importantly he emphasised that a precise situation was being addressed: the conditions in the Madurai mission (he specifically distinguished it from Goa) under which the Gospel must be preached if *these* people were to be converted to Christ. De Nobili worked away from the main areas of Portuguese power, in the middle of brahmanical society where the protection of colonial structures did not provide a ready base for mission. The Portuguese authorities complained that, in deliberately distancing himself from the Church they dominated, he was risking schism; de Nobili replied that, so far from setting up an élitist Church for convert Brahmins, he was seeking to overcome the high-caste perception of the Church as *de facto* 'fit only for low castes'.[33]

De Nobili's practice was élitist only in the sense that he knew that without the conversion of at least some Brahmins the mission would be a failure. And he remained always primarily a missionary whose main aim was the conversion of India to Christ – as he made clear on many occasions. In the letter he wrote to Pope Paul V after the crucial Goa conference of 1619, he says that 'we are all bound . . . to facilitate the conversion of those people and to imitate the tolerance and tenderness of our Holy Mother the Church, by throwing wide open to all men the door of salvation instead of driving them to perdition'.[34]

Viewed as purely theological documents, the two major Latin treatises with which he sought to defend his practice appear, for all their erudition, pragmatic and even calculating.[35] But, as Halbfass puts it, he was motivated by the 'uncompromising *desire to be understood*'.[36] His assumption was that whatever was not directly contrary to the Gospel could be employed in its service. Despite considerable opposition, his meticulously documented arguments eventually won papal approval in 1621.[37]

---

[33] Saulière 1995:187, quoting the 'manifesto' which de Nobili sent to Errama Setti, brother of one of the four governors of Madurai, in 1610.

[34] Saulière 1995:291.

[35] See de Nobili's *Informatio de quibusdam moribus nationis indicae* (1613), (Rajamanickam 1972b); and *Narratio fundamentorum quibus Madurensis Missionis institutum caeptum est et hucusque consistit* (1618–19), (Rajamanickam 1971).

[36] Halbfass 1988:53; emphasis in original.

[37] Saulière 1995:311–31.

In due course, his principles became official Roman policy. In 1659, *Propaganda Fide* echoed de Nobili by stating unequivocally that European missionaries were to take with them not 'France, Spain, or Italy or any part of Europe' but the Faith 'which does not reject or damage any people's rites and customs, provided these are not depraved'.[38]

The significance of de Nobili for the Indian Church

Today, de Nobili gets a mixed press in India, regarded by some as the prophet of Vatican II, by others as a forger and charlatan who encouraged caste and untouchability.[39] As de Certeau would remind us, like many historical judgments these say as much about the contemporary world as they do about the epoch they are addressing. In retrieving the significance of de Nobili for today's Church, it is important to avoid the sort of anachronistic judgment which would turn him into some proto-orientalist projecting an image of India as Europe's compliant other. It is true that he appealed to St Paul's practice on the Areopagus by teaching people 'that law which is said to have been lost'.[40] As Halbfass says, he 'had no fundamental questions as to the intercultural communicability of his message'; he was simply following in the footsteps of the Church Fathers who 'accepted the "natural light" of Greek learning'.[41] It is also true that, as Halbfass goes on to comment, the readiness to find 'a common basis of "natural religion" in India' could appear as 'a potential threat to the missionary impetus itself'.[42] It does not follow, however, that he was actively promoting a rationalist thesis about some universal 'religion' shared by all people. An early Tamil text, the 'Dialogue on Eternal Life', is written in the form of a traditional Hindu dialogue between guru and pupil, but its theology and philosophical principles are thoroughly

---

[38] *Sacrae Congregationis de Propaganda Fidei Collectanea*, volume 1; Rome, 1907; p. 42. The statement is reassuringly reminiscent of Vatican II's refusal to reject 'those things which are true and holy in these religions'(NA 2).

[39] Compare, for example, Wilfred 1993:9–18, with Massey 1995:87–9. A considerable literature on de Nobili has been opened up by the recent research of S. Rajamanickam (see especially Arockiasamy 1986).

[40] Saulière 1995:78, quoting a letter to de Nobili's Provincial, Fr. Albert Laerzio, 1608.

[41] Halbfass 1988:43.

[42] Halbfass 1988:43. The detailed reports of Jesuit missionaries, published in the first half of the eighteenth century as *Lettres Édifiantes et Curieuses*, were seized upon especially by deist philosophers anxious for material to support their critique of Christianity (see Halbfass 1988:44–6; Schwab 1984:146–8).

Thomistic. De Nobili was no forerunner of the Enlightenment approach to religion. He was thoroughly opposed to idolatry, subordinated the 'missing Veda' to Christian revelation and, as Clooney points out, was careful to counter the typical Hindu imagery of rivers mingling in a single ocean or roads leading to a single town.[43]

Bernard McGrane argues that it was typical of the Enlightenment to identify the other in terms of ignorance – or, to be more precise, ignorance of the causes of ignorance, the failure to enjoy that global view of the totality of experience which was regarded as the touchstone of truth.[44] The Christian religion, universal, unchanging, ordered and timeless truth, was fixed over against what were, at best, shifting and, at worst, degenerate 'other' religions. Such a perception arises from the Enlightenment shift from a philosophy rooted in practical issues, such as clinical medicine, juridical procedure, moral case analysis, the rhetorical force of argument, to a much more 'theory-centred' style of philosophy.[45]

It is not here that de Nobili belongs but in a world fascinated with the exotic and unusual, a world, says Toulmin, which 'never set ecclesiastics and secular writers against one another'.[46] De Nobili's novice-director, Nicolo Orlandini, the first historian of the Society of Jesus, was a man 'inclined towards the mild scepticism of the later Italian Humanism'.[47] Little is known about de Nobili's studies, except that he excelled at them; but the Roman College at the beginning of the seventeenth century was famous not just for its philosophy and theology but for classical learning, particularly Greek.[48] In his missionary work, de Nobili himself was mainly concerned with translation, not polemic, producing free versions of scripture in Sanskrit, Tamil and Telugu.[49] The better-known of his Latin apologias, the *Narratio fundamentorum*, intended for a very different audience in Rome, lays down basic principles for preaching the Gospel which begin not with a concept of religion but with the person of the

---

[43] See 'Roberto de Nobili's *Dialogue on Eternal Life* and an early Jesuit Evaluation of Religion in South India', in O'Malley *et al.* 1999:402–17.

[44] McGrane 1989:43–76.

[45] Toulmin 1990:30–5.

[46] Toulmin 1990:28.

[47] H. E. Barnes, *A History of Historical Writing*, New York, 1963; p. 132 (quoted in Amaladass 1988:4).

[48] See Garcia-Villoslada 1954:158–60.

[49] See, for example, de Nobili's version of the prologue to the Fourth Gospel, following the model of the *Bhagavadgītā*: the *Śrī Khristu Gita*, in Rajamanickam 1972a:86–90.

preacher himself.[50] The basic premise is that people will only listen to one whose manner of life is worthy.[51] De Nobili thus saw himself as the guru around whom disciples would gather, an enlightened one or *jñani*, come to teach the 'lost' part of the spiritual law.[52] As Arockiasamy says, de Nobili's theories of adaptation were not a 'clever strategy' but sprang from a 'humanism which enabled him to appreciate genuinely the value of another culture'.[53]

What makes de Nobili such a significant figure for the post-conciliar Church, especially in India, is that he embodies just those qualities and dispositions of faith needed for a re-reading of the Gospel tradition which are recommended by Vatican II for the renewal of religious life.[54] In brief: he saw that, without a personal adaptation of his life to the ideals and spiritual values expected of an Indian holy man, no adaptation of his message was likely to be effective.[55] The question to ask of de Nobili is not, therefore, the essentially 'modern' question of how different languages of faith correspond, but a prior question about subjectivity or self-appropriation – what allows for self-understanding in face of the other? It is in the addressing of this more 'post-modern' question that we are taken back to de Nobili's 'pre-modern' world and to the religious principles and practice of the Society of Jesus which inspired a new approach to mission.

The motivation for mission: responding to the gift of God's love

What was it that motivated men like Roberto de Nobili? At the heart of the *Spiritual Exercises of St Ignatius of Loyola* is a sacramental contemplative vision of the grace of God at work transforming the world, a work in which the Father asks human beings to co-operate as companions of the

---

[50] There is no equivalent for the word 'religion', in its post-Enlightenment sense, in Hinduism. As understood by de Nobili, the polyvalent term *dharma* is both 'truth', the knowledge that comes from God, and 'virtue', the right practice which follows from this revelation, but is not to be identified in any uncritical way with civil customs and laws (see Arockiasamy 1986:289ff.).

[51] For example, *Narratio* 1.1: 'Evangelicus concionator illam institutere debet vivendi rationem, qua dignus judicetur ab iis inter quos versatur, qui audiatur', Rajamanickam 1972b:6ff.

[52] Arockiasamy 1986:350–7.

[53] Arockiasamy 1997:805.

[54] Although asking religious orders to return to their own founding documents, the Council's 'Decree on the appropriate renewal of religious life', insisted that the ultimate norm was the gospel (see Sandra Schneiders, 'Religious Life', in Hastings 1991:157–62).

[55] See E. Hambye, 'De Nobili and Hinduism', in Gispert Sauch 1973:326–7.

Son.[56] Essentially, the *Exercises* are a way of entering into the Gospel story, a process of recognising and responding to the love of God made manifest in Christ.[57] Thus in the final exercise, the '*contemplatio ad amorem*', the exercitant asks for 'interior knowledge' that 'all that is good and every gift descends from on high'.[58] This is the high point of a contemplative sensitivity inspired by the gratuitous gift of God; yet the same exercise begins with the note that 'love ought to find its expression in deeds more than in words'.[59] The point is that the formula 'finding God in all things' – which, as de Certeau reminds us, dominated Ignatius's life – is to be taken with utter seriousness.[60] The interior movements of the Spirit of prayer 'in me' are a necessary starting point, but they open up a more universal vision of God found in the events and encounters which take place 'before me' – in the world of the other. In other words, what the *Exercises* encourage is a dialectic of 'intention' and 'mission', or what de Certeau calls the 'subjective' and 'objective' orders, the one responding to the interior movement of the Spirit, the other to the Word of God revealed through the Church.[61]

This dialectic developed in the early Society a 'style' of mission which was almost synonymous with 'pilgrimage', a term which, says O'Malley, recalls the particular circumstances of Ignatius's own personal journey.[62] Hence the strong motivation towards 'finding God through searching'.[63] But it is also written into the text of the *Exercises*, both into the rules for discernment[64] and into the various notes, additions and supplementary considerations. These also have a specific apostolic or missionary purpose – in particular the short paragraph called the 'presupposition', a brief statement which precedes the *Exercises* proper. It sets the tone for the

---

[56] In this account I have followed the translation of the original texts, including the *Spiritual Exercises* and the *Autobiography*, in Munitiz and Endean 1996. Ignatius's life and the origins of the Society of Jesus are well covered in a number of secondary works, especially Dalmases 1985 and Ravier 1987.

[57] For a clear overview of the structure of the *Exercises* and the pivotal points of the retreat, see Lonsdale 2000:126–41.

[58] *Exx* 237.

[59] *Exx* 230.

[60] De Certeau 1966:173–83.

[61] De Certeau 1966:176.

[62] O'Malley 1993:270f. See also O'Malley 1994.

[63] See E. Przywara, *Deus Semper Maior*, Fribourg, 1940, volume 3; pp. 404, 427 (quoted in de Certeau 1966:173).

[64] *Exx* 313–36.

retreat and forms a climate of mutual respect between director and exercitant favourable to the disclosure of thoughts and feelings:

> So that the director and the exercitant may collaborate better and with greater profit, it must be presupposed that any good Christian has to be more ready to justify than to condemn a neighbour's statement. If no justification can be found, one should ask the neighbour in what sense it is to be taken, and if that sense is wrong he or she should be corrected lovingly. Should this not be sufficient, one should seek all suitable means to justify it by understanding it in a good sense.[65]

There is something of Ignatius's own history reflected in this brief text.[66] The ecclesiastical world he confronted was deeply suspicious of any form of personal revelation or 'illuminism' which appeared to bypass the mediation of the Church. Thus the text reflects Ignatius's desire to re-assure the authorities about his orthodoxy.[67] But he is also concerned with the promotion of an atmosphere of trust – and to that extent the text is deeply subversive. Contemporary norms of engagement with the other were built on confrontation. As Walter Ong's analyses of the rhetorical tradition in the West have demonstrated, the predominant style of teaching and learning in medieval universities 'remained basically oral and deeply agonistic in life-style and intellectual style'.[68] This was the academic system which Ignatius himself underwent, a system of adversarial disputations in which the other's 'proposition' was the enemy to be defeated. His text is an exhortation to temper the tendency to polarise opinions with a conscious attitude of openness and mutual respect. But, set alongside the 'Rules for thinking with the Church', which express Ignatius's strict sense of orthodox belief and obedience to authority,[69] it is striking in its insistence on a fair and open attitude to the other. The

---

[65] *Exx* 22. Studies based on the sixteenth-century directories (originals in *Monumenta Historica Societatis Iesu*, volume 76; collection translated by Palmer 1996) show that the presupposition antedates the annotations proper (*Exx* 1–20), and was intended to safeguard the quality of the retreat relationship. By 1599, however, with the publication of the official directory, the purely apologetic function of the presupposition has taken over and it is only to be given where necessary (see Palmer 1996:244, 311; Arzubialde 1991:61–7; Ivens 1998:22–5).

[66] The anonymous 'E.D.' suggests that the text's origins lie in the harassment Ignatius received from the Inquisition and his realisation that human beings are only too ready to condemn rather than defend one another (see 'El Presupuesto', *Manresa*, 44 (1935), 327–42; see also *Autobiography*, 67–72, in Munitiz and Endean 1996:46–8).

[67] See Palmer 1996:232.

[68] Ong 1981:126.

[69] *Exx* 352–70; the tension between obedience and openness is discussed by Lonsdale 2000:166–9.

underlying assumption is that both parties are concerned with allowing 'the Creator to work directly with the creature, and the creature with the Creator and Lord',[70] not with debate or argument in which attack and defence of prepared positions was the mark of academic prowess.

It is significant that Ignatius speaks of defending or saving the other's *statement* from error. The point is that, if God works directly in the well-disposed individual, then truth is communicated through what is actually articulated in the discernment process with the director.[71] This is not to give some mystical status to language as such, nor to deny that careful discernment of the conversation is needed, but to say that without an honestly sustained conversation there can only be, at best, a vague approximation to truth or, at worst, the triumph of the more forceful speaker. For the first generations of Jesuit missionaries, the experience of the *Spiritual Exercises* was a powerful motivation not just to follow Christ as companions on pilgrimage, but also to recognise in the other a basic good will which allowed communication to take place.[72] That de Nobili and others saw their vocation in terms of witness to Christianity as the true faith is clear; it could scarcely have entailed anything else. But respect for the person, and for what the person says, is more than a prudential attitude, a necessary prelude to conversion. In the course of the transactions during the *Exercises*, *both* the director and the retreatant are made responsible for examining the limits of their understanding of what is being communicated between them. What Ignatius proposes in the *Exercises* is an ethical principle which is to apply, by extension, to all forms of encounter and conversation with the other.[73]

Missionary practice from a 'place' of weakness

That the presupposition and the spirit of the *Exercises* had a powerful influence on the intellectual and religious ethos of the early Society is clear from the emphasis which came to be put on that ministry called

---

[70] *Exx* 15.

[71] Annotation 15 makes it clear that the director's role is to remain 'in the middle like the pointer of a balance'. The early directories reflect Ignatius's insistence that the exercitant interpret 'whatever is said or done in his regard in good part' (see Palmer 1996:19,166).

[72] On the sources of theological motivation for mission, see Barnes 1992:53–60. The article takes as examples Matteo Ricci and Ippolito Desideri – the latter responsible for a short-lived Jesuit mission in Lhasa in the early eighteenth century.

[73] Nicolau 1980 discusses the presupposition as a necessary dimension of contemporary ecumenism.

'devout conversation'.[74] This was a certain practical skill which Ignatius expected Jesuits to acquire – an ability to raise ordinary encounters to an intellectually more serious and edifying level. It also typified the patient and rigorous engagement with people from different religious and cultural traditions whom Jesuit missionaries encountered, especially in India and the Far East. What makes de Nobili such a powerful model for contemporary missiology in India is that he lived and worked, like Ricci before him, away from the centre of colonial power, in a world defined by the other. To invoke a distinction of de Certeau's, the missiology of the Portuguese was based on a *strategy* of establishing a place which would erode time, whereas de Nobili relied on the *tactics* of adjustment – 'a clever *utilization of time*, of the opportunities it presents and also of the play that it introduces into the foundations of power'.[75]

This 'micro-discourse' illustrates the working of 'the heterological law', how the 'returning other' which insinuates itself back into the discourse of the same subtly influences and changes that discourse. De Certeau shows how ownership of place is challenged by a 'tactical' use of time. Without a 'place to stand' the powerless still find ways to negotiate through the skilful use of time. Their tactic of resistance precludes any 'totalising attempt' on the part of the powerful to stand above or outside time. If the powerful have a place which can be considered their own, an environment which they control, the powerless operate from a position of weakness yet maintain the freedom to move across boundaries in order to adapt to present needs.

De Nobili's desire to distance himself from the political influence of the Portuguese was easily misinterpreted. In fact, he was only acting out of the spirit of Ignatius's presupposition and the sacramental contemplative theology on which it was based. If he himself had received the truth of the Gospel quite gratuitously, then the same would apply to the other. And this would have implications for the way the Gospel is presented. It must be explained without violence and without unnecessarily

---

[74] See Ignatius's own account in *Autobiography*, 21, 34, 65, 88, in Munitiz and Endean 1996. For the early history of Jesuit practice, see Clancy 1978; O'Malley 1993:110–14; see also de Certeau 1966:178–9.

[75] See de Certeau 1984:xviii–xx, 29–42 (quotation from pp. 38–9; emphases in original). The distinction seeks to account for the practice of *bricolage*, 'artisan-like inventiveness', and *braconnage* – literally 'poaching', a way of operating 'in the shadows'. For Certeau a strategy is a calculus of force-relationships which becomes possible when the subject of power assumes its 'proper place'. A tactic is a calculus which cannot count on any border distinguishing it from the other.

violating social practices.[76] For de Nobili to communicate with anyone –
let alone with people who already lived within a sophisticated religious
community such as he found amongst the Brahmins of Madurai – would
take time and demand much painstaking effort at learning to understand
their culture and customs. He sought actively to witness to the Gospel,
but he also recognised the need for a certain passivity, a waiting within
the world of the other.

Spirituality and the practice of inculturation

Some of de Nobili's most significant successors are to be found in the contemporary ashram movement in India. Undoubtedly, for the Roman
Catholic Church, Vatican II's call to return to the sources of tradition
brought a new freedom to experiment.[77] New foundations in India recalled the efforts of the Bengali brahmin Brahmabandhab Upadhyay at the
turn of the century to establish a contemplative community which would
become the source of a new Hindu–Catholic spirituality.[78] The British
Benedictine monk, Bede Griffiths, leader–*acarya* of the Saccidananda
Ashram at Śantivanam, Tamil Nadu, has enjoyed a reputation for daring
experiment in the 'dialogue of religious experience' far beyond the bounds
of India itself. Like Brahmabandhab, he advocated the removal of theology
from the exclusive ambit of seminaries and theological colleges and for it
to be incarnated in the religious life of the people. A controversial figure,
whose frank and heart-felt views often risked the disapproval of the more
conservative in the Church, he nevertheless represented for many years the
best of what has come to be known as ashramic spirituality.[79]

This is an approach to inculturation which arises from the conviction
that Indian theology must be founded not just on Indian thought-forms,
but, as de Nobili insisted, on a properly Indian lifestyle as well. Although
popularly associated with the place where the *guru* lives and therefore
sometimes translated as 'monastery', the word *aśrama* in Sanskrit refers

---

[76] See Rajamanickam 1971:31–5.

[77] The literature on Christian ashrams is immense. The more significant publications
include Monchanin and le Saux 1956; Griffiths 1966; Vandana 1978; see also Wilfred 1993:41–69.

[78] Brahmabandhab was convinced that Christian faith had to be expressed through the
language and philosophical categories of Vedanta. His famous declaration that he was a 'Hindu
Catholic' stretched the limits of adaptation almost to breaking point and contributed to his
personal tragedy (see the account in Staffner 1985:89–109). Largely rejected by the Catholic
community in his lifetime, he is now celebrated as a pioneer (see Lipner and Gispert-Sauch 1992).

[79] See Griffiths 1978; 1983; and the biography by du Boulay 1998.

primarily to what *happens* in the place, to the spiritual environment which enables the act of striving for release or *moksha*. The refusal to dichotomise theology and spirituality or religious practice is perhaps the greatest strength of the ashramites' approach to inculturation. What they propose is a new way to make Christ present – through a thoroughly Indian form of religious life animating the heart of an Indian Church.

In fact, the form of Catholic missiology known as ashramic spirituality predates the Council. The first of the modern Catholic ashramites, the French diocesan priest Jules Monchanin, never wanted to be a missionary in the traditional sense. He always insisted that his vocation was to work in an ordinary parish under the local bishop, at the same time giving himself to a contemplative life of study and prayer which would root the Church in the life and culture of India. If de Nobili's overriding concern was, in Halbfass's words, to 'be understood', Monchanin saw the need, first and foremost, *to understand*, to become himself more and more steeped in the cultures and traditional religions of India. With Henri le Saux, known as Swami Abhishiktananda, he founded Śantivanam in 1950. In the story they told about the ashram, they spoke of the life of contemplation, 'borrowing their prayers from [the Church's] divinely inspired liturgy', as essential to the missionary task of bringing Christ to India.[80] It was Monchanin's tragedy never to see the fruit of his labours. He had to struggle to be allowed to come to India, arriving eventually in 1939, just as the war began. No great communicator, dogged by poor health, and apparently lacking in basic organisational skills, he died in 1957 before the Council made his theological vision a reality.[81]

Abhishiktananda, on the other hand, another seminal figure in the recent history of Catholic India, lived to enjoy the post-conciliar 'spring'.[82] His relations with Monchanin were never easy. If Monchanin was first and foremost a Catholic theologian in the classical mould, Abhishiktananda wanted a more radical form of inculturation, to enter as fully as possible into the *advaitic* experience described in the Upanishads.[83] The

---

[80] Monchanin and le Saux 1964:10–11.

[81] See the very full biography by Jacquin 1996, the briefer account by Rodhe 1993, and the memoir by de Lubac 1966. For letters (to his mother) see Jacquin 1989. The only collection of Monchanin's writing in English is Weber 1977 (a translation of *Écrits Spirituels*, edited by Monchanin's close friend Edouard Duperray; see Monchanin 1965).

[82] For an account of Abhishiktananda's life and writing told through his letters, and bibliography, see Stuart 1995; see also Vattakuzhy 1981.

[83] See especially Abhishiktananda 1974a:41–50.

failure of the Church in India, he said, was that 'real Hindus' perceived in her little more than an efficient administration.[84] The latter years of his life were spent as a wandering *sannyasi*, committed to bringing to eschatological completion God's ancient Covenant with humankind.[85] We will return to the contrasting theologies which inspired Monchanin and le Saux in the penultimate chapter where the differences between them will be taken as illustration of the theological dimensions of the 'dual responsibility' of Christian faith. In concluding this chapter, I want only to point to a further dimension of the ashramites' response to the inculturation debate in India, a dimension which will be further explored in the next chapter: its lack of social context.

Abhishiktananda's reference to 'real Hindus' has distinctly élitist overtones. There is more to Hinduism than the sophisticated philosophy of the Vedanta and more to the culture and social reality of India than the ritually ordered round of life in the villages. In recent years, ashramic spirituality has come under attack. The most influential of contemporary Asian theologians, Aloysius Pieris, criticises it for being divorced from the economic and political reality of the mass of ordinary people. By training and inclination a buddhologist, Pieris brings a very precise experience of dialogue with a deeply ethical tradition to his theological writing. He is as critical of what he sees as the naive Marxist-inspired activism of much 'imported' liberation theology as he is of an equally 'foreign' obsession with Eastern 'mysticism'.[86] An even more trenchant critic is the much respected biblical exegete George Soares Prabhu. Ashrams, he says bluntly, are just not suitable places for doing theology. In a subtle way, they are still dominated by largely Western concerns:

> What are the Christian ashrams trying to do? . . . Are they trying to cure the sickness of a post-Christian Western society by giving them anti-consumerist values from a highly idealized 'book' Hinduism; or are they addressing themselves to a decaying Indian society in order

---

[84] Abhishiktananda inspired a whole generation of Indian priests and religious. The reference to 'real Hindus' and the opinion that only those 'on the fringes of the Hindu world' have listened to the Gospel is from a twenty-three-page letter, dated 13.10.69, sent to Fr. X. Thamburaj SJ, then a student of theology, in response to questions about a possible Indian Christology.

[85] See especially Abhishiktananda 1974b:168ff., with its cosmic vision of the vocation of monk and priest, preparing the way for the coming of Christ through the practice of mystical prayer and the celebration of the Eucharist.

[86] See in particular, 'Western Models of Inculturation: Applicable in Asia?' in Pieris 1988a:51–8.

to share with them the Christian experience of liberation and give them the healing values that Christianity has to offer?[87]

For Soares Prabhu, to speak of inculturation in the language of incarnation is only valid if it enables an encounter with the mainstream of Indian society – which includes the structures of oppression at its heart.[88]

De Nobili's practice of inculturation is a graphic illustration of that adaptability to changed circumstances which is demanded of life in the 'middle' shared with the other. Clearly more is involved than a translation of the language of faith. But how much more? De Nobili's example represents a conversion, a 'translation' of the self in face of the other as it becomes a 'border-crosser', moving over the threshold into the world of the other. His experience, and that of other early Jesuit missionaries, waiting and learning within the boundaries set by the other, raises the possibility of an alternative to the Orientalist or – in de Certeau's terms – 'strategic' identification of the other by an approximation of the unknown to the known. For de Nobili and Ricci before him, what a later generation refers to as inculturation involves a constant 'tactical' rediscovery *in* the known of what is unknown, *in* the same of what is other. However such an account is to be given – and my argument is that this can only be done in and through the actual practice or engagement with the other and not before – the starting point lies with what was described earlier as the retrieval of a contemplative awareness of the Spirit of God sanctifying the world. But it cannot end there. At some point, the project of inculturation has to acquire an ethical 'edge' which may become distinctly political. Hard-hitting critiques of ashramic spirituality raise serious question marks over the value of a dialogue with high-caste Indian religion which is blind to issues of justice. But is a more politically conscious dialogue simply expressing a faithfulness to the prophetic nature of the Gospel? Or, by taking a stand on principle, does it make any sort of engagement with the other that much more risky?

---

[87] From a letter to the participants in the Ashram Aikiya Satsang, November 1991, published as an appendix to Vandana 1993:153–6. For the ashramites' spirited response see *ibid.* pp. 157–60; also Vandana's more extensive discussion of the contemplative-active tension in Vandana 1982.

[88] Soares Prabhu argues that in a society as culturally diverse and socially divided as India inculturation can only be achieved through the model of conversion (see Soares Prabhu 1984, and 'From Alienation to Inculturation', in John 1991:55–99). For the influence of Soares Prabhu on the Indian Church, see D'Sa 1997.

6

Reflecting on 'an other' experience

My point in introducing the 'micro-discourse' of Roberto de Nobili negotiating the complex socially and historically conditioned 'middle' of inter-religious relations was to retrieve a very specific pre-modern context for Christian mission, a context governed by a Catholic humanist spirit of contemplation. This chapter continues the story. Here, however, the emphasis shifts from the contemplative to the more ethical dimension of Christian personhood.

The question raised by the dialogue between Levinas and Ricoeur asks how a certain passivity can be reconciled with the Christian commitment to prophetic speech before the other. So far, my reflections have remained very much at the level of the lone individual 'taking time' within the space controlled by the other to respond to the interior movement of the Spirit. De Certeau himself joined the Society of Jesus intending to be a missionary. There can be little doubt that the spirituality of Ignatius, with its guiding image of the apostolic 'contemplative in action', formed de Certeau's vision of the Christian life as a constant departure.[1] Like Roberto de Nobili in the seventeenth century, he embarked on a lonely Levinasian 'Abrahamic journey' into the unknown. I finished the last chapter by extending the Christian's 'horizons of contemplation' to include the wider social reality, thus raising more intractable ethical questions about power, visibility and resistance. The subject of our next 'micro-discourse' is the wider ethical and political 'context of otherness' within which the Church must find its own place.

---

[1] On de Certeau as theologian see especially Bauerschmidt in Ward 2000:209–13 and Bauerschmidt 1996a.

This chapter begins with the shift in India from an inter-faith dialogue based on religious experience and ashramic spirituality towards forms of liberation or *dalit* theology, a populist movement of solidarity with the poor and oppressed of caste society. Much of the impetus behind liberation theology comes from a recovery of the sense of God revealed in the other – the poor, the stranger, the marginalised. As Metz reminds us, one expects to find God not in 'the system' or the established institution but in the voice which breaks into and challenges the system.[2] The catalyst for theology of religions in Europe was the Shoah. In India, the dispossessed of caste society have added an ethical dimension to inter-faith dialogue. In presenting a brief overview of the Indian experience my aim is not, however, to attempt a critique of a movement which is still very much in its infancy. It is, in the first place, to draw attention to the way the Indian churches have sought appropriate forms of inculturation into the full social and historical reality that is contemporary India. Thereby I hope to show how the theological sensitivity towards the living tradition of Judaism initiated by *Nostra Aetate* works itself out in an ethical response to other relations as well. As Felix Wilfred puts it, Indian theology is not concerned with 'comparing and contrasting various religions vis-à-vis Christianity' but with focusing attention on 'the specific contribution which Christianity can make today to India and to humankind at large, which will also make evident its unique character'.[3]

Indian Church and Indian society

Not only does India present an extraordinary array of communities and peoples amongst which the Church has sought to 'inculturate' itself for centuries, but to contemplate any form of mission in India today is very quickly to enter into a sometimes contentious intra-Church debate about the place of Christian revelation in the wider debate about India itself.[4] Christians have always had to face the charge of being non- or anti-Indian, the agents of some colonial conspiracy. And in many quarters the suspicion remains that, despite – and even because of – the move towards local inculturation, as instanced in the introduction of the vernacular and Indian symbolism

---

[2] Metz 1990, an article entitled 'With the eyes of a European Theologian'.

[3] Wilfred 1993:237.

[4] See e.g. Amalorpavadass 1981 for a comprehensive record of the conference held at the NBCLC in that year; see also the essays collected in van Leeuwen 1984 and Kunnumpuram and Fernando 1993. For an account of Christianity's part in the nationalist movement and contribution to the emergence of independent India, see Padinjarekuttu 1998.

into the liturgy, the Christian churches have a divided allegiance.[5] Schools, hospitals, colleges and other highly prestigious institutions give Christians a prominence out of all proportion to their numbers. But to many, both in and outside the Church, they speak of foreign power rather than disinterested identification with the needs of the people of India as a whole. Over the years, a lengthy and at times highly sophisticated dialogue has produced forms of local Indian theology, both Catholic and Protestant, which respond to the thought patterns inherent in Indian culture and religion.[6] Much of this theology is now under suspicion. Not only is it regarded as reflecting an orientalist ideology of an India constructed by European, and particularly British, interests, but, more importantly, rejected as too dependent on high-caste Brahmanical Hinduism – and therefore colluding with the systemic injustice which is endemic to contemporary India.

In a rapidly changing national and international scene, the patterns described by Indian politics do not resolve themselves straightforwardly. India, of course, has a secular constitution, a fact which seems curiously anomalous in a nation of so many religions and raises as many awkward questions as it presumes to solve.[7] Various lines of critique, each seeking to reconcile the demands for some level of cultural unity with the reality of religious pluralism, have been proposed.[8] In what follows I want to focus on one major dimension, the tension between two cultural–religious forces: militant Hindu revivalism and an increasingly strident low-caste insurgency.

This volatile mix of extreme nationalism, on the one hand, and conflictive liberation movements, on the other, represents a struggle for Indian identity with its roots fixed in different perceptions both of the past and of the contemporary reality to which it has given rise. The extent to which the encounter between India and Europe, more particularly

---

[5] See, for example, the polemic by Shourie 1994, which originated from an invitation to address and participate in a CBCI consultation on *Paths of Mission in India Today*, held at Pune in 1994, and the equally vigorous responses by Narchison 1996 and Mangalwadi 1995. Shourie takes the line that missionaries have only ever sought to destroy Hinduism. Narchison points to changes in ecclesiology, quoting the CBCI declaration at Pune which stressed the importance of the dialogical attitude: 'a courageous open perception and recognition of others as others' (p. 60). Mangalwadi tries to show that what the missionaries experienced as the 'conflict of duty and interest' is a crucial issue for the future of contemporary Indian civilisation (p. 51).

[6] The most detailed account of Indian theology remains Boyd 1975. More recently the story, with greater weight on the Catholic tradition, has been brought up to date by Wilfred 1993.

[7] On the tension between 'secularism' and religion in Indian politics, see especially Nandy 1990, 'The Politics of Secularism and the Recovery of Religious Tolerance'; also Juergensmeyer 1993 and Larson 1995.

[8] See especially the six positions identified by Sen 1996.

between Indian religion and the Christianity of evangelical missionaries in the early nineteenth century, was responsible for the construction of 'Hinduism' remains a topic of some debate. Nor is it my main concern here. The wide variety of responses to Western ideas, from the rationalist 'father of modern India', Ram Mohan Roy, to spokesmen for a universalist Hindu *Dharma*, such as Swami Vivekananda, argues against any easy categories.[9] It is, however, quite plausible to argue that, in the words of Halbfass, the British presence in India represented an 'encounter between tradition and modernity' which meant 'the advent of a new type of objectification of the Indian tradition itself, an unprecedented exposure to theoretical curiosity and historical "understanding", and to the interests of research and intellectual mastery'.[10] In the nineteenth century, a new self-consciousness of 'India' emerged, mirroring the Orientalist preoccupations of Europe. Ashis Nandy describes it as a psychological invasion which followed in the wake of the establishment of the Raj. Christianity and Western liberal values began to make more than a political impact on Indian self-consciousness.[11] Nandy argues that Hindu religious reformers succumbed to the colonial discourse, interiorising the values of Christianity, and accepting a version of the Hindu tradition which was actually formed by the colonialist myth of an ancient Aryan past lost in the decline into decadence.

Be that as it may, the debate about Indian nationhood has been dominated by different ideas about the relationship of its main religious tradition to minority or other cultural groups.[12] Paul Griffiths, drawing on Halbfass, notes three characteristics of what is often loosely referred to as neo-Hinduism: Westernisation, nationalism, and the 'tendency toward an inclusivistic view of the relations between Hinduism and non-Hindu religions'.[13] Such 'inclusivism', however, could take radically different forms. Vivekananda, so often regarded as the open-minded prophet of a

---

[9] Lipner 1994 gives a refreshingly broad reading of Hinduism as a 'multi-level edifice' in which the nineteenth-century revival of the Vedic tradition is one form taken by a vast and proliferating growth.

[10] Halbfass 1988:217.

[11] Nandy 1983:1–63. The first of these two essays, on the 'psychology of colonialism', presents a psychological reading of the different reactions to the influence of British colonial hegemony. In the second essay, Nandy turns to the Indian 'uncolonized mind', beginning with Kipling as an example of the pathology of the colonial ruler.

[12] Hence the most popular (or populist) of Sen's six critiques of Indian secularism, that which insists on a 'shared cultural outlook, which in India can only be a largely Hindu view' (see Sen 1996:16).

[13] Griffiths 1990:194.

harmony of religions, was more the advocate of a dominant Hinduism which he asserted *against* the West while yet incorporating Western forms of reflection and critique for his own ideological purposes.[14] Gandhi, on the other hand, with his conviction of the validity of all religious traditions, advocated *ahimsa*. Usually translated as 'non-violence', *ahimsa* has a more positive connotation and is inseparable from what Gandhi called *satyagraha*, an active 'holding fast to truth' in the face of violence of all kinds. Both Vivekananda and Gandhi were opposed to the materialism they associated with Western modernity, but, whereas Vivekananda's version of neo-Hinduism tended to reverse the power-relations, Gandhi's concept of an India free from British oppression was defined by *svaraj* (literally 'self-rule' but with connotations of moral restraint and self-control) in which all communities had a place.[15] Gandhi developed a critique of the colonialist mentality, making it a fundamentally ethical issue, not one based on the innate superiority of one culture. His moral sense retained an authentically Indian activism which avoided the masculine aggressivity of colonial culture. He thus raised, says Nandy, the possibility of people 'choosing their futures here and now – without heroes, without high drama and without a constant search for originality, discontinuous changes and final victories'.[16]

Since Independence, Gandhi's vision of India as a community of communities has suffered something of an eclipse. The ideal of a 'secular symmetry' seems much harder to achieve as what Sen calls the 'lines of separation' are accentuated by the myriad contrasts which divide the country.[17] The foundation of the Rashtriya Svayamsevak Sangh (RSS) as a defence of Hinduism against its enemies – Islam as much as the West – was based on a very different notion of the place of Hinduism in national life.[18] Contemporary political parties such as the Hindu

---

[14] See the sections from *The Complete Works of Swami Vivekananda*, volumes 1–8, Calcutta: Advaita Ashrama, 1970; quoted in Richards 1985:79–90.

[15] Margaret Chatterjee, 1983:32–3, draws attention to the influence of Jain ethics and concepts on Gandhi's thought, notably the 'theory of *anekantavada*, the many-sidedness of reality [which] provides the metaphysical basis of his conception of democracy, including that of a democracy of religions'.

[16] Nandy 1983:62.

[17] Sen 1996:38–43.

[18] The RSS, established in 1925 by Dr K. B. Hedgewar as a militant defence of Hinduism, is based on an ideology which makes it clear that India is first and foremost Hindu; members of other communities which have grown up on Indian soil are to be assimilated. Thus, according to Hedgewar's successor, M. S. Golwalkar, they should be 'wholly subordinated to the Hindu nation' (*We or Our Nationship Defined*, Nagpur: Bharat Prakashan, 1947; pp. 55–6; quoted in Michael 1996a:302).

Mahasabha and the Bharatiya Janata Party (BJP) find their roots in the same revivalist stream, but have taken the spirit of Hindu nationalism which influenced Vivekananda in a much more dangerously chauvinist direction. Their sloganising centres round the term *hindutva* – described tendentiously as a 'unifying principle which alone can preserve the unity and integrity of our nation'.[19] In its origins, *hindutva* means something like 'hinduness' and refers to the totality of historical and cultural aspects of Indian identity.[20] As used by the BJP, however, it has become a description of Hinduism as the defining religion of the nation, a description with a clear political sub-text.[21]

Searching for a post-colonialist historiography

As minority communities, the Christian churches feel less threatened than Muslims by the more extreme strands of this Hindu nationalism, but they find themselves in an ambiguous position with regard to the more recent phenomenon of low-caste insurgency. This has been given direction through the influence of various figures who, in different ways, fought for an alternative vision of Indian nationhood. First and foremost, however, it represents a diffuse and ill-defined movement of agitation against the hegemonic culture of the Brahmanically dominant élite.[22] If the 'Hindu nationalists' are united by the controlling ideology of *varnashramadharma*,[23] the insurgents are essentially an oppositionalist movement – opposed, that is, to what they perceive as a narrow

---

[19] From the 1996 election manifesto of the BJP. Quoted in *Muslim India*, a monthly journal of reference (Delhi); March 1996; 113–14.

[20] See Lipner 1993; 1994:179.

[21] Thus in the 1996 manifesto, *hindutva* is commended as 'the antidote to the shameful efforts of any section to benefit at the expense of others'. The target here is the concept of separate 'interests' in general, and the interests of the Muslim community in particular. For a perceptive analysis of the political consequences of the *hindutva* ideology for the Church in India see Menamparampil 2000.

[22] According to Michael 1996a:303, the major figures representative of 'this larger non-Aryan and anti-Brahmin vision of Indian nationalism are Jotiba Phule, E. V. Ramasami "Periyar" and Babasaheb Ambedkar, with many others throughout India . . . They attacked the system of exploitation at all levels, culturally, economically and politically.' For a different account of challenges to the caste system see Amaladoss 1994:53–75.

[23] The 'duties in accordance with class and stage of life'. According to the orthodox Brahmanical ideal described in the classical *Manusmrti*, each person finds salvation within a *varna* or social group by adhering to the tradition of the appropriate *ashrama*.

interpretation of Indian culture, derived from Vedic times as a creation of the Aryan people. In the search for a more adequate post-colonialist historiography of India, not only are the stories of hitherto forgotten protest movements now being retrieved, but the influence of both orientalist and Hindu–nationalist concepts of 'Indian identity' are being held up to an increasingly critical scrutiny.[24]

It is to this work of revision which the project of the *Subaltern Studies* group of historians is dedicated.[25] The editor, Ranajit Guha, states in the first volume of the series that the general aim is the recovery of a *'politics of the people'* – the subaltern classes and groups constituting the mass of the labouring population. Rather than a 'vertical response' to the still dominant discourse of the British Raj, what is now called for, says Guha, is a 'horizontal response' which mobilises whole groups along the lines of traditional kinship and territoriality. Such an ideology, he says, will reflect a legitimate diversity of outlook, but an invariant feature will be the notion of resistance to élite domination.[26] This project, with its self-consciously subversive agenda, has become the subject of intense debate about the nature of post-colonial, anti-orientalist discourse.[27]

This response restates the philosophical question about the representation of the other which was raised in the last chapter. Can the subaltern speak? How can the other be represented, except in the language controlled by the same? The work of interpretation, historical or theological, presumes a relation with the past but also depends on it. For the historian, as de Certeau puts it in speaking of the relation between history and theology, any reading of the past

> is driven by a reading of current events. Readings of both past and present are effectively organized in relation to problematic issues which a historical situation is imposing. They are haunted by

[24] Thus Romila Thapar, 1992:1–2, comments on the influence of Orientalist historiography that its 'resulting theories frequently reflected, whether consciously or not, the political and ideological interests of Europe, the history of India becoming one of the means of propagating those interests'.

[25] *Subaltern Studies* began in 1982 as a collection of monographs (New Delhi: Oxford University Press).

[26] Guha 1982:4–5 (emphasis in original).

[27] A critical overview of the first volumes of the project is contained in O'Hanlon 1988; see also O'Hanlon and Washbrook 1992. For the discussion provoked in India, see Alam 1983; Partha Chatterjee 1983; Upadhyay 1988; Kaviraj 1992.

presuppositions, in other words by 'models' of interpretation
that are invariably linked to a contemporary situation of
Christianity.[28]

To apply the point to the subaltern historians and the 'contemporary situation' of Indian politics: how can they presume to stand above or outside the dominant discourse of Hindu nationalism when the repressed voice of the outcaste other is *already* conceptualised as resistant to it? In fixing the other within a discourse, it becomes less than other, subordinate to the same. This aporia of the other, which was raised in the two readings of Levinas, makes any sort of 'theory of the other' contradictory.[29] Hence, in trying to develop de Certeau's concept of heterology, I have tried to interpret it not as a theoretical construct but as a phenomenology, a description of the way the other 'returns' or insinuates itself within the very linguistic structures designed to encompass and therefore overcome it. To repeat: a certain logic is always at work, not in the way the other makes itself known, but in the *practices* by which the same seeks to relate to the other.

So far, all I have done is illustrate the process with regard to the 'microdiscourse' of de Nobili and questions which it raises for the post-Vatican II missiology of 'inculturation'. If I now consider further the experience of the Indian Church in relating to a social reality which is itself fragmented and always in search of redefinition, my intention is again to fix the theoretical question in practice. But this time attention shifts to the diffuse process of self-scrutiny which goes on within, as much as between, communities.

Communalism, caste society and dalit insurgency

First, however, attention must be given to the politics of dalit insurgency which has provoked the response of an indigenous Indian theology. What 'sign of the times' is the Church discerning here and how to account for the marked shift away from the movement of inculturation through liturgy and ashramic spirituality?

The fundamental issue is acknowledged to be caste and the influence which communalism or caste-dependency has on society and Church in

---

[28] De Certeau 1988:23.

[29] 'Levinas's problem' is well stated by Buchanan, 1996:487: '[H]ow can a victim become a plaintiff?'

India.[30] The vast collection of dalit or 'Scheduled Castes'[31] are at the very bottom of the hierarchy which makes up caste society. While there is no general agreement about the origins of caste, or even about its fundamental nature, its all-pervading influence on Indian culture and society is beyond doubt.[32] Two Sanskrit terms need to be distinguished: *varna*, literally colour but meaning exterior covering or character, and *jati* or birth. The former refers to the traditional fourfold division of Vedic society[33] and corresponds very roughly to the Western notion of class; the latter is more strictly caste (originally a Portuguese term – 'casta', literally chaste, and meaning 'apart'), and refers to groups the membership of which is controlled essentially by birth. Family loyalties, economic status, traditional crafts and professional skills are all safeguarded by caste and may have contributed in some way to the present highly stratified social complex. In the course of time, a large number of 'outcastes' has added an extra 'level'.[34] Whatever its place in the system – and the ranking or degree of 'respectability' of individual castes is open to considerable variation – each caste or sub-caste is a closed social group. Its members

---

[30] A clear overview of the issues is provided by Amaladoss 1994; see also the collected essays in Arockiasamy 1991 and Part I of Wilfred 1995.

[31] According to the Indian Constitution there are 138 million people classified as 'Scheduled Castes' in India – about 17% of the population. Some 60% of Christians are dalits; in places, the proportion is as high as 90%. See 'Dalit Organisations: Reconstituting Reality' by F. Franco and Vijay Parmar, in Fernandes 1996:81–108.

[32] Quigley, 1993:2–3, makes a distinction between materialist and idealist explanations. According to the former, caste is simply 'a rationalization and obfuscation of more base inequalities . . . According to the idealist explanation caste is a cultural construct, the product of religious ideas.' A similar distinction is made by Forrester 1980 between the 'purely' sociological explanation of F. G. Bailey (see Bailey, 'Closed Social Stratification in India', *Archiv. europ. sociol.*, 4 (1963); 107–24) and the 'ideological' of Louis Dumont's classic *Homo Hierarchicus* (see Dumont 1970). Quigley is mainly concerned with a critique of Dumont, using the earlier work of Hocart 1950.

[33] The classical form is given in the *Manusmrti* 1.87ff: *brahmans*, or priestly caste at the head, followed by *ksatriyas*, 'warriors', *vaiśyas*, 'traders', with the *śudras*, 'servants', below; the classic theological justification of caste appears in the *Purusa Sukta*, the 'song of the cosmic person', at Rg Veda x. 90.

[34] Once independent, or tribal, groupings, they eventually had to surrender to the growing political and economic influence of the higher *varnas* who controlled the hierarchy of caste relations. Mukherjee 1988 concludes that the 'untouchable' castes and sub-castes were the result of a fluid development which had its origins within the already stratified Vedic society. Set against the three *dvija*, 'twice-born', castes was the *śudra* who acted as a sort of 'safety valve' accommodating all non-Aryans, the *dasas* or 'slaves' of the Veda. Although a further *varna* is excluded by the *Manusmrti* on a priori grounds, a *pañcama* or fifth grouping eventually arose *within* the system probably, says Mukherjee, because the power of the Brahmanical hierarchy sanctioned it. The 'fifth caste' became a way of classifying and controlling anomalous groups – which is why it has various names, *candala* etc. The practice by which deviants and 'misfits' were given a place within, but kept at the desired distance from, the social scheme was 'strengthened at the ideological level by the doctrines of *karma* and the transmigration of souls' (p. 96).

usually practise the same profession or trade and have common festivals and customs. The individual's role in wider society – and therefore identity – is determined by membership of the caste. The individual will be constrained not just by the trade or work of the membership, but also by the need to adapt to the canons of purity and impurity, the standards of religious and social life, set by the Brahmin *varna* which heads and controls the hierarchy. It is this process of social exclusion which has made the dalits the caste system's 'other'.

The Sanskrit word '*dalit*' means broken, trampled or destroyed.[35] It is the title which dalits give themselves, in preference to the more traditional vocabulary of 'untouchables' or 'outcastes'. Its current popularity is ascribed to Dr B. R. Ambedkar, Gandhi's colleague and adversary, who was bitterly opposed to the caste system as such. Gandhi's ideal was a purified Hinduism in which untouchability was abolished and *harijans* – 'children of God', as he called them – were guaranteed entry into temples.[36] It is important, however, to remember the political origins of the current usage which go back to the Dalit Panther Movement in Maharashtra. The Panthers' 1973 manifesto speaks of dalits as 'members of scheduled castes and tribes, neo-Buddhists, the working people, the landless and poor peasants, women and all those who are being exploited politically, economically and in the name of religion'.[37] A considerable descriptive literature of all kinds on dalits is available; novels, books of poetry and more popular writing stand side by side with anthropological and sociological works. To this must be added a rapidly growing theological literature.[38]

---

[35] Some theologians trace the root of the word dalit to both the Indo-European and the Semitic linguistic families. Massey, 1994:4ff., argues on the basis of 'their possible historical link' to the identification of dalits with the faithful poor of the Old Testament – more precisely those who exist in a reduced or oppressed state.

[36] Dr B. R. Ambedkar, architect of the Indian Constitution, is today regarded as almost the 'patron saint' of the dalit movement. See e.g. Irudayaraj 1990:80ff.; Fernandes 1996:9ff. Ambedkar's extensive works have been edited by Vasant Moon, *Writings and Speeches*; Education Dept, Government of Maharashtra; 1991–   . The use of the term 'dalit' to refer to the 'outcastes' is apparently derived from the nineteenth-century Maharashtrian reformer, Mahatma Phule, one of very few Hindu reformers concerned for untouchables – though the schools he established seem to have been ineffective. On Phule, see Heimsath 1964; O'Hanlon 1985.

[37] Quoted in Joshi 1986:141–2.

[38] Theology draws on a large number of broadly sociological accounts of the 'dalit reality' – for example, the detailed studies collected in Fernandes 1996 and the more variable quality of material in Massey and Bhagwan Das 1995. Briefer, more derivative and decidedly more polemical are Raj 1992ab and Manickam 1995. Some of the more important theological works and collections available in English include: Wilson 1982; Prabhakar 1988; Irudayaraj 1990; Nirmal 1990, n.d. (*A Reader in Dalit Theology*) and n.d. (*Towards a Common Dalit Theology*); Devasahayam 1992ab; Massey 1994, 1995; Arulraja 1996.

The politics of dalit insurgency: the history of dalit Christians

Dalit theology is usually interpreted as an Indian form of liberation theology.[39] For the Roman Catholic Church, however, it derives more directly from the Council's call for a dialogue with culture which highlights the structures of injustice at the heart of society. To appreciate the link between the present dalit movement and dalit theology brief attention must first be paid to the history of the dalit Christians.

According to John Webster, three overlapping periods in that history can be distinguished: the nineteenth and early twentieth centuries' mass movements of conversion, a transitional period between the two world wars which Webster refers to as 'the politics of numbers', and the period since Independence marked by 'the great experiment in "compensatory discrimination" set forth in the constitution'.[40] This third phase has seen the development of dalit theology proper – that is to say a theology developed *by* dalits themselves from what is implicit in their expressions of Christian faith.[41] The catalyst, both in Protestant churches and, more dramatically, in the Catholic Church, has been the scandal of the injustice suffered by dalits within the Christian community itself. This injustice is summed up in a phrase often used of the Christian dalits: they are 'doubly disadvantaged' or 'twice alienated'.[42] Firstly Christian dalits do not enjoy the same constitutional rights as are guaranteed by the Indian Constitution to the scheduled castes and tribes generally. These include reservation of seats in Parliament and the state legislative assemblies and claims to a whole series of civil service and government posts.[43] Through such positive discrimination, the aim of the legislation is to ensure that dalits can progress. However, such rights are not guaranteed

---

[39] Very few Catholic Indian theologians fit the Latin American pattern. Even those given to Marxist analysis, such as Sebastian Kappen, see the need for an approach more appropriate to the context of Indian religious pluralism. See Kappen 1977, and 'Towards an Indian Theology of Liberation', in Puthanangady 1985:301–18. In the post-conciliar era there was much talk of the need for liberation theology in India, but most of the praxis, as Wilfred, 1993:79–84, notes, was set in a liberal developmental mode. The 1981 All India Research Seminar began a more radical process of identification with the concerns of the poor and marginalised. See Amalorpavadass 1981. The split between 'liberationists' and 'ashramites' can be dated from this time.

[40] Webster 1992:x–xii.

[41] Webster 1992:199ff.

[42] See e.g. Wilson 1982; Raj 1992a:8ff.

[43] Arulraja 1996:17ff.

to non-Hindus.[44] The disabilities suffered by the scheduled castes are held not to exist in Christianity – which, according to the witness of its own scriptures (Galatians 3.26–28 is most often quoted), is an egalitarian religion.[45] By being identified by those *outside* the Church according to their *religion*, Christian dalits lose out on the legitimate aid guaranteed to dalits who belong to the same sub-caste but profess a different religion.

This first level of disadvantage arises from the assumption behind the constitutional arrangement that there are no caste divisions in Christianity. *Within* the Church, however, dalits are still identified according to their caste. Rather than being accorded their rightful dignity as members of what, at least in theory, is a casteless institution, the Church is seen to collude in the injustice of a discriminatory system. Dalit Christians, in other words, suffer the worst of both worlds. The discrimination which is rife in society at large runs right through the Church itself and reveals a second level of disadvantage.[46] As Walter Fernandes points out, in an insightful article on the origins of present-day conflicts within the Roman Catholic Church in Tamil Nadu, the problem is rooted in history and in the conservative and assimilative structure of the caste system which affects all religions and communities. According to Fernandes, the converts to Christianity who date from de Nobili's time had found a new identity in the caste hierarchy before those dalits who were converted in the mass movements two centuries later. The former had already taken the positions of influence before the latter arrived, and have been defending their vested interests ever since.[47] Now, says the dalit activist and Jesuit sociologist, Antony Raj, a Church

---

[44] Article 15 outlaws discrimination on grounds of 'religion, race, caste, place of birth', but Article 341 empowers the president to issue Orders identifying which sections of the population need special concessions. The effect of legislation is actually to reinforce the degree of caste dependence. See Webster 1992:139f.; Amaladoss 1994:76ff. The Order of 1950 specifically provided only for those scheduled castes which are Hindu; i.e. dalits were defined by *religion* and tied into the system – albeit, as Massey, 1995:164, points out, by the old negative title of *pañcama* or 'fifth' caste. Subsequently this provision was extended by Parliament, in 1956, to include Sikh dalits, and in 1990 to include Buddhists. Muslims and Christians are still excluded.

[45] Massey 1995:81ff.

[46] It should be noted that there is a rapidly growing dalit feminist movement which draws attention to a 'third level' – discrimination against dalit women, both within and outside the dalit castes. See Devasahayam 1992b; Kumud Pawde, 'The Position of Dalit Women in Indian Society' in Massey and Bhagwan Das 1995:145–64; Ruth Manorama, 'Downtrodden among the Downtrodden', in Massey and Bhagwan Das 1995:165–76; Persis Ginwalla and Suguna Ramanathan, 'Dalit Women as Receivers and Modifiers of Discourse', in Fernandes 1996:36–62; Aruna Gnanadason, 'Dalit Women – the Dalit of the Dalit', in Nirmal, *Reader*, pp. 129–38.

[47] 'Conversion to Christianity, caste tensions and search for an identity in Tamil Nadu', in Fernandes 1996:140–65.

supposedly fired by an ideology of 'a common fatherhood' and 'common brotherhood' faces the prospect of violence and even schism.[48]

To speak in this way of 'double discrimination' warns against a simplistic account of the dalit issue as based on a juxtaposition of exploiters and exploited. There are, rather, two sets of issues, intra- and extra-ecclesial, which rub up against each other. Recent surveys, such as that made by Raj of some 9,000 respondents in Tamil Nadu, produced a socio-economic profile the cumulative impact of which he describes as 'one of felt powerlessness'.[49] Apart from a wealth of details about the plight of dalits, the report draws attention to discriminatory practices in the Roman Catholic Church generally. Such surveys could be interpreted as no more than angry complaints about the all too common inability of large institutions to deal with petty injustice. The story they uncover, however, goes beyond intra-Church politics; the injustice lies at the heart of a social system with which the Church is seen to have colluded for centuries. In response to the 'double discrimination', dalit theology has emerged as an 'authentically Indian' form of indigenous liberation theology.[50] For Roman Catholic theologians especially, it represents a new development, which involves a revisioning of history and a demand to come to terms with the ethical issue of discrimination at the heart of the Church.[51]

---

[48] 'A dalit Jesuit speaks to the Tamil church', report in the Jesuit newsletter *Jivan*, January 1992; pp. 26–7. For further accounts of Raj's work amongst dalits in the Madurai area of Tamil Nadu see de Charentenay 1994; Maier 1996.

[49] 'The presence of two chapels in the same village . . . Separate seating arrangements within the same chapel . . . Two separate cemeteries . . . Separate queues to receive communion.' Authority structures of the Church are kept within the power of the élite; dalits form nearly 70% of the Catholic population, but among the total number of priests and nuns in Tamilnadu dalits number 3.5% and 2% respectively (see the summary in Raj 1992a:10–11; see also Raj 1992b).

[50] See Arvind Nirmal, 'Towards a Christian Dalit Theology', in *Reader*, pp. 53–70; also in Irudayaraj 1990:123–42.

[51] By and large Roman Catholic missionaries were more accommodating to caste distinctions, seeing them as social and not religious in character. The evangelical missionaries who followed the example and teaching of William Carey were much more radical. In their opposition to caste, which they saw as inseparable from the 'idolatry' of Hinduism as a whole, they were quite uncompromising. Coming from a background of religious dissent in England and antagonistic to matters of class, their egalitarian zeal found a ready target. Theological and ethical objections were all of a piece; the Gospel challenged the other by its very nature. In the later nineteenth and early twentieth centuries the very complexity of the issue led to more nuanced strategies; the strengths and virtues of the system gained acceptance in some, more liberal, circles. But, as Forrester concludes, there was a 'well-nigh unanimous unease concerning caste'; most Christians found it 'offensive to a greater or lesser degree'. See Forrester 1980:199. The only reference to caste in Cracknell 1995 records the statement of the liberal Robert A. Hume (according to Cracknell a forerunner of J. N. Farquhar's 'fulfilment' theology) that 'though it was "not uncommon to consider the caste system as wholly a device of the devil, it can be shown that, in this institution too, can be seen the hand of God. Few institutions which have very wide acceptance and long life in a large community are wholly bad"' (p. 351); quotation from Hume's *An Interpretation of India's Religious History*, New York, 1911; pp. 134–5.

But it also raises awkward questions about the various responsibilities of the theologian.

Dalit theology and the responsibility of the theologian

Dalit theologians, both Catholic and Protestant, find themselves on the horns of a dilemma more complex than that noted in the last chapter with regard to inculturation: not just when and how to affirm or oppose culture, but *which* culture? A great deal of attention is paid to social analysis and the recounting of particular stories and incidents which illustrate the dalits' sense of grievance.[52] Faced with what they see as the oppressive chauvinism of the Hindu majority, dalits look for – and enjoy – a solidarity in oppression which crosses *religious* boundaries. Theologians often articulate this experience in terms of polemic, setting Old Testament prophecy and the moral teaching and actions of Jesus alongside dalit experience to express the anger which, it is felt, represents the authentic voice of Christ in contemporary India.[53] One of the Roman Catholic dalit voices, the Jesuit exegete Arul Raja, bases the charismatic 'legitimate voice of dissent' of the dalits on a careful reading of the Gospel narrative which yields a 'spirituality of confrontation'.[54] Arvind Nirmal, in a summary of the development of Indian theology against the background of changes in Indian society, makes the important point that dalits are not so much a low caste but, strictly speaking, are *outside* the system altogether. They are non-persons who lack their own story. Scripture – especially in the denunciations of the prophets and the words and actions of Jesus Christ himself – gives them an identity of their own.[55] For James Massey, however, another story has to be told: the history of caste oppression sanctioned by Brahmanical texts. For Massey contemporary dalits are identified as objects over against the dominant subject.[56] They are made to represent the 'non-Aryan' element in Indian culture, the 'other' which

---

[52] See, e.g. the rudimentary analysis by the influential Abraham Ayrookuzhiel, 'Dalit Struggle and Religious Renaissance in India', in Puthanangady 1985:178–83, which emphasises the ambiguity of religion, strangling yet liberating.

[53] See especially George Koonthanam, 'Yahweh the Defender of the *Dalits* – a Reflection on Isaiah 3.12–15'; reprinted in Sugirtharajah and Hargreaves 1993:229–39; see also Michael 1996b:105–22.

[54] Arul Raja 1995:136.

[55] See e.g. articles in Nirmal, *Reader* pp. 53–70, 71–83; Devasahayam 1992a.

[56] Massey 1995:121ff.

leads through a history of racial supremacy to communalism and Hindu revivalism.

This, however, is where the language of 'otherness' can become part of the problem rather than its solution, raising again the complex hermeneutical issue of the 'otherness' of the other. What we have in much dalit theology is a reverse Orientalism which encourages a type of 'oppositionalist' thinking.[57] If the Orientalist is dominated by a certain universalising and self-validating historicism, which objectifies the oriental other according to set European categories, dalit revisionism rewrites the same history from a different perspective. A constant theme is a largely negative reading of Indian religion; the 'high' Sanskritic culture of caste Hindus is contrasted with that of the poor majority whose aspirations the élite seeks always to stifle.[58] In reaction against this perception, dalits are sometimes referred to as the original inhabitants of India.[59] The conclusion follows that, since most Indian liturgy and theology are couched in the culture and thought forms of a minority of Christians, for the majority they have failed and must needs be rejected.[60]

It is easy to understand the rejection of a theology which by locking itself into the language of brahmanical religion has become detached from the justice issues which affect Indian society. Religion in India has often been used to entrench caste divisions. As Walter Fernandes puts it, given the effect of the fundamentalist revival in the country today, 'interreligious dialogue can, in reality, play in the hands [sic] of the vested interests that are attempting to use religions for their own purposes'.[61] Small wonder that activists direct attention towards the destructive nature of the political forces inscribed in Indian culture and society and dismiss inter-faith dialogue as an irrelevant pastime for a few ashramites and academics. The aim of dalit theologians is to develop a sense of dalit identity – in Massey's terms to restore a lost dignity by enabling them, as he puts it, 'to get their own face back'.[62] Their problem is how to do so without subtly substituting one ideology for another. How far the

---

[57] A point sharply observed by Menamparampil 2000.

[58] For a thoughtful critique of the tendency to demonise the Sanskritic tradition in a way which ignores the 'complex processes through which a culture grows' see Amaladoss 1994:90–4.

[59] See e.g. Massey 1995:21ff.; 121ff.

[60] See e.g. Massey 1995:169ff.; Fernandes, 'Social Action and Inter-Religious Dialogue', in Irudayaraj 1989:37f.

[61] In Irudayaraj 1989:37.

[62] Massey 1995:128.

'dialogue of action' can be integrated into a wider inter-religious and inter-cultural dialogue in a way which overcomes rather than creates oppositional dualisms remains to be seen.[63]

This is where the ethical responsibility of the theologian becomes more than a theoretical issue. For protest and confrontation are inextricably tied into, and even determined by, the structures which they oppose. Is it inevitable that the subtle systemic violence of the Brahmanically dominated caste society must come up against the more manifest violence of dalit insurgency? Does the one somehow imply the other? The message of history is not encouraging. Communal violence seems endemic to the sub-continent. For today's Church, with its manifold responsibilities, the dilemma – to collude with injustice or to be committed to political agitation – is fraught with risk. How to witness to the Gospel before a divided Church and a divided society?

Learning to live in relationship

In directing attention to the shift from one theological response to Indian culture, the contemplative way of the ashramites, to another, the commitment to justice by dalit theologians, my intention is not to provide answers for questions particular to the situation faced by Christians in India. Rather I am concerned to draw out the ethical and political implications of that encounter and to point to the conceptual issues which confront the theologian engaged in inter-religious encounter – in any part of the world.

Given the agenda of the Vatican Council, the displacement described above is easily understood. Vatican II's call to an open encounter with other religions and cultures released in the Roman Catholic Church in India a new and powerful awareness of the level of discrimination both within society at large *and* in the Church itself. The emphasis placed on the missionary responsibility of local churches brought about a greater sensitivity to ecumenical relations and to what was to be learned from the experience of other Christian churches. At the Council, there began an inexorable process of uncovering the hidden layers of otherness which haunt the history of Christian mission. Since the Council, as the experience of the Indian Church as a whole indicates, the call to read the 'signs

---

[63] For discussion of this point see Irudayaraj 1989, especially the articles by T. K. John, 'Interfaith Dialogue in Justice Perspective', pp. 45–63, and Samuel Rayan, 'Spirituality for Inter-Faith Social Work', pp. 64–73.

of the times' has extended that process from people of different faiths to the poor, the forgotten and the politically marginalised. Is not the same response demanded in comparable situations once the theologian has become sensitised to the constant and disarming 'return' of the other within the world of the same? In addressing this question, my argument is not that the Indian churches set a paradigm for theological response to the other. Again that would be to fall into the trap of turning de Certeau's concept of heterology into a theory. Rather, the particular Indian context of religious pluralism and contentious post-colonialist politics illustrates the way in which the other always insinuates itself back into the process of reflection.

In the course of this discussion of dalit theology, the intentionality of the 'resistant other' has been noted as the crucial issue. The Indian Church, seeking to cast off its Orientalist inheritance in favour of the diverse symbols and language of rich and sometimes sophisticated local traditions, is now struggling to come to terms not just with the possibilities contained in a host of new dialogues, but also with the pathology of existing and, more often than not, broken relations. From whatever part of the spectrum they come, Indian theologians are united in their inheritance of a dual religious tradition, the Judaeo-Christian and the Indian. The latter cannot be summed up in terms of Brahmanical Hinduism nor reduced to some form of dalit 'popular religion'. It contains elements of both, and more besides: an ever-proliferating growth in which the encounter with Christianity has played an important role. Relating to the other in such complex circumstances cannot, therefore, be 'strategic' – an act of power – without being ethically compromised. The alternative would appear to be some form of 'tactical' accommodation, the inventiveness of the powerless which keeps alive the ethical demand of another history or another culture and seeks to live *within* the relations which are set by history and politics. But can the subject of the discourse be identified in a way which both avoids the 'strategic' self-centred domination of Orientalism *and* recognises the risks of the discordant relativism contained in a 'tactical' accommodation to a plurality of voices?

The 'organic' conception of relationality

In the last section of this chapter I want to develop a response to this version of Levinas's problem which complements the philosophical discussion in Part I. So far we have considered the responsibility of the Indian

Church for wider society. Here the key question is not *whether* a community of faith can be understood in relational terms (for clearly in some sense all can), but *how* within particular communities, or between different communities, relationships are to be established and maintained.[64]

One creative response, which tries to keep both the local and universal perspectives in view, comes from Felix Wilfred. Searching out the 'world views, modes of action, cultural patterns etc.' on which an Indian theology of 'liberating dialogue' will be based, Wilfred draws a distinction between the Eastern 'organic' and the Western 'architectonic' conceptions of reality. In the former, the various constituent parts are so inter-related that unity is not extraneous to the web of relationships; in the latter, the various parts are seen as 'steps or stages leading to a pre-conceived unity'.[65] Wilfred does not develop the point and his distinction reads, at first sight, suspiciously like another version of oppositional thinking. But his meaning becomes a little clearer when he turns to Gandhi as his exemplar of the 'organic mind-set'. Gandhi knew what he wanted to achieve but refused to subordinate the means to the end; the intermediate stages were just as important to the pursuit of truth.[66]

As developed by Wilfred, Gandhi's carefully reflective pragmatism is reminiscent of de Certeau's account of the ethics of everyday conduct and his distinction between 'strategies' and 'tactics'. De Certeau, of course, understands the distinction as essentially between the practices of the powerful who defend existing places and those of the powerless who work within categories of time. Wilfred, however, is more interested in the terms of a 'legitimate pluralism' which emphasises the complexity of the process of negotiation. Goals follow from means, not because there is no clarity about the goal but because, for the Gandhian 'organic mind-set', the goal is forever being reappropriated. Much as with Levinas's talmudic commentary, workable solutions for present dilemmas are sought through recapitulating the wisdom of the past. The provisional and pragmatic is not, however, merely 'second best'; it recognises that the goal is 'something on which we cannot claim mastery'.[67] With his sketch of an

---

[64] See the distinctions between forms of communalism made by the sociologist T. K. Oommen in Arockiasamy 1991:7–12.

[65] Wilfred 1995:290. The distinction is taken from Bowes 1986 who emphasises that 'both terms connote unity among a lot of things which are *in some sense* separate and different from one another' (p. 112).

[66] Wilfred 1995:291–2, quoting from Margaret Chatterjee 1983:159.

[67] Wilfred 1995:291.

organic 'web of relationship' in which all human beings – and the land – are caught up, Wilfred is looking for a properly Indian response to the obsession with the modern project of development and progress, but he is also seeking a rapprochement with a Western post-modernism which takes seriously the reality of pluralism and the voice of the marginalised. He can therefore happily embrace 'the postmodern with teeth' – not the 're-assertion of a conservative, integralist theology of restoration' but a 'centrifugal movement towards the other, towards what is different'.[68] The post-modern clears a space for the exploration of fresh avenues. The 'teeth' Wilfred sees emerging from an ethical response to those 'other' voices suppressed by the modern project of Enlightenment rationality: especially '[t]he mystics and those who suffer oppression'.[69]

What Wilfred describes is a version of Ricoeur's project of 'oneself as another', a process of dialogical or *mutual* construction in which same and other are not fixed and static polarities but always responsive to the pressures of history, culture and politics. It finds support in Homi Bhabha's allusive and deeply rhetorical analyses of colonial subjectivity and in the second of the two essays by Ashish Nandy noted earlier (see p. 160).

Bhabha argues that identities are established not by the dominant same over against the other, nor by a compliant other in response to the same, but by a complex process of identification, which 'only emerges in-between disavowal and designation'.[70] My action affects the other, but I am also affected *by* the other. At the heart of the colonial relationship, he says, the native undergoes a splitting of the self through his desire to 'stand in two places at once': set against the master who is responsible for constructing his identity as other yet at the same time seeking to be independent.[71] According to Nandy, looking at the pathology of the 'other side' of the colonial relationship, Kipling was personally split between a deep sense of imperial responsibility and an affection for the India of his childhood days. His dilemma had to be resolved one way or another: he could not 'stand in two places at once', be both British and Indian. However much the other was respected and even admired, the subject of fascination from whom there was so much to be learned, ultimately the 'strategic' demands of Empire were paramount. The Westerner was

---

[68] The title of the last chapter of Wilfred 1995:327–45. Quotations from pp. 332, 334.

[69] Wilfred 1995:339; emphasis in original.

[70] Bhabha 1994:50.

[71] See Homi Bhabha's introduction to Fanon 1986:xv–xvi.

'definitionally non-Eastern'; the otherness of the Indian had to be erased and controlled, his religiousness occluded as superstition, his cleverness as deviousness. As a result, otherness became a fixed category within European self-identification: that over against which the same identified itself. Once locked into such concepts of 'negative identity', it became unnecessary to speak about oneself in more positive terms.[72]

Radical exteriority and radical interiority

The great merit of these analyses is that they do not end up replacing one a priori theory with another. Bhabha, Nandy and Wilfred himself all begin with the particularity of Indian experience and with a radical form of relationality in which same and other are forever engaged in the negotiating of the shared space of the 'middle'. They reflect the concerns of de Certeau's heterological project – to allow the other to speak as other.

What is at stake here is not just the particular problematic of postcolonialist discourse in India and the effect of oppositionalist thinking on dalit consciousness, which I noted earlier, but the whole question of how identities are established. If Bhabha and Nandy are right, the subjectivity of the colonised arises from *both* the coloniser's attempt to prescribe the public reality of the colonised, *and* the latter's more private, or 'tactical', struggle to resolve a sense of displacement by seeking indigenous processes of identification. To speak, as Bhabha does, of binary or two-part identities, made up of the image that confronts us and the desire for an intuition of totality, reminds us that the inter-religious relationship – which can also be described in terms of the desire to 'stand in two places at once' – can be profoundly disorientating, but may also, as Wilfred would argue, become a source of liberation.

The dialogue with Indian culture which straddles the Vatican Council, from Monchanin and Abhishiktananda to the dalit theologians, has witnessed both. In the eyes of the Orientalist, the other is fundamentally alien and must be domesticated by the system controlled by the same. What this discourse achieves is a reduction of otherness to difference within the same genus. There remains, however, the alternative of discourses which emerge *from* the encounter with the other, not prior to it. Here the other is recognised, as Ricoeur would remind us, as the

---

[72] Nandy 1983:71. Nandy refers here to the psychology of Erik Erikson (see *Young Man Luther*, New York: Norton, 1958).

horizon of knowledge and a source of self-criticism: the one whose very presence challenges the sufficiency of concepts and stereotypes of otherness. Typically, as Bhabha shows, such discourses look in two directions. The colonised object of Orientalist discourse reacts both by interiorising the values of the coloniser and by resisting them; radical interiority tends therefore to go hand in hand with a radical exteriority. Nandy's account of the psycho-pathology of colonialism makes fundamentally the same point about the formation of the colonised 'resistant subjectivity'. He acknowledges a 'new universalism' and pays tribute to those who 'construct a West which allows them to live with the alternative West while resisting the loving embrace of the West's dominant self'.[73]

If theology is to avoid the violence of totalising discourses, whether of the Orientalist or the oppositionalist variety, and respond to Wilfred's post-modern agenda, it must develop some version of such a 'new universalism': not – to return to an earlier distinction – a theology *for* dialogue, based on what O'Leary calls a 'comprehensive explanatory scheme', but a theology *of* dialogue, one which brings the 'horizons of contemplation'[74] opened up by the Gospel into the inter-personal encounter itself. In Wilfred's Gandhian terminology, 'goal' must never be separated from 'means'; rather goal must become 'something that naturally flows from the means'.[75]

Learning to negotiate the space 'between'

A theology which would reflect this Gandhian 'organic' approach, responding to the experience of dialogue with the other, will be a reflection on the practice of engagement with the other. Wilfred's 'mystics and those who suffer' offer an alternative to the oppositional approach of much dalit theology. Working within the dominant tradition, rather than against it, they illustrate de Certeau's account of the myriad ways the powerless operate 'in the shadows' of space controlled by the powerful.[76] Typically, the binary or hybrid character of subaltern identity described by Bhabha is no oppositionalist mirror-image but a subjectivity which is

---

[73] Nandy 1983:xiv.

[74] O'Leary 1985:79ff.

[75] Wilfred 1995:291.

[76] De Certeau 1984:38–9 and de Certeau *et al*. 1998.

at the same time resistant and compliant, active yet passive. Ravindra Khare's study of the *chamar* caste of Lucknow, for example, turns them into somewhat unlikely post-moderns.[77] Employing the language of deconstruction to explain how the untouchable is both part of yet separate from the caste system, Khare argues that the traditional opposition of 'active' caste Hindu and 'passive' untouchable needs to be rethought in terms of the myriad 'differing' and 'deferring' devices employed by the latter in order to maintain the relationship. Alongside the rhetoric of the activists is to be found a sense of the provisional which seems quite content to live 'in the middle', with all the dichotomies and the lack of system. Other examples, further 'micro-discourses', could be given.[78] They further illustrate my account of subjectivity in which the self exists always in uneasy synchronic relationship with the diachronic incursions of the other. Might it not be that such a subjectivity reflects something of the Indian 'organic' or – better – relational ideal, a tacit acceptance that no one institution, still less individual, is allowed to monopolise the sources of authority or cultural value?

Such a possibility is suggested by the terms of Nandy's psychopathology. India, he says, is often identified as 'spiritual', but underlying much Indian spirituality is a 'hard self-interest'. There are two interdependent sides to Indian self-consciousness; 'materialism' and 'spirituality' are mutually conditioning. Not all victims react to violence by a 'spiritualising obfuscation'. More typically, Indians have sought to live with suffering by a defiant faith which only *seems* passive. The common form taken by the 'Indian self' is the non-heroic way of the archetypal survivor. When survival is at stake, polarities break down and become irrelevant; the experience of, and spontaneous resistance to, suffering becomes more direct. There emerges in the victim of the system a vague awareness of the larger wholes which transcend the system's analytic categories, standing them on their head, as it were. Such a 'spirituality of the weak' is paradoxical, to be sure, but the basic refusal on the part of the Indian to make the choice that damaged Kipling, the choice *between* one culture and another,

---

77 Khare 1984:147. 'As democratic India attenuates his social disability, deferment of resentment permits accommodation between him and the caste Hindu. As both sides betray their double-bind . . . they discover themselves beyond a simple opposition. *Différance* also questions the general structures of binary oppositions, a genre of question congenial to the Untouchable's ideological position and experience.'

78 See e.g. Clarke 1998 who describes how the *peraiyars* engage in an imaginative appropriation of symbolic resources which form what the author calls 'a jigsaw-like religious configuration' (p. 128).

is what makes for the 'uniqueness of Indian culture'. This, concludes Nandy, consists

> not so much in a unique ideology as in the society's traditional
> ability to live with cultural ambiguities and to use them to build
> psychological and even metaphysical defences against cultural
> invasion. Probably the culture itself demands that a certain
> permeability of boundaries be maintained in one's self-image and
> that the self be not defined too tightly or separated mechanically
> from the non-self.[79]

If this is true of the Indian experience of the other, there is also a lesson here for other religious communities and for the subjectivity which is developed in face of the other – *within or without* their own community. All religious traditions seek to develop some sort of comprehensive pattern of life which provides universal norms for the community, or indeed for society as a whole. What seems comprehensive from the point of view of the powerful, however, may appear very differently to the powerless – those whom the community excludes or regards as marginalised. There will, therefore, always be some measure of resistance to such a comprehensive pattern, a measure of heterodoxy within or a counter-tradition without – especially from those who, for whatever reason, find themselves in subaltern positions.[80] Any 'unitary definition' of so diffuse a phenomenon as Indian religion, for instance, will only be a unity in the sense that in order to maintain its hegemonic position the brahmanically dominated power vested in the caste system must constantly be renegotiating the terms of the relationships on which it is built.

No doubt something analogous can be said of other religious traditions. A religious community seeks to retain its sense of identity by defining whatever is other over against the same; but, in being so named and identified as a sort of 'shadow' or 'mirror' image, the other always returns. Not only does the other challenge the self-sufficiency of the same; the very strangeness of the other within the space of the same leaves open the possibility of change, of something new. Same and other are not, as Ricoeur emphasises, polar opposites, but are related always by particular constructions which have their roots in history and politics. This can lead, as I have tried to point out in this chapter, to a displacement within the

---

[79] Nandy 1983:107.
[80] See Chatterjee 1989.

resultant discourse, from one dialogue to another – from an engagement with the Sanskritic culture to one with the dalit or non-Sanskritic. To this extent the terms of the relationship may change as resistance to domination develops its own intentionality. Put negatively, this involves the refusal to choose between competing opinions. More positively, it represents a consistent commitment to reflection on the terms of the relationship itself and the concept of a 'suffering' or 'non-heroic' subjectivity, one which refuses to make choices 'between' but is content to live with ambiguity. The very act of faithfully writing history or theology, therefore, invites the risk of actually naming that other – and learning something that is new.

Many Indian Christians have begun an engagement with the Indian religious tradition which responds to what might be called its 'cultural ambiguities' by rejecting a priori strategies in favour of some form of resistant subjectivity. This dimension or quality is what Wilfred and Nandy, in their different ways, find so admirable in Gandhi: the capacity to improvise – not an unprincipled relativism, but an empathy which can transform situations and turn them to advantage. It is akin to what the anthropologist Talal Asad considers the particular skill of the 'mobile personality' – the ability to live in and negotiate the 'middle', the space between.[81] Is it possible for theologians to develop a version of a Gandhian suffering 'non-heroism' which values all cultural options and seeks to keep them alive while yet remaining committed to Ambedkar's fierce denunciation of injustice? Wilfred's 'organic conception of reality', which avoids assimilation, on the one hand, and oppositional violence, on the other, expresses something of this ideal.

The ethics of inter-faith relations

Earlier I described inter-faith dialogue as a multi-layered practice which negotiates the shared space of the 'middle'. The argument I have sought to develop is that a theology of dialogue is to be based not on the strategy of placing the other 'somewhere else', by unilaterally drawing the boundaries, but on the tactical retrieval of an ethically demarcated sense of the other. In this I have been guided by de Certeau's psycho-analytically inspired image of the past which returns to 'haunt' the present. His perspectives on the practices of everyday life, in which the powerless work

---

[81] Talal Asad 1993:11.

within the constraints of the dominant cultural economy in order to adapt it to their own interests, were used to develop the post-conciliar concept of 'inculturation'. This was seen to be significant in linking the recovery of the early missionary practice of de Nobili in India with the more recent engagement of the Indian Church with issues of justice and human rights, issues which have occasioned the development of dalit theology.

My critique of this phenomenon has argued that, in seeking a reversal of the oppositional consciousness which it perceives in much eurocentric theology, dalit theology risks similar strategies of domination of the other. My conclusion is that any theology which would be more than an accommodation within the terms set by the culture of modernity raises both theological and ethical questions about how inter-faith relations are to be conducted. The implication for the contemporary Church is that Christian mission must manifest an ethical character; an active witness in the face of the other must go hand in hand with a more passive willingness to wait within the space shared with the other.

The aim of this chapter has been to develop de Certeau's 'heterological law', but to move from the contemplative to the ethical and political dimensions. By focusing on the experience of the Indian Church I have tried to draw attention to an engagement with the other which is more naturally 'at home' negotiating the middle ground, and which avoids polarities and oppositions by proposing a dialogical understanding of relationality. This was in line with the analysis of the 'returning other' which insinuates itself back into discourse about the same developed in the two readings of Levinas's ethical philosophy. Enough has been said to describe how the Church's 'primary otherness' is overlaid or enhanced by further levels, in much the same way as Ricoeur's account of 'oneself as another' builds upon degrees of otherness or passivity. My earlier question which led to these Ricoeurian detours was how Christians are to learn 'a certain passivity' which is one with the responsible speech they are called to exercise before the other. The next chapter returns to the liturgy of the Church to ask how such a subjectivity is to be grounded within the formative practices of Christian faith.

7

Forming the school of faith

De Certeau's project of heterology describes what happens to the self when it engages with the other in such a way as to be altered – to *become* other. This was the point of the lengthy excursus on the liberative praxis of dalit theology. Theology of religions in India does not develop directly as a response to the Shoah. But it does mirror and intensify the catalytic effect which the Shoah has had on the way inter-faith relations are conceived. To that extent, the shift from ashramic spirituality to liberation theology has made the Indian Church aware of the ethical demands of the 'context of otherness'. Once what Levinas would call the priority of the other is taken seriously, the Church finds itself called not just to speak of what it knows in faith to be true but to exercise a responsible discernment of the traces of God – 'seeds of the Word' – in its own forgotten or occluded experience of the other.

This focus on the other which continues to haunt the present underlies a theology of dialogue, a theology which emerges from reflection on the relational experience itself. However, this does not make such a project merely an alternative to, or extension of, the threefold paradigm of the 'normative pluralism' project. Despite its insistence on tolerance, openness and respect, pluralism begs the question of motivation. While it is, no doubt, true that some theory of meaning is necessary to the understanding of religious diversity, there can be no such thing as a value-free 'view from nowhere'. The not-so-hidden assumption in the pluralist reading of theological approaches to other faiths is that inter-religious encounter will enable a complete theory of meaning once the means and methods of communication have been clarified. In this account, dialogue is a means to an end. One all-important factor is ignored: the encounter with the irreducible mystery of otherness. There can be no end to the engagement because the middle, in Gillian Rose's image, is always 'broken'. Religious traditions are not, therefore, to be understood as complete systems of meaning. Rather, they enable people of faith to go on creating meaning by responding to the diverse 'others' which confront them. To a 'market-place' model of religious diversity I am, therefore, opposing that of Lash's 'schools' – 'whose pedagogy', he says, 'has the twofold purpose . . . of weaning us from our idolatry and purifying our desire'.[1]

How is such a 'school' formed? How do Christians learn to negotiate the 'broken middle' of inter-faith relations? That is the theme of this chapter. In engaging with the dialogue between Levinas and Ricoeur, my argument has been that experiences of passivity, dislocation and vulnerability in face of the other are to be understood not as invitations to the mourning narratives of post-modernity but, more positively, as 'something to do with God'. In other words, the very difficulty of becoming a 'border-crosser' can be envisioned as itself a salutary – in the best sense – experience, which both enables the 'naming' of the other and allows the other to speak. The examples of heterologies I have recounted in the last two chapters illustrate this possibility. Such 'micro-discourses' do not provide an overarching theory of religious meaning; indeed, as responses to Levinas's warnings about the totalising tendencies in Western thought generally, they are intended precisely to subvert such a project.

The question asked by a theology of dialogue is not how to develop theories of religious meaning, but how to shift attention from theory altogether to the skills, dispositions and virtues which sustain persons in their pursuit of meaning. Where the practice of such virtues is learned is in the living out of the heritage which grounds and gives coherence to the faith of communities. This begins with the liturgical celebration of memories, and continues with the never-ending narration of life-giving stories of faith in face of the other, stories which are passed from one generation to another and enable people to 'plot' their way through the exigencies of time. Classically, the Christian theological virtues of faith, hope and love have God as their object; according to Aquinas they 'relate us to God'.[2] But for

---

[1] Lash 1996:21.

[2] *ST* 1a2ae 62,2. Strictly speaking, for Aquinas the theological virtues are distinct from moral virtues such as prudence or temperance since the former are the pure gift of God. In a postmodern context, however, my concern is essentially with the role played by all kinds of virtues, but particularly the theological, in the formation of character and hence with what MacIntyre regards as the qualities 'the possession and exercise of which tends to enable us to achieve those goods which are internal to practices' (1985:191).

the virtues to become habitual, to be properly 'ordered to the good',[3] they have to be practised. Through the practice learned from the discipleship of Christ, they motivate Christians to develop a contemplative sensitivity to 'seeds of the Word' which informs not just inter-faith dialogue but the whole life of faith – study and prayer as much as catechesis and theology.

This is what gives a theology of dialogue a different logical status from the three positions of the 'threefold paradigm'. Rather than reduce theology to a series of 'isms', ranked according to their tolerance of the other, it makes better sense to understand them as each embodying a theological virtue essential to the understanding of the relationship between *any* faith community and those which it perceives as other. 'Exclusivism' witnesses to that faith which speaks of what it knows through the specificity of tradition. 'Inclusivism' looks forward in hope to the fulfilment of all authentically religious truths and values. 'Pluralism' expresses that love which seeks always to affirm those values in the present. A theology of dialogue sets out to shift attention from consideration of the specific *objects*, or traditional themes, of theological study to the nature of the theological *subject*, the community of faith whose identity is to be found in the response it seeks to make to the self-revealing Word of God – wherever and whenever that revelation is to be discerned.[4]

Learning from the 'otherness' of faith

In this chapter, I want to argue that the gathering of the Christian community of faith to be taught by God through the liturgy and the sacraments provides that unity of life within which the theological virtues of faith, hope and love are formed. But, before proceeding any further, two dangers need to be noted. Firstly, any theology which takes its stand on liturgical practice can be accused of merely returning all human experience to some originating all-dominating narrative. Secondly, any recourse to 'the sacramental' as a theological principle risks what Rowan Williams calls a 'rather bland appeal to the natural sacredness of things'.[5] The risk in both cases is that 'the other' – whether understood as relations with other persons or with the world as a whole – is totalised into 'more of the

---

[3] *ST* 2a2ae 23,7.

[4] See Barnes, 'Religious Pluralism', in *Penguin Companion*, Hinnells ed.; for the three paradigms as representing the theological virtues, see Mathewes 1998:87.

[5] Williams 2000:210.

same'. The virtue of faith can become self-righteousness; love can be patronising; while hope can be reduced to a prosaic and predictable expectation that 'all will be well'. In a multi-faith world, where the other is easily accommodated by deferral within some eschatological scheme, it is this last virtue which tends to be the most seductive. How are we to ensure that the 'absolute optimism' of Christianity – to use Karl Rahner's term – does not become the naive optimism which turns all human religiosity into some generalised revelation of the divine?[6]

What is demanded is an approach to liturgy and 'the sacramental' which, following the direction of the last chapter, is not just contemplative but ethical; or, to summarise what was said there, one which responds to the demands of the other by avoiding a cosy accommodation between gospel and culture comfortably settled in a controllable present. Love – the 'pluralist' virtue which seeks to affirm all genuine manifestations of God's Spirit – expresses this ethic of a generous yet critical discernment. But love cannot be separated from faith and hope any more than statements of religious belief can be set apart from the practices of faith which give them life. To emphasise the point once again: the more difficult challenge for a theology of dialogue is not the comparatively straightforward question of how 'seeds of the Word' are to be discerned in the present, as if they are distant and obscure projections of what is clearly available in the Christian revelation. It is, more awkwardly, how the open-ended process of negotiation with an often quite explicit threat to the stability of faith can reveal 'something of God'. The truly generous, but more discomforting, response to the other is to recognise that faith is only ever completed in hope. Once the 'primary otherness' at the very heart of the experience of faith is accepted not as a threat to faith but as revealing faith's object, the 'possibility of God', it holds open a promise of engagement with further dimensions of otherness. To hope is to be ready to be surprised, to be challenged and maybe threatened, yet never to lose a sense that the present and future, as much as the past, for all their pain and awfulness, are still of God. In these terms, to speak of a contemplative sensitivity does not imply a semi-gnostic intuition which would risk ascribing some indiscriminate capacity to objects and persons to bear

---

[6] In an article in which he uses the controversial term 'Anonyme Christentum' for the first time, Rahner asks 'what reason should I have for not being a Christian, if Christianity means taking possession of the mystery of man with absolute optimism?' (see 'Thoughts on the Possibility of Belief Today', Rahner 1966a:8).

divine meaning.[7] Rather it describes a God-given grace which enables human beings to reach beyond themselves, to imagine the unimaginable, to live with the provisional, to enter into a demanding engagement with others.

I am, however, beginning to run ahead of myself. The God who is revealed in the engagement with the other is the subject of the next chapter. My theme here is the contemplative, ethical and now liturgical dimensions of the formation of Christian faith. If Ricoeur's response to Levinas is correct, human subjectivity is always and already affected by the relationship with alterity. History, language and culture are not, therefore, distractions which theology must somehow surmount by a tactical adaptation, but the *only* material – albeit at times other and strange – by which human beings can identify themselves. The self that is summoned by the voice of the other learns a willingness to accept that *in* the very otherness of faith are to be discerned signs of what Rahner calls the 'universal and supernatural will of God which is really operative in the world'.[8] This, of course, still leaves open the question as to how any such willingness – the Ignatian 'presupposition' – is to be learned. This, I shall argue, comes from participation in the life of a community formed by the liturgy of the Eucharist.

Let me indicate the direction in which this chapter will go. What I am proposing is a theological examination of the working of what de Certeau, following Pierre Bourdieu, calls *habitus*: the process by which external practices of everyday life arise from learned responses and attitudes.[9] Such a term comes close to what was described earlier as a new experience for the Church, the experience of 'inculturation' – not the pragmatic translation of 'words' but, more importantly for the Church's self-understanding, theological reflection on the process of communication itself, both on the more active speaking of the Word and on the more passive discernment of the 'seeds of the Word' in the world of the other. What impresses de Certeau is the way groups or communities at any point in time live out of concealed subjective motivations which yet give practices some sort of social legitimation. As a short-hand for such

---

[7] See Williams, 2000:218, who argues against a 'sacramental principle' which supposedly recognises the 'divine *presence* in all things' on the grounds that it risks an instrumentalising of creation and an 'anthropocentrism that denies difference or integrity to the material environment'.

[8] Rahner 1978:313.

[9] De Certeau 1984:45–60. For an insightful account of the Eucharist as 'a condensation of the Christian habitus', see Ford 1995, 'What happens in the Eucharist?'.

practices, the process of inculturation presumes upon a traditional 'store of memories' which are forever being adapted as challenges to identity come under pressure from without. For the community called Church, the conviction of bearing a vision of the harmony of creation is constantly disrupted by what is strange and other. How is the Church to develop new ways of conceiving old ideas?

The ideal, of course, is clear. The Church speaks of the possibility of God's action elsewhere on the basis of what it knows of God's action *here*, within that 'school of faith' which is the Church. In its liturgy, by celebrating the self-giving of Christ, the Church acknowledges the whole of the created order as pure gift and, by reimagining the possibilities for human community, anticipates the new creation gathered to its fullness in Christ. In practice, any contemplative sensitivity which would discern 'seeds of the Word' and negotiate the space of the middle has to be learned. I have tried to argue that the origins of Christian faith are always inscribed elsewhere; that is to say, they are always in need of being recalled, as if for the first time. What are the terms of this '*docta ignorantia*' – what de Certeau calls 'a cleverness which does not recognize itself as such'?[10]

The sacramental 'mystery' of the Church

In shifting attention to the liturgical and sacramental basis of Christian faith, my initial dilemma perhaps needs to be restated. How to avoid the ritualised and defensive repetition of the known and familiar which simply ignores the ethical challenge of the other? How, on the other hand, to avoid a bland accommodation of the story the Church is called to tell within the pluralism of other stories? A model is provided by Paul's passionate faith in the constancy of God which leads him to a celebration of the Good News of God's self-giving in Christ. Paul is prepared to wait patiently upon the fulfilment of God's promise; his hope in what remains God's work is expressed in praise for what he knows God has already done. The faith of the contemporary Church in its dialogue with other 'schools of faith' will be expressed in a similar theology of thanksgiving.

In pursuing such a theology, it is instructive to note that Vatican II's ecclesiology begins not with the now-familiar image of the People of God on pilgrimage, but with the mystery for which the Church gives thanks:

---

[10] De Certeau 1984:56.

the Good News of Christ the 'light of the nations'. The Church, in other words, is always pointing towards another reality, towards the God whom it perceives revealed in Christ. This is what identifies the Church as itself 'in the nature of sacrament, a sign and instrument, that is, of communion with God and unity among all people' (LG 1). It is important to note, however, that it is not being suggested that the Church is 'another sacrament'. A more ancient tradition is being recalled, a reminder that the sacraments are not a discrete series of private rituals or Christian 'rites of passage'. Rather, they spring from the practice of the whole community of faith, pointing to the single mystery of the inner life of the Trinity made manifest in the world. Thus, as Walter Kasper points out, when the Council reintroduced the Latin Patristic usage of *sacramentum* to describe the Church, itself a translation of the scriptural *mustērion*, the aim was 'anything but a bid for [the Church's] ideological elevation', as if the essential reality of the Church is constituted by some sort of primal sacramental reality.[11] The extraordinary richness of imagery used of the Church in Vatican II – for example, People of God, sheepfold, cultivated field, temple, bride of Christ, Body of Christ (LG 6f.) – is not intended to provide some exhaustive definition of the Church. On the contrary, the intention is to show that the Church is itself a mystery which cannot be exhausted. The words 'in the nature of' are key. The term sacrament is used analogically of the Church. But analogy is analogy; whatever the similarity to which the analogy points, as Kasper says, 'a difference remains'.[12]

The Council is careful to avoid the triumphalism which would imply that the Church is some sort of autonomous agent of salvation, independent, that is, of the life-giving work of the Spirit of Christ. In this context, if the word sacrament is appropriate, it is because Christ is the sacrament or *mustērion* of God.[13] Kasper's brief account of the crucial conciliar debate over the text of *Lumen Gentium* is a reminder that the rejection of the first draft of the conciliar schema 'On the Church' was prompted by the renewal of scriptural and Patristic studies which was among the less likely results of the Modernist crisis.[14] In the New

---

[11] Kasper 1989:113.

[12] Kasper 1989:114.

[13] Thus Schillebeeckx, following Aquinas, 1972:16f.

[14] The first draft, drawn up by Sebastian Tromp, the main author of Pius XII's 1943 encyclical, *Mystici Corporis*, remained within the tradition of scholastic theology. It was withdrawn after demands were made for something less legalistic, in which the 'mystery' of the Church would be more adequately expressed.

Testament, the context in which the term 'sacramentum' or *mustērion* appears is always Christological. Thus, in the Synoptics, Jesus speaks of revealing to his disciples the 'secret of the Kingdom of Heaven', while for those outside the rest is in parables.[15] Here the term has apocalyptic overtones, referring to an unveiling which will only be completed at the end of time.[16] In the Pauline tradition, *mustērion* refers to the mystery of that 'hidden wisdom' which expresses God's resolve to unite all things in Christ.[17] One of the Council's prophets, Henri de Lubac, made the Christological context plain when he said in his influential first book, *Catholicism*, that '[i]f Christ is the sacrament of God, the Church is for us the sacrament of Christ'.[18] This is the meaning intended by the Council: the Church is 'sacrament' only in a derived sense, in so far as it reflects and mediates the light which is Christ. As the Council's text puts it:

> For just as the assumed nature serves the divine Word as a living instrument of salvation inseparably joined with him, *in a similar way* the social structure of the Church serves the Spirit of Christ who vivifies the church towards the growth of the body (Ephesians 4.16).[19]

The Church finds in Christ alone the means of salvation; the Church is the servant of the poor and persecuted and the sign of the new unity God wants for all people in Christ. To speak of the Church as being *like* a sacrament is not to say that the Church acts like some sort of prolongation of the Incarnation. Rather it is the Spirit which works through the Church, and the Spirit which brings all things to their completion in Christ. This image of the Church as the universal sacrament of salvation – 'instrumental sign of intimate union with God and of the unity of all humanity' (*LG* 1) – mediates between two aspects of the Church's 'one complex reality' (*LG* 8): its visible structure as a human society and its

---

[15] Mark 4.11. The synoptic parallels, Matthew 13.10 and Luke 8.10, both speak of 'mysteries' in the plural.

[16] The problematic note of misunderstanding and division struck in the Marcan saying (which gave rise to Wrede's 'Messianic secret') is made more explicit in the Fourth Gospel where, according to Ashton 1991:189–93, 383–406, the apocalyptic dimension, implying times and stages of revelation, has become a significant element of the Gospel genre itself.

[17] E.g. 1 Corinthians 2.7; Romans 16.25; Colossians 1.26.

[18] *Catholicism*, a seminal work in pre-Vatican II theology, was originally published as part of a series inaugurated by Yves Congar in 1937 concerned to promote the cause of Christian unity; see de Lubac 1950. In the Introduction, de Lubac says his aim is to follow out the logic of the Gospel which is 'obsessed with the idea of the unity of human society' (quoting a 'believer and theologian' (E. Masure, conference in *Semaine sociale de Nice*, 1934; p. 229) Introduction, p. x).

[19] *LG* 8; emphasis added. The role of the Church as 'sacrament of unity' is described in *LG* 1, 9, 48; *SC* 5, 26; *GS* 42, 45; *AG* 1, 5.

spiritual nature as the faithful interpreter of the mystery of God's self-communication. It is from this 'double-sided' mystery that the Church's dual responsibility springs: to speak of what it knows and to be open to what it does not know – but which may be revealed in the world of the other.[20] As Kasper suggestively puts it, reminding us of the original context from which the language of sacramentality emerges, '[s]acraments are an emblematic manifestation of the liturgy of the world'.[21] The Church is charged with the celebration of that mystery through its liturgy of remembrance and learning. This is what makes the Church, if not a sacrament, then the mediator of the sacramental.[22]

Mediating the mystery of Christ

To describe the Church in sacramental terms is to raise the question of how the meaning of the Church's experience of estrangement and election continues to be mediated *within* the Church, before it is mediated outside. This mediation recalls Ricoeur's use of the three categories – same, other and analogous – with which he seeks to close the 'gap' between historical and fictional writing. Ricoeur's point is that the 'debt owed to the past' is paid by a rhetoric sensitive to the trace of the other which haunts the present.[23] To put the point once again in Levinas's terms: for liturgy not to be reduced to 'mere' ritual it must become ethical, '*for*-the-Other'. It is not enough simply to repeat past formulae; as Levinas the Talmudic commentator might put it, we have to develop a faithful commentary on the tradition carried out responsibly before the community of faith *and* in face of the other. In performing such a mediation, recalling and re-imagining its identity, the Church maintains both the continuity and the discontinuity in its own memory and experience. Same and other are not, therefore, *superseded* by a third category but – to use Ricoeur's terms – conjoined or redescribed through the imaginative

---

[20] See last paragraph of chapter 1, p. 28.

[21] Kasper 1989:126. Kasper's discussion here focuses on Rahner's attempt to reverse a way of thinking which made sacraments 'point-like' divine interventions in an otherwise 'secular' world and to restore an older perspective, before the medieval dichotomising of Church and world. As Rahner himself puts it elsewhere, 1978 : 411–12: '[w]hat we call church and what we call the explicit and official history of salvation, and hence also what we call the sacraments, are only especially prominent, historically manifest and clearly tangible events in a history of salvation which is identical with the life of man as a whole'.

[22] Bouyer 1965:51–2.

[23] Ricoeur 1988:142–56.

use of the tropes of classical rhetoric. To put it another way: through re-sorting to narrative and metaphor, the dialectic of identity-in-difference which characterises the relationship between same and other, Church and world, is constantly being restored.[24]

In the first move in the dialectic, the Church makes a return to the foundational events inscribed in the texts of tradition – to the Gospel record which opens up the 'horizons of contemplation'.[25] This, how-ever, necessitates a second move, for Christian origins are 'other'; the Church's Jewish 'primary otherness' subverts any finality for Christian-ity itself. Otherwise the Church would face the danger of a certain over-objectification, the tendency to find in the symbols and images of scriptural language a more universal meaning than they can properly bear. As William Burrows points out, Christian theology can easily lose the richness and nuance of the originating narrative structure of faith if it shifts 'without sensitivity' from 'first-order religious language closely linked to events, symbols, words, and persons in one socio-historical context to second-order doctrinal language in different con-texts'.[26] The Church is therefore committed to the process of relearning the language, images and concepts it uses – not *despite* the fact that they are always being disturbed by the other, but precisely *because* they are questioned and therefore remain forever provisional. This rhythm of repetition and critique, especially when provoked by the destabilising relationship with people of different faith traditions, does not enable a tidy theological synthesis. In fact, any finished analogical resolution is made impossible by the very nature of the relationship with the other. The self, as Ricoeur insists, is not constituted by categories of perma-nence of substance but, in relationship with the other, by categories of self-constancy and responsibility.

---

[24] As noted in chapter 4, p. 127, Ricoeur's account of 'successive filters' lays himself open to what he calls the 'Hegelian temptation' – the position, 'reiterated by every great philosophy of time, of the oneness of time'. By assuming historical time into 'the eternal present' the 'unsurpassable character of the significance of the trace' disappears; however much the Other is conserved, the ultimate victory of the Same is assured and 'any reason for having recourse to the leading kind of the analogous disappears'. See Ricoeur 1988:193ff. Ricoeur recognises the danger inherent in any historical synthesis and argues for an incomplete mediation with no totalising *Aufhebung*.

[25] O'Leary 1985:79ff. See chapter 2, note 56.

[26] Burrows 1996:125. Writing from a missiological perspective, Burrows is here concerned with the way Christian soteriologies set divides between same and other by getting locked into 'objectivist doctrines' which tend to '*reify* and *instrumentalize* the mystery of what took place on Calvary' (emphases in original).

To admit that the analogising process, the building of bridges between same and other, is inherently unstable is not to conclude that it is impossible, only that it is laborious and time-consuming, a work never complete. Nor is it to make of such negotiation no more than a preliminary tactical adjustment to an indefinable otherness which will eventually be overcome once better concepts, better translations, even a better self-understanding, are somehow available. The question is not whether the negotiators can find some elusive bedrock of certainty – whether within their respective traditions of faith or, more dubiously, 'between' them – but what is to be said of the experience of mediation or relationality itself. To say that such an activity of mediation lies at the very heart of the Church's nature is not to presume upon its possession of an esoteric knowledge which exalts the Church above the other, nor to suggest that its identity is bound up with successful witness to, or defence of, a *finished* vision of salvation in an essentially hostile environment. Rather the Church shares with others what this particular community of faith has experienced in its own 'primary otherness': that access to God depends not on moral value or religious privilege but on a purely gratuitous acceptance by God. In other words, what the Church knows in faith is the story which it is called to narrate, the story of how this people, gathered in space and time, has been reconciled to God.

What the Church does not know is the extent of God's salvific action. Which is where a healthy and humble reticence is in order. The corollary of the faith formed by God's grace is the conviction – more exactly the hope – that this same God goes on drawing people together irrespective of their moral worth. Inseparable, therefore, from these two theological virtues is the third. The mediation which Christians practise is motivated by the Spirit of love, in imitation of God's own action of welcome and hospitality towards all people. The God whom Christians celebrate is the source of the gift which they presume to communicate to others *and* the means by which the gift is shared. To put it another way, God is himself both host and guest, the one who invites all people to the abundance of God's life yet becomes present in an act of self-giving *kenosis* amongst a particular people. God is the generous host, celebrated in the Psalms as the one who 'prepares a table for me in the sight of my foes' (Psalms 23.5). But it is the same God who inspires the practice of hospitality – for instance in Abraham's receiving the Lord in the form of the three visitors by the oaks of Mamre (Genesis 18.1-8) – the God who, in the words of the Johannine Prologue, 'dwelt among us, full of grace and truth' (John 1.14).

In illustration of that theme there is no need to labour the obvious, that in the New Testament Jesus is depicted as the one who has no home and is frequently a guest (Luke 7.36ff., 9.51ff., 10.38ff.; Mark 1.29ff., 2.25ff.). More to the point is that when Jesus is himself the host, as at the Last Supper, the roles are reversed; the washing of the feet of the disciples is a parable in action, a graphic image of the nature of loving service, and points the way forward to the real cost of the new commandment to love 'as I have loved you'. Jesus becomes our guest, present wherever 'two or three are gathered in my name'. At the same time, he issues an invitation to share in the messianic banquet (Matthew 8.11; Luke 14.15ff.). The Last Supper points forward to that meal which Jesus promises to share in the Kingdom of the Father (Matthew 26.29; Luke 22.16), thus making every celebration of the Eucharist not just a remembrance of Jesus's submission to the will of the Father, but very much an anticipation of the abundance of God's self-giving.

This is what makes the Church 'sacramental', a sign of the 'hidden wisdom' of God: its continuing celebration of God's gratuitous action. The people of Israel met to renew the Covenant and to celebrate the Passover, thereby renewing the foundational event of their history; so the Church finds its identity through repeating and reliving the words and actions of Jesus. This, however, is no mechanical process, the simple recall of a memory. For the memory is of a terrible paradox: the event in which God's Messiah is deserted and killed by God's own people.[27] In saying this, I am not making a naive and anachronistic distinction between Judaism and Christianity,[28] but pointing to the tension at the heart of the 'horizons

---

[27] It is worth recalling here the crucially important visit made by Jules Isaac to Pope John XXIII, on 13 June 1960, in which he drew attention to the orthodox Catholic tradition, set out in the *Roman Catechism*: 'sinners were the authors and the ministers of all the sufferings that the divine Redeemer endured' (1.5,11). The point is repeated in the recent *Catechism of the Catholic Church* (1994), where it is said that Christians bear the responsibility for the death of Christ – 'a responsibility with which they have all too often burdened the Jews alone' (598) (see Oesterreicher 1985:105–8).

[28] An ahistorical account of Jewish–Christian relations almost inevitably reifies 'Judaism' and 'Christianity' into separate and opposed religious 'systems'. Whatever the truth in the distinction, it is clearly anachronistic in the first century. Nor does it reflect the complexity of religious relations in which the 'early Church' participated. Thus Robert Murray argues for a distinction between the 'Jerusalem establishment' and various strands of what he calls the 'disaffected' within the wider Jewish tradition, many elements of which, particularly through apocalyptic texts such as Enoch, influenced early Christianity. See Murray 1985:263–81. The Fourth Gospel is most obviously marked by an anti-Jewish polemic, but again it would be anachronistic to take the designation 'the Jews' as referring to the Jewish people as a whole. As Ashton shows, 1991:151, the context is the growing antagonism between the Johannine community and a 'conservative segment within the broad band of a common religious tradition'.

of contemplation' recorded in the New Testament. On the one hand, God promises to reveal himself through the history of a chosen people; on the other, when the chosen Messiah appears, he encounters rejection by the same people. Such is the *historical* story: not the triumph of one particular group over 'the others', but the clash of God's purposes and human misunderstanding. Christian faith is based – as Paul reminds us – on what it knows of the constancy of God, the conviction that God has overcome this rejection and in the middle of weakness and confusion fashions something unexpectedly new.

Finding the source of hope

The lesson, however, has continually to be relearned as Christians find themselves in a space 'haunted' by the other. Whenever the Church gathers to celebrate its faith, and whenever Christians are reminded of the 'primary otherness' of their relationship with the living tradition of the people of the Old Covenant, the 'question of the other' is raised. This response to the other in the middle of the familiar is enabled by a liturgical action, the Eucharist, which, by recalling the most important of the signs by which Jesus points to God's action in the world, enables the Church to live, as David Ford puts it, 'in the face of this imperative person and event'.[29]

The supremely paradoxical moment of the Last Supper is itself coloured by an inevitable otherness; the cost of resurrection lies in Jesus facing the otherness of death. How does this amount to something more than a vague and aimless passivity before the unknown? The Eucharist – with its historical resonances of the Last Supper pointing to the meaning of Jesus's approaching Passion, and vice versa, as Williams puts it, 'the death of Jesus metaphorized as a breaking and sharing of bread'[30] – allows the community to enter into and to be formed by this encounter. The Last Supper sums up a whole series of face-to-face encounters between Jesus and his disciples. It is significant that very often these encounters include meals, in which argument, disagreement and even – and especially – betrayal are as central as Jesus's words of instruction and healing. This is no serene moment of peaceful isolation; still less some

---

[29] Ford 1995:370.
[30] Williams 2000:214.

prototype of a nostalgic post-modern mourning narrative. The Last Supper, most importantly, is a meal taken in the face of death – and paradoxically an expression of genuine hope.

Here I would recall Levinas's contestation of Heidegger, for whom death is the 'supreme virility'. For Levinas, death is always future, always other and therefore *ungraspable*. 'Now' is the suffering which endures the nearness of death and which marks the reversal of the subject's activity into passivity.[31] Death is significant for Levinas not because it brings the final test of our heroic capacity, but because it marks the onset of that moment when we are no longer, as he puts it, '*able to be able*'.[32] The true hero is the one who accepts the 'end of virility' and, at the same time, the paradox that with the destruction of hope there is yet hope. For Levinas, the source of this hope is the other; in the face-to-face encounter with another person I become a responsible subject. For Ricoeur, of course, the extreme nature of such a substitutionary *kenosis* leaves us with an aporia; for the philosopher it may be impossible to name the other.[33] This is not to say that the task of the theologian is to supply that name, as if from some secret gnosis. Rather it is – to repeat my theme – to give a Christian account of relationality, a dialectic which refuses to totalise same or other, but to go on re-reading the New Testament witness as a narrative of Jesus's encounter with the other and, thereby, to learn how to live according to his relationship with the Father.

However Jesus's identification with the bread and the wine is to be interpreted theologically, there is no doubting that his words, 'my body *broken* for you . . . my blood poured out', as repeated in the liturgy have an extraordinary power over the imagination. They are, first and foremost, a narrative which inspires hope.[34] Standing in continuity with the predictions of the Passion which highlight the Gospel narrative, the Last Supper is the centre of the drama, the axis around which the Gospel can be said to revolve. This is the last occasion that the disciples will meet together as a group before being scattered. And in every subsequent

---

[31] Levinas 1987a:70–1.

[32] '*Nous ne pouvons plus pouvoir*' (Levinas 1987a:74). The translator, Richard Cohen, explains in a note that: 'Levinas's idea seems to be that in the face of the mystery of death, the subject not only loses its various powers, it loses its very ability to have powers, its "I can" – that is to say, its very self-constitution as an existent.'

[33] Ricoeur 1992:355.

[34] See FitzPatrick 1993 for a reminder of the context which scholastic discussion of Aristotelian categories tends to forget: 'Whatever else the Eucharist is, it is a *rite* of some kind' (p. 47).

celebration of the Eucharist the memory of that moment of betrayal of the leader and the breaking of the community is present. The Eucharist forms the community of faith in the image of that first community; in so doing it enacts a potential not just for transcending all boundaries, of race and nation, but for bringing creation into a new unity.[35]

This may be why, in John's Gospel, the account of the washing of the feet is substituted for the usual story of the institution of the Eucharist. This parable in action of the service Jesus demands of his Church brings into a stark juxtaposition the new commandment to love 'as I have loved you' and the brokenness which is the real cost of that service. John, of course, has already given us the lengthy Bread of Life discourse which, significantly, is framed by stories of acceptance and rejection. According to Raymond Brown, John's meditation reflects the antagonism between the Johannine community and those who do not share its strongly sacramental view of the Eucharist.[36] Chapter 6 begins, against the backdrop of the Passover, with the 'sign' of the multiplication of the loaves, and leads up to John's version of Peter's confession of faith: 'Lord, to whom shall we go? You have the words of eternal life; and we have believed and have come to know, that you are the Holy One of God'(6.68–9). Between these two points comes Jesus's discourse which provokes hostility from the 'Jews' and dissension among the disciples.

At first sight this makes for a clear division amongst Jesus's hearers. And there is no doubt that the theme of judgment, the separation between those who come to the light and those who prefer to remain in darkness, is central to the theology of an evangelist who, as Ashton puts it, 'had dualism in his bones'.[37] John's dualism, however, is complex. The division which runs through the Gospel, between insiders and outsiders, is not a narrow apologia for membership of the Johannine community over against the 'others', but goes hand in hand with a prior division between two ages or times of revelation: what is now at least partially concealed is to be revealed in the fullness of time.[38] In none of the Gospels is faith a 'gnosis', a final and complete knowledge of God. Nor is the faith

---

[35] For a remarkable account of the transformative power of the Eucharist, see Cavanaugh 1998, especially pp. 203–52.

[36] Brown 1979:74.

[37] Ashton 1991:237.

[38] A point made most dramatically in John chapter 9, the story of the man born blind, which juxtaposes two movements: on the part of the Jews, from self-regarding 'knowledge' to self-condemning blindness, and on the part of the man, from blindness to faith in the Messiah.

which is formed through the liturgical repetition of the Gospel story anything other than Peter's hesitant confession or the Emmaus disciples'
amazed glimpse of a truth half-concealed. Again, it is not gnosis, but
the very lack of knowledge which provokes the defining moment
in Christian faith – Jesus' own facing of the immediacy of death in
Gethsemane and on the Cross.

Here a Christian reading of Levinas's enigmatic 'for-the-Other' becomes
possible. When Jesus, at the end of the first part of the farewell discourse
in the Fourth Gospel, prepares his disciples for the final departure he says
'as the Father has commanded me, so I do'(14.31). He takes responsibility in
face of the other. His passion is only a form of passivity in so far as it expresses a prior activity: of putting everything into the Father's hands.[39] The
future is unknown – in Levinas's terms: 'what is in no way grasped . . .
absolutely surprising'[40] – and can be known only in analogical terms, as a
projection from the past which is configured in liturgical form in the present. 'Now' is the liturgical moment when the Christian community is made
aware of being 'for-the-Other'. The Eucharist, if we follow Ricoeur, is a re-
rooting *in* time, but it is also – and much more disconcertingly – if we follow
Levinas, a placing on the frontier *of* time. The Christian is never allowed a
'panoptic vision' which is not also immersed in the immediate world of suffering temporally bound relations. It is in the 'now', this moment of faith,
that the Church learns to be itself through participation in the sacrament
or *mustērion* of God's self-communication – that is to say in the Death and
Resurrection of Christ which is celebrated in the liturgy of the sacraments
generally and, quintessentially, in the Eucharist.[41]

Forming the community of faith in this present moment the Eucharist
also points to the fulfilment of God's promise. In the last part of this chapter, however, my intention is not to work out the terms of a Eucharistic
theology which, as an articulation of the Paschal Mystery, might be
accused of covertly totalising the other into a Christian finality, but to
argue that, as a liturgical practice, the Eucharist encourages the learning

---

[39] There is, therefore, something profoundly appropriate about John's version of the
Passion narrative which replaces the synoptics' language of suffering with that of exaltation
and triumph. In John there is no agony in the garden and a shout of triumph rather than the
cry of desolation from the Cross. But, as Ashton, 1991:485ff., argues against Käsemann, the
Passion story is not an 'embarrassment' to be tacked on at the end of an otherwise serene
narrative, but all of a piece with the complex theology of the revelation of God's 'glory' which
is stated in the Prologue.

[40] Levinas 1987a:76.

[41] Bouyer 1965:24–5, 38–9.

of those dispositions necessary if the Church is to act in accordance with the mystery of Christ's continuing presence. If Levinas's insight is correct, if death is not to be grasped but only faced in hope, then it is in liturgy that such a Christian *habitus* is practised – that set of habitual ways of behaving which structure behaviour, attitudes and instincts.[42] Here, in other words, the community of faith is encouraged to persevere in the inevitably laborious process of discerning what is of God in the world of the other.[43] To suggest, therefore, that it is in the practice of liturgy that Ricoeur's 'analogical resolution' of same and other is made possible is not to replace theology with the ritual of sacred ceremony, locking a community into a well-sealed enclave. Nor is it to imply that by participating in a ritual act a community of faith is somehow given a formula or intellectual grid which 'places' the other within a system of mastery. It is, rather, to recognise the liturgical nature of theology: a practice which is rooted in the constant study and celebration of the tradition.

Forming a worshipping community for mission

The sort of theology I am seeking to develop in this book is not a speculative investigation into other-worldly verities, but a reflection on a people's life and experience which begins with doxology, the praise and thanks due to God for what God had done on behalf of sinful humankind. To explore the significance of this retrieval for a theology of dialogue, let me first return to the theological 'event' of Vatican II and set it alongside the Church's experience of the 'context of otherness'.

The Council's Constitution on the Liturgy, *Sacrosanctum Concilium*, was the first document to be promulgated – not because it was considered the strategic key to the rest, but because the long-term theological work of preparation had been done well before the Council was summoned.[44] It

---

[42] See Ford 1995:360–62.

[43] Rowan Williams, 1988:50, reflecting on difficulties incurred by models of interiority and the 'inner life' which emphasise the placing of the self over against the other, comments that '[m]y obscurity to myself, yours to me, and mine to you, are not *puzzles*, waiting for fruitful suspicion to uncover the real script, Marxian, Freudian, sociobiological . . . They are to do with the inescapability of taking time.'

[44] See Bouyer 1965; Jones *et al.* 1978:285–94. The 'liturgical movement' in the Roman Catholic Church was well established by the time of the Council thanks to the work of scholars like J. A. Jungmann, P. Parsch and G. Diekmann, and the pastorally oriented reforms encouraged by such official statements as Pius XII's *Mediator Dei* in 1947. The foundation of the document in solid theological learning is stressed in Aidan Kavanagh's introduction in Hastings 1991:68–73, who also notes the complete lack of attention to anthropological research into ritual and culture.

reflected the growing consensus, amongst theologians and liturgical scholars, of the need both for a reform which would encourage a wider and more active participation in the worship of the Church and, more importantly, for a sound theology linking the Eucharist with the celebrating community, the Church.[45] Although essentially a programme for reform, this Constitution nevertheless brings together a number of theological perspectives – especially on the Church as a worshipping community for mission – which mirror what were to become the central concerns of the Council. The major emphasis in the Constitution is on the 'eucharistic sacrifice of [Christ's] Body and Blood' which initiates people into a closer union with God (SC 47), but the context is the liturgical, sacramental and devotional life of the Church as a whole. Liturgy does not exhaust the activity of the Church; first comes conversion and subsequently comes mission (SC 9). Nevertheless, the liturgy is the 'high point towards which the activity of the Church is directed' and 'the source from which all its power flows' (SC 10). In the 'public service' or 'function (ergon) undertaken on behalf of the people (laos)' – as Jungmann explains the classical meaning of leitourgia[46] – the worship offered to God is set within the context of a community of faith called to be an 'ensign raised for the nations'.[47]

To speak of liturgy as the 'work of the people' should not obscure the crucial prior truth, that before becoming a 'work' of worship and celebration liturgy is God's work, what is accomplished in the community of faith before it is accomplished by it.[48] All liturgy, in other words, is a response to the prior initiative of the other. Orthodox Jewish life, for instance, continues to be organised as a liturgy which expresses the people's response to God's Covenant as if they are the contemporaries of ancient Israel.[49] God has formed his people and continues to hold them together. As that particular liturgy which gathers the community for worship and sends it out to share the Good News, the Eucharist is the focal point which

---

[45] The execution of reforms was not enacted by the Constitution itself; its purpose was to lay down 'normas generales et altiora principia'. The reform which led to the revision of the Roman Missal in 1969 by Paul VI was only one, albeit the most far-reaching, of reforms in process since the beginning of the century. See the commentary on the text by J. A. Jungmann, in Vorgrimler 1967 I:1–87; also Bouyer 1965; McManus 1967.

[46] Jungmann 1975:851.

[47] SC 2: 'signum levatum in nationes '(Isaiah 11.12).

[48] As Purcell, 1997:148, puts it, '[T]he recourse to liturgy reveals the true nature of subjectivity, beyond the limits of the autonomy of the self and the freedom which rationality imposes, as a heteronomy.'

[49] E.g. Deuteronomy 29.14–15.

intensifies the relationship not just with the 'primary otherness' of Judaism but with all those 'other others' who can claim a place in the ethical and political conversations which make up wider society. Through the celebration of the Eucharist, the Church becomes what it is: the source of that communion which makes it the sacrament of the unity of humankind. In de Lubac's words, recalling the perspective of the Fathers, notably Augustine and Origen, the Eucharist makes the Church.

As Paul McPartlan has so clearly demonstrated, de Lubac's ecclesiology seeks to correct an exaggerated emphasis on the Eucharist as almost an end in itself and to restore its original meaning as the life-giving heart of the Church.[50] In the first place, de Lubac aims to restore a social dimension to the liturgy, to counter individualism and to build a vision of the Church as genuinely 'Catholic' – the *'congregatio generis humani'*, which, in celebrating the Eucharist, 'gathers together the whole world'.[51] With his vision of the Church as the visible and imperfect community which yet points the way to the definitive completion of the Kingdom of God, de Lubac anticipates the Council's rejection of any simplistic equation of the visible community of the Roman Catholic Church with the Mystical Body of Christ.[52] Rather, he allies himself with the Patristic tradition which saw in the Eucharist the sacrament of a new creation: as grains of wheat are formed into bread to become the 'Body of Christ', so is the Church 'moulded into one sole body in Christ, feeding on one flesh alone. One Spirit singles us out for unity, and as Christ is one and indivisible we are all no more but one in him'.[53]

The same theme, shifting the doctrinal priority from the 'mystical body' of the Church to the 'mystical body' of the Eucharist, is given a more substantial treatment in a later book, *The Splendour of the Church*.[54] Just as

---

[50] McPartlan 1993. De Lubac's major historical labour, *Corpus Mysticum* (Aubier: Paris, 1949) shows how the term 'mystical body' was transferred from the Eucharist to the Church. According to McPartlan, 'De Lubac says that the adjective "mystical" was dropped in reference to the Eucharist in the mid-eleventh century, in reaction to Berengarius. Then followed a period in which both the Eucharist and the Church were simply called the *Corpus Christi*, with the adjective *mysticum* unattached. It was during the second half of the twelfth century that, in order to distinguish the *ecclesial* Body of Christ, *it* came to be qualified as the *corpus mysticum*' (1993:76–7).

[51] De Lubac 1950:26, 49.

[52] Notably in the change from 'is' to 'subsists in' to avoid the identification of Body of Christ with the Catholic Church in *LG* 8.

[53] De Lubac 1950:38–40; quotation from Cyril of Alexandria, *Dialogue on the Trinity*, Patrologia Graeca, lxxv, 695.

[54] De Lubac 1979. The influence of this book on the ecclesiology of the Council is noted by McPartlan 1995:30–2;73–7; see also Jungmann in Vorgrimler 1967 I:33.

Lumen Gentium considers the mystery of God's self-revelation before turning to the visible society which makes up the People of God, so de Lubac begins not with the Church itself but with the mystery of the restoration of humanity revealed by God in Christ. Here he speaks of the active and passive aspects of the Church – sanctifying and sanctified. Church and Eucharist stand 'as cause to each other. Each has been entrusted to the other, so to speak, by Christ; the Church produces the Eucharist, but the Eucharist also produces the Church.'[55] In saying this, de Lubac is making more than the obvious point, that Church and Eucharist are interdependent. He is, rather, recalling a thoroughly Patristic vision of humanity reconciled and sanctified by God in Christ. In recovering this unity, the 'Mystical Body of Christ', that is to say the Church gathered around the Eucharist, is not the means but the goal.[56] In this way, the dialectic – de Lubac would have preferred the term paradox[57] – between the active and passive aspects of the Church reflects the tension I described earlier in the documents of Vatican II. By remaining faithful to what is known, the revelation of God in the Word, and full of hope about what is unknown, the 'seeds of the Word', the Church as the eschatological pilgrim People of God looks forward to the perfection of the relationship with God which Christ promises and the Church itself anticipates in its liturgical, ethical and social life.

Thus what I called earlier the 'catholic instinct', which typifies Catholic Christianity at its best, is neither a pious individualism nor what de Lubac refers to as a 'false collectivism'.[58] It is, rather, characterised by a particularity responsible before the specific historical circumstances of its origins, and by a universality responsible before the 'seeds of the Word', the traces of the other which continue to haunt the present. This paradox is only ever resolved when the Church learns how to be itself: through the practice of return and repetition which, in giving thanks for *God's* act of welcome and hospitality, links the faithful liturgical practice of *this* community here and now with the story of its origins and the promise of its fulfilment.

---

[55] McPartlan 1995:92.

[56] De Lubac's achievement, says Milbank, 1990a:226, is to show how salvation is *inherently* social and historical, that is to say '[t]he individual is always saved in a *particular manner*, according to his situation with regard to the Christian past, and in prospect of the Christian future'.

[57] Whereas dialectic moves an argument forward by alternation, paradox seeks the 'simultaneity of the one and the other' (see McPartlan 1993:11–12, quoting de Lubac's *Paradoxes of Faith*, San Francisco: Ignatius, 1987).

[58] See de Lubac 1950, chapter 11, 'Person and Society'.

The aim of de Lubac's historical studies, McPartlan observes, is 'to re-instate the Church as the "marvel" and to understand the Eucharist as the "mystical principle, permanently active" to realise it'.[59] This, however, is very far from commending an ahistorical model of the Church safely re-moved from the action. To use a phrase of Jules Monchanin's, the liturgi-cal cycle of the Church makes present in a 'sacrificial *moment*' the whole of human history and points it towards its completion.[60] At the same time, however, the Eucharist is also a '*sacrificial* moment', the re-membering, the putting back together, of the *broken* body of Christ. As liturgy, the Eucharist anchors the community in its own history, but, as a story which can be traced back to earlier traumatic experiences, of Exodus and Exile, it also interacts with, and stimulates imaginative variations upon, more recent memories, such as the horrors of the Shoah and the sufferings of dalits, the 'broken' of caste-ridden India.[61] As the re-presentation of the broken Body of Christ–again in both senses of the term–the Eucharist disposes all Chris-tians to remain waiting in hope, but also confident that the constant re-newal of the sources of a universalist tradition enables the reimagining of its meaning for others. In this sense, the 'Eucharist makes the Church' not by continuously rescuing a fallible community from its own sense of fail-ure, still less by giving a particular group a sense of identity set apart from others, but by bringing the community back to the full implications of *God's story*, the *missio Dei*, that sending out and return which refigures all human existence. Christians find themselves gathered *ad intra* as the People of God by the celebration of the Eucharist, but the same practice of remembering and rereading sees them dispersed *ad extra* on a mission which is the ex-pression of God's continuing dialogue with the whole of humanity.

Learning from the story of Christ

This is what makes the Eucharist 'ethical': the relationship which it es-tablishes with the other. As an action of the Church, the liturgy of the Eucharist expresses Levinas's Abrahamic journey, 'a movement of the same unto the other which never returns to the same'.[62] In the first place,

---

[59] McPartlan 1993:79, quoting *Corpus Mysticum*, p. 103.

[60] Monchanin 1965:167–9 (emphasis added).

[61] See Devasahayam 1992a:54: 'Jesus allows his body to be broken as a representative of the broken humanity in order that through his breaking, all the broken will find healing and succour.'

[62] Levinas 1986:348.

the Eucharist brings to mind and celebrates the story of the Church's origins in the people of Israel. More profoundly, however, the Church is reminded that this story told about origins is itself other. It is, in an obvious sense, the story of another people which may not be colonised without doing it violence. What the Eucharist remembers, therefore, is more than a trace of the distant past but, more accurately, that past as it is refigured by the Paschal Mystery of the Death and Resurrection of Christ. The Church is formed in the present after the manner of Christ facing the otherness of his own death.[63] The Eucharist is thus the centre of the 'school of faith' which is Christianity, and the focal point around which those ideas and concepts central to an understanding of the Christian virtues – and therefore of Christian personhood – formed in response to God's continuing initiative may gather.

It is, no doubt, easier to recognise in the unfolding of the liturgy the God who gathers a people for himself by an act of self-sacrifice than it is to search for 'seeds of the Word' in the more infuriatingly diffuse forms of inter-faith dialogue. And yet, if the Eucharist is the 'school' where a generous hospitality towards the other is learned, then the former inspires the latter. Both in their different ways are manifestations of that continuous dialogue of God with humankind which begins with God's initiative and returns to a completeness in God. Both tell a similar story of hospitality and welcome, a story which teaches Christians how to act as host and to respond as guest. In the different stages of inter-faith dialogue, and in the celebration of the Eucharist which gives rise to this and all other practices of Christian faith, is to be discerned a similar movement and a similar response to the hospitable God. Subjectivity, as described earlier, is a project of engagement with areas of passivity and otherness which continually arise and return. Dialogues and conversations with people of other faith traditions usually begin with the familiar, show a progressive encounter with the unfamiliar and lead to a gradual and sometimes painful resolution. They involve a movement – literal as much as metaphorical – over the threshold into a world where one's sense of identity is questioned. The stages which are discernible in this process have already been noted; they mirror Ricoeur's use of the three categories – same, other and analogous. Seen as a process of engagement with the other they have an almost ritual-like quality: a response to the welcome and invitation to enter; a temporary initiation into the life of a

---

[63] Bouyer 1965:11ff.

new and strange society; a confrontation with something which is 'other' about oneself; a return to the familiar which is effected by translating the experience of being altered into a form comprehensible in the familiar world. But what makes the ritual a liturgy, a 'work which makes the people', is its ethical quality: it is never simply 'for itself' but, in Levinas's sense, 'for the other'. The Christian liturgy is never a neat and finished process, a mechanism for capturing the Word in a formula of words. As Levinas goes on warning us, every attempt to close the 'gap' between same and other risks betrayal, the act of Saying becoming encased in the Said. Thus it is that even the most ethical of all rituals, the liturgy of the Eucharist which makes and remakes the community of faith in response to the ever-welcoming and hospitable God, must be repeated. The Christian '*habitus*', whether understood as the theological virtues of faith, hope and love, or as the more practical dispositions of generous welcome and hospitality to the other, springs from a '*docta ignorantia*': a responsible reticence which waits upon God. In this way, the Church becomes properly sacramental, sensitised to the call God goes on making to be a 'sign and instrument' of the unity of all creation.

The task for a Christian theology of dialogue is to discern 'seeds of the Word' – not so much, as noted earlier, incipient or 'cut-down' versions of the Word, as signs of the Christ who leads all people to the Father. Christ, the 'image of the unseen God', is the one who enables Christians to bring into a single focus experiences which inspire faith, hope and love *and* all those more disarming and threatening experiences, of loss, confusion and abandonment which are inseparable from *any* human relationship. The question is not, therefore, how Christians can find a way of including the other within a single story, still less a theological scheme, but whether they can discern in their own experience of being *altered* – made other – something of the mystery of Christ's Death and Resurrection. Liturgy, the celebration of God's act of welcome to his people, inspires a faith which would welcome others to share God's gifts. But it also enables Christians to renew their hope in the God who promises always to remain whenever faith enters the darkness of loss and incomprehension. It is this latter experience, the more passive experience of the guest who must wait upon the initiative of the host, which takes us from the question of Christian personhood to the nature of the self-revealing God.

8

Contemplating the depths of God

The confession, that in Jesus of Nazareth is revealed the very presence and promise of God for humankind, is made against the background of what I have called a 'context of otherness'. By this term I do not refer only to the originating story of the one who challenges all human logic and wisdom by undergoing death – though it is clearly this story which takes the lead in the formation of Christian faith. I also mean the continuing story of a community of faith which recognises in its own sometimes fraught and broken relations with people of other faiths a trace of the God who is always other and beyond all imaginings. In the previous chapter, I tried to bring these two dimensions together. When the Christian community gathers to celebrate the Eucharist, it does not enact a ritual which subsumes all meaning into some predetermined interpretive scheme, but is itself formed and reformed by God's own work of 're-membering', in the literal sense of putting back together. Liturgy – the 'work of the people' – makes the Church. It thus enables the Christian *habitus*: notably, in a world of many faiths, a contemplative and ethical sensitivity to the action of God's Spirit wherever it is to be discerned. A measure of passivity or patience is, therefore, intrinsic to Christian personhood. Or, to put it the other way round, a properly Christian response to the God who speaks requires time and discernment. In continuing to confess its faith, the Church recognises that God's self-revelation in the economy of creation and in the history of salvation is a unity, yet is never reducible to a single straightforward narrative. Thus any attempt to recount the Christian story as it continues to unfold in our contemporary world means returning to the Church's own experience of God in Christ in order to rehearse what it is that gives *this* particular story a universal reference.

Yet any notion of 'return' is, of course, problematic. If the Eucharist can be said to 'make the Church', it is not because it allows a nostalgic retrieval which mends the 'broken middle' but because the action of telling the story reminds Christians that the middle is – precisely – broken. For de Certeau, the Church is haunted, indeed defined, by a sense of loss and separation, to the extent that he can speak of Christianity as 'founded on the *loss of a body* – the loss of the body of Jesus Christ, compounded with the "loss" of the body of Israel, of a "nation" and its genealogy'.[1] Compared with the living body of the Jewish people which remains anchored in its original social reality, continuing to draw life from the Covenant of Sinai, Christian faith begins with a rupture, a break with the past symbolised in the New Testament account by the tearing of the veil of the temple (Mark 15.38; Luke 23.45; Matthew 27.51). The God who raises Jesus from the dead has done something new; the touchstone of Christian faith lies not with fidelity to the practice of the Torah, but with a life lived in hope of the Resurrection. And yet, as Paul insists, the old has not been effaced. Indeed, the Church can only understand this sense of something new by relating it to what is past, what has been lost yet somehow remains. When the disciples encounter the Risen Lord, he still bears the marks of the Crucifixion. The new life of transformation does not overwhelm but lives in a sometimes disconcerting tension with what has gone before.

As the early Christian community begins to come to terms with its initial loss, new texts – or, to be more accurate, new relationships with old texts – are born, and with them new 'bodies', new practices of remembrance, new structures, new doctrines, all making for a new way in which believers in God's gracious self-revelation can understand themselves. In these terms, to say that Christian faith begins with a sense of loss is, more positively, an extrapolation from the Resurrection experience in which the one who was intimately known as companion and friend is always changed, strangely different, same yet other, known yet unknown. Recognition of such otherness depends now on Jesus's initiative, his words and actions: they know him 'in the breaking of the bread' (Luke 24.35). The Eucharist is thus no communion of privileged initiates, but a sign that the Spirit of Christ is at work, constantly calling the Christian community back to responsibility to the God who calls.

Like all religious traditions, Christianity seeks to recover what is always bound to be lost. And, perhaps more than most, Christianity runs the risk of

---

[1] De Certeau 1992:81.

seeking a premature finality for itself. Liturgy can easily be reduced to 'mere' ritual, or – as Levinas would put it – the act of Saying is always in danger of betrayal by the Said. My point, however, is that loss, distance, a sense of the provisional, a certain passivity before the other, are of the essence of Christian faith. In coming to terms with this truth, I first noted two complementary dimensions of a Christian practice of faith – the 'interior' and the 'social' – which go to make up a contemplative and an ethical sensitivity to the demands of the other. The aim has been to show that Christian subjectivity is formed neither through a 'passive' interiority nor an 'active' exteriority which exist independently of each other. To be 'oneself as another' entails a participation in the mystery of God's self-giving which alone can mend the 'broken middle' of inter-faith relations. Hence a third dimension. Celebrated in the liturgy, the gap opened up by the 'loss of the body' is not so much closed as renewed; the action of Christ facing death is mirrored in the everyday experience of Christians learning how to relate to the other.

Having spent some time discussing the Christian *habitus*, with these contemplative, ethical and liturgical dimensions, I now want to argue that the whole issue of what makes for Christian integrity and personhood invites us back into the doctrine of the self-revealing God and, more specifically, into what might be called the 'originating conversation' which expresses the inner life of the Trinity. Again, however, the danger of a totalising of the other looms, so let me begin this penultimate meditation by invoking another version of de Certeau's 'ethical heterology'. The micro-discourses I shall use allow for an illuminating comparison of different approaches to the returning other: the two founders of the Śantivanam Ashram, Jules Monchanin and Henri le Saux.

The immanence of one in all

As McPartlan points out, Henri de Lubac's mystical theology of the Eucharist owes much to Monchanin's inspiration.[2] Some years after his

---

[2] McPartlan 1993:21–2. In a conference which de Lubac addressed soon after the Council on the topic '*Lumen Gentium* and the Fathers', he brackets Monchanin with 'another precursor', Teilhard de Chardin, linking the latter's mysticism of the 'Eternal Feminine', who addresses humankind as biblical Wisdom, with Monchanin's meditation on 'the Virgin in India' (see proceedings edited in Miller 1966:153–75). Monchanin and Teilhard, who first met in 1925, maintained a mutual esteem and engaged in critical correspondence. According to Ursula King, 1980:185, Monchanin was among the first to compare Teilhard's thought with the evolutionary vision of Śri Aurobindo. See also the notes of the lecture, 'Teilhard et Śri Aurobindo', in Monchanin 1974:315–17.

death, de Lubac produced a brief personal memoir. In it he pays tribute to this scholarly 'man of the Church' whose destiny was to live out the 'great Christian paradox, that of "the Church placed in the tomb" '.[3] Theirs was a friendship founded on mutual esteem and a genuine passion to renew the Church with the forgotten teaching of the Fathers.[4] At their first meeting, in 1930, Monchanin introduced de Lubac to Indian religions. De Lubac was clearly impressed by Monchanin's learning, but more so by the depth of his personal mysticism which, according to de Lubac, was always anchored in the Trinity and nourished by the liturgy of the Church.[5] To Monchanin he ascribes a succinct if enigmatic formula which expresses for him the true nature of Christian personhood, the life of a world 'ruled by the mysterious immanence of one in all, and of all in each one'.[6]

De Lubac uses these words to speak of the difficult resolution which Catholic spirituality proposes to the 'alternating rhythms' of an 'interior' and a 'social' tendency, the poles of individualism and collectivism which so much occupied him in *Catholicism*.[7] Detachment and solitude are not an invitation to solipsism, but the means by which the individual person recovers the image of God, and learns how to respond to the invitation to live a life of relationship with the other – a relationship which is expressed theologically by the notion of the circumincession of the Persons of the Trinity.

The same guiding idea is to be found in the book which Monchanin co-authored with Henri le Saux to explain the goals of the Śantivanam Ashram.[8] Monchanin's writing, spread through a series of articles, lectures and posthumous papers and notes, is not systematic.[9] Yet he

---

[3] De Lubac 1966:117. The text includes a comparison between Monchanin and Teilhard; pp. 119–51.

[4] According to Françoise Jacquin, 1996:99–100, de Lubac always insisted to the end of his life that he was the one who gained most from their exchanges.

[5] 'Christian mysticism, he would say, "is trinitarian or it is nothing" ' (see de Lubac 1966:19–21). Monchanin frequently referred to India as the 'land of the Trinity' (see e.g. 1965:9, 18f. etc.) and named the Śantivanam Ashram by the upanishadic title of *Saccidananda*, a combination of *sat*, being, *cit*, thought, and *ananda*, bliss.

[6] In de Lubac 1950:187; quotation from 'De la solitude à Dieu', in *Médecine et Adolescence*; Lyon: Lavandier, 1936; p. 293.

[7] De Lubac 1950:188.

[8] See Monchanin and le Saux 1956. Subtitled 'un essai d'intégration de la tradition monastique de l'Inde', this book is essentially an expanded edition of the much shorter booklet *An Indian Benedictine Ashram*, Tiruchirapalli, 1951; revised as *An Indian Ashram*; Douglas, 1964. According to Rodhe 1993:51, Monchanin wrote the first chapter and Le Saux most of the rest (see also Stuart 1995:48 n13).

[9] The fullest bibliography, with some secondary literature, is in Mattam 1975:197–200.

is guided by an intense theological vision of a world already being 'assumed, purified and transformed' by the Spirit of Christ which animates the Church and dwells in each person.[10] In the Church, to which all people are called to belong, each individual receives a unique vocation for the sake of the whole. Monchanin saw this clearly: without the contemplative the Church would lose its vision of the ultimate future of a life shared with the divine Persons. In a series of densely argued paragraphs, Monchanin finds in the life of the Trinity not just the prime analogue of the communion between the members of the Church, but – he muses – 'perhaps the beginning of a solution' for the philosophical problem of inter-subjectivity.[11] However, his main concern lies elsewhere. Dominating all Monchanin's meditations is the antinomy in Hinduism between a personal and an impersonal God, between the personalist communion of *bhakti* and the impersonal fusion of *Advaita*. Only in the Trinitarian God, essentially a God of love, is a reconciliation to be found; in the Holy Spirit, the 'completion' of the Trinity who leads the Church back to the communion of love, India awaits her fulfilment.[12]

However similar their theological vision, de Lubac and Monchanin lived it out very differently – de Lubac by developing in systematic fashion a theological account of the 'essential passivity' of mystical experience, Monchanin by pioneering a model of the contemplative life adapted to the missionary needs of India.[13] A life of prayer and study, sharing the customs and culture of local people in the manner of an Indian ascetic, was not aimed at dialogue, in the narrow sense of the term, still less at proselytism, but at the evangelisation of Indian culture and religion. Although steeped in the classical texts of Christianity and Hinduism and dominated by a profound Trinitarian vision, he

---

[10] At a conference to celebrate the centenary of his birth, held at Lyon in April 1995, Monchanin's biographer Françoise Jacquin expressed his project in terms of the three words '*assumer–purifier–transformer*'. India would only be evangelised when all its spiritual values and experiences had been assumed, purified of sin, and had their deepest meaning transformed into a universal message. See report in Matus 1996.

[11] Monchanin and le Saux 1956:20ff.

[12] See Weber 1977:122. Monchanin finds in the New Testament the *sensus plenior* of the upanishadic texts, the 'fulfilment' to which they point (see Mattam 1975:168f.).

[13] McPartlan, 1993:51f., tells us that, in his introduction to André Ravier's *Mystique et les mystiques* (Paris: Desclée de Brouwer; 1965), 'de Lubac said that there is "an essential passivity in true mysticism" and that the Catholic position hinges upon the distinction and relation of the two terms in his title, "Mysticism and Mystery". His account bears the marks of his study of grace in the same year, with its painstaking precisions.'

seems content to contrast concepts with a rigorous clarity which makes the differences between them – and the philosophical complexity of interpretation – seem at times insurmountable.[14] This leads Michael Amaladoss to comment that Monchanin was never able to 'resolve the tension between his Cartesian mind and his artistic and mystic instinct'.[15] Joseph Mattam is more generous. Monchanin, he says, 'has done us a great service in shaking us out of our complacency'.[16] He wrote during the early years of Indian independence, long before the issues of nationhood, endemic poverty and caste discrimination gave rise to dalit theology. The limitations of a theology still steeped in the classical patterns of Patristic tradition and European philosophy reflect the tensions in the pre-Vatican II Catholic Church rather than the self-imposed demands of the scholarly academic.[17]

Monchanin's concerns are similar to those of de Nobili: to understand in order 'to be understood'. In an Indian Church which at that time was still deeply suspicious of anything 'pagan', Monchanin saw the need to develop a prior and more fundamental familiarity with the religious language of the people of India. He does not establish a *theory* of interreligious relations, but is more concerned for sound practice rooted in 'adoration, an act which is but an anticipation, foretaste and rehearsal of eternal life in the bosom of the Holy Trinity'.[18] Although there is an idealist tinge to his project – 'to recapture Christianity in its original outpouring . . . to isolate the essence . . . of the civilisation to be christianised'[19] – it would be wrong to dismiss him as an Orientalist intellectual. He was quite prepared to accept the demands of an 'age-long vigil', for – as he put it – 'very often "Love can enter where the intellect must stand at the door" '.[20]

---

[14] Thus, for example, despite the constant focus on spirituality and religious practice he has grave reservations about Yoga: 'Today it is almost always associated with pelagianism, virtual atheism, and questionable *tantric* practices' (see Weber 1977:120; see also 'Yoga et hesychasme', in Monchanin 1974:109–17).

[15] Amaladoss 1995:315.

[16] Mattam 1975:172.

[17] Particularly in the Church in France. Françoise Jacquin, 1996:261–7, notes the effect that Pius XII's encyclical *Humani Generis* had on French missionaries everywhere - especially those, like Monchanin and the French Jesuits of the Madurai Province, who were close to Henri de Lubac and others who were suspended from teaching.

[18] Monchanin and le Saux 1964:10.

[19] Monchanin 1965:132.

[20] See 'The Quest of the Absolute', in Weber 1975:132.

Love lived by waiting in a dark night

Monchanin never deviated from the central conviction, which he shared with de Lubac, that all things had to be rethought in the light of theology and theology itself through mysticism.[21] He saw himself not as a traditional missionary or 'convertisseur', but as a Christian sannyasi, a witness to the timeless and eternal at the heart of Christianity and Hinduism.[22] Like de Nobili before him, he rejected the strategy of a 'proper' place from which to exercise power, and chose instead to wager on the tactic of 'temporal relations' – to use de Certeau's terminology. The experience of having to wait in the 'crucifying dark night of the soul' makes time for him more than an intellectual conundrum.[23] Whether he is speaking of the contrast with Hindu cyclic ideas, or linking it more speculatively with the Teilhardian 'christosphere', he is always drawn back to the moment of the Incarnation which gives meaning to the whole of history. In a typically allusive essay, which recognises the impossibility of a purely philosophical account of time, he finishes with a brief account of the 'double economy' which characterises what he calls the 'Christic becoming':

> In so far as it is visible, the *body* of the Word Incarnate, it belongs to the economy of the becoming of the Church, of the Spirit, of life, of the world. In so far as it is invisible, the body of the *Word*, it belongs to the eternal circumincession 'which expands unity into Trinity and gathers Trinity into unity". The Incarnation saturates time with the eternal (the Johannine *kai nun*) and confers on becoming ontologized by Christ the absolute gift of the eternal.[24]

For Monchanin, this Augustinian vision of eternity entering into and giving meaning to the flux of time is identified with the early Christian community's experience of the mystery of the Passion and Resurrection which, through the celebration of the Last Supper, continues to guide them as they look forward to the parousia.[25] It is of the very essence of

---

[21] See letter to Mme Adiceam commenting on conversation with de Lubac, Lyon, 20 April 1939; in Monchanin 1974:146.

[22] Monchanin and le Saux 1956:63.

[23] Amongst the 'notes' collected by Duperray is the comment: 'The problem of time is one that obsesses me . . . A philosophy and a theology of time are one of the crying needs of our age' (see Monchanin 1965:129 and ET in Weber 1977:120).

[24] Quoted in Weber 1977:136.

[25] See 'Le temps selon l'hindouisme et le christianisme', in Monchanin 1974:104f.

Christianity to enjoy the unity of a life always lived 'in time' but which is also lived 'in Christ', and therefore manages to anticipate the eternity which is God's.

Mention of the liturgical act which allows the Church to find itself within, yet also above, the passage of time takes us back to the point with which this chapter opened: the 'loss of the body' and the constant return of the other. In many ways, Monchanin's project – which combines the intensity of de Lubac's commitment to historical theology with his own fascination with the otherness of Indian culture – can be described as 'mystics', in de Certeau's sense of the term.[26] For de Certeau 'mystics' arises within a particular historical context, ultimately to be traced back to the split between Church and State resulting from the European wars of religion in the first half of the seventeenth century. The loss of a familiar sense of Church led to a shift within Christian discourse, from what de Certeau calls a 'long Socratic and spiritual tradition of the "know thyself" ' to questions which arise from a new experience of dislocation and 'otherness': ' "Who else lives inside of you?" and "To whom do you speak?" '[27] What de Certeau is describing here is the ever-growing complexity of the Christian life as it responds to 'other voices'; layers of otherness are forever dislocating that fundamental sense of the 'loss of the body'. At the same time, he is only reminding us of the 'mystic' quality of *all* Christian discourse, a discourse which originates in the call of God, *the* Other, which may not simply be reduced within the familiar patterns of history. Here I recall de Certeau's vision of the historian's task, that of 'calming the dead', paying the debt to the past by setting out its 'regularities and their modifications' according to a largely linear temporal pattern. The mystic, on the other hand, de Certeau refers to as 'seized by time', by what erupts and transforms.[28] Theology, especially a theology which is rooted in an act of liturgical praise and thanksgiving, seeks to combine these two concepts of time – or, in de Certeau's terms, to overlay the one with the other. In these terms Monchanin can be seen as grappling with a version of the dual responsibility which has run through this book. For him, however, the task is to go on narrating the Christian story not in

---

[26] See translator's note in de Certeau 1992:ix–x. The translation of de Certeau's *la mystique* by 'a made-up English term, *mystics*' is intended to avoid the 'essentialist' connotations of the term 'mysticism' and addresses the 'historical specificity' of de Certeau's object of study: the reification of an original adjectival usage which in the early 17th century assumed a life of its own.

[27] De Certeau 1992:195.

[28] De Certeau 1992:11.

distinction from the disturbance wrought by the returning other in this present moment, but by seeing in the latter a trace or sign of the Spirit of Christ, the 'possibility of God' which in its very challenge to faith confirms the Christian vocation.

Life far from the familiar can appear as a threat to the stability of the self. Like de Nobili before him, Monchanin lived with his own sense of vulnerability. But for neither of them was the 'loss of a body', their experience of distance and separation, translated into a mourning nostalgia. Rather, Monchanin echoes a theme familiar from the Fourth Gospel: the paradox of the Lord who leaves the disciples to go to the Father yet promises that they will be 'where I am'.[29] The promised Spirit is more than a consoler, but precisely the one who will lead the disciples into all the truth. Such an eschatological emphasis is very far from providing the Church with some all-powerful explanation of the totality of truth, still less of the mystery of God. Something more humble yet more radical is envisaged. By referring to the Eucharist as the 'completion of the Incarnation . . . the coming of the Paracletophany',[30] Monchanin makes clear that he is not proposing a finality for the community which gathers to renew itself in the liturgy of faith – making it a triumphant ritual of consolation in the midst of darkness and misunderstanding. Rather, the Eucharist is the 'prefiguration, the sacramental realisation' of the Parousia, which brings to mind for succeeding generations the meaning and achievement of the redemption won by Christ and celebrates his return.[31] The Church is only brought to a fulfilment by God's own Spirit in God's own time. Which is not to say that the same Spirit is not at work in *this* time, this decisive moment. Christians act now as mystics, constantly reinscribing the experience of the other within the texts of their own history.

Contemplating the depths of God

This is what makes Monchanin emblematic of the acting and suffering self formed before the broken Body of Christ – taking the image in both the ecclesial and eucharistic sense. What Ricoeur discusses in terms of differing levels of passivity, Monchanin discovered in his attempt to think through

---

[29] See, for example, John 7.34, 12.26, 14.3, 17.24.

[30] Weber 1977:164.

[31] Monchanin and le Saux 1956:83.

his Christian faith in dialogue with Hinduism. He anticipated the Council, and the contemporary Church's attempts to come to terms with its relationship with the other: faithful to the best of tradition yet always open to the demands of the destabilising relationship with the irreducibly other. He thus represents the best qualities of Talal Asad's 'mobile personality', committed to living in and negotiating the 'middle', the space between.[32] That he should be broken in the attempt does not take away from the integrity of that commitment, nor does it invalidate the central argument of this book, that the Christian self finds its identity as 'oneself as another' in response to the God who speaks from the 'context of otherness'.

Monchanin was dominated by a Teilhardian vision of a world in process of transformation: the immanence of 'one in all and all in one'. To his strongest critic, his colleague Henri le Saux, Swami Abhishiktananda, what this amounted to was a policy of 'wait and see'.[33] It is clearly possible, as I have noted in my first reading of Levinas, to overemphasise passivity before the other. What of that testimony to the abundance of God's self-gift to which the Christian is committed? If Monchanin's version of 'mystics' is to wait faithfully upon the completion of what is always God's work, the endless journeying of Abhishiktananda is emblematic of the openness dimension of the inter-faith dilemma: a thoroughgoing commitment to follow the homeless Christ who, to quote de Certeau again, is 'the one continually "converted" to the inaccessible Father who says to him "come" '.[34] Together, Monchanin and Abhishiktananda remind us of what we have learned from the dialogue between Levinas and Ricoeur, that Christian subjectivity is formed neither through a 'passive' interiority nor an 'active' exteriority which exist independently of each other, but through participation in the mystery of God's self-giving which alone can mend the 'broken middle'. Here I seek only to draw a certain contrast between Monchanin and Abhishiktananda while setting them within the same frame of reference: what has come to be described as the 'inculturation' of a fully Indian Church. Abhishiktananda fully embraced what Monchanin could never attempt. He soaked himself in the world of *advaitic* Hinduism – with all its attendant risks to faith and identity.

---

[32] Talal Asad 1993:11.

[33] Abhishiktananda's words in a letter prior to his leaving Śantivanam in March 1957 (see Stuart 1995:102).

[34] De Certeau 1987a:289.

Even the briefest account of one of the most colourful and influential figures in the history of the post-Vatican II Church in India would
fail to do justice to his complex and, as he would admit, inconsistent
theological vision.[35] Unlike Monchanin, Abhishiktananda took very
easily to writing, but his theology still has to be prised from the passionate outpourings of his voluminous correspondence and from the often very personal reflections in his many books and articles.[36] Although
very much the restless explorer, he is also conscious of the need to pur-
ify and prepare the Church for its mission in India. He begins a small
book intended as remote preparation for the All India Seminar of 1969
with the Vatican Council's description of the Church as 'the universal
sacrament of salvation' (LG 48), and argues in language reminiscent of
Monchanin for the 'primacy of spiritual values and contemplation'.[37]
The future of the Indian Church will depend on a priestly ideal modelled on the Hindu *guru* or *jñani*, a spiritual teacher who 'knows' through
his own experience of God. Together with Monchanin, Abhishiktananda had already introduced many aspects of Indian culture and
practice into their daily living and prayer. He thus takes the use of Vedas
and Upanishads in Christian worship for granted. But he is also clear
that adequate studies and preparations must be made.[38] Translation of
words is not enough; an Indian rite will require a 'total transformation
of the Church'.[39] This, however, raises an almost insoluble problem, for
Indian worship is 'cosmic', while the 'Eucharistic anaphora is of course
the recapitulation of the history of salvation'.[40] As he writes to Raimon
Panikkar:

> Will the transformation of Christianity into Vedantin formulas leave
> it any other reality than the (provisional) reality of the cults which
> have succeeded each other on the soil of Bharat? And if Christianity
> cannot be expressed in the religious–cultural terms of India without

---

[35] Not the least difficulty in making any such assessment is the number of different
editions of his work. He was rarely satisfied, and even his most carefully worked-over text,
Saccidananda, he dismissed at the end of his life as 'outmoded' (see Stuart 1995:286).

[36] See Stuart 1995:xii who comments in his Preface that an account of Abhishiktananda's
life through his letters 'enables him to "speak for himself", and to reveal himself as he was – deeply
committed, yet always vulnerable'.

[37] Abhishiktananda 1970:1–5.

[38] Abhishiktananda 1970:24ff. See also Abhishiktananda 1969 (subtitled 'an Essay in
Christian Self-Criticism').

[39] Stuart 1995:192.

[40] Stuart 1995:192.

dissolving away, then it is not *catholic*. I do not see how one can escape from this dilemma.[41]

Abhishiktananda's 'solution' is to practise a form of encounter which, he repeats, can only take place at the level of 'interiority', between people committed to silence and prayer.[42] Soon after settling at Śantivanam, he went to the Hindu shrine at Arunachala and met the great Hindu saint Ramana Maharshi.[43] The experience of encountering such extraordinary holiness in someone totally untouched by Christianity marked him for the rest of his life. He always hankered after the life of total immersion in *Advaita* and only seemed genuinely content in the company of other wandering sannyasis or, as he recalls in a personal account of a pilgrimage to the source of the Ganges, when integrating elements of Hindu devotion and liturgy into his own spirituality.[44] The result is the often expressed conviction that the insights of the Upanishads are 'the highest experience of the mind'.[45] The Christian liturgy and *Advaita* are on 'different planes'—wherein lies the 'agonizing tension'.[46] In what Stuart calls the 'middle stage' of his pilgrimage (the years which coincided with the Council and its immediate aftermath), Abhishiktananda argued for a relationship expressed in terms of a 'theology of fulfilment . . . assuming the convergence upon the historical Christ and the Church, of all the religious and spiritual experiences of mankind'.[47]

Continuing to narrate the Christian story

By the end of his life, however, Abhishiktananda seems almost to have abandoned any attempt to develop an 'inculturated' theology. Thus he begins his best-known work, *Saccidananda*, with the powerfully stated conviction that the biblical 'mystery of darkness and silence which Jesus has

---

[41] Stuart 1995:217; letter of 10 July 1969.

[42] See e.g. Stuart 1995:135; letter of 29 April 1961 addressed to Canon Lemarié.

[43] See Stuart 1995, especially pp. 28–32. The story of Ramana (1879–1950) is told in Mahadevan 1977. For Abhishiktananda's own account of Ramana's Vedantic experience, 'Death Transcended', see 1974a:19–29. After his second stay at Ramana's ashram, Abhishiktananda wrote that his heart was 'now divided between the sacred river (Kavery) [on the banks of which Śantivanam was situated] and the sacred mountain (Arunachala)' (see Stuart 1995:32).

[44] See Abhishiktananda 1966ab; reproduced in Abhishiktananda 1974b:137–74. See the account in Stuart 1995:162, which identifies his priest–companion as Raimundo Panikkar.

[45] Stuart 1995:206. 'For me everything is in the Upanishads' (see Stuart 1995:284).

[46] Stuart 1995:111.

[47] Introduction to Abhishiktananda 1974a:xv.

revealed to us as the bosom of the Father' and the upanishadic symbolism of the 'untouched, undivided Brahman' discovered in the 'cave of the heart' are set together as 'the very same mystery'.[48] In the final pages of the same book, he admits that the Christian's certainty of faith and the Hindu *jñani*'s intuition into the nature of Brahman are 'quite different'.[49] The inconsistency, however, is due less to the difficulty of inculturating faith than to different, and perhaps incompatible, approaches to the practice of dialogue and the theology of religions. What begins as a project to integrate *Advaita* into Christian faith leads to a more Pauline confession that the Lord 'does not play with us, and his gifts once given are irrevocable'.[50] As Paul wrestled with the question of the consistency of God's promises to his people, so Abhishiktananda struggled to express his own faith in a God whose mystery surrounded him in the world of the other. In one of his final letters, he returns to what he calls the 'essential teaching' of his guru Ramana Maharshi: 'there is no such thing as "realization" '.[51] For the Christian, what faith demands is not the pursuit of some new syncretic form of interiority. Rather Abhishiktananda is drawn back to the living out of the responsibilities of faith with a renewed intensity. In the end, he says, the faith of the Christian 'rests on the experience of his Lord and *Sadguru*, Jesus. But there is also something else – the testimony of the Spirit who has awakened him in the depths of his soul to the mystery of Jesus, the Son; but this is a secret between him and God (Rev 2.17).'[52]

The fact that Abhishiktananda never resolved his dilemma does not lessen his significance as a prophet of Vatican II's call to 'recognise, preserve and promote those spiritual and moral good things' found amongst people of other faiths. For all his criticism of Monchanin, he continued the older man's project by pursuing it to its logical conclusion. With Abhishiktananda, inculturation takes on its most radical form: not a translation of the language of faith but of the subject himself. To become a 'border-crosser' means passing over the threshold and living no longer in one's 'own place' but in the world of the other. However, to set Monchanin

---

[48] Abhishiktananda 1974a:12.

[49] Abhishiktananda 1974a:198.

[50] Abhishiktananda 1974a:198.

[51] Stuart 1995:320; letter to Marc Chadue 23 November 1973.

[52] Abhishiktananda 1974a:201. Abhishiktananda explains the term 'Sadguru' as 'the Master of Truth pre-eminently' who 'alone introduces others to the Real, to *sat*'; see 1974a:202 n5.

as a more passive 'mystic' in dialectical tension with Abhishiktananda the active 'prophet' would be to miss the crucial point.[53] In de Certeau's terms, mystics *are* prophets because they are the ones who keep alive the Word which in its otherness constantly returns to disturb the world of the same. Recognising the danger of reducing Saying to Said, of encompassing the other within a theological totality, they go on following after and searching out the traces of the homeless Christ which always exceed the effort to inscribe him in a formula of words. In this sense, both Monchanin and Abhishiktananda struggled with the dilemma and the dual responsibility which have run through this book.[54] What they both discovered is that there is no neat, predictable way in which Christian faith can be practised, let alone spoken about when facing the other, any more than the darkness and the richness of our talk about God can ever be definitively spoken. In lives which constantly oscillated between two different worlds, they went on telling the Christian story of *kenosis* and resurrection and celebrating it in the Eucharist where the action of the self-communicating God receives its most poignant and vivid account.

In the previous chapter, I spoke about the dispositions which arise from the Eucharist in terms of the theological virtues. The evangelical responsibility of Christian faith is learned in that liturgical act of praise and thanksgiving which inspires a contemplative and ethical sense of the presence of the hospitable and welcoming God at the heart of all creation. But the Eucharist is also an effective sign of what God goes on doing in our midst. For Monchanin, the Eucharist prefigures the Parousia and anticipates the coming of the Spirit on all creation. For Abhishiktananda, it is the sign of the communion of the faithful and an anticipation of what the Church is yet to become. As he puts it, while remembering a simple celebration in the open air at the source of the Ganges:

> The Eucharist must be celebrated in every part of the globe in order
> to make actually present in time the Resurrection, the Ascension, and

---

[53] This is not to deny that this disjunction expresses something of the different *emphases* in religious traditions and, as such, is a useful heuristic device in the complex task of understanding the other. Problems arise, however, when it is given an almost determining status within theology. David Tracy sees the contemporary theological task as an inter-religious hermeneutical practice which 'can best be described as "mystical–prophetic"', but the two 'types' that he brings into dialogue are not persons in relationship but two forms of rhetoric (see Tracy 1990, especially pp. 9–26, 95–123).

[54] Expressed in the titles of the two opening chapters of their joint work *Ermites du Saccidananda*: Monchanin's tight and tortured 'Au nom de l'Église' and Abhishiktananda's more lyrical 'Et au nom de l'Inde'.

Christ's return in glory, here the sign for Christians which is already realized, there the sign of the invincible hope of the Church. The bread and wine which I shall offer here in my Mass will be the calling towards God of all these pilgrims at the sacred sources of the rivers in the Himalayas, of all the priests, all ascetics, those of our time, of days gone by, and of the future, for the Eucharist transcends all time. Through the sacramental word, they will, so to speak, pass into the Body and Blood of the Lamb, the one who alone adores the Father in spirit and in truth. By this *Word* they will finally attain their true and perfect being. By it the glory of the Trinity will finally be proclaimed in these holy places.[55]

For both, the Eucharist gathers the whole of creation to God, for, as Abhishiktananda puts it, the Eucharist, and the whole sacramental character of the Church, is 'both the promise – and also the foretaste here and now – of the last day, the return in the Spirit to the Father of all that has been made, the completion of the cycle of Love'.[56] And yet, for all the grand visions which inspire hope in what God promises, the Church is not yet gathered to that fullness which is God's. It exists now 'in between', as much part of the 'broken middle' as any other community of faith. For all that that fullness is sacramentally anticipated, same and other, known and unknown, remain to a great extent hidden from each other within the infinity of God's continually unfolding purposes.

Founding Catholicity

I have argued that there is more to theology of religions than resolving the 'problem' of religious pluralism. Rather, the Christian theologian in dialogue with the other is called faithfully to reflect on the experience of tracing a pilgrimage of constant departure which is also an entry into this fullness which God promises. My contention is that the eminently pragmatic commitment of 'mystic–prophets' like Monchanin and Abhishiktananda to the telling of the Christian story of the Death and Resurrection of Christ comes much closer to illustrating this experience than a theology concerned for the strategic placing of a problematic other. But to make them prophets of the contemporary practice of inter-faith dialogue does not imply that they represent a completely novel approach

---

[55] Abhishiktananda 1974b:169.

[56] Abhishiktananda 1974a:58.

to Christian mission. Rather, they seek to relive, as much as reread, the sources of Christian tradition – in particular that first decisive break faced by the early Church and its engagement with Graeco-Roman civilisation.[57] As I showed in an earlier chapter, Jesuit missionaries such as de Nobili developed a similar reflective capacity to work within the terms set by the other. Like Paul the ex-Pharisee, whose wrestling with the God of Israel led him to engage with Athenian philosophers, they all share the conviction that God 'did not leave himself without witness' (Acts 14.17) but is already at work through his Spirit in the 'context of otherness'. This is why, to 'be understood', they first have to understand;[58] to give faithful witness to the Gospel it is first necessary to acknowledge the 'seeds of the Word', signs of the Spirit which is already there before them. In the West, as Monchanin says, various theological 'constellations' have gathered around the 'nucleus' of the Christian revelation. Rahner's 'world Church', now finding its own voice through local churches such as I have described in India, is beginning to repeat the same process in a different way, a way appropriate to a very particular situation. Something similar can be said for the conversations being developed between Christians and their neighbours from other faiths in so many once mono-cultural Western cities.

This 'micro-discourse' of Monchanin and Abhishiktananda is not some sort of substitute for a theory of the other. What I have called 'ethical heterology' describes not a programme *for* engagement, but a process of prayerful reflection *on* engagement – a theology of dialogue. My point is that such examples of contemplative living and learning will enable something quite different from the traditional forms of proclaiming the Gospel to arise from the sacramental heart of the Church. As Monchanin puts it with characteristic intensity: '*Catholic unity* rests on this gravitational centre, and *Catholicity* is this undefined firmament'.[59] In today's multi-faith world, the complex nature of this 'undefined firmament', the 'broken middle' shared with the other, has become more challenging both within the Church as a whole and, indeed, between the churches. Subsequent to the efforts of ashramites like Monchanin and Abhishiktananda, the more recent development of dalit theology has sought to respond to the ethical and political questions which attend the practice of inter-faith relations. The story could be expanded and taken further; many more examples

---

[57] Monchanin 1965:132.

[58] Halbfass 1988:53.

[59] Monchanin 1965:134; emphases in original.

could be given of the competing demands of more 'contemplative' and more 'active' forms of dialogue. The two, however, are not opposed, as radical interiority to radical exteriority. They reflect different challenges put to a Church seeking constantly to renew its own understanding of its God-given origins, while yet responding to the promise of its fulfilment, to learn 'something of God' in the face-to-face encounter with the Other.

What links them together is the emphasis, which I have sought to maintain throughout this book, on the practice of many forms of inter-personal encounter rather than on a priori theories about 'religion'. This is not to replace the 'strategic' translation of the known with a 'tactical' adjustment within what is unknown, nor to develop a form of inculturation which seeks an accommodation between situation and tradition. Rather, an ethical heterology – the practice of remembrance which seeks ways to allow the other to speak as other – expresses those virtues of faith, hope and love which arise from, and return to, the eucharistic celebration of the self-giving God of Jesus Christ. Here the Church learns that it is the mystery of God's self-giving which alone can mend the 'broken middle' of inter-faith relations. This reminds us again that the whole issue of Christian integrity and personhood, a self formed in face of the other, has to be understood within the doctrine of the Trinitarian God.

The depths of God

Although I have spoken of a dual responsibility – a faithfulness to an evangelical responsibility which speaks of a truth for all people and that respect for the other which would 'recognise, preserve and promote those spiritual and moral good things' in a religiously plural world – and although they will be worked out in myriad different practices, they represent in reality what de Certeau calls a single 'logic of action'.[60] The virtue of faith and the virtue of hope coexist within the virtue of love. Just as the lover cannot reduce the beloved to an object of knowledge nor tolerate separation so, says de Certeau, is it impossible to be Christian 'without the others'.[61] In this he is simply reiterating the best of the

---

[60] In the essay 'How is Christianity Thinkable Today?' in Ward 1997:154.

[61] De Certeau 1987a:112,213. For de Certeau the 'double negative' in the two words 'pas sans' expresses the response of Christian faith to the experience of loss, of 'not there' or 'not yet'. De Certeau finds forms of the expression in the liturgy (especially the prayer 'may I never be separated from you') and in Heidegger's concept of 'nicht ohne'. This is quoted from Heidegger's essay published as 'Temps et être', in L'endurance de la pensée, Paris, 1968. See also the introduction to de Certeau 1992:1–2, and the commentary by Bauerschmidt in Ward 1997:137–8.

'Catholic instinct', to respond generously to the other. The Christian community is 'authorised' not just by a necessary relation to its past but by the necessity of living alongside, and witnessing in love to, other existing communities.

De Certeau's account of Christianity springs directly from his historiography which he applies to the Gospel record as the history of Jesus's own relationship with the otherness of the Father. In seeking to be faithful to the past, Christians must face the irreducible difference of the inaugurating event of Jesus Christ. They will do this after the manner of Jesus's act of loving self-effacement in obedient witness to the Father – yet perforce they will do it differently. Thus every Christian, and Christianity as a whole, is called to be the *'sign of that which is lacking'*.[62] De Certeau does not mean by this that the Christian is to make up the 'lack' by somehow colonising or filling up 'other' spaces, but that the fundamental Christian experience of loss and separation demands a response which springs from the conviction that the only way to remain faithful to the 'author of faith' is precisely to live like him in 'the middle'. For de Certeau, the security of home has to give way to a living with loss if the *'living* God' is to be discovered.[63] The formality of Christian practice, therefore, cannot be stated by an opposition of 'the one *or* the other', nor by the universalising of 'the one *and* the other', but by what de Certeau calls the 'logic of "neither the one nor the other" [. . . which . . .] opens a future but without fixing that future'.[64] The double negative makes the point that something other, something different, will emerge from a practice which will take its rise from faithfulness to its origins, but precisely because it can never return to, let alone encompass, those origins, must look for the fullness of its meaning elsewhere. Christian living, therefore, depends not on occupying a 'place' alongside others, but on practising faith face to face with others; as de Certeau – and Levinas – would have it, by constantly departing for another place.[65]

In my final chapter, I intend to return to some of the more practical issues surrounding the 'negotiation of the middle'. Practical yet also theological. For, however the 'logic' of practices of face-to-face encounter with others is described, it is important to understand them as

---

[62] In Ward 1997:150; emphasis in original.

[63] In Ward 1997:155; emphasis in original.

[64] In Ward 1997:154.

[65] See Bauerschmidt 1996a and b; Ward 1996.

'something to do with God'. Throughout this book, I have been arguing that there is an intrinsically theological value to the various forms of inter-faith encounter. The other is not a 'problem' to be encompassed within the same, but the one who raises ethical and therefore theological questions for the same. In this sense, what I have called the 'context of otherness' reveals the 'possibility of God'. Indeed, the heterologies discussed in this book show that so often it is only when faith becomes 'inter-faith', or, as de Certeau might have put it, when faith-as-hope departs for 'another place', that God encounters us precisely as God, as *the* Other. How do we recognise such a God? In the same way as we account for *any* dimension of otherness: not by naively identifying the other as an object 'out there', but by learning how to discern those traces of the other which inspire an endless refiguring of traditional language, metaphor and symbol. In Ricoeur's terms, theology is an exercise in refiguration which arises out of the ethical dimension of human engagement and the constant movement which it inspires between address and response, listening and reply. In Christian terms this is, strictly speaking, the work of the Spirit of love, the Spirit of Christ.

God and the other

Working out of a very different context, but one which addresses the same fundamental issue of how Christian theology must always keep open a sense of the transcendent, William Placher puts it like this:

> We can know the transcendent God not as an object within our
> intellectual grasp but only as a self-revealing subject and even our
> knowledge of divine self-revelation must itself be God's doing.
> Christian faith finds here confirmation of God's Triune character:
> We come to know this gracious God not merely in revelation but in
> self-revelation in Jesus Christ, and we come to trust that we do know
> God in Christ through the work of the Holy Spirit.[66]

Revelation here is no unveiling of a hidden truth but God's act of loving self-communication accomplished through the reciprocal action, the 'double mission', of *Logos* and Spirit. The doctrine of the Trinity is not a peculiarly Christian scheme of thought which is to be contrasted with other equally particular ways of speaking about the Absolute or

---

[66] Placher 1996:182.

Ultimate Mystery. But neither can it be treated as a speculative thesis about the way all of reality, all forms of religious consciousness, all ideas of God, are to be configured. It speaks, rather, of the God who communicates – and *goes on* communicating – himself. As Nicholas Lash puts it with characteristic bluntness, 'the doctrine of the Trinity simply *is* the Christian doctrine of God'.[67] Lash is not claiming here a totalising finality for the Trinity which turns all belief into Christian belief. What he is arguing for is a communicational rather than a speculative model of theological discourse – one rooted not in the dualist abstractions more proper to Enlightenment thought but in the liturgical language of doxology, praise and thanksgiving. Understood, therefore, in terms of what Lash calls a 'grammar of faith', a Trinitarian conception of God allows Christians to go on telling the story of the God revealed in Christ while, at the same time, preserving what it is tempting to call a 'theological template' with which to hear, to measure and to interpret the stories told by others.

Again, the question is how to speak of the 'possibility of God' in a non-totalising way; the 'catholic instinct' has to be careful not to reduce the other to a passive non-participant at an exclusively Catholic spectacle. This is what makes one aspect of Raimon Panikkar's otherwise wonderfully evocative account of the Trinity as 'theandric mystery' somehow unsatisfactory.[68] Panikkar makes admirably persuasive efforts to cross the religious frontiers by speaking of multiple spiritualities rather than mutually exclusive 'religions'. And he rightly insists that spiritual practices

---

[67] Lash 1986:183.

[68] The Trinity is the central theme of Panikkar's thought. His classic study in Christology, *The Unknown Christ of Hinduism*, which appears in two editions 1964 and 1981, deals with the relation of the Father and the Son as reflected in Hindu thought. His all too brief book on the Trinity first appeared as 'Toward an Ecumenical Theandric Spirituality', *Journal of Ecumenical Studies*, 1968; pp. 507–34; and subsequently as *The Trinity and World Religions* (Madras: Christian Literature Society, 1970) and as *The Trinity and the Religious Experience of Man* (New York: Orbis; London: Darton, Longman and Todd, 1973). His 1989 Gifford Lectures, entitled 'Trinity and Atheism: the Housing of the Divine in the Contemporary World', are to be published by Orbis. Given the range of Panikkar's interests, and the scope and depth of his thought, it is not altogether surprising that such commentary that exists varies from the adulatory to the antagonistic. MacPherson 1996, for instance, contains a useful bibliography of secondary material but is so polemical as to be positively misleading. Ramachandra 1996:76–108 is more balanced and makes many shrewd observations. The Festschrift edited by Joseph Prabhu 1996 contains some useful theological studies, especially Francis D'Sa, 'The Notion of God', pp. 25–44, and Ewert Cousins, 'Panikkar's Advaitic Trinitarianism', pp. 119–30. See also Cousins's much longer study, 'Panikkar: the Systematic Theology of the Future', in Cousins 1992:73–104. Rowan Williams's essay, 1990:3–15, describing Panikkar's *Trinity* as 'one of the best and least read meditations in our century', manages to be both appreciative and critical.

must complement each other if the 'deviations' encouraged by a narrow particularism are to be overcome. But the double move, first from spiritualities to the persons of the Trinity and then from the Trinity to 'theandrism' – in his words, 'a spirituality which combines in an authentic synthesis the three dimensions of our life on earth as well as in heaven' – risks turning itself into an essentialist scheme which totalises all religious meaning.[69]

More persuasive is the fundamental insight which Panikkar shares with Monchanin, that the Being of God is a 'Being with'. As Monchanin puts it, God's *esse* is a *'co-esse'*, an *'esse ad alterum*, a being for and towards the other as other'.[70] This is why Panikkar can speak of the Trinity as 'the ultimate paradigm of personal relationships'.[71] His reflections swing sometimes uneasily between the 'fundamental unity of reality' and the 'diversity of the whole universe', but this should not take away from the emphasis he wants to give to an account of relationality which is grounded in the 'Christic fact', the Paschal Mystery of the Death and Resurrection of Christ.[72] In Panikkar's terms, just as the human person is neither 'monolithic oneness nor disconnected plurality', so the Trinity 'as pure relation epitomises the radical relativity of all that there is'.[73] This reflects something of the dynamic of the mystic Monchanin's experience of a certain passivity in face of the 'context of otherness'. Understood in Trinitarian terms as the mystery of God's twofold mission in the world – as *Logos* and as Spirit – the Christian experience of the 'loss of the body' acts as motivation to grapple with the Pauline paradox of what has been given but is never complete – in Ricoeurian terms, the 'superabundance' which, precisely because it is pure gift, can never be constrained.

---

[69] Although not developed in any detail it is revealing to note that Panikkar cannot but accommodate the *de facto* existing religious traditions to the three persons. The result is a curiously essentialist scheme in which the 'apophatic' spirituality of the Father finds its closest analogue in Buddhism, the 'personalist' spirituality of the Son is instantiated in Christianity, and the 'advaitic' spirituality of the Spirit is represented, as the chosen descriptor indicates, by the dominant Advaita Vedanta school of classical Hinduism.

[70] In Weber 1977:132.

[71] Panikkar 1973:xv.

[72] This is why Rowan Williams can speak of Panikkar as 'an uncomfortable ally' for the pluralist school. He nevertheless voices two reservations which would correct Panikkar's ahistorical approach and provide the basis for an 'authentic *theology* of interreligious engagement'. They 'have to do with the need to keep in view the specific process of discovery whereby the Trinitarian, logos–spirit pattern is brought to light, and with the *critical* responsibility of Christian witness . . . toward the traditions it encounters'(1990:12).

[73] Panikkar 1973:xv.

The *Logos* made flesh in Jesus represents in a concrete form the God-given potential for bringing the whole world together in a new unity and intelligibility. This is what Christians know in faith to be true. At the same time, this potential remains always a potential, never complete in time; it can only be worked for in a hope-filled imitation of Jesus's own freedom before God.

The various forms of inter-faith dialogue are always set uneasily between these two terms, or – perhaps – two times, the determination and the generation of meaning. As with all practices of faith, Christians are asked to face the challenge of learning through the relationships they establish with others about the complex yet single and irreducible mystery of God which supports and challenges the lives of all people. Putting it in the sort of Trinitarian language which Panikkar would recognise, dialogue can be understood as a response to a self-revealing source, the one whom Christians name as the Father of Jesus Christ, which is expressed in a never-ending dialectic between form or *Logos* and the inexhaustible life of Spirit. My point in saying 'never-ending' and 'inexhaustible' is to recall a point from the introductory chapter, namely that inter-faith dialogue is rarely, if ever, about establishing agreement between partners. It will always seek for the clarification of meaning. But, so often, there is discovered in the human relationship itself a lack of completeness, a disarming sense of radical otherness, which demands a return and yet further engagement. The other can no more be included within the same than the diversity of human experience can be totalised into an overarching universal theory. To give a Christian account of the experience of being in relationship with the other, committed always to living 'in between' *this* concrete position within history and the fullness of meaning which comes at the end of history and which can only be anticipated in hope, is only possible if one is willing to take the risk of crossing the threshold, of encountering the other person.

In these terms, living 'in the middle', there can be no single starting point for reflection on the Christian experience of God. Christians will naturally feel at home with the sort of perspective developed in the last chapter, one which responds to the self-revelation of God in the Paschal Mystery. But, as William Burrows observes, there is always a danger of working from 'a *categorical*, Father–Son theology of Christian existence and not a Trinitarian understanding of the economy of salvation'.[74] The

---

[74] Burrows 1996:128.

Spirit introduces a *'non-categorical'* dimension into our theology – which is not to say that the Spirit is invoked as some 'last resort' to account for the mysterious 'other' quality of all our knowing. Rather, the Spirit both leads us into the truth and, at the same time, subverts all our pretensions to mastery. In the Fourth Gospel, the Spirit blows where it wills (John 3.8) but also witnesses to the Son (John 15.26). In Luke, Jesus himself is guided by the Spirit (e.g. 3.22, 4.1,14, 10.21) and throughout the Acts the Spirit goes ahead of the apostles, inspiring them as they witness to what God has already accomplished (e.g. 1.8, 2.3ff., 4.8, 8.14ff. etc). At the very least, it is the work of the Spirit to remind Christians that the *Logos* makes God's meaning concrete and tangible for the world; but it does not exhaust that meaning.

If God is, in Panikkar's phrase, 'pure relation', then any particular perspective on God's act of self-communication needs to be submitted to others – not in order to be supplemented or fulfilled, so as to develop a more adequate 'scheme', but to be led back into the matrix of religious practices of communication – from liturgy to catechesis to inter-faith dialogue – from which the Church lives. It is the Spirit who nourishes this process of continual conversion. Provided the self-revelation of God through the Word and God's continuing presence as Spirit are regarded not as independent but as the *single mystery* of the self-communicating God, then – following Panikkar – God may be understood equally well as the silent source of all, as the personal partner in dialogue, and as immanent life-giving mystery.[75] The doctrine of the Trinitarian God is not, therefore, an obscure intellectual conundrum accessible to an élite few, but an invitation to listen, to learn and to participate in God's own mission. In professing faith in 'God one and three', Christians do not seek to gather up all religious meaning into a Church-centred totality. Rather, the Trinity is the 'grammar' which allows the Church to speak of what it knows, to seek to communicate, both within the community and outside, both as a community gathered to praise God for what it knows and as a people committed to sharing the abundance of what it has received with others.[76]

---

[75] See Williams 1990. For very different versions of this thesis of the complementarity of Trinitarian persons, see the Epilogue to Rahner 1978 which describes 'three brief creedal statements' and, less gnomically, Lash 1992, especially pp. 83–120.

[76] The distinction between a 'speculative' theology about the nature of God, in which the language of Trinity becomes almost inevitably problematic, and one which is rooted in doxology and discipleship is admirably made by Lash 1986 (see the discussion in Barnes 1999:95–110).

Finally, then, how can the doctrine of the Trinity enable a theology of dialogue which does not simply include everything in an essentialist scheme? In imitation of that conversation which is revealed within the Trinity, Christian life – and therefore theology – is intrinsically dialogical. Christians exist in relationship with the other; that is to say, they are always committed to living 'in between' *this* concrete moment in history and the fullness of meaning which lies with God alone. The model for such a life and for crossing the threshold of any relationship is Jesus's relationship with the Father. Through participating in that relationship – Father and Son united by the Spirit of love – Christians learn how to relate to others. The analogy of a mutual indwelling, or *perichoresis*, of the divine persons within the Godhead teaches the virtues and practice of hospitality and welcome. It is not, then, that the doctrine of the Trinity somehow allows Christians mysteriously to speak of some 'triple dimension' to Being; rather it enables them to speak in three ways of a vision of the interdependence of all things which permeates every dimension of reality. The *Logos* made flesh in Jesus reveals, as well as reinterprets, the 'Emanuel' who in his act of self-communication forms the faith of Israel. That faith is remembered in the present as the community gathers now around the Eucharist which is the sign of Christ's love for his friends, prefiguring a new unity, a promise of a fullness which is anticipated in the life of the Spirit of God. And it is the Spirit who inspires the endless and unpredictable forms of imitation of Jesus of Nazareth which are found to be possible in the lives of human beings. As Lash puts it:

> It is 'in the Spirit' that we learn to hear God's message, recognize
> our brother, Jesus Christ; in the Spirit that we discover all the world
> to be the labour of God's fruitful love, learn to relate to the creator of
> all things as to a parent; and it is the Spirit who educates us into
> humanness, trains us in the virtues.[77]

It is this last point which takes Christians irrevocably out of any narrow ecclesiocentric 'totality'. If Christian identity is found only in generous-hearted relationship, in learning to see 'oneself as another', then it will be through trust in the Spirit that constant conversion is made possible. Faith, love and hope are reciprocal dimensions of the Christian life, manifestations of God's own self-giving, the grace which makes for human flourishing. Earlier, I suggested that these three theological

---

[77] Lash 1992:97.

virtues could be associated with the positions of the threefold paradigm.[78] More precisely, once understood as qualities which make up the Christian *habitus* of 'regulated improvisation',[79] they remind Christians that the God of the Covenant is revealed in form or meaning as *Logos* and in the ever-continuing reworking of that meaning which is inspired by *Pneuma*. Faith can be understood as the virtue which expresses a response to the unoriginated God who as Father invites us into the Covenantal relationship; love is the gift associated with the Son who gathers us in the present to celebrate the unity which has already been achieved; hope belongs more exactly to the Spirit who shows us how the fullness of the promise is always there to be discovered – or rather re-discovered – in the discerning of 'seeds of the Word'.

These, however, are not three separate ways any more than the persons to whom they can be loosely accommodated are to be set apart. My point is that they are interdependent and equally necessary qualities or dispositions without which there can be no understanding of the mystery of the Death and Resurrection of Christ – whether that mystery is apprehended within the familiar experience of the liturgical and sacramental practice of the Church, or more dimly sensed in those more kenotic moments which accompany the crossing of the threshold into the world of the other.

---

[78] See chapter 7, p. 184, n4.

[79] Pierre Bourdieu, *Outline of a Theory of Practice*, Cambridge University Press, 1977; p. 8, quoted in Ford 1995:361.

9

Negotiating the middle

This book has been addressed primarily to the Christian community. What I have argued, however, is that Christian identity cannot be understood in isolation from other communities of faith. If the lengthy route which I have traced from the 'context of otherness' to the *perichoresis* of the triune God is anything like an adequate account of the philosophical and theological issues surrounding alterity and subjectivity, then to be Christian is to exist in relationship. That may be considered a fairly meagre outcome for so much effort; in some sense all communities, all societies, all persons, need to be considered in relational terms. But, to repeat a point made in the chapter on the experience of the Indian Church, the question is not *whether* identity can be understood relationally, but *how* within or between particular societies or communities relationships are to be developed and how they are to change.[1] Any relationship with the other is particular. What my use of descriptive heterologies has shown is that, as long as persons continue to exist in time, the other always returns to disturb the self-sufficient world which they create. For Levinas, it is this ethical primacy of the other which challenges any totalising account of relationality. Being in relationship means seeing oneself 'in the accusative', attending not to strategies which maintain mastery of the other across time, but to the more awkward and demanding experience of waiting before what he would call the 'face of the Other'.

This face is never an unchanging phenomenon which can be incorporated within the 'system' of the same, but an epiphany, a revelation, which always points away from self towards the Infinite Other. To take on board the full implications of such a 'possibility of God' is to understand Christian

---

[1] Chapter 6, p. 174.

identity in intrinsically relational terms. Once the primary and irreducible relationship with Judaism has been accepted as the matrix out of which Christianity arises, a different way of thinking, a more ethical or relational approach to 'the other', begins to assert itself. But it is only the one who waits in hope – patiently but not passively – who can see this face. Through such a 'facing' of the Risen Lord the self is transformed. As David Ford puts it:

> The risen face of Jesus is a 'revelation' not in the sense of making him plain in a straightforward manner. Rather, what is 'unveiled' is a face that transcends simple recognisability, that eludes our categories and stretches our capacities in the way in which God does . . . It generates a community whose life before this face is endlessly interrogative, and whose response to it leads into ever new complexities, ambiguities, joys and sufferings.[2]

'Joys and sufferings' together have been the catalyst for my theology of dialogue which seeks to give a faithful account of the engagement with the 'context of otherness': experiences of gift and loss, abundance and emptiness, familiarity and strangeness. In this final chapter, it is time to return to the community formed before this face and to the labour of negotiation which, responding to the face of the other, would build a 'community of communities'. Catholic Christianity, as I have sought to describe it, remains always committed to a particular vision of the way God reveals God through the Word and goes on acting in the world through the sanctifying work of the Spirit. Such a work is never finished and never predictable. Hence Ford's ever new complexities and ambiguities. Christians may be called to anticipate the working of the Spirit through discerning 'seeds of the Word', the patterning of God's continuing self-revelation. But Christians speak always of what they know; they have to be careful about speaking of what they do *not* know, what always remains other and utterly mysterious. Such reticence is supported by a remark of Christopher Butler on the ecclesiology of the Vatican Council. Commenting on the 'lack of clarity' yet 'richness and nuance' of *Lumen Gentium*, '[p]erhaps we could say with a distinguished Orthodox theologian, "We know where the Church is; it is not for us to judge and say where the Church is not" '.[3]

Thus, although I speak from a Christian theological perspective, I am primarily concerned with an account of dialogue as the 'negotiation of

---

[2] Ford 1999:172.

[3] See Butler 1981:119; quoting Paul Evdokimov's *L'Orthodoxie*, p. 119. See also McPartlan 1995:66–7.

the middle', a mutual process of learning, of critical questioning and respectful listening, which 'imagines the possibility of harmonious difference'.[4] That, at least, has been the aim. The test, of course, comes with practice and the experience of inter-faith relations. Many a big book could, no doubt, be written on such a topic. Nothing ambitious can be attempted here. This chapter seeks only to make some elementary application of de Certeau's account of 'strategy' and 'tactics' to the four forms of inter-religious dialogue which were described earlier.[5] What I want to show is that time and space are more than the theoretical constructs which inform a theology of dialogue; they are essentially practical categories which underpin all acts of faithful witness before the face of the other. Formed by the liturgy and its sacramental tradition, the Church learns how to co-operate in God's work of sanctifying the space of the world. But the work of negotiation which the Spirit inspires, the mending of the 'broken middle', takes time and can never be reduced to a few ever-reliable precepts and rules.

Living in the middle

I have spoken of the importance of an inculturation which is always 'local' and particular. It would, therefore, subvert the whole project of dialogue if I were to presume to pin down some 'multi-faith reality' with a few statistics or a general survey. There is, however, room for one final heterology, a brief micro-discourse which will take up some of the points noted in the chapter on the Indian Church's experience of the other. To approach this example we must first briefly retrace our steps.

In discussing Wilfred's 'mystics and those who suffer' I drew attention to the way that Indian communities of faith often manage to develop a sense of the provisional which enables them to cope with dichotomies and the lack of system. By working within the given tradition, rather than by outright opposition to it, they develop what is needed for their own continued survival. Such eclectic *braconnage* witnesses, however, not to de Certeau's somewhat romantic image of the powerless adjusting 'tactically' to the terms set by the powerful, but to something more deeply rooted in Indian culture: what I described, using Nandy's

---

[4] Loughlin 1996:21.

[5] See chapter 1, p. 21, n42.

psychopathology, as the non-heroic way of the archetypal survivor. To repeat his point:

> [T]he culture itself demands that a certain permeability of boundaries be maintained in one's self-image and that the self be not defined too tightly or separated mechanically from the non-self.[6]

Coming from a very different angle, but one similarly concerned to reject any theory about self-identification which would set same over against other, is Dharampal's account of what he calls Indian 'civilisational consciousness'.[7] According to this conservative Hindu historian, Indian identity is not bound up with the pursuit of some distant mystical truth. In what is essentially a commentarial tradition like Hinduism, there is an abiding faith in the past as providing workable solutions for present dilemmas. This is not simply a matter of correlating tradition and situation, a pragmatic reinterpreting of ancient texts. As with Gandhi's refusal to subordinate the means to the end, the actual *process* of reinterpretation is more important than the result. Underlying the readiness to 'keep asking questions' and to 'keep finding provisional answers', is what Dharampal calls a 'way of continuous awareness and continuous reflection [which] is perhaps the essence of the Indian way of life'.[8]

This book opened with a description of life in a multi-faith town dominated by a population – Sikh, Muslim and Hindu – originating in the Indian sub-continent. The 'Indian way of life' is more apparent in the cultural trappings of temples, curry-houses and sari-shops than in any discernible 'essence'. Indeed, there is something faintly contradictory about any 'essence' whose most salient characteristic is the deliberate attempt to avoid being categorised. More persuasive is the concept of a 'resistant subjectivity', the sort of Gandhian self-image in which same and other are forever engaged in the negotiating of the shared space of the 'middle'. Indian communities tend to resist assimilation, but this is not to say that they cannot and do not adapt. Whatever the problems of adjusting to a Western secularised culture in which religion is acceptable as

---

[6] Nandy 1983:107.

[7] Dharampal 1993:64. The author seeks to restore a sense of Indian identity by rescuing Indian culture from what he regards as the destructive incursions of the West. The 'world-picture of modernity', for instance, is totally at odds with the perspective of most Indians who 'may not be living even in the eighteenth century of the West'(p. 19). So much that is distinctive about the Indian psyche is rooted in a vision of creation dominated by cycles of time which move gradually and inexorably from perfection to destruction (see the extensive reviews and discussion in *Hindu–Christian Studies Bulletin*, 8 (1995); 2–19).

[8] Dharampal 1993:40.

long as it remains a matter of private opinion, self-confident communities of faith are beginning to emerge marked by a sense of loyalty to their own traditions and an attitude of civic responsibility towards wider society. The Christian churches have, of course, initiated much of the dialogue and encounter which has taken place in recent years. Thanks to their efforts, such practices as inter-faith pilgrimages and walks are now commonplace in cities like London.[9] But they are by no means the exclusive preserve of a few committed Christians and hardened inter-faith groupies. Other faiths are involved, especially in facilitating visits to places of worship. The quality of hospitality and welcome is typical of traditions which, at their best, are less concerned with resisting 'the other' than with finding their own place alongside others in a sometimes fraught and volatile multi-faith mix.

One particularly striking example of such an adjustment is the Valmiki Sabha.[10] Their temple, serving some five-hundred families from all over London, is one of the more unusual places of worship in a town remarkable for its religious and cultural diversity. The Valmikis have managed to flourish in a thoroughly pluralist environment by learning how to resist assimilation into caste Hinduism while at the same time using its religious resources to tell their own particular story. Although their regular ritual focuses very much on readings from sacred texts, they have developed a strong sense of the visual in their religious practice. All around the walls and ceiling of the *mandir* are depictions of scenes from the two great epics, the *Ramayana* and the *Mahabharata*. Hovering over the sanctuary is a large painting of a bearded sage-like holy man; in the sanctuary itself sits a life-size statue of the same figure. For the Valmiki Sabha the central manifestation of Brahman is the poet Valmiki, the author of the *Ramayana*. Like many formerly untouchable castes, the Valmiki Sabha see themselves as heirs to a tradition more ancient than the Aryan Vedas. But they are also conscious of having to adjust to the typical perceptions of Indian religion in a Western context. Thus the stories associated with Valmiki are used sometimes in a separatist, sometimes in an assimilationist, fashion, making for a practice of faith which manages to avoid both the totalising rhetoric of caste ideology and the sometimes strident oppositionalism of the

---

[9] For an account of a typical inter-faith pilgrimage, see Thorley 2000.

[10] For the history of what in its origins is something of a Punjabi Hindu–Sikh hybrid consisting largely of members of the sweeper caste, see Juergensmeyer 1982:169ff.; and for the wider social and political context, Mendelsohn and Vicziany 1998.

dalit minority.[11] In Britain, they see themselves as a consciously 'non-Hindu' community, but their sense of identity has been given more positive connotations by a 'tactical' retrieval of one of the most popular of Indian stories and by a rereading of an ancient epic dialogue, the *Yogavaśistha*. This Valmiki community accepts its own difference but, unlike some dalit communities, refuses the 'oppositionalism' which would set one particular caste identity over against others. Such a compliant-yet-resistant 'middle way', continuous with the wider world of Indian religion yet notably particular in its interpretation, has allowed the Valmikis to develop their own integrity.

Ambiguities and complexities

Of course, not all communities of faith manage to retain their independence in such a positive way. In a strange environment the pressures are enormous – not just from the dominant 'host' community but from the historical antagonisms which continue in, and in many ways are heightened by, an alien environment. Meanwhile a generation gap is appearing: older folk who still live on the fringes of British society and younger people with divided, and in many ways confused, allegiances. 'Globalisation' is an ambiguous experience, especially when immigrant communities find themselves caught between different worlds of discourse. For every successful 'tactical' adjustment to the terms set by the other, there are just as many examples of 'strategic' refusals which encourage retreat and isolation. Nevertheless, even where communities withdraw behind cultural barricades, their sense of identity often acquires distinctly ragged edges. Thus, any account of inter-faith engagement as an unequivocal process of communication between monolithic 'systems' is bound to be simplistic. Not only does any such approach underestimate the very real difficulty of communication across cultures, it also circumvents the need for genuine and time-consuming negotiation of the 'space' which communities of faith share in a pluralist and secular society.

I will return to the broader political implications of this 'broken middle' shortly. For the moment, let us stay with the Christian experience and the truth which Christians in the post-modern West are, all too painfully, beginning to learn. Whether or not de Certeau is correct to point to a future

---

[11] Juergensmeyer 1982:180.

for believers in which Christianity is 'shattered',[12] there can be little doubt that they will exist in a space where they are no longer 'at home'. To live and work in close proximity with the other means recognising the complex ambiguities of the experience. Time spent with other persons of faith usually proceeds successfully enough for a while on the naive assumption that there is plenty to agree about. Whether in the actual conversation or in subsequent reflection, the visual impression made by symbols and artefacts and the affective resonances provoked by the language and metaphor of another tradition can lead to imaginative reconstructions and improvisations on the more familiar themes of Christian faith. Most Hindu temples, for instance, have a distinctly old-fashioned 'Catholic' feel to them; Sikh gurdwaras, on the other hand, with the single focus of the Holy Book, the Guru Granth Sahib, are reminiscent of more sober Protestant churches. But the presumed similarities never quite fit. When the comfortable 'family resemblance' approach to religious pluralism comes up against the flesh-and-blood reality of particular communities, the stereotypes break down and a diffuse and mysterious other begins to reassert itself. Which is why de Nobili's 'desire to be understood' leads to the 'desire to understand'.[13] Putting his experience in more contemporary terms, the inculturation of the Gospel always demands attention to the particularity of context.[14] The 'global' pretension to encompass commonalities within the ideal conceptual scheme is always being subverted by local needs, the demands of *this* specific situation.

Such ambiguities are not easily resolved. If Christians are to be mediators, they will need to learn not just how to welcome and practise hospitality to the stranger. As I have argued, they will also need to develop the virtues appropriate for a new situation: different forms of adaptation, different skills of adjustment, and different ways of reimagining and retelling the story of Christ.

Although there are plenty of elements of this 'multi-faith reality' which are unfamiliar to Christians more used to the monocultural world of the recent past, there is nothing particularly novel about the experience of

---

[12] De Certeau and Domenach 1974. As Ahearne, 1996:503 n4, points out, to translate the title of this book (a transcription of a radio debate) as 'shattered Christianity' loses the connotations of 'brilliant light or enduring radiance carried by the adjective *éclaté*'.

[13] Halbfass 1988:53.

[14] See the references in Burrows 1996:130–2 who notes the tension between a long-standing Catholic tradition of 'radical contextualization–inculturation–dialogue' and the centralising tendencies of Vatican authority.

facing the other. Every time human beings enter into the sometimes disarming relationship with the other, we are altered, that is to say we *become* other by having to learn to adjust to the demands made by the other. The forms this alteration takes will vary according to how the shared space between us, 'the middle', is perceived. Shortly, I will need to consider the responses associated with different forms of dialogue. But, whatever the form of encounter, engagement with the other entails certain appropriate forms of behaviour and response. When the other crosses my threshold, I become actively responsible for his or her well-being: I may not manipulate the trust shown in me to my advantage. When I become a 'border-crosser' and allow myself to be taken into the confidence of the other, I must expect to play a more passive role in the relationship; once I have passed over the other's threshold I wait on his or her initiative.

For the sake of good inter-faith relations, some such distinction between giving and receiving and some more or less explicit rules of conduct are essential, if only to respect sensitivities and curb unrealistic expectations. But I do not want to imply that the only role for the theologian is to justify certain pragmatic 'principles of engagement'. Earlier I spoke of the Eucharist as the energising heart of the Christian 'school of faith'; by constantly returning to the liturgy, the 'work of the people' which celebrates the hospitable and welcoming God, Christians learn how to act as host and respond as guest. For the Christian, the task is to evoke and focus the Christian understanding of God in the midst of everyday relationships with persons who belong to other faith traditions. This means serious and sustained attention not just to the 'dual responsibility' of Christian faith – faithfulness and openness – but to the sometimes dark ambiguities which the encounter with the other both reveals *and* conceals. The most rewarding dimension of inter-faith dialogue is to develop ways in which Christians can constructively and with integrity unite with others in the serious business of reconciliation in a pluralist society. But there will always be times when the question is how they can critically resist the subtle manipulations and covert restrictions which can, in any community, substitute human interests for the demands of God.

Again, there is nothing particularly novel here for Christian faith. Wherever Christians attempt to speak about God, the words they use do not reveal the Word without faithful and sometimes laborious interrogation. Or, to put it more accurately, the Church only overcomes the temptation to substitute its own words for the Word of God when it allows itself to be interrogated by the Word. In Vatican II, the Church as the People of God on pilgrimage is described as being 'like a sacrament', bearing God's question for the world in a way which makes the Church a microcosm, sign and instrument, of the unity of the whole human race. But, at the same time, the Church is – in de Certeau's terms – committed to ever more radical departures in search of the Word which no community, however privileged, can presume to command, still less reduce to the words of its own narrative. At its best, through liturgy, the preaching of the Word, inter-faith dialogue and other practices of discipleship, the Church celebrates and transforms the diversity of human culture. The reality, of course, is often less than ideal. But this is only to echo de Certeau's words about the need for 'successive conversions'. It is through existing at the very heart of the world in all its beauty and tragedy that the Church witnesses to what it knows: that in Christ all people are united in God. De Certeau himself would probably have put it more radically by reminding Christians that to belong to the Church entails a commitment to *belonging elsewhere*.

Discovering the face of Christ

Here, surely, there is something which is new: the discipleship which – even, perhaps especially, in the midst of ambiguity – sanctifies the 'context of otherness' by waiting patiently upon the Father after the manner of the active-yet-passive Christ. This is the Christ who does not grasp power, but who stands before the complexities and ambiguities of the future with serenity and with hope. Filled with the Spirit of the Christ of Gethsemane, Christians learn that in face of the other there is yet hope beyond hope.

In what sense can this 'face of the other' be said to reveal the face of Christ? Paul reminds the Corinthians that 'it is the God who said "Let light shine out of darkness", who has shone in our hearts to give the light of the knowledge of the glory of God in the face of Christ' (2 Corinthians 4.6). If it is the case that the hope, which the act of facing the other inspires, returns Christians to the anarchic – the 'beginningless' – roots of their own faith in Moses' encounter with the God of the Covenant at Sinai, can we not speak of Christ as present, if not in the face of the other, then in the *act* of facing?

Such a thought is purely speculative. In this book, I have not tried to develop anything resembling 'inter-faith Christology' or to do anything other than raise the most tentative questions about the meaning of Christ in a multi-faith world. My main concern has been with what I see as a prior task: establishing the credentials of a theology of dialogue, a theology which would engage with the meaning of the providential mystery of otherness for the life of the Church as a whole. An open engagement with people of other faiths is itself deeply theological – and specifically Christological – because it is informed by a vision of the Trinitarian God who acts as both host and guest – the source of the gift which Christians presume to communicate to others and the means by which the gift is shared. Such a vision informs the 'Catholic instinct', a spirit of generous inclusiveness, on which the theological virtues and the practices to which they give rise are based. To go right back to my opening remarks, theology of religions is mistakenly conceived as a reflection on the 'problem of the other'. It is, much more radically, a reflection from *within the context of otherness*. In the middle of manifest ambiguities and ever new complexities, it takes its stand on the biblical story of the God who is 'Emanuel', Christ the Word spoken in the 'broken middle' of the world, who still goes on speaking through the Spirit which leads disciples into all the truth. A theology of dialogue is not, therefore, intended to solve some inevitably obscure conundrum about the 'hidden' or 'anonymous' Christ. It is about forming the community of faith with those Christlike virtues and qualities which listen and respond to the Spirit, which enable a facing of the other with critical respect. And for those prepared to listen with generosity, it is sometimes surprising what they hear.

I give but one example, an example of the 'dialogue of religious experience', the sort of para-liturgical inter-faith 'event' which brings people of different faiths 'together to pray' around a common focus or symbol.[15] To celebrate the new millennium, some three-hundred persons met at a central London church to listen to readings from non-Christian sources which were none the less inspired by the person and teaching of Jesus. The reflections came from the Qur'ān, from the Baha'i scriptures, from Hindu, Sikh and Buddhist teachers. For many Christians, many of the words they heard were strange but also had a certain familiarity. The Qur'anic version of the nativity, for instance, tells of how fresh dates fell from a tree so that Mary would be refreshed. A modern meditation master,

---

[15] The distinction between 'coming together to pray' and 'coming to pray together' stems from the most celebrated and influential of these events, the meeting of religious leaders hosted by Pope John Paul II at Assisi on 27 October 1986. For the texts see Gioia 1997:340–54. Some important characteristics of different forms of 'inter-religious prayer' are discussed by M. Thomas Thangaraj in a conference report published by the PCIRD, *Pro Dialogo*, 98 (1998); 186–96.

the peace activist Śri Chinmoy, much given to poetic aphorisms, writes that 'Jesus's human birth was the question. His divine Death was not only the answer but The Answer.' The Sikh statesman Gopal Singh wrote a moving meditation on 'the man who never died', while the contemporary Zen Buddhist teacher Thich Nhat Hanh confessed that he found no problem in speaking of Jesus as 'the Son of God who was resurrected and who continues to live'.[16]

What was the object of this celebration? None of the texts speaks the language of the New Testament or the great Church Councils. They come out of very different religious worlds and reflect a sometimes obscure process of incorporation of Christian ideas into another idiom. Nevertheless, they can be taken as responses to the question about his identity which Jesus put to the disciples at Caesarea Philippi – albeit responses which complexify rather than resolve what Ricoeur calls 'narrative identity'. Noting that 'several plots' can be woven from the 'same incidents' depending on how the different roles of historical and fictional writing are developed, Ricoeur reminds us that

> narrative identity continues to make and unmake itself, and the question of trust which Jesus posed to his disciples – Who do you say that I am? – is one that each of us can pose concerning ourself, with the same perplexity that the disciples questioned by Jesus felt.[17]

In other words, Jesus's 'Christological question', which leads on, of course, not to some straightforward statement of Jesus's significance, but to the deeply perplexing prediction of the Passion, goes on being asked wherever people find themselves interrogated by the Word of God. Their responses remain, like any form of 'narrative identity', inherently unstable and liable to change.

Reading a text – or on this particular occasion listening to one – is a challenge to the imagination to 'inhabit worlds foreign to us', a provocation 'to be and act differently'.[18] Like so many of the somewhat diffuse activities which make up inter-faith dialogue, the celebration was concerned with beginnings not endings, with bringing people together to share a prayerful experience, not with defending Christian orthodoxy

---

[16] The passages which were used on this occasion are included in a much bigger collection of some seventy texts published as *Celebrating Jesus: a Multifaith Appreciation,* edited by Daniel Faivre with an introduction by Michael Barnes; published by the editor, Southall 1999.

[17] Ricoeur 1988:249.

[18] Ibid.

against the inadequate formulations of others. The people who attended were not particularly interested in speculation – about whether, for instance, Sanskrit terms such as *avatar* and *bodhisattva* offer scope for reinterpreting the more familiar titles of Messiah and *Logos*. It was, more simply, an opportunity not to practise theological debate, but to test the imagination by exercising a certain theological hospitality. The premise on which such hospitality is based is that what others say has its own integrity – a version, in other words, of the 'Ignatian presupposition'. The passages, both the insightful and the quaintly endearing, witness to the profound influence which the person, the teaching and the mission of Jesus of Nazareth have always had outside the familiar bounds of the Christian tradition. From the revelations of the Holy Qur'ān to the humblest picture in a Hindu home, Jesus is there, a figure to inspire a sense of mystery and challenge, devotion and love, courage and questioning.

The book in which these passages were collected does not, therefore, presume to be anything as pretentious as a 'multi-faith Christology'; the contributions are essentially devotional reflections, not high theology. It is, however, a good illustration of what can happen when the Vatican Council's call to discern and respect what is 'true and holy' in other religious traditions is taken with utter seriousness. Christian dialogue with other persons of faith becomes anything but a muted exercise in impressing the Gospel story on some pristine 'tabula rasa'. As the celebration showed, the faith of others has, in so many ways, already been touched by the Gospel; new conversations in temples and mosques and on the streets of our inner-cities do not take place in an historical and cultural vacuum. If the evidence of one afternoon's exchange is anything to go by, Christ is already there, exercising an extraordinary influence over the religious imagination.[19] For Christians and non-Christians alike, the occasion showed how Christ continues to question and disturb the same by speaking with the voice of a disarming otherness.

In imitation of this homeless Christ, the Church exists as an historically bound people on pilgrimage, albeit seeking to preserve *in hope* a vision of a fullness which is yet to come. Jesus's question to his disciples begins a process of living with the 'loss of a body' which speaks not just of the Church's experience of 'God-with-us' but also of a God who is 'other' and 'elsewhere'. Indeed, it is precisely in so far as Christians allow the Paschal Mystery to speak of God's presence in the world of the other that they will

---

[19] For a full report see *The Tablet*, 8 January 2000, p. 10.

answer Jesus's question – 'Who do you say that I am?' – most faithfully. In practice, if the other is not to be totalised into a Christian conceptual strategy, then it is not simply a matter of my representing Christ to the other; I must also find some way in which the other can be Christ *to me*. In some way, two movements have to be held together. What I say *of Christ* questions the other; but I must also allow that what the other says may well be spoken *about Christ*, questioning me. This present moment does not, therefore, give Christians a privileged position 'above the action', from which they can presume to judge or control the whole, but it does make them more humbly conscious of being *with God*, rooted in God in the middle of things.

The identity which this God confers comes not through an assertion of power but by negotiating a whole series of relationships with various 'others'. If, as I have argued, human identity is not a 'given' to be maintained by rational reflection so much as a goal to be achieved through the experience of learning how to communicate, then 'seeds of the Word' do not necessarily grow from any specific 'inter-religious insights' which may be communicated between the persons in dialogue; they are born from the actual process of communication itself. To hear others speak about the significance of Jesus, in the language of another culture and another religion, can be consoling; it can also be profoundly disconcerting. But, then, the face of the Risen Lord is not the face the disciples expected.

Practising dialogue

This 'negotiation of the middle' is not limited to what goes on between religious communities. It also takes place within a particular community of faith as it learns to adjust to the wider culture. Throughout this book, I have tried to resist forms of reductionism which seek to reconcile the conflicting truth claims of different religious traditions by extracting some supposedly timeless ethical essence. I have, therefore, argued for a rereading of traditions rather than some high-minded exercise in rewriting them. Essentially, inter-faith dialogue is such a rereading – a common enterprise in which, at a number of different levels, schools of faith can learn to co-operate. In this sense dialogue and 'inculturation' are correlative terms, different ways of speaking about the complex way in which the comprehensive pattern of a tradition learns to communicate with and adjust to whatever is perceived as other.

The four types of inter-faith dialogue – the dialogue of life, the dialogue of common action, the dialogue of religious experience and the dialogue of theological exchange – all represent different dimensions of a familiar human experience, the everyday encounter with another person which opens up new vistas and new possibilities. People of faith begin by living alongside one another, learning to accept each other as neighbours, sharing the same streets and schools and shops. They start engaging with each other in shared projects which express their common concerns – for the welfare of children and old people, for the needs of immigrants and strangers. They become interested in each other's religious texts and traditions; the familiarity of places of worship generates a willingness to listen in silence or even to experience for themselves something of the other's meditative practices. Such 'core-to-core' dialogue, as Aloysius Pieris calls it,[20] may eventually lead to conversation about the coherence of their images of ultimate truth and their hopes for the humanity they share. One type of dialogue almost inevitably leads to or implies, at some level, one of the others. But, whether considered independently or as a single process of negotiation, they also imply, at some level, the four dimensions of a theology of dialogue which have underpinned the last four chapters of this book. What I have described, mainly in terms of heterologies which retrieve some occluded aspect of the ever-returning other, is a theology which seeks to be contemplative, ethical, liturgical and Trinitarian.

I am not suggesting that each of the four types of dialogue can be neatly correlated with the fourfold character of a theology of dialogue. In theory, specialist lectures, seminars, conferences and formal dialogues are concerned with achieving theological understanding and philosophical clarification. Occasional events such as the multi-faith celebration of Jesus are, more obviously, forms of the 'dialogue of religious experience'. At a different 'level' of engagement, local inter-faith groups may well be concerned with 'common action', with encouraging specific commitments to collaboration in a neighbourhood project. But this is not to neglect the more prosaic but vitally important task with which all dialogue begins – learning how to live alongside neighbours from different communities. In practice, of course, rarely do these types of engagement with the other define such neat categories. Racism, for instance, is the ever-present dark side of a multi-cultural society, and 'common action' builds

---

[20] Pieris 1988b:110ff.

on 'common life' as part of the educational process without which ignorance, the seed-bed of racism, only breeds fear and contempt. Nor can the more theological dialogue be conducted at an abstract intellectualist level which fails to acknowledge the complex yet intimate links between theology, spirituality and religious practice of all kinds.

Clearly the 'negotiation of the middle' can begin with, and grow from, any of these four forms. It will, however, be obvious from the example of a multi-faith celebration of Jesus discussed above that I consider the 'dialogue of religious experience' to have some central significance in mediating the constant exchange which goes on between the ethical and the theological. I called it 'theological hospitality' – not an invitation to some crude syncretism but the willingness to listen, even to become perplexed by others' responses. Liturgy, as I have described it, is the source of all theology; the community is gathered by the formal recounting of sacred memories. But the context of Christian liturgy always includes the other, both the language and symbolism of the Jewish other *and* the more recent history of further engagements with 'other others'. The same must apply to the simplest of para-liturgies and inter-faith gatherings where people listen to each other in the silent support of faith. For Levinas, the face of the other challenges the very capacity to know, and so to appropriate to the same. When understood as a face-to-face encounter, dialogue is 'not merely a way of speaking. Its significance has a general reach. It is transcendence.'[21] Even the most hesitant and ill-defined exchanges of word, gesture and symbol between people of different faiths provide the basis for mutual understanding, a mutual self-transcending. Moving around this 'fulcrum', as it were, what the many different practices of dialogue have in common is not some a priori theological scheme but the encounter with another person–Panikkar's 'dialogical dialogue' which is logically prior to the 'dialectical dialogue', the exchange of concepts and ideas.[22]

A theology of dialogue, then, is no attempt to justify some putative 'common ground' between religions; still less is it some vaguely Christian musing on time spent listening to somebody else's religious imaginings. It is, more exactly, a theological account of de Certeau's 'heterological law', the way the other returns, insinuating itself back into the world previously controlled by the same, disrupting the status quo and

---

[21] Levinas 1998b:147.

[22] Panikkar 1984.

demanding further interpretation.[23] If Ricoeur's narrative structure – the 'successive filters' of 'same', 'other' and 'analogous' – provides a helpful way forward, describing something of this process of retelling the community's story, it is not – to repeat Levinas's strictures – a straightforwardly synchronic process. No neat pattern of 'progress' is possible. Rather, a Christian theology which would seek to grapple with the 'context of otherness' will be contemplative in discerning possible 'seeds of the Word'; it will be ethical in its responsibility before the face of the other; it will be liturgical in constantly returning its experience of the 'broken middle' to the formative experience of the community; and, if it is to be properly Christian, then it will be Trinitarian in the way it discerns in that dialogue between Father and Son, which is eternally generated in the love of the Spirit, the prime analogue of all human encounter and relationship. In seeking to respond faithfully to other stories in which the community sees itself dimly mirrored and reflected, these dimensions build on one another. However, this is precisely *not* to import a covert Christian totality. It is, more humbly, a reminder that, wherever Christian deliberation on the mystery of the self-revealing God starts, there is more to be said; wherever it ends, there will always be other routes back to the beginning, there to start again. Similarly, Christians who seek to reflect prayerfully and theologically on their experience of 'crossing the threshold' will find that there can be no single way of attending to the very diverse forms in which the 'possibility of God' manifests itself.

Responding to the theological

I began this book with a dilemma, and much has been said about the responsibility of the theologian in living and working in a 'context of otherness'. A certain pluralism of response to other faiths is inevitable; a theology in dialogue with Theravada Buddhism, for instance, will be very different in form from one which speaks to Muslims – or even from one which engages with the language of Tibetan or Chinese traditions of the Mahayana. Nevertheless, the celebration of the Paschal Mystery which gives voice to all theology is nothing if not the renewal of a universalist tradition, a repetition which is, therefore, always the same yet ever different. The form – ultimately, of course, the form of God's Word – is both particular and concrete, yet under the influence of the Spirit

---

[23] See Ahearne 1991:21.

always fluid and flexible. What liturgy inspires, therefore, is a constant reimagining of the story which Christians seek to tell in response to the other. The two 'movements' demand each other. The former without the latter would be 'mere' ritual; the latter without the former an exercise in rootless speculation.[24]

Like the historian, the theologian is expected to discern and order the patterns of human experience – which is not to imply the linking of different religious traditions as if with a single unifying thread. Strictly, just as an historical narrative can no more 'think origins' than it can predict the future, so theology cannot avoid its own 'anarchic' character or presume to speak of the totality of truth; its starting-point, and its ending, lie beyond, with God. In that sense at least, theology, so far from seeking to pronounce a 'timeless truth', is the most time-bound, because history-bound, of religious practices. Every encounter with the other takes place in time, and therefore precludes any 'totalising attempt' to stand above or outside time. Yet this is very far from embracing a tacit relativism. On the contrary. But the universal truth, to which such a never-ending process of negotiation points, is vested not in some 'essence' of Christianity but in the vision of a redeemed humanity to which Christian faith points. The work of communication across the 'broken middle', which demands such a complex interaction of theological 'dimensions', is due not so much to the inadequacy or incompleteness of the language and cultural idioms which are used, but to the fact that, in a much more profound sense, the persons who seek to communicate are themselves incomplete. While it is always tempting to think of the other as lacking something essential which I possess, the truth is that a certain darkness or otherness or lack of self-presence manifests itself in all human beings – especially in face-to-face dialogue. Paradoxically, perhaps, the truly universal experience in inter-faith dialogue is of that moment of disruption or surprise before the other which at certain moments in time reveals my own perplexity or incompleteness. As Terry Eagleton, in the middle of a withering demolition of the post-modern fashion for a certain type of cultural relativism, puts it:

> It belongs to the human situation to be 'out of joint' with any specific situation. And the violent disruption which follows from this connecting of the universal to a particular content is what we know

---

[24] For a particularly impressive example of an imaginative rereading of the Christian tradition in dialogue with Hindu texts, see the 'comparative theology' developed by Francis Clooney, especially 1993, 1996, and 'Reading the World in Christ' in D'Costa 1990a:63–80.

as the human subject. Human beings move at the conjuncture of the concrete and the universal, body and symbolic medium; but this is not a place where anyone can feel blissfully at home.[25]

Responding to the ethical

The prospect of not feeling 'at home' provokes different responses from religious communities – from the reactionary backlash against threats to internal stability to the romantic nostalgia which would recreate the long-lost paradise. As de Certeau might explain it, there are those who react to a loss of power by a 'strategic' manipulation of place, while there are others who have never had power and spend their time in a 'tactical' 'utilization of time'.[26] The reality, as always, is a lot more complicated – and the theologian's responsibility more demanding. Even so innocuous a term as 'community' can turn out to be problematic, being based on the assumption that all people experience similar degrees of belonging within similar culturally determined groupings. But this is only to repeat, once again, that the crucial question is *how* within particular societies, communities, religions, or whatever, *relationships* are established and maintained.

However else we might describe the great world religions, they are 'schools' which seek to form people according to the norms of age-old customs and practices. All people of faith have to live with a certain tension, between the ideal comprehensive pattern which the tradition promises and the resistance which the pressures and challenges of daily life in a less than ideal environment so often deliver. If my earlier analysis is correct, the energies and allegiances which religious commitment encourages are channelled through an uneasy dialectic between foundational stories and varieties of commentarial traditions which seek to address whatever is recognised as other. That ill-defined phenomenon, fundamentalism, which affects almost all the major world religions in some respect, is an expression of the 'enclave culture' which, due to a whole variety of social, political and economic factors, results in a breakdown in the dialectic.[27]

---

[25] Eagleton 2000:97.

[26] De Certeau 1984:38–39.

[27] See especially Emmanuel Sivan, 'The Enclave Culture', in Marty and Appleby 1995:19. In 'Politics, Ethnicity and Fundamentalism', the final article of this final volume of 'The Fundamentalism Project' (five volumes in all, from the University of Chicago), Gabriel A. Almond, Emmanuel Sivan and R. Scott Appleby conclude that 'fundamentalist movements are inherently interactive, reactive and oppositional – that is, they are inexorably drawn to some form of antagonistic engagement with the world outside the enclave' (p. 503).

In short, fundamentalism refuses the labour of 'negotiating the middle'. This is not to hide the negativity of fundamentalism – its aggressive rejection of modernity – or to ignore the very real danger that the 'myth–reason' tension will be manipulated by short-term vested interests. It does, however, recognise that the rhetoric of pluralism is part of the problem, not the solution.[28]

Where faith meets faith, the major ethical and political issue is how to give difference its proper place without risking a disintegration into competing, or even warring, factions. Levinas is undoubtedly correct that most Western philosophy, and therefore explicit and implicit political ideology, is totalising of the other. A structure of thought which will keep 'the other' under the control of 'the same' is to be imposed on consciousness. To that extent, there is always likely to be a bias in a multi-faith society towards establishing a basis of supposedly 'common values'. Even apart, however, from the fact that such an approach can be subtly coercive – concerned more to avoid conflict than to encourage positive contributions to the national culture – little attention is paid to the pressing question of how what is 'common' and 'global' can grow from the 'particular' and 'local'. Well-meaning exhortations towards a tolerant multiculturalism not only fail to touch the life-giving heart of a religious faith, but may actually do violence to the wider fabric of story, ritual, devotion and custom, on which faith depends to give it real energy and motivation. No religious group or community of faith enjoys being slotted away into someone else's minimalist categories. The patronising assumption in a secular post-modern society that religion is yet another marketable commodity, albeit part of some 'spiritual' economy of aesthetic values and cultural practices, forgets that religions are whole ways of life, 'schools of faith' which teach politics as much as forms and methods of prayer. Clearly any school is open to all sorts of corruption; but this is only to repeat that communities exist through a process of constant self-identification in face of the other and are no more complete and blissfully at home than any individual person.

It is all too easy, in a multi-faith world, to seek to reconcile conflicting truth claims by attempting to reduce them within the framework of some overarching panoptic vision. The more demanding challenge is to work

---

[28] According to D'Costa 2000:19–52, on closer examination much of the typically pluralist rhetoric can be deconstructed into disguised forms of exclusivism or modernist Enlightenment agnosticism.

within and between the living traditions – not to seek to extract from them some supposedly timeless ethical essence, but to enable them to 're-read' their own stories and to learn from each other. Essentially inter-faith dialogue, as I have sought to describe it, is such a rereading – a common enterprise in which, at a number of different levels, schools of faith can learn how to speak, how to listen, how to co-operate. But, for this to work, communities have to be given sufficient space and encouragement to reach down into their own fund of collective wisdom and to rediscover their own strengths and sources of energy. At the same time, if they are not to become alienated from wider society (and wider society not to be alienated from them), this needs to be done consciously *in relationship* with whatever they take to be 'other' – whether other religious groups and communities or secular society. The 'dual responsibility' applies not just to Christians but to all people of faith, to be fully and faithfully 'them-selves' within a commitment to the harmony of civic society as a whole.

Facing the other – times and places

This vision of a 'school of schools' takes us back to where we started, with Christians in a multi-faith society learning how to become mediators and bridge-builders. In this book, I have tried to sketch the terms of a 'theol-ogy of dialogue', a Christian reflection on an intrinsically relational exis-tence – with 'learning about learning', as Rowan Williams neatly puts it.[29] To conclude, then, we might ask what has been learned from the post-modern 'context of otherness', from the Church's experience of a present 'haunted' by traces of an anarchic past, from our 'liturgical' reading of the post-modern concern with alterity, from 'micro-discourses' of the re-turning other and the Christian story of the welcoming and hospitable God?

Christians claim to know and to name the source of salvation; guided by God's Spirit they know something of what it costs to become 'border-crossers' after the manner of Christ. At the same time, 'it is not for us to judge and say where the Church is not'.[30] Or, as I put it at the end of the introductory chapter, the Church speaks of what it knows to be true; what the Church does *not* know is the total reality of what always remains other and utterly mysterious. The process of negotiation is never

---

[29] Williams 2000:132.
[30] Butler 1981:119.

straightforward, if only because borders, the limits of the enclave, often turn out to be difficult to define, let alone discern. It is, therefore, impossible to predict in advance what the outcome of any particular form of inter-faith dialogue is going to be. This is precisely *not*, however, to espouse some unprincipled exchange from which 'truth' will inevitably emerge if only the partners practise sufficient tolerance and respect for the other. Whatever the importance of such practices, I have argued that a Christian theology of dialogue is founded not on the accommodation of tradition and situation, but ultimately on the doctrine of the self-revealing God. Living in the Spirit who, as Monchanin repeatedly puts it, draws all things back to the Father,[31] Christians are committed to the practice of breaking the borders by constantly departing for 'elsewhere' in imitation of the homeless Christ.

The implication of the Christian story of the hospitable God who acts both as host and as guest is that it is not for us to predict in advance where God is to be found and how God is to act. Speaking very much out of the Asian experience, Aloysius Pieris makes a distinction between two missiologies, one which 'defines mission as somehow or other *procuring a place for Christ in Asia*' and another which, as he puts it, 'spells out the missiological consequences of recognizing and proclaiming *Christ as the one who has no place in Asia*'.[32] Pieris's aim is to identify a new christology which he sees emerging amongst the poor and displaced peoples of Asia. The Asian Church, he says, has to learn how to '*discover* the Christhood of the Asian poor who, like Jesus, have no decent place to be born in (Lk 2.7), no reputable place to live and work in (Jn 1.46), no safe place in their own country to hide from oppressive rulers (Mt 2.13-14) or no honourable place to die in (Lk 23.23) and no place of their own to be buried in (Mt 27.59)'.[33] Pieris is highly critical of a missiology of 'conquest' which presumes to 'place' Christ in territories which are alien to him. Rather, he argues, Christ is already there before Christian missionaries succeed in establishing a special place for him.

Although bound up very much with Pieris's constant concern – how to make the Church *in* Asia the Church *of* Asia – his remarks are curiously apposite for the Christian Church in the post-modern West. On the streets which I have been describing, Christians often find themselves a

---

[31] See e.g. in Weber 1977:122, 136, 146, 153, 155, 164–5.

[32] Pieris 1993a:43; emphases in the original.

[33] Pieris 1993a:44.

minority, facing questions about the practice and limits of inculturation every bit as difficult as those which so much preoccupied Ricci and de Nobili and the early Jesuit missionaries. Not only is there an ever-growing proliferation of 'other places', but many mosques and temples were once churches or church halls. The number of redundant churches turned into flats, theatres and museums makes for a potent symbol of a post-Christian society. That there has been a sea-change in the religious profile of late modernity is obvious. And yet, if the distinction Pieris makes is valid, does it not follow that the Church's 'evangelical responsibility' in such a world is not to spend energy and effort defending or reclaiming the 'old' places, but to acknowledge the Christ already making himself present in the space shared with other people of faith?

Much of what I have said has focused attention on the space, the 'between', the 'middle', which is always broken and always mended. This is, nevertheless, the space of the unpredictable, the only space within which to await in patient hope the revelation of the face of Christ. The language of incarnation roots Christians firmly in space and time – even if they cannot claim a 'place' of their own in the sense of a geographically distinct home. When Jesus speaks of being present where 'two or three are gathered together in my name' (Matthew 18.20), still more when he tells them to 'do this in memory of me', he is not exhorting the disciples to some sentimental memory, but enacting the promise of the God who is 'Emanuel', the one he calls Father. This God is understood to be 'with us' by gathering up and representing the history of Israel in a radically new way, a radically *present* new way. It is not, as the Gospel story constantly reiterates, that Jesus points the way forward to a future fulfilment in a particular place. Rather, he announces the in-breaking of the Kingdom at this moment and for all people. The Paschal Mystery, the Death and Resurrection and the outpouring of the Spirit, marks the beginning of a new community, a new gathering of humankind, the 'harmonious difference' which transcends all divisions, of slave and free, male and female, Jew and Gentile. This is what has begun but, of course, it is not yet completed. A distinction has to be made between the time of the inauguration of this new world and the time of its fulfilment. But, similarly, if the inauguration of the Kingdom is not to be reduced to the triumphant mastery of one particular institution, culture or community, then some distinction has to be made between *this particular place* in which Christians find themselves as the people of God sharing a pilgrimage with others, and the *space of the world* which has already been sanctified and dedicated to God.

Christian eschatology overturns any notion of a privileged place or a privileged moment of time. Now every place and every moment speaks equally of God to those who learn how to discern and witness to the 'seeds of the Word', the signs of the in-breaking of the Kingdom. How to recognise those signs? That is where Christians do need a 'place' of their own. This, however, is not a place of power which, as de Certeau warns us, can end up as a self-defining border to be defended against the other. In a sense, the purpose of Christian places is that they become 'non-places', to be places of *kenosis* and negation which impel disciples away from an attachment to the concrete and a desire for the familiar, to go 'elsewhere' in obedience to Christ's call to follow. Of course, care has to be taken that from being centres of power Christian places do not end up as mere centres of retreat from the world, and that the time of waiting does not become a pretext for the covert manipulation of the other. The more insidious danger, however, is that the 'lost body' of the Lord is substituted by some theoretical construct or system rather than 'found' by response to the Word which God goes on speaking. Christians find by searching, for, in the words of the Resurrection narrative, Christ 'is not here . . . He has been raised from the dead and is going ahead of you to Galilee' (Matthew 28.6–7). Putting the point quite pragmatically, Christian places – churches and chapels which, like the empty tomb, are essentially signs of the 'lost body' – continue the work of sanctification which *God* begins in God's people and seeks to extend throughout the whole space of creation. This they do by acting as places of hospitality, places which celebrate the welcoming God made manifest in Christ.

There is little need to say more about the way this celebration inspires practices of facing the other in generosity and freedom. When Christians gather to celebrate the Eucharist, they are confronted by the Word which speaks not in confirmation of human expectations but precisely to subvert them. As ritual, the repetition of the narrative form enacts memory, the life-blood of all religion. More particularly, as *liturgy* – the 'work which makes the people' – the Eucharist enacts an ethical relation with the other. The indicative, the story which is told, is mixed with the imperative, the commands of Jesus which bestrew the Gospel narrative. Thus, at the end of the celebration the people God has formed are sent out not just to follow, to go elsewhere, but to share the Good News of what God can do in human weakness. That is the source of, and motivation for, the negotiation of the middle, the desire freely to share with others what the ever-welcoming God has strangely yet freely shared with God's people.

Christian places – and this term must surely apply not just to cathedrals and schools but to all the many visible sites of Christian presence in the world – have but one purpose: the sanctification of time and space. This begins with the Eucharist and the celebration of the sacraments. But my argument is that the identity which God gives his people through the formal celebration of the Paschal Mystery is inseparable from the much more diffuse process of engagement with the other, from being sent as the Spirit is sent to witness to the love of God made manifest in Christ. The Church is the People of God on pilgrimage through a world which is shared with others. But it is also the sacrament of unity, the sign of what God intends for the whole of humanity.

These two aspects of the Church's inner life would seem to commend two principles for facing the other. The homelessness of Christ, with its profound witness to God's gracious blessing of this present moment, is more than a wonderful ideal which motivates a few extraordinary individuals like the early Jesuit missionaries and more recent Indian ashramites. All Christians are called to a life of active-yet-passive detachment, if not some form of departure for 'elsewhere'. The homeless Christ's inner freedom before the Father is also a reminder that there can be no absolute demand to defend any place, church structure or territory, for the peace which God promises is pure gift and can never be constrained by particular moments in time or particular places. Christians cannot *depend* on place.

But the radical following of the Christ who has nowhere to lay his head can encourage not the patience of Christ who waits in hope but a bland passivity which lacks any purchase on the real messy world of sin and broken relationships. To return for one last time to the multi-faith streets of London, there is something attractive about the project of 'walking the city', seeking out opportunities to meet and converse with people. But it can also be delightfully, and insidiously, aimless. The establishing of places of welcome is important if Christians are to learn how to act as hosts to the other and to respond as guests, and thus to enable God's work of sanctification of space to proceed. There are, however, a hundred and one ways in which human short-sightedness, collusion with sinful structures, and compromise with short-cuts and easy answers, all seek to subvert that work. Places are needed not just to celebrate faith and to welcome the other, but to act as sites of critique and resistance. Something similar can be said about the use of time. Without places of celebration and service, Christians have no visibility, no basis from which they can engage with the wider space of multi-faith society. Without the time to wait upon the action of God's Spirit, they will never develop those inner dispositions of faith, hope and love, which allow God to work in God's own time.

We live in a post-modern world which is defined by a 'context of otherness', haunted by the other who is always returning, seeking to disturb the short-term comfort which human beings always seek to construct for themselves. There will, therefore, be times when it will be appropriate to speak and to resist; there will also be times when it is right to listen and to leave alone. In this sense, Christian discipleship will be marked not just by a constant attention to the 'tactics' which take time and wait upon the right moment, but also to the sort of place which makes possible both the time of waiting and the time for resistance.

Christians wait upon God after the manner of the homeless Christ. Jesus, we are told, often withdrew to a 'place apart' in order to be with the Father. But he did so only to return, strengthened by the Spirit, to confront and to console. Similarly, the only place that Christians really need to be is in Christ with the Father. There, through the liturgical participation in the Paschal Mystery, they learn the *habitus* of inter-faith, that generous yet critical facing of the other which is always prepared to negotiate the middle by discerning possible 'seeds of the Word'. In this book I have not, therefore, sought to defend some form of Christian identity over against the other. My subject has been the experience of relationality, the properly relational experience of Christian faith in the self-revealing God. 'God is known', as Lash says, 'by participating in that movement which he is. And it is this participation which constitutes the reality, the life and history, of everything that is.'[34] To that extent, all theology is a response to that dialogue which God initiates. But it is also properly heterological: a response to the otherness of God who alone can enable the other to speak. Understood in this way, as an ethical meeting of persons and as much a moment of God's self-revelation as liturgy and prayer, dialogue opens the partners without limit towards that Infinite horizon of their being which is God.

---

[34] Lash 1996:86.

References

Abbott, Walter (ed.) (1966), *Documents of Vatican II*, London: Chapman.

Abdel-Malek, Anouar (1963), 'Orientalism in Crisis', *Diogenes*, 44; pp. 102–40.

Abhishiktananda, Swami (Henri le Saux) (1966a), *Une Messe aux Sources du Gange*, Paris: Éditions du Seuil.

(1966b), *The Mountain of the Lord*, Bangalore: CISRS. (ET of 1966a)

(1969), *The Church in India*, Madras: Christian Literature Society.

(1970), *Towards a Renewal of the Indian Church*, Bangalore: Dharmaram College.

(1974a), *Saccidananda*, Delhi: ISPCK.

(1974b), *Guru and Disciple*, London: SPCK.

Ahearne, Jeremy (1991), *Michel de Certeau: Interpretation and its Other*, Cambridge: Polity.

(1996), 'The Shattering of Christianity and the Articulation of Belief', *New Blackfriars*, 909; 493–504.

Alam, Javeed (1983), 'Peasantry, Politics and Historiography: a Critique of a New Trend in Relation to Marxism', *Social Scientist*, 117; 43–54.

Alberigo, Giuseppe (1987), *The Reception of Vatican II*, edited by Jean-Pierre Jossua and Joseph A. Komonchak; Washington DC: Catholic University of America Press.

(1995) (ed.), *History of Vatican II*, volume 1: *Announcing and Preparing Vatican Council II, Toward a new Era in Catholicism*; volume 2: *The Formation of the Council's Identity*, (1997); volume 3: *The Mature Council* (2000); English version by Joseph A. Komonchak, Maryknoll: Orbis; Leuven: Peeters.

Amaladass, Anand (1988), *Jesuit Presence in Indian History*, Anand: Gujarat Sahitya Prakash.

Amaladoss, Michael (1990), *Making All Things New: Dialogue, Pluralism and Evangelization in Asia*, Maryknoll NY: Orbis.

(1994), *A Call to Community*, Anand: Gujarat Sahitya Prakash.

(1995), 'The Theological and Missionary Project of Monchanin in Today's Indian Theological Context', *Indian Theological Studies*, 32.4; 307–20.

Amalorpavadass, D. S. (ed.) (1981), *The Indian Church in the Struggle for a New Society*, Bangalore: NBCLC.

Arockiasamy, Soosai (1986), *Dharma, Hindu and Christian according to Robert de Nobili*, Rome: Pontificia Università Gregoriana.

(1991) (ed.), *Responding to Communalism: the Task of Religions and Theology*, Anand: Gujarat Sahitya Prakash.

(1997), 'Moral Theological Perspectives in Evangelisation', *Vidyajyoti*, 61; 800–8.

Arulraja, M. R. (1996), *Jesus the Dalit*, Hyderabad: Volunteer Centre.

Arul Raja (1995), 'The Authority of Jesus: a Dalit Reading of Mark 11.27–33', *Jeevadhara*, April; 123–38.

Arzubialde, Santiago (1991), *Ejercicios Espirituales de S Ignacio: Historia y Anàlisis*, Bilbao–Santander: Colección Manresa.

Ashton, John (1991), *Understanding the Fourth Gospel*, Oxford University Press.

Barnes, Michael (1989), *Religions in Conversation*, London: SPCK.

  (1992), 'Evangelization and other Faiths: the Motivation for Mission', in *Many Mansions: Interfaith and Religious Intolerance*, edited by Dan Cohn-Sherbok; London: Bellew; pp. 53–60.

  (1999), *Walking the City*, New Delhi: ISPCK.

  (2000), *Traces of the Other: Three Philosophers on Inter-Faith Dialogue*, Chennai: Satya Nilayam.

Bauerschmidt, F. C. (1996a), 'The Abrahamic Voyage: Michel de Certeau and Theology', *Modern Theology*, 12.1; 1–26.

  (1996b), 'Walking in the Pilgrim City', *New Blackfriars*, 909; 504–18.

Bell, David (1990), *Husserl*, London: Routledge.

Bergman, Shmuel Hugo (1991), *Dialogical Philosophy from Kierkegaard to Buber*, Albany NY: State University of New York Press.

Bernasconi, Robert (1995), ' "Only the Persecuted . . ." ', in *Ethics as First Philosophy: the Significance of Emmanuel Levinas for Philosophy, Literature and Religion*; edited by Adriaan Peperzak, London, Routledge; pp. 77–86.

Bernasconi, Robert and Critchley, Simon (1991), *Re-reading Levinas*, Bloomington: Indiana University Press.

Bernasconi, Robert and Wood, David (eds.) (1988), *The Provocation of Levinas: Rethinking the Other*, London: Routledge.

Bhabha, Homi (1994), *The Location of Culture*; London: Routledge.

Biernatzki, William E. (1991), *Roots of Acceptance: the Intercultural Communication of Religious Meanings*, Rome: Pontificia Università Gregoriana.

Bosch, David (1991), *Transforming Mission*, New York: Orbis.

Bouyer, Louis (1965), *The Liturgy Revised: a Doctrinal Commentary on the Conciliar Constitution on the Liturgy*, London: Darton, Longman and Todd.

Bowes, Pratima (1986), *Between Cultures*, New Delhi: Allied Publishers.

Boyd, Robin (1975), *An Introduction to Indian Christian Theology*, revised edition; Delhi: ISPCK.

Brooks, Roger (ed.) (1988), *Unanswered Questions: Theological Views of Jewish–Christian Relations*, Notre Dame University Press.

Brown, Raymond (1979), *The Community of the Beloved Disciple*, New York and London: Paulist.

Buber, Martin (1958), *I and Thou*, ET Ronald Gregor Smith; 2nd edition; Edinburgh: T. and T. Clark.

Buchanan, Ian (1995), 'Heterology: Towards a Transcendental Approach to Cultural Studies', Ph.D. dissertation, Murdoch University, Western Australia.

  (1996), 'What is Heterology?' *New Blackfriars*, 909; 483–93.

Buckley, James J. (1992), *Seeking the Humanity of God: Practices, Doctrines and Catholic Theology*, Collegeville: The Liturgical Press.

Bulman, Raymond F. and Parella, Frederick J. (eds.) (1994), *Paul Tillich: a New Catholic Assessment*, Collegeville: The Liturgical Press.

Burrows, William (1994) (ed.), *Redemption and Dialogue: Reading Redemptoris Missio and Dialogue and Proclamation*, Maryknoll NY: Orbis.

Burrows, William (1996), 'A Seventh Paradigm? Catholics and Radical Inculturation', in *Mission in Bold Humility: David Bosch's Work Considered*, edited by Willem Saayman and Klippies Kritzinger; Maryknoll NY: Orbis.

Butler, B. C. (1981), *The Theology of Vatican II*, 2nd edition; London: Darton, Longman and Todd.

Byrne, James (1998), 'The Category "Religion" Reconsidered', *Way Supplement*, 92; 102–12.

Cantwell Smith, Wilfred (1962), *The Faith of Other Men*, New York: Harper.

(1963), *The Meaning and End of Religion*, New York: Macmillan.

(1981), *Towards a World Theology: faith and the comparative history of religion*, London: Macmillan.

Cavanaugh, William T. (1995), '"A Fire Strong Enough to Consume the House": the Wars of Religion and the Rise of the State', *Modern Theology*, 11.4; 397–420.

(1998), *Torture and Eucharist*, Oxford: Blackwell.

Chatterjee, Margaret (1983), *Gandhi's Religious Thought*, London: Macmillan.

Chatterjee, Partha (1983), 'Peasants, Politics and Historiography: a Response', *Social Scientist*, 120; 58–65.

(1989), 'Caste and Subaltern Consciousness', *Subaltern Studies* 6; 169–209.

Chenu, Marie-Dominique (1965), 'Les signes des temps', *Nouvelle Revue Theologique*, 87; 29–39.

Clancy, Thomas (1978), *The Conversational Word of God*, St Louis: Institute of Jesuit Sources.

Clarke, Sathianathan (1998), *Dalits and Christianity*, Delhi: Oxford University Press.

Clooney, Francis X. (1993), *Theology after Vedanta*, Albany: State University of New York Press.

(1996), *Seeing through Texts*, Albany: State University of New York Press.

Cohen, Richard (1986) (ed.), *Face to Face with Levinas*, Albany: State University of New York Press.

(1994), *Elevations: the Height of the Good in Rosenzweig and Levinas*, Chicago University Press.

Cousins, Ewert (1992), *Christ of the Twenty-First Century*, Shaftesbury: Element.

Cracknell, Kenneth (1995), *Justice, Courtesy and Love, Theologians and Missionaries Encountering World Religions, 1846–1914*, London: Epworth Press.

Critchley, Simon (1992), *The Ethics of Deconstruction*, Oxford: Blackwell.

Cronin, Vincent (1959), *A Pearl to India*, New York: Dutton.

Dalmases, Candido de (1985), *Ignatius of Loyola, Founder of the Jesuits*, St Louis: Institute of Jesuit Sources.

Daniélou, Jean (1948), *Le Mystère du Salut des Nations*, Paris.

(1962), *The Advent of Salvation*, Glen Rock: Paulist.

Davis, Colin (1996), *Levinas: an Introduction*, Cambridge: Polity.

D'Costa, Gavin (1985), 'Karl Rahner's Anonymous Christian – a Reappraisal', *Modern Theology*, 1.2; 131–48.

(1986), *Theology and Religious Pluralism*, Oxford: Blackwell.

(1987), *John Hick's Theology of Religions, a Critical Evaluation*, Lanham: University Press of America.

(1990a) (ed.), *Christian Uniqueness Reconsidered: the Myth of a Pluralistic Theology of Religions*, Maryknoll NY: Orbis.

(1990b), 'One Covenant or Many Covenants? Toward a Theology of Christian Jewish Relations,' *Journal of Ecumenical Studies*, 27.3; 441–52.

(1990c), 'Taking Other Religions Seriously: Some Ironies in the Current Debate on a Christian Theology of Religions', *The Thomist*, 54; 519–29.

(1991), 'John Hick and Religious Pluralism: Yet Another Revolution', in *Problems in the Philosophy of Religion: Critical Studies of the Work of John Hick*, edited by Harold Hewitt; London: Macmillan; pp. 3–18.

(1996), 'The Impossibility of a Pluralist View of Religions', *Religious Studies*, 32; 223–32.

(2000), *The Meeting of Religions and the Trinity*; Edinburgh: T. and T. Clark.

de Beauvoir, Simone (1970), *The Second Sex*, ET H. Parshley; New York: Bantam Books.

de Certeau, Michel (1966), 'L'universalisme ignatien; mystique et mission', *Christus*, 13; 173–83.

(1984), *The Practice of Everyday Life*, ET Steven Rendall; Berkeley: University of California Press.

(1986), *Heterologies: Discourse on the Other*, ET Brian Massumi; Foreword Wlad Godzich; Manchester University Press.

(1987a), *La Faiblesse de Croire*, Paris: Seuil.

(1987b), 'The Gaze: Nicholas of Cusa', *Diacritics*, Fall 87; 2–38.

(1988), *The Writing of History*, ET Tom Conley, NY: Columbia University Press.

(1992), *The Mystic Fable: Volume I – the Sixteenth and Seventeenth Centuries*, ET Michael B. Smith; Chicago University Press.

de Certeau, Michel and Domenach, J.-M. (1974), *Le Christianisme Éclaté*, Paris: Seuil.

de Certeau, Michel, Giard, Luce and Mayol, Pierre (1998) *The Practice of Everyday Life*, ET Timothy J. Tomasik; Minneapolis: University of Minnesota Press.

de Charentenay, Pierre (1994) 'D'une inculturation à "l'autre"', *Études*, 209–18.

de Lubac, Henri (1950), *Catholicism: a Study of Dogma in Relation to the Corporate Destiny of Mankind*, ET from the French 4th edition, 1947; London: Burns and Oates.

(1966), *Images de l'Abbé Monchanin*, Paris: Aubier.

(1979), *The Splendour of the Church*, ET Michael Mason from the French 2nd edition; London: Sheed and Ward.

Derrida, Jacques (1978), *Writing and Difference*, ET Alan Bass; London: Routledge.

(1992), *Given Time*, ET Peggy Kamuf; Chicago University Press.

Descombes, Vincent (1980), *Modern French Philosophy*, ET L. Scott-Fox and J. M. Harding; Cambridge University Press.

Devasahayam, V. (1992a), *Outside the Camp*, Madras: Gurukul.

(1992b), *Dalits and Women*, Madras: Gurukul.

Dharampal (1993), *Bharatiya Chitta Manas and Kala*, ET from the Hindi by Jitendra Bajaj; Madras: Centre for Policy Studies.

Di Noia, J. A. (1992), *The Diversity of Religions: a Christian Perspective*, Washington DC: Catholic University of America Press.

Doran, Robert (1990), *Theology and the Dialectics of History*, University of Toronto Press.

D'Sa, Francis X. (1997), *The Dharma of Jesus*, Anand: Gujarat Sahitya Prakash.

Du Boulay, Shirley (1998), *Beyond the Darkness*, London: Rider.

Dulles, Avery (1992), 'John Paul II and the "New Evangelization"', *America*, February 1992; 52–9; 69–77.

Dumont, Louis (1970), *Homo Hierarchicus*, ET; London: Weidenfeld.

Dunn, James (1983), 'The New Perspective on Paul', *Bulletin of John Rylands Library*, 65; 95–122.

(1988), *Romans 1–8, 9–16, Word Biblical Commentary*, volumes 38ab; Dallas: Word Books.

Dupuis, Jacques (1997), *Toward a Christian Theology of Religious Pluralism*, Maryknoll NY; Orbis.

Dussell, Enrique (ed.) (1992), *The Church in Latin America*, London: Burns and Oates.

Eagleton, Terry (2000), *The Idea of Culture*, Oxford: Blackwell.

Eckardt, Roy (1986), *Jews and Christians: the Contemporary Meeting*, Bloomington.

Ellis, Marc H. (1997), *Unholy Alliance: Religion and Atrocity in our Time*, London: SCM.

Eminyan, Maurice (1960), *The Theology of Salvation*, Boston.

Fackenheim, Emil (1982), *To Mend the World: Foundations of Future Jewish Thought*, New York: Schocken Books.

Faivre, Daniel (ed.) (1999), *Celebrating Jesus*, Southall: privately published.

Fanon, Frantz (1986), *Black Skin White Masks*, London: Pluto Press.

Farrugia, Joseph (1988), *The Church and the Muslims*, Gozo: Media Centre.

Fernandes, Angelo (1997), *Vatican Two Revisited*, Anand: Gujarat Sahitya Prakash.

Fernandes, Walter (ed.) (1996), *The Emerging Dalit Identity*, Delhi: Indian Social Institute.

Fitzpatrick, P. J. (1993), *In Breaking of Bread: the Eucharist and Ritual*, Cambridge University Press.

Fodor, James (1995), *Christian Hermeneutics: Paul Ricoeur and the Refiguring of Theology*, Oxford: Clarendon Press.

Ford, David (1995), 'What Happens in the Eucharist?', *Scottish Journal of Theology*, 48.3; 359–81.

(1997) (ed.), *The Modern Theologians*, Oxford: Blackwell.

(1999), *Self and Salvation: Being Transformed*, Cambridge University Press.

Forrester, Duncan (1980), *Caste and Christianity*, London: Curzon.

Gadamer, Hans-Georg (1989), *Truth and Method*, ET Joel Weinsheimer and Donald G. Marshall; 2nd revised edition; New York: Crossroad.

Gallagher, Michael Paul (1997), *Clashing Symbols*, London: Darton, Longman and Todd.

Garcia-Villoslada, Riccardo (1954), *Storia del Collegio Romano*, Rome: Pontificia Università Gregoriana.

Giard, Luce (1991), 'Epilogue: Michel de Certeau's Heterology and the New World', *Representations*, 33; 212–21.

Gibbs, Robert (1992), *Correlations in Rosenzweig and Levinas*, Princeton University Press.

Gioia, Francesco (ed.) (1997), *Interreligious Dialogue – the Official Teaching of the Catholic Church (1963–1995)*, sponsored by the Pontifical Council for Interreligious Dialogue; Boston: Pauline Books.

Gispert Sauch, George (ed.) (1973), *God's Word Among Men*, New Delhi: Vidyajyoti.

Glatzer, Nahum (1953), *Franz Rosenzweig, His Life and Thought*, New York: Schocken Books.

Griffiths, Bede (1966), *Christian Ashram*, London: Darton, Longman and Todd.

(1978), *Return to the Centre*, London: Fount.

(1983), *The Marriage of East and West*, London: Fount.

Griffiths, Paul (1990), *Christianity through Non-Christian Eyes*, Maryknoll NY: Orbis.

(1991), *An Apology for Apologetics: a Study in the Logic of Interreligious Dialogue*, Maryknoll NY: Orbis.

Guha, Ranajit (1982), 'On some Aspects of the Historiography of Colonial India', *Subaltern Studies*, 1; 1–8.

Hahn, Lewis E. (ed.) (1995), *The Philosophy of Paul Ricoeur*, The Library of Living Philosophers Volume XXII; Chicago: La Salle.

Haight, Roger (1990), *Dynamics of Theology*, New York: Paulist.

Halbfass, Wilhelm (1988), *India and Europe: an Essay in Understanding*, Albany: State University of New York Press.

Handelman, Susan A. (1991), *Fragments of Redemption: Jewish Thought and Literary Theory in Benjamin, Scholem and Levinas*, Bloomington: Indiana University Press.

Harrington, Daniel J. (1992), *Paul and the Mystery of Israel*, Glazier.

Harrison, Peter (1990), *'Religion' and the Religions in the English Enlightenment*, Cambridge University Press.

Hastings, Adrian (1991), *Modern Catholicism: Vatican II and After*, London: SPCK.

Hebblethwaite, Peter (1977), 'The Status of Anonymous Christians', *Heythrop Journal*, 18; 47–55.

(1993), *Paul VI: the First Modern Pope*, London: Fount.

(1994), *John XXIII: Pope of the Council*, revised edition; London: Fount.

Heidegger, Martin (1962), *Being and Time*, ET John Macquarrie and Edward Robinson; Oxford: Blackwell.

Heimsath, Charles (1964), *Indian Nationalism and Hindu Social Reform*, Princeton University Press.

Hennelly, Alfred T. (ed.) (1990), *Liberation Theology: a Documentary History*, Maryknoll NY: Orbis.

Henry, A.-M. (ed.) (1966), *Les Relations de l'Église avec les Religions Non Chrétiennes*, Paris: Cerf.

Hick, John (1974) (ed.), *Truth and Dialogue*, London: Sheldon Press.

(1977), *God and the Universe of Faiths*, London: Fount.

(1989), *The Interpretation of Religion*, London: Macmillan.

Hick, John and Knitter, Paul (eds.) (1987), *The Myth of Christian Uniqueness*, London: SCM.

Hocart, A. M. (1950), *Caste: a Comparative Study*, ET London: Methuen.

Husserl, Edmund (1950), *Cartesian Meditations*, ET Dorion Cairns; Dordrecht: Kluwer. French translation, *Méditations Cartésiennes*, by Gabrielle Peiffer and Emmanuel Levinas; Paris: Armand Colin, 1931.

Irudayaraj, Xavier (ed.) (1989), *Liberation and Dialogue*, Bangalore: Claretian Publications.

(1990), *Emerging Dalit Theology*, Madurai: Tamil Theological Seminary.

Ivens, Michael (1998), *Understanding the Spiritual Exercises*, Leominster: Gracewing.

Jacquin, Françoise (1989), *Abbé Monchanin: Lettres à sa Mère*, Paris: Cerf.

(1996), *Jules Monchanin, Prêtre*, Paris: Cerf.

Jai Singh, Herbert (ed.) (1967), *Inter-Religious Dialogue*, Bangalore: CISRS.

John, T. K. (ed.) (1991), *Bread and Breath*, Anand: Gujarat Sahitya Prakash.

Jones, C., Wainwright G. and Yarnold, E. J. (eds.) (1978), *The Study of Liturgy*, London: SPCK.

Joshi, Barbara (1986), *Untouchables – Voice of the Dalit Liberation Movement*, New Delhi.

Juergensmeyer, Mark (1982), *Religion as Social Vision*, Berkeley: University of California Press.

(1993), *The New Cold War: Religious Nationalism Confronts the Secular State*, Berkeley: University of California Press.

Jungmann, J. A. (1975), 'Liturgy', in *Encyclopedia of Theology*, edited by Karl Rahner; London: Burns and Oates.

Kappen, Sebastian (1977), *Jesus and Freedom*, New York: Orbis.

Kasper, Walter (1989), *Theology and Church*, London: SCM.

Kaviraj, Sudipta (1992), 'The Imaginary Institution of India', *Subaltern Studies, 7*; 1–39.

Kearney, Richard (ed.) (1996), *Paul Ricoeur, the Hermeneutics of Action*, London: Sage Publications.

Khare, Ravindra S. (1984), *The Untouchable as Himself: Ideology, Identity and Pragmatism among the Lucknow Chamars*, Cambridge University Press.

King, Ursula (1980), *Towards a New Mysticism: Teilhard de Chardin and Eastern Religions*, London: Collins.

Knitter, Paul (1985), *No Other Name? A Critical Survey of Christian Attitudes to World Religions*, London: SCM.

(1995), *One Earth Many Religions: Multifaith Dialogue and Global Responsibility*, Maryknoll NY: Orbis.

Kuhn, Thomas (1970), *The Structure of Scientific Revolutions*, 2nd edition; Chicago University Press.

Küng, Hans (1993), *Christianity and the World Religions*, 2nd edition; London: SCM.

Küng, Hans and Kuschel, Karl-Josef (eds.) (1993), *A Global Ethic*, London: SCM.

Kunnumpuram, Kurien and Fernando, Lorenzo (eds.) (1993), *Quest for an Indian Church: an Exploration of the Possibilities opened up by Vatican II*, Anand: Gujarat Sahitya Prakash.

Lakeland, Paul (1997), *Postmodernity: Christian Identity in a Fragmented Age*, Minneapolis: Fortress.

Larson, Gerald (1995), *India's Agony over Religion*, Albany: State University of New York Press.

Lash, Nicholas (1986), 'Considering the Trinity', *Modern Theology*, 2.3; 183–96.

(1992), *Believing Three Ways in One God*, London: SCM.

(1996), *The Beginning and the End of 'Religion'*, Cambridge University Press.

(1997), 'The Church in the State we're in', *Modern Theology*, 13.1; 121–38.

Laurentin, René and Neuner, Joseph (1966) *Declaration on the Relation of the Church to non-Christian Religions of Vatican II*, Glen Rock NJ: Paulist Press.

Levinas, Emmanuel (1969), *Totality and Infinity*, ET Alphonso Lingis; Pittsburgh: Duquesne University Press.

(1978), *Existence and Existents*, ET Alphonso Lingis; Dordrecht: Kluwer Academic Publishers.

(1982), *De l'évasion*, Montpellier: Fata Morgana.

(1983), 'Franz Rosenzweig', translated by Richard A. Cohen; *Midstream*, 29.9; 33–40.

(1985), *Ethics and Infinity*, ET Richard A. Cohen; Pittsburgh: Duquesne University Press.

(1986), 'The Trace of the Other', in *Deconstruction in Context*, edited by Mark C. Taylor; Chicago University Press.

(1987a), *Time and the Other*, ET Richard A. Cohen; Pittsburgh: Duquesne University Press.

(1987b), *Collected Philosophical Papers*, ET Alphonso Lingis; *Phaenomenologica*, volume 100, Dordrecht: Nijhoff.

(1989), *Levinas Reader*, edited by Sean Hand; Oxford: Blackwell.

(1990a), *Difficult Freedom*, Essays on Judaism, ET by Sean Hand; London: Athlone Press.

(1990b), *Nine Talmudic Readings*, ET Annette Aronowicz; Bloomington: Indiana University Press.

(1991), *Otherwise than Being or Beyond Essence*, ET Alphonso Lingis: Dordrecht: Kluwer Academic Publishers.

(1993), *Outside the Subject*, ET Michael B. Smith; London: Athlone Press.

(1994a), *In the Time of the Nations*, ET Michael B. Smith; Bloomington: Indiana University Press.

(1994b), *Beyond the Verse*, ET Gary D. Mole; Bloomington: Indiana University Press.

(1995), *The Theory of Intuition in Husserl's Phenomenology*, ET André Orianne; Evanston IL: Northwestern University Press.

(1996), *Basic Philosophical Writings*, edited by Adriaan T. Peperzak, Simon Critchley and Robert Bernasconi; Bloomington: Indiana University Press.

(1998a), *Entre Nous: Thinking-of-the-Other*, ET Michael Smith and Barbara Hershav; London: Athlone.

(1998b), *Of God who Comes to Mind*, ET Bettina Bergo; Stanford University Press.

(1999), *Alterity and Transcendence*, ET Michael Smith; London: Athlone.

Lindbeck, George (1984), *The Nature of Doctrine*, London: SPCK.

Lipner, Julius (1993), 'On "Hindutva" and a "Hindu-Catholic" with a moral for our times', *Hindu–Christian Studies Bulletin*, 5; 1ff.

(1994), *Hindus*, London: Routledge.

Lipner, Julius and Gispert-Sauch, George (eds.) (1992), *The Writings of Brahmabandhab Upadhyay*, volume 1; Bangalore: United Theological College.

Lloyd, Genevieve (1993), *Being in Time: Selves and Narrators in Philosophy and Literature*, London: Routledge.

Lochhead, David (1988), *The Dialogical Imperative: a Christian Reflection on Inter-Faith Encounter*, Maryknoll NY: Orbis.

Lonergan, Bernard (1971), *Method in Theology*, London: Darton, Longman and Todd.

Lonsdale, David (2000), *Eyes to See, Ears to Hear*, London: Darton, Longman and Todd.

Loughlin, Gerard (1990), 'Prefacing Pluralism: John Hick and the Mastery of Religion', *Modern Theology*, 7.1; 29–55.

(1991), 'Squares and Circles: John Hick and the Doctrine of the Incarnation', in *Problems in the Philosophy of Religion: Critical Studies of the Work of John Hick*, edited by Harold Hewitt; London: Macmillan; pp. 181–205.

(1996), *Telling God's Story: Bible, Church and Narrative Theology*, Cambridge University Press.

Macann, Christopher (1991), *Presence and Coincidence: the Transformation of Transcendental into Ontological Phenomenology*, Dordrecht: Kluwer.

McDade, John (1990), 'The Continuing Validity of the Jewish Covenant: A Christian Perspective', *SIDIC*, 23.3; 20–5.

McDonagh, Enda (1985), 'A Church for the World', in *Freedom to Hope?* edited by Alan Falconer, Enda McDonagh and Sean Mac Reamoinn; Dublin: Columba Press; pp. 82–93.

McGrane, Bernard (1989), *Beyond Anthropology: Society and the Other*, New York: Columbia University Press.

MacIntyre, Alasdair (1985), *After Virtue*, 2nd edition; London: Duckworth.

Maclean, Ian (1987), 'The Heterologies of Michel de Certeau', *Paragraph*, 9; 83–7.

McManus, Frederick R. (1967), *Sacramental Liturgy*, New York: Herder and Herder.

McPartlan, Paul (1993), *The Eucharist makes the Church: Henri de Lubac and John Zizioulas in Dialogue*, Edinburgh: T. and T. Clark.

(1995), *Sacrament of Salvation*, Edinburgh: T. and T. Clark.

MacPherson, Camilia Gangasingh (1996), *A Critical Reading of the Development of Raimon Panikkar's Thought on the Trinity*, New York: University Press of America.

Mahadevan, T. M. P. (1977), *Ramana Maharshi, the sage of Arunacala*, London: Unwin.

Maier, Martin (1996), 'Die Unterührbahren und das Christentum in Indien', *Stimmen der Zeit*, 214; 99–110.

Mangalwadi, Vishal (1995), 'Missionary Conspiracy? A Response to Arun Shourie', *Dharma Deepika*, 1.2; 51–65.

Manickam, S. (1995), *Conspiracy of Silence*, Madurai: Tamil Theological Seminary.

Maranhao, Tullio (ed.) (1990), *The Interpretation of Dialogue*, Chicago University Press.

Marty, Martin and Appleby, R. Scott (eds.) (1995), *The Fundamentalism Project*, Chicago University Press. (Five volumes: *Fundamentalisms Observed, Fundamentalisms and Society, Fundamentalisms and the State, Accounting for Fundamentalisms, Fundamentalisms Comprehended.*)

Massey, James (1994), *Towards Dalit Hermeneutics*, Delhi: ISPCK.

(1995), *Dalits in India*, Delhi: Manohar.

Massey, James and Bhagwan Das (eds.) (1995), *Dalit Solidarity*, Delhi: ISPCK.

Mathewes, Charles T. (1998), 'Pluralism, Otherness, and the Augustinian Tradition', *Modern Theology*, 14.1; 83–112.

Mattam, Joseph (1975), *Land of the Trinity*, Bangalore: Theological Publications in India.

Matthews, Eric (1996), *Twentieth Century French Philosophy*, Oxford University Press.

Matus, Thomas (1996), 'Jules Monchanin (1895–1957): An International Colloquium on the Occasion of the Centenary of his Birth', *Pro Dialogo*, 91; 55–62.

Maurier, H. (1965), *The Other Covenant: a Theology of Paganism*, New York.

Menamparampil, Thomas (2000), 'Christian Response to Harassment: a Deeper Commitment to the Gospel', *Vidyajyoti*, 64; 328–41.

Mendelsohn, Oliver and Vicziany, Marika (1998), *The Untouchables: Subordination, Poverty and the State in Modern India*, Cambridge University Press.

Metz, J. B. (1990), 'With the Eyes of a European Theologian', *Concilium*, 90.6; 113–19.

Michael, S. M. (1996a), 'The Cultural Context of the Rise of Hindutva and Dalits Forces', *Vidyajyoti*, 60.5; 294–310.

(1996b), 'Dalit Vision of a Just Society in India', *Vaiharai*, 1.2; 105–22.

Milbank, John (1990a), *Theology and Social Theory*, Oxford: Blackwell.

(1990b), 'The End of Dialogue', in *Christian Uniqueness Reconsidered*, edited by Gavin D'Costa, Maryknoll NY: Orbis; pp. 174–91.

(1991), ' "Postmodern Critical Augustinianism": a Short *Summa* in forty two Responses to Unasked Questions', *Modern Theology*, 7.3; 223–37.

(2000), 'The Programme of Radical Orthodoxy', in *Radical Orthodoxy? A Catholic Enquiry*, edited by Laurence Hemming; Aldershot: Ashgate.

Miller, John H. (ed.) (1966), *Vatican II: An Interfaith Appraisal*, University of Notre Dame Press; 1966.

Moltmann, Jürgen (1977), *The Church in the Power of the Spirit*, London: SCM.

Monchanin, Jules (1965), *Écrits Spirituels*, edited by Edouard Duperray; Paris: Centurion.

(1974), *Mystique de l'Inde, Mystère Chrétien*, Paris: Fayard.

Monchanin, Jules and le Saux, Henri (Swami Abhishiktananda) (1956), *Ermites du Saccidananda*, Paris: Casterman.

(1964), *A Benedictine Ashram*, revised edition; Douglas IoM.

Moran, J. F. (1993), *The Japanese and the Jesuits: Alessandro Valignano in Sixteenth Century Japan*, London: Routledge.

Morgan, Michael (ed.) (1989), *The Jewish Thought of Emil Fackenheim*, Detroit: Wayne University Press.

Mortley, Raoul (ed.) (1991), *French Philosophers in Conversation*, London: Routledge.

Mukherjee, Prabhati (1988), *Beyond the Four Varnas*, Delhi: Motilal Banarsidass.

Munitiz, Joseph and Endean, Philip (eds.) (1996), *Saint Ignatius of Loyola: Personal Writings*, London: Penguin.

Murray, Robert (1985), ' "Disaffected Judaism" and Early Christianity', in *'To See Ourselves as Others See Us': Christians, Jews, 'Others' in Late Antiquity*, edited by Jacob Neusner and Ernest S. Frerichs; Chico CA: Scholars Press; pp. 263–81.

Nandy, Ashis (1983), *The Intimate Enemy: Loss and Recovery of Self Under Colonialism*, Delhi: Oxford University Press.

(1990), 'The Politics of Secularism and the Recovery of Religious Tolerance', in *Mirrors of Violence*, edited by Veena Das; Delhi: Oxford University Press; pp. 69–93.

Narchison, J. Rosario (1996), 'Missionaries in India: an Appraisal of Arun Shourie's Book', *Indian Church History Review*, 30.1; 45–72.

Neusner, Jacob (1978–9), 'Comparing Judaisms', *History of Religions*, 18; 177–91.

Nicolau, Miguel (1980), 'El "Presupuesto" de San Ignacio y el diálogo ecuménico', *Manresa*, 52; 87–90.

Nirmal, Arvind (1990), *Heuristic Explorations*, Madras: CLS.

(n.d.) (ed.), *A Reader in Dalit Theology*, Madras: Gurukul.

(n.d.), *Towards a Common Dalit Theology*, Madras.

Novak, David (1989), *Jewish–Christian Dialogue: a Jewish Justification*, New York: Oxford University Press.

Nys, H. (1966), *Le Salut sans L'Évangile*, Paris: Cerf.

O'Collins, Gerald (1993), *Retrieving Fundamental Theology*, London: Chapman.

Oesterreicher, John M. (1971), *The Rediscovery of Judaism*, New Jersey: Seton Hall University.

(1985), *The New Encounter Between Christians and Jews*, New York: Philosophical Library.

Ogden, Schubert (1992), *Is there Only One True Religion or are there Many?* Dallas: Southern Methodist University Press.

O'Hanlon, Rosalind (1985), *Caste, Conflict and Ideology*, Cambridge University Press.

(1988), 'Recovering the Subject: Subaltern Studies and Histories of Resistance in Colonial South Asia'; *Modern Asian Studies*, 22.1; 189–224.

O'Hanlon, Rosalind and Washbrook, David (1992), 'After Orientalism: Culture, Criticism and Politics in the Third World', *Comparative Studies in Society and History*, 34.1; 141–67.

O'Leary, Joseph S. (1985), *Questioning Back: the Overcoming of Metaphysics in Christian Tradition*, Minneapolis: Winston.

O'Malley, John (1971), 'Reform, Historical Consciousness, and Vatican II's Aggiornamento', *Theological Studies*, 32; 573–601.

(1983), 'Developments, Reforms, and Two Great Reformations: Towards an Historical Assessment of Vatican II', *Theological Studies*, 44; 373–406.

(1993), *The First Jesuits*, Cambridge MA: Harvard University Press.

(1994), 'Mission and the Early Jesuits', *The Way Supplement*, 79; 3–10.

O'Malley, John *et al.* (eds.) (1999), *The Jesuits: Culture, Science and the Arts 1540–1773*, Toronto University Press.

Ong, Walter (1981), *Fighting for Life: Context, Sexuality and Consciousness*, Ithaca: Cornell University Press.

(1983), *Ramus: Method and the Decay of Dialogue*, Cambridge MA: Harvard University Press.

Ormerod, Neil (1996), 'Quarrels with the Method of Correlation', *Theological Studies*, 57; 707–19.

Padinjarekuttu, Isaac (1998), 'Christianity in Independent India', *Jñanadeepa: Pune Journal of Religious Studies*, 1; 77–92.

Palmer, Martin (1996), *On Giving the Spiritual Exercises*, St Louis: Institute of Jesuit Sources.

Pandey, Gyanendra (1994), 'The Prose of Otherness', *Subaltern Studies*, 7; 188–221.

Panikkar, Raimundo (1973), *The Trinity and the Religious Experience of Man*, New York: Orbis; London: Darton, Longman and Todd.

(1984), 'The Dialogical Dialogue', in *The World's Religious Traditions*, edited by Frank Whaling; Edinburgh: T. and T. Clark; pp. 201–21.

Peperzak, Adriaan (1983), 'Emmanuel Levinas: Jewish Experience and Philosophy', *Philosophy Today*, 27; 297–306.

(1993), *To the Other*, West Lafayette: Purdue University Press.

Peperzak, Adriaan (ed.) (1995), *Ethics as First Philosophy: the Significance of Emmanuel Levinas for Philosophy, Literature and Religion*, London: Routledge.

Pickstock, Catherine (1998), *After Writing: on the Liturgical Consummation of Philosophy*, Oxford: Blackwell.

Pieris, Aloysius (1988a), *An Asian Theology of Liberation*, Edinburgh: T. and T. Clark.

(1988b), *Love Meets Wisdom*, New York: Orbis.

(1993a), 'Does Christ have a Place in Asia? A Panoramic View', *Concilium*, 2; 33–47.

(1993b), 'An Asian Paradigm: Interreligious Dialogue and Theology of Religions', *The Month*, 26; 1993.

Placher, William (1989), *Unapologetic Theology*, Louisville: Westminster.

(1996), *The Domestication of Transcendence*, Louisville: Westminster.

Prabhakar, M. E.(ed.) (1988), *Towards a Dalit Theology*, Delhi.

Prabhu, Joseph (1996), *The Intercultural Challenge of Raimon Panikkar*, New York: Orbis.

Purcell, Michael (1997), 'Liturgy: Divine and Human Service', *Heythrop Journal*, 38; 144–64.

Puthanangady, Paul (ed.) (1985), *Towards an Indian Theology of Liberation*, Bangalore: NBCLC.

Quigley, Declan (1993), *The Interpretation of Caste*, Oxford University Press.

Race, Alan (1983), *Christians and Religious Pluralism*, London: SCM.

Rahner, Karl (1966a), 'Thoughts on the Possibility of Belief Today', *Theological Investigations (TI)*, volume 5, London: Darton, Longman and Todd; pp. 3–22.

(1966b), 'Christianity and the non-Christian Religions', *TI*, volume 5, London: Darton, Longman and Todd; pp. 115–34.

(1974), 'Anonymous Christianity and the Missionary Task of the Church', *TI*, volume 12, London: Darton, Longman and Todd; pp. 161–78.

(1978), *Foundations of Christian Faith*, London: Darton, Longman and Todd.

(1979a), 'Anonymous and Explicit Faith', *TI*, volume 16, London: Darton, Longman and Todd; pp. 52–9.

(1979b), 'The One Christ and the Universality of Salvation', *TI*, volume 16, London: Darton, Longman and Todd; pp. 199–224.

(1979c), 'Towards a Fundamental Theological Interpretation of the Second Vatican Council', *Theological Studies*, 40; 716–27.

(1983), 'On the Importance of non-Christian Religions for Salvation', *TI*, volume 18, London: Darton, Longman and Todd; pp. 288–95.

Raj, Antony (1992a), *Children of a Lesser God (Dalit Christians)* Madurai: Dalit Christian Liberation Movement.

(1992b), 'The Dalit Christian Reality in Tamil Nadu', *Jeevadhara*, March; 95–111.

Rajamanickam, S. (1971) (ed.), *Roberto de Nobili on Adaptation*, ET of Roberto de Nobili, *Narratio fundamentorum quibus Madurensis Missionis institutum caeptum est et hucusque consistit* (1618–19), Palayamkottai: St Xavier's College.

(1972a), *The First Oriental Scholar*, Tirunelveli: St Xavier's College.

(1972b) (ed.), *Roberto de Nobili on Indian Customs*, ET of Roberto de Nobili, *Informatio de quibusdam moribus nationis indicae* (1613), Palayamkottai: St Xavier's College.

Ramachandra, Vinoth (1996), *The Recovery of Mission*, Carlisle: Paternoster.

Ravier, Andre (1987), *Ignatius of Loyola and the Founding of the Society of Jesus*, San Francisco: Ignatius Press.

Reader, John (1997), *Beyond Reason: The Limits of Post-modern Theology*, Cardiff: Aureus.

Reed, Charles William (1986), 'Levinas's Question', in *Face to Face with Levinas*, edited by Richard Cohen; Albany: State University of New York Press; pp. 73–82.

Richards, Glyn (1985), *A Sourcebook of Modern Hinduism*, London: Curzon Press.

Ricoeur, Paul (1967), *Husserl: an Analysis of His Phenomenology*, ET Edward G. Ballard and Lester E. Embree; Evanston: Northwestern University Press.

(1984), *Time and Narrative*, volume 1; ET Kathleen McLaughlin and David Pellauer; Chicago University Press.

(1985), *Time and Narrative*, volume 2; ET Kathleen McLaughlin and David Pellauer; Chicago University Press.

(1988), *Time and Narrative*, volume 3; ET Kathleen Blamey and David Pellauer; Chicago University Press.

(1991), 'Life in quest of narrative', in *On Paul Ricoeur – Narrative and Interpretation*, edited by David Wood; London and New York: Routledge; pp. 20–33.

(1992), *Oneself as Another*, Chicago University Press.

(1995), *Figuring the Sacred: Religion, Narrative and Imagination*, ET David Pellauer; edited by Mark I. Wallace, Minneapolis: Fortress Press.

(1996), 'Love and Justice', in *Paul Ricoeur: the Hermeneutics of Action*, edited by Richard Kearney, London: Sage Publications; pp. 21–39.

(1998), *Critique and Conviction*, Cambridge: Polity.

Rodhe, Sten (1993), *Jules Monchanin: Pioneer in Christian–Hindu Dialogue*, Delhi: ISPCK.

Roest-Crollius, Ary A. (1978), 'What is so New about Inculturation? A Concept and its Implications', *Gregorianum*, 59; 721–38.

Roos, Heinrich and Neuner, Joseph (compilers) (1967), *The Teaching of the Catholic Church*, edited by Karl Rahner; Cork: Mercier.

Rose, Gillian (1992), *The Broken Middle: Out of our Ancient Society*, Oxford: Blackwell.

(1993), *Judaism and Modernity*, Oxford: Blackwell.

(1996), *Mourning Becomes the Law*, Cambridge University Press.

Rosenzweig, Franz (1970), *Star of Redemption*, ET William W. Hallo; London: Routledge.

Ross, Andrew C. (1993), *A Vision Betrayed: The Jesuits in China and Japan 1542–1742*, Edinburgh University Press.

Roth, John K. and Berenbaum, Michael (eds.) (1989), *Holocaust: Religious and Philosophical Implications*, New York: Paragon House.

Rubenstein, Richard (1966), *After Auschwitz: Radical Theology and Contemporary Judaism*, 1st edition; Indianapolis: Bobbs-Merrill.

(1992), *After Auschwitz: History, Theology and Contemporary Judaism*, 2nd edition; Baltimore: Johns Hopkins University Press.

Ruether, Rosemary R. (1974), *Faith and Fratricide: the Theological Roots of Antisemitism*, New York.

Ruokanen, Miika (1992), *The Catholic Doctrine of Non-Christian Religions*, Leiden: Brill.

Rynne, Xavier (1966) *The Fourth Session*, London: Faber.

Said, Edward (1978), *Orientalism*, New York: Vintage Books.

(1986), 'Orientalism Reconsidered', in *Literature, Politics and Theory: Papers from the Essex Conference*, edited by Francis Barker *et al.*; London: Methuen; pp. 210–29.

(1993), *Culture and Imperialism*, London: Chatto and Windus.

Sallis, John C., Moneta, Giuseppina and Taminiaux, Jacques (1988), *The Collegium Phaenomenologicum: the First Ten Years*, Dordrecht: Kluwer.

Sanders, E. P. (1977), *Paul and Palestinian Judaism: a Comparison of Patterns of Religion*, London: SCM.

(1991), *Paul*, Oxford University Press.

Saulière, A. (1995), *His Star in the East*, revised and re-edited by S. Rajamanickam; Anand: Gujarat Sahitya Prakash.

Schillebeeckx, Edward (1972), *Christ the Sacrament of Encounter with God*, London: Sheed and Ward.

Schroeder, Brian (1996), *Altared Ground: Levinas, History and Violence*, New York and London: Routledge.

Schutte, Josef Franz (1980/85), *Valignano's Mission Principles for Japan*; ET John Coyne SJ; 2 volumes; St Louis: Institute of Jesuit Sources.

Schwab, Raymond (1984), *The Oriental Renaissance: Europe's Rediscovery of India and the East, 1680–1880*, ET Gene Patterson-Black and Victor Reinking; New York: Columbia University Press.

Schwerdtfeger, Nikolaus (1982), *Gnade und Welt: Zum Grundgefuge von Karl Rahners Theorie der Anonymen Christen*, New York: Herder.

Sen, Amartya (1996), 'Secularism and its Discontents', in *Unravelling the Nation: Sectarian Conflict and India's Secular Identity*, edited by Kaushik Basu and Sanjay Subrahmaniam; London: Penguin.

Shapere, Dudley (1964) 'The Structure of Scientific Revolutions', *The Philosophical Review*, 73; 383–94.

Shorter, Aylward (1988), *Towards a Theology of Inculturation*, London: Chapman.

Shourie, Arun (1994), *Missionaries in India: Continuities, Changes, Dilemmas*, New Delhi: ASA Publications.

Silverman, Hugh J. (ed.) (1988), *Philosophy and non-Philosophy since Merleau-Ponty*, London: Routledge.

Smith, Jonathan Z. (1998), 'Religion, Religions, Religious', in *Critical Terms for Religious Studies*, edited by Mark C. Taylor; Chicago University Press; pp. 269–84.

Smith, Steven G. (1983), *The Argument to the Other: Reason Beyond Reason in the Thought of Karl Barth and Emmanuel Levinas*, American Academy of Religion: Academy Studies 42; Chico CA: Scholars' Press.

Soares Prabhu, George (1984), *Inculturation, Liberation, Dialogue*, Pune: Jñana-Deepa Vidyapeeth.

Spivak, Gayatry Cakravorty (1988), 'Can the Subaltern Speak?', in *Marxism and the Interpretation of Culture*, edited by Cary Nelson and Lawrence Grossberg; Basingstoke: Macmillan; pp. 271–313.

Stacpoole, Alberich (ed.) (1986), *Vatican II: by Those Who Were There*, London: Chapman.

Staffner, Hans (1985), *The Significance of Jesus Christ in Asia*, Anand: Gujarat Sahitya Prakash.

Stendahl, Krister (1976), *Paul among Jews and Gentiles*, Philadelphia: Fortress Press.

Stuart, James (ed.) (1995), *Swami Abhishiktananda: His Life Told Through His Letters*, revised edition; Delhi: ISPCK.

Suenens, Leon Joseph (1965), *The Gospel to Every Creature*, Westminster: Newman Press.

Sugirtharajah, R. and Hargreaves, C. (eds.) (1993), *Readings in Indian Christian Theology*, volume 1; London: SPCK.

Sullivan, Francis A. (1992), *Salvation outside the Church? Tracing the History of the Catholic Response*, London: Chapman.

Surin, Kenneth (1990), 'A Certain "Politics of Speech": "Religious Pluralism" in the Age of the McDonald's Hamburger', *Modern Theology*, 7.1; 67–100.

Swidler, L. (1987), *Toward a Universal Theology of Religion*, Maryknoll: Orbis.

Swidler, L., Cobb, J., Knitter, P. and Hellwig, M. (1990), *Death or Dialogue?*, London: SCM.

Talal Asad (1993), *Genealogies of Religion*, Baltimore and London: Johns Hopkins University Press.

Tanner, Kathryn (1993), 'Respect for Other Religions: a Christian Antidote to Colonialist Discourse', *Modern Theology*, 9.1; 1–18.

(1997), *Theories of Culture: a New Agenda for Theology*, Minneapolis: Fortress.

Tan See Kam (1996), 'Making Space for Heterologies', *Social Semiotics*, 6.1; 27–44.

Thapar, Romila (1992), *Interpreting Early India*, Oxford University Press.

Theunissen, Michael (1984), *The Other, Studies in the Social Ontology of Husserl, Heidegger, Sartre and Buber*, ET Christopher Macann; Cambridge, MA: MIT Press.

Thorley, Sarah (2000), 'Inter Faith Pilgrimage: Journeys across Boundaries' *The Way*, 40; 181–90.

Tillich, Paul (1951), *Systematic Theology*, volume 1; Chicago University Press.

Toulmin, Stephen (1990), *Cosmopolis: the Hidden Agenda of Modernity*, Chicago University Press.

Tracy, David (1982), *The Analogical Imagination: Christian Theology and the Culture of Pluralism*, London: SCM.

(1990), *Dialogue with the Other: the Inter-Religious Dialogue*, Louvain: Peeters; Grand Rapids: Eerdmans.

Turner, Victor (1967), *The Forest of Symbols*; Ithaca: Cornell University Press.

(1969), *The Ritual Process*; Ithaca: Cornell.

Upadhyay, Prakash Chandra (1988), 'Subaltern Studies III and IV: a Review Article', *Social Scientist*, 178; pp. 3–40.

Vandana (1978), *Gurus, Ashrams and Christians*, London: Darton, Longman and Todd.

(1993) (ed.), *Christian Ashrams: a Movement with a Future?* Delhi: ISPCK.

van den Hengel, John (1994), 'Paul Ricoeur's *Oneself as Another* and Practical Theology', *Theological Studies*, 55; 458–480.

van Leeuwen, G. (1984), *Searching for an Indian Ecclesiology*, Bangalore: Asian Trading Corporation.

Vattakuzhy, Emmanuel (1981), *Indian Christian Sannyasa and Swami Abhishiktananda*, Bangalore: Theological Publications in India.

Vorgrimler, Herbert (ed.) (1967–69), *Commentary on the Documents of Vatican II*; volumes 1–5; London: Burns and Oates; New York: Herder.

Ward, Graham (1995), *Barth, Derrida and the Language of Theology*, Cambridge University Press.

(1996), 'The Voice of the Other', *New Blackfriars*, 909; 518–28.

(1997) (ed.), *The Postmodern God*, Oxford: Blackwell.

(2000), *The Certeau Reader*, Oxford: Blackwell.

Weber, Joseph G. (ed.) (1977), *In Quest of the Absolute*, Kalamazoo: Cistercian Studies Publications.

Webster, John C. B (1992), *The Dalit Christians: a History*, Delhi: ISPCK.

Wilfred, Felix (1993), *Beyond Settled Foundations*, University of Madras.

(1995), *From the Dusty Soil*, University of Madras.

Williams, Raymond (1987), *Culture and Society*, new edition; London: Hogarth.

Williams, Rowan (1988), 'The Suspicion of Suspicion: Wittgenstein and Bonhoeffer', in *The Grammar of the Heart: New Essays in Philosophy and Theology*, edited by Richard H. Bell; San Francisco: Harper; pp. 36–53.

—— (1990), 'Trinity and Pluralism', in *Christian Uniqueness Reconsidered*, edited by Gavin D'Costa, Maryknoll NY: Orbis; pp. 3–15.

—— (1995), 'Between Politics and Metaphysics: Reflections in the Wake of Gillian Rose', *Modern Theology*, 11.1; 3–22.

—— (2000), *On Christian Theology*, Oxford: Blackwell.

Wilson, K. (1982), *The Twice Alienated – Culture of Dalit Christians*, Hyderabad.

Wiltgen, Ralph (1967), *The Rhine flows into the Tiber*, New York: Hawthorn Books.

Wright, Tamra (1999), *The Twilight of Jewish Philosophy*, Amsterdam: Harwood.

Index